AQA

KS3

Activate
Know • Apply • Extend
1

Teacher Handbook

Simon Broadley
Philippa Gardom Hulme
Jo Locke
Mark Matthews
Helen Reynolds
Victoria Stutt
Nicky Thomas

Assessment Editor
Dr Andrew Chandler-Grevatt

OXFORD
UNIVERSITY PRESS

Contents

Introduction

About the series

AQA Activate for KS3 is designed to support every student on their journey through secondary science with AQA.

Each Big Idea in the AQA KS3 syllabus is fully covered, and support and extension is provided to help students achieve and exceed the mastery goals. *AQA Activate for KS3* sparks students' curiosity in science, whilst gradually building the maths, literacy, practical, and enquiry skills needed for progression to AQA GCSE.

This two-part series is accompanied by flexible schemes of work to enable varying Key Stage lengths. All of the content in the *AQA Activate for KS3* series has been written and reviewed by our expert author and editor teams, all of whom have significant teaching experience, and our Assessment Editor, a school-assessment expert. You can be confident that *AQA Activate for KS3* provides the best support for the AQA KS3 syllabus.

Your Teacher Handbook

This Teacher Handbook aims to save you time and effort by offering lesson plans, differentiation suggestions, and assessment guidance on a page-by-page basis that is a direct match to the Student Book.

You can use the Openers to see the knowledge required of students from Key Stage 2 for each Big Idea at a glance. You can also use the Checkpoint Lessons at the end of each Big Idea to support students who have yet to master key concepts from that Big Idea. Lesson plans are written for 55-minute lessons but are flexible and fully adaptable so you can choose the activities that suit your classes best.

Opener

Overview
Each Big Idea starts with an Opener spread providing an overview of the Big Idea and how it links to Key Stage 2 and AQA GCSE.

Curriculum links
An overview of the topics and how they link to the AQA KS3 syllabus.

Preparing for Key Stage 4 success
This table provides an overview of the Key Stage 4 skills and underpinning knowledge that are covered in the Big Idea. It also provides details of where AQA-style assessment questions can be found throughout the Big Idea.

Key Stage 2 catch-up
This table outlines the Key Stage 2 knowledge that is a pre-requisite for each Big Idea. This can be assessed using the automarked Pre-test on Kerboodle or the baseline assessment.

For each Key Stage 2 statement, a suggestion for how you can help students to catch up is provided, as well as an index of which section each statement links to.

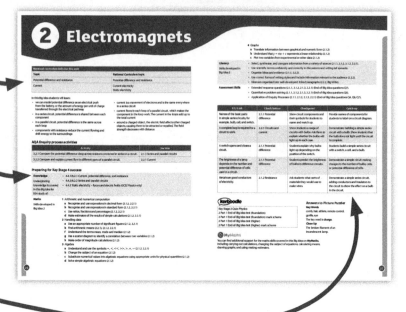

Lesson

AQA KS3 syllabus links
This indicates the area of the 2014 Programme of Study this lesson covers. An Enquiry Processes link is also given for most lessons. This indicates the main enquiry focus of the lesson.

Differentiated outcomes
This table summarises the possible lesson outcomes. They are ramped and divided into three ability bands (Know, Apply, Extend). The three ability bands are explained on the following page.

An indication of where each outcome is covered is given in the checkpoint table, helping you to monitor progress through the lesson.

Maths and Literacy
These boxes provide suggestions of how Maths and Literacy skills can be developed in the lesson. They also indicate when a Maths or Literacy activity is given in the Student Book and include MyMaths links.

Maths and Literacy skills are ramped throughout the series. A Progression Grid and Progress Tasks are supplied on Kerboodle. MyMaths suggestions are also included.

Preparing for GCSE
Links to AQA Separate Sciences and Trilogy GCSEs are provided for each lesson.

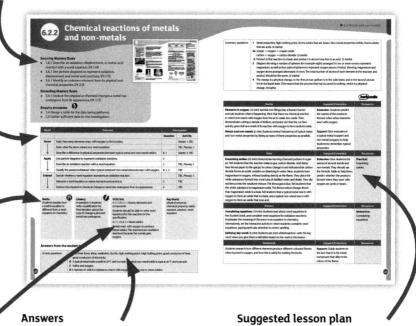

Answers
Answers to the Student Book activities and questions can be found here. For extended response questions, only the correct scientific points for marking are given. When marking these questions, attention needs to be given to the quality of the writing in the answer.

Suggested lesson plan
A suggested route through the lesson is provided, including ideas for support, extension, and homework. The right-hand column indicates where Kerboodle resources are available.

Each lesson plan is supported by an editable lesson presentation on Kerboodle.

Checkpoint Lessons

Overview
The Checkpoint Lesson is a suggested follow-up lesson after students have completed the automarked Checkpoint Assessment on Kerboodle. There are two routes through the lesson, with the route for each student being determined by their mark in the assessment. Route A helps students to consolidate what they have learnt through the chapter, whilst Route B offers extension for students who are yet to master key concepts.

Checkpoint routes
A summary of the two suggested routes through the lesson.

Progression table
This table summarises the outcomes covered in the Revision Lesson, and provides guidance for how students can make progress to achieve each outcome.

The tasks outlined in the table, resources for the Extension Lesson, and detailed Teacher Notes are all available on Kerboodle.

Answers
Answers to the questions in the Student Book.

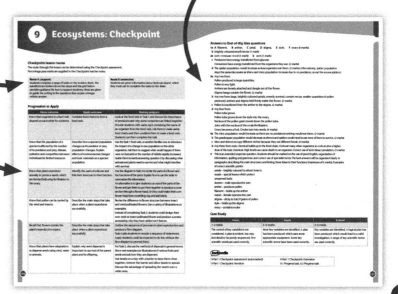

Assessment and progress

Welcome

from the Assessment Editor

Welcome to your *AQA Activate for KS3* Teacher Handbook. The Teacher Handbooks, together with Kerboodle and the Student Books, provide comprehensive assessment support for the new curriculum.

The AQA syllabus has provided an exciting framework to assess and support progress at Key Stage 3 and prepare for AQA GCSE. It builds on Activate's Developing, Secure and Extending assessment model, with a greater focus on the knowledge required to Apply scientific knowledge, understanding, and skills to the demands of the National Curriculum for Science.

It has been straightforward to rearrange Activate's content into the AQA Big Ideas. The shift of assessment focus moves from Activate's Pathways based on descriptors for Developing, Secure and Extending to a mastery approach.

Throughout the development and authoring of *AQA Activate for KS3* we have followed our core assessment principles.

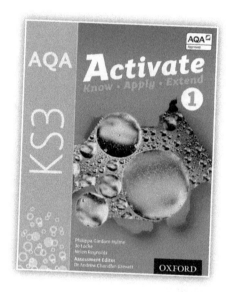

Activate assessment principles

All of our assessment aims to:

- inform teaching and/or learning directly (have a formative function)
- assess agreed and shared objectives
- provide opportunities for peer- and self-assessment
- provide opportunities for specific feedback to be given to and acted upon by individual students
- provide usable data or information that informs teachers of progress of classes and individuals.

I have been working closely with our expert author teams across all components of this series to ensure consistency in the assessment material, meaning you can be confident when using Activate to monitor your students' progress.

5-year assessment for AQA

With *Activate*, we supported teachers to move from National Curriculum levels to the Activate Bands of Developing, Secure and Extend. This model is more in line with the mastery approach to teaching and learning, which has 'Apply' as the benchmark of success for AQA KS3.

When using this new approach, we may move away from thinking of 'level equivalence' and instead use band descriptors, but numbers or grades may still be needed for reporting. Our assessment across AQA KS3 and GCSE is therefore also mapped to GCSE grades, for easy 5-year tracking.

Key stage 3	Band	Know		Apply		Extend	
	Level	3	4	5	6	7	8
	Band	Aiming for 4		Aiming for 6		Aiming for 8	
GCSE	Grade	1	2	3	4	5	6	7	8	9
	Demand	Low		Standard		High	

Flexible assessment that works for you

Assessment in *AQA Activate for KS3* is designed to be flexible, formative, and summative, allowing you to choose what best suits your students and school. All paper assessments are fully editable for you to adapt to your chosen approach.

All automarked assessments have the option of providing either formative feedback (where students receive feedback on each question and additional attempts) or summative feedback (with one attempt at each question and feedback at the end).

Know, Apply, Extend	Grades	Levels	Comment only
All outcomes are banded throughout this book and in progress tasks. Use this model to assess if students have mastered key concepts.	The 5-year assessment model can be used to help you monitor progress against target GCSE grades. Summative assessments are accompanied by a Test Score Converter that outputs an approximate GCSE grade (to be used in conjunction with teacher judgement).	Level matching has been included online in Kerboodle and in the Test Score Converter so you can compare results of your AQA KS3 cohort with previous cohorts.	Some schools have adopted the 'no grades or marks' approach to assessment, opting for comment-only feedback. Interactive assessments provide comments and feedback to facilitate progression, and all paper assessments are fully editable, so banding and levelling can be removed.

The Checkpoint system

At the end of each Big Idea, there is an automarked online assessment. It will help you to determine if your students have mastered key concepts.

Activities for a follow-up Checkpoint Lesson are provided on Kerboodle. There are two recommended routes through the lesson for students, depending on the percentage they achieve in the assessment. Revision and Extension routes can be followed in the same lesson, allowing students to either consolidate their understanding or attempt an extension task.

Each lesson also includes informal checkpoints to track progress through a lesson.

Follow assessment with learning

AQA Activate for KS3
The checkpoint assessment system:

1 Use the automarked Checkpoint Assessment at the end of each Big Idea to determine next steps.

2 Use the Checkpoint Lesson and resources to support and extend your students as needed.

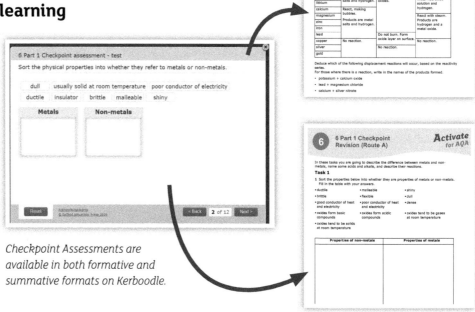

Checkpoint Assessments are available in both formative and summative formats on Kerboodle.

Differentiation and skills

Maths skills 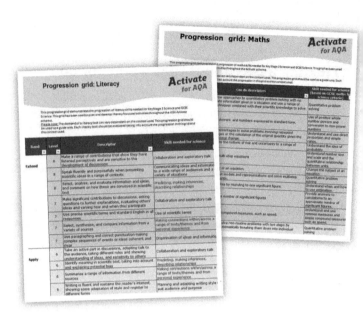 MyMaths

Maths skills have always been important for science but with the introduction of the new GCSEs, competence in maths in scientific contexts will be vital for success.

Key Maths skills for science include quantitative problem solving, use of scientific formulae, and the calculation of arithmetic means. Each skill has been integrated across the series, with progress in each skill mapped out. You can view the Progression Grid for Maths in Kerboodle.

The **Student Books** contain maths activities and hints to support and develop Maths skills as students work from their books. There are also Maths challenges at the end of some Big Ideas, focussing on quantitative problem solving skills.

In **Kerboodle**, you will find maths Skills Interactives that are automarked and provide formative feedback. Maths questions are also incorporated into other assessments where appropriate, and designated Progress Tasks for Maths will help you track progress. Kerboodle also includes exclusive links to MyMaths for MyMaths schools.

In this **Teacher Handbook**, you will find Maths suggestions for most lessons, linking to the Student Book where relevant. By using *AQA Activate for KS3*, students will gain plenty of experience in a range of Maths skills that have been identified as vital preparation for AQA GCSE.

Literacy skills

Literacy skills enable students to effectively communicate their ideas about science and access the information they need. Since the introduction of extended response at GCSE, Literacy skills are now more important than ever.

Literacy skills are vital for success in any subject but key Literacy skills for science include understanding meaning of scientific texts and identifying supporting ideas and evidence, adapting writing styles to suit audience and purpose, and the organisation of ideas and information.

The **Student Books** contain literacy activities and hints to support and develop Literacy skills as students work from their books. There are also Big Writes at the end of some chapters, focussing on extended writing skills. Extended response questions are provided on most spreads, and Key Words and a Glossary help students get to grips with scientific terms.

In **Kerboodle** you will find Skills Interactives and Progress Quizzes that will help assess Literacy skills, including spelling of key words. Question-led Lessons offer an alternative approach to some lessons, focussing on the Literacy skills needed to answer a Big Question. Progress Tasks for Literacy will help you track progress in key skill areas throughout the key stage. You can view the Progression Grid for Literacy in Kerboodle.

In this **Teacher Handbook**, you will find Literacy suggestions for most lessons, linking to the Student Book where relevant. By using these resources, students will gain plenty of experience in a range of Literacy skills that have been identified as good preparation for GCSE.

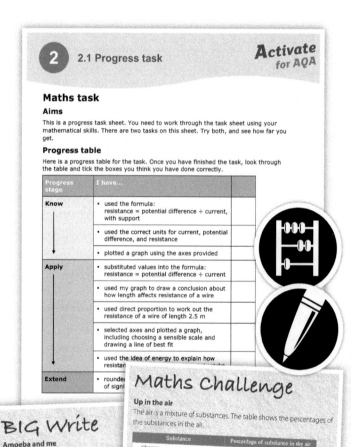

Enquiry Processes

Enquiry Processes are new in the AQA syllabus. They cover the Working Scientifically criteria in the 2014 Key Stage 3 Programme of Study, and help prepare for GCSE:

Analyse, consisting of presenting data, analysing patterns, drawing conclusions and discussing limitations.

Communicate, consisting of constructing explanations, communicating ideas, critiquing claims and justifying opinions.

Enquire, consisting of devising questions, testing hypotheses, planning to control variables and collecting data.

Solve, consisting of estimating risks, examining consequences, interrogating sources and understanding how scientific ideas change over time.

Enquiry Processes are integrated throughout the **Student Book**, which contains activities and hints to help students build their investigative skills and understand the process of Enquiry Processes. A dedicated Enquiry Processes Section is also provided in *AQA Activate for KS3* .

In **Kerboodle** you will find Practicals and Activities, each with their own Enquiry Processes objectives, as well as Interactive investigations, Skills Interactives, Skill Sheets, and Progress Tasks.

The **Teacher Handbook** lessons often have an Enquiry Processes focus in mind for the activities of that lesson. Enquiry Processes outcomes are ramped and included as part of the lesson outcomes.

Differentiation

AQA Activate for KS3 will help you to support students of every ability through Key Stage 3. A variety of support is available, combining opt-in differentiation, ramped questions and tasks, and differentiation by task, as appropriate for each type of activity.

Differentiation using the Checkpoint system
- The Checkpoint lessons will help you to progress students of every ability.
- The revision tasks are designed to be used with students in need of support. Teacher input will help them grasp important concepts.
- The extension tasks provide an opportunity to stretch students who require an extra challenge. Students can work independently.

Teacher Handbook
Lesson outcomes are differentiated, including Enquiry Processes. Suggestions for activities throughout lesson plans are also accompanied by support and extension opportunities.

Student Book
The Summary Questions and Big Idea Questions in the Student Book are ramped. The level of demand of each question is indicated by the number of conical flasks depicted at the beginning of the question.

Practicals and Activities
Each Practical or Activity includes an extension task. Support Sheets or Access Sheets are available as an extra resource for most Practicals and Activities. Support Sheets offer opt-in differentiation, providing additional support with a difficult area of the task. Access Sheets offer alternative lesson activities where the main Practical or Activity is not accessible by some students.

Skill Sheets may also be used in tandem with Practicals and Activities to provide extra support. These can be found in Additional support in Kerboodle.

Interactive Assessments
Interactive Assessments are ramped in difficulty and support is provided in the feedback.

Written assessments
- End-of-Big Idea Tests have Foundation and Higher versions.
- Progress Tasks each contain two tasks and a progress table to cater for all abilities.

Kerboodle

Kerboodle is packed full of guided support and ideas for running and creating effective Key Stage 3 Science lessons, and assessing and facilitating students' progress. It's intuitive to use, customizable, and can be accessed online.

Kerboodle consists of:
- Lessons, Resources, and Assessment (includes teacher access to the accompanying Kerboodle Book)
- Kerboodle Books.

Lessons, Resources, and Assessment

Kerboodle – Lessons, Resources, and **Assessment** provides hundreds of engaging lesson resources as well as a comprehensive assessment package. Kerboodle offers flexibility and comprehensive support for both the course and your own scheme of work.

You can **adapt** many of the resources to suit your students' needs, with all non-interactive activities available as editable Word documents. You can also **upload** your existing resources so that everything can be accessed from one location.

Kerboodle is online, allowing you and your students to access the course anytime, anywhere. Set homework and assessments through the Assessment system, and **track** progress using the Markbook.

Lessons, Resources, and Assessment provide:
- Lessons
- Resources
- Assessment and Markbook
- Teacher access to the Kerboodle Book.

Lessons

Click on the **Lesson tab** to access the Lesson Plan and Presentation (with accompanying notes).

Ready-to-play Lesson Presentations complement every spread in the Teacher Handbook and Student Book. Each lesson presentation is easy to launch and features lesson objectives, settlers, starters, activity guidance, key diagrams, plenaries, and homework suggestions. You can further **personalize** the lessons by adding in your own resources and notes. This means that the Lesson Presentations and accompanying notes sections are 100% customizable. Your lessons and notes can be accessed by your whole department and they are ideal for use in cover lessons.

Every lesson is accompanied by teacher notes that provide additional support and extension opportunities, to fully support lesson delivery.

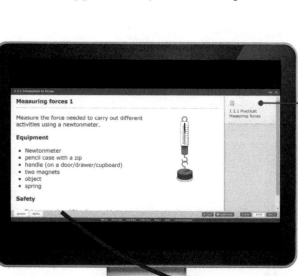

Resources are built into each lesson presentation so that associated interactive content, practical, or activity worksheets are ready to launch.

Measuring forces (20 min)

Introduce students to the idea of a newtonmeter and measuring forces in newtons. Students measure the force needed to carry out different activities (e.g., to lift a pencil case) and record these in a table. Students should compare readings with each other, explaining differences. For accurate readings, the newtonmeter hook should be in line with its spring.

Fully-editable resources and Teacher and Technician Notes (offering further guidance on this practical and answers to the questions on the practical sheet) are available from the resources tab under 1 Forces - Part 1> 1.1 Speed> 1.1.1 Introduction to forces.

Resources

Click on the **Resources tab** to access the full list of *AQA Activate* lesson resources.

Fully customizable content to cater all your classes. Resources can be created using the create button.

Existing resources can be uploaded onto the platform using the upload button.

Page navigator shows resources matching to particular pages in the Student Book and Kerboodle Book.

Navigation panel and search bar allow for easy navigation between resources by Big Idea, Topic, and Section.

Resources matching every lesson in the series are shown here.

The resource section contains:

Practicals and Activities Fully editable resources to develop Enquiry skills. In addition to an Activity Sheet and a Support or Access sheet, a set of Teacher and Technician Notes is provided to offer further ideas on differentiation, answers, and a list of resources required by technicians.

Interactive Screens Starters and plenaries to accompany each lesson, as an interactive alternative to maximise student participation.

Skill Sheets Targeted and supportive skill sheets focus on crucial Maths and Enquiry skills. These sheets are generic and provide guidance and examples to help students whenever they need to use the particular skill. You can find the Skill Sheets in the 'Additional support' folder, and they are referenced in relevant lessons in the Teacher Handbook.

Animations Animations focus on explaining difficult concepts using real-life contexts, engaging visuals, and narration. They are structured to clearly support a set of learning objectives and are followed by an Interactive Screen to help consolidate key points.

Videos Videos help students to visualise difficult concepts using engaging visuals and narration. They are structured to clearly address a set of learning objectives.

Skills Interactives Automarked interactive activities with formative feedback focus on key Maths, Literacy, and Enquiry skills. You can use these activities in class to help consolidate key skills relevant to the lesson.
They can also be set as homework by accessing them through the Assessment tab.

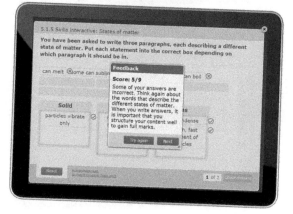

Kerboodle

Assessment and Markbook

All of the Assessment material in Kerboodle has been quality assured by our expert Assessment Editor. Click on the **Assessment tab** to find a wide range of assessment materials to help you deliver a varied, motivating, and effective assessment programme.

It's easy to import class registers and create user accounts for your students. Once your classes are set up, you can assign them assessments to do at home, individually, or as a group.

A **Markbook** with reporting function helps you to keep track of your students' results. This includes both automarked assessments and work that needs to be marked by you.

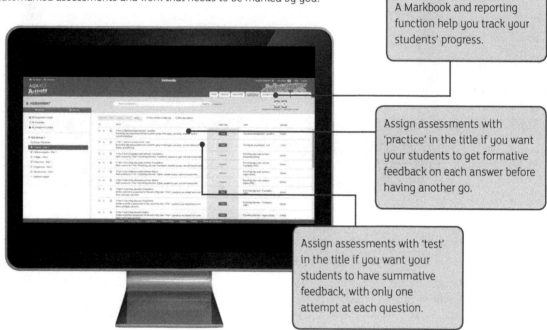

A Markbook and reporting function help you track your students' progress.

Assign assessments with 'practice' in the title if you want your students to get formative feedback on each answer before having another go.

Assign assessments with 'test' in the title if you want your students to have summative feedback, with only one attempt at each question.

Practice or test?

Each automarked assessment in *AQA Activate for KS3* is available in formative or summative versions.

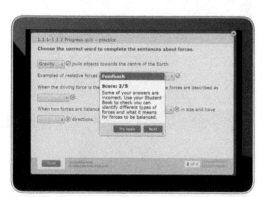

Practice versions of the assessment provide screen-by-screen feedback, focussing on misconceptions, and provide hints for the students to help them revise their answer. Students are given the opportunity to try again. Marks are reported to the Markbook.

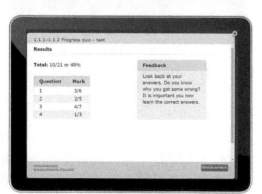

Test versions of the assessment provide feedback on performance at the end of the test. Students are only given one attempt at each screen but can review them and see which answers they got wrong after completing the activity. Marks are reported to the Markbook.

The Assessment section provides ample opportunity for student assessment before, during, and after studying a unit.

Start of the course

 Key Stage 2 quizzes These automarked tests revise and assess students' knowledge of Key Stage 2 content. Students are given feedback on their answers to help them correct gaps and misconceptions.

 Baseline assessments These two-part paper-based assessments have separate tests for content and enquiry skills. They assess Key Stage 2 and are accompanied by follow-up intervention lessons.

Through each chapter

 Progress Quizzes These automarked assessments focus on content at regular intervals within a Big Idea to help you keep track of students as they move through the course.

 Skills Interactives These automarked interactives focus specifically on Maths, Literacy, and Enquiry skills.

 Interactive Investigations These automarked assessments are set in the context of an investigation. Each screen assesses a different Enquiry Processes skill.

 Progress Tasks These written task-based assessments focus on progress in Maths, Literacy, and Enquiry skills. Each task uses a real-life scenario and comes with a progress ladder for students to self- or peer-assess their work.

 Checkpoint Assessments These automarked assessments determine whether students have mastered key concepts from the Big Idea. These assessments are ramped in difficulty and can be followed up by the Checkpoint Lesson revision and extension activities.

Summative assessment

 Big Idea and End-of-year tests These written assessments mimic examination-style questions. They include extended response, practical, and maths questions and are available in two tiers. Both sets of tests have a Foundation and a Higher tier. You can use the Test Score Converter to convert scores to levels, bands, or grades.

 Big Practical Projects These written assessments focus on Enquiry Processes and Literacy skills. Students plan and complete an investigation based on a given scenario and then answer exam-style questions about their work. These are great preparation for the new practical requirements of the GCSEs.

Zoom in and spotlight any part of the text

Use different tools such as sticky notes, bookmarks, and pen features to personalize each page

Kerboodle Book

The *AQA Activate for KS3* Kerboodle Book provides a digital version of the Student Book for you to use with your students at the front of the classroom.

Teacher access to the Kerboodle Book is automatically available as part of the Lessons, Resources, and Assessment package. You can also purchase additional access for your students.

A set of tools is available with the Kerboodle Book so you can personalize your book and make notes.

Like all other resources offered on Kerboodle, the Kerboodle Book can also be accessed using a range of devices.

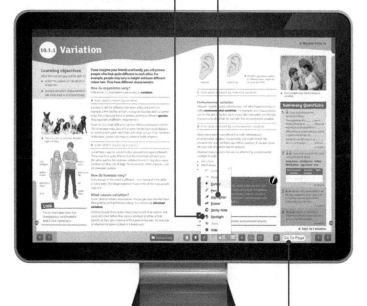

Every teacher and student has their own digital notebook for use within their Kerboodle Book. You can even choose to share some of your notes with your students, or hide the from view – all student notes are accessible to themselves only

Navigate around the book quickly with the contents menu, key word search, or page number search

Asking scientific questions

Enquiry processes

- 2.10 Identify an observation that could be recorded or measured over time.
- 2.10 Identify a dependent variable, an independent variable, or two variables which may show a correlation.
- 2.10 Write an observation, fair test, or pattern seeking enquiry question.
- 2.12 Think up a hypothesis, and make an experimental prediction.
- 2.12 Identify and record key features of an observation.
- 2.12 Conclude if hypothesis is correct.

Band	Outcome	Checkpoint	
		Question	Activity
Know	State some questions that can be investigated.		Starter 2, Main 1
	Name variables that can vary in an investigation.		Starter 1, Main 1
↓	Name some types of enquiry question.		Main 1
Apply	Describe how scientists develop an idea into a question that can be investigated.	2	Starter 2, Main 1
	Identify independent, dependent, and control variables.	A, B	Main 1
↓	Suggest ways to investigate different types of enquiry question.	3	Starter 2, Main 1
Extend	Explain how and why some questions can be investigated and why some cannot.	3	Main 1
	Suggest examples of independent, dependent, and control variables in an unfamiliar situation.		Main 1, Plenary 1
↓	Explain in detail why a specific question cannot be investigated, suggesting alternative questions that can be investigated.	3	Main 1

Literacy
Use of scientific terms when asking questions and describing variables.

GCSE link
WS 2.1 Use scientific theories and explanations to develop hypotheses.

WS 2.2 Plan experiments or devise procedures to make observations, produce or characterise a substance, test hypotheses, check data or explore phenomena.

Key Words
observation, investigation, data, **evidence, variable, independent variable, dependent variable, control variable, prediction, hypothesis, scientific enquiries, correlation,** fair test, observation enquiry, pattern seeking enquiry

Answers from the student book

In-text questions	**A** independent, dependent
	B control

Summary questions	**1a** independent variable - What you change in an investigation to see how it affects the dependent variable. dependent variable - What you measure or observe in an investigation. control variable - One that remains unchanged or is held constant to stop it affecting the dependent variable. (3 marks) **b** fair test enquiry - Questions to check that all the control variables been kept the same. observation enquiry - Questions relating to what you see happen in the experiment. pattern seeking enquiry - Questions to determine if there is any link or pattern in the observations that you made. (3 marks) **2a** For example, how does the temperature of the water affect how long it takes the ice cube to melt? (1 mark) **b** It is a question that you can collect data for by measuring the temperature and the time. (2 marks) **3** Extended response question (6 marks). Example answers: **Questions scientists could investigate:** What is the energy content each food? Because you could measure the energy content to answer it. What is the vitamin content of different foods? Because you could measure the vitamin content to answer it. What type of foods do different animals eat? Because you could watch different animals to answer it. **Questions scientists could not investigate:** What is the best food? Because it depends on what you mean by best – you cannot collect data. Why do different people like different food? Because you could not collect data to answer it – it is a matter of opinion. Is there enough food to feed everyone in the future? Because you could not collect data to answer it.

kerboodle

Starter	Support/Extension	Resources
What varies? (5–10 min) Students make a list of things that could change in an investigation. The investigation could be one they have done or are planning to do, for example, 'How quickly does a drink cool?' **Asking questions** (10 min) Students make lists of questions they could ask if they were given something to investigate, for example, 'Melting ice-cream' or 'Floating or sinking'. Pick out examples of questions that can be investigated and examples that cannot.	**Support**: Provide a list of different things connected with an investigation for students to choose from.	

Main	Support/Extension	Resources
Asking scientific questions (35 min) Introduce the idea that there are different types of enquiry question (fair test, observation, pattern seeking). Discuss the different methods that you can use to answer these types of question, using examples from the starter. For each example of the fair text questions, introduce the independent variable, dependent variable, and control variable. Explain that the type of variable something belongs to depends on the question and how it is asked. Work though the activity sheet and encourage students to share their ideas. They should describe how controlling variables is important if you are to obtain evidence to answer your question.	**Support**: A support sheet is available where students focus on the ideas, questions, and variables of two stations, instead of four. Try to decrease the number of technical terms used. For example, ensure students understand that you can choose the values of some variables, rather than stressing the term independent variable. **Extension**: Students can consider how to collect evidence to answer the other two types of question.	**Activity**: Asking scientific questions

Plenary	Support/Extension	Resources
Identifying variables (5–10 min) Students are given a hypothetical investigation for which they must categorise variables as independent, dependent, and control using the interactive resource. **Grouping variables** (5–10 min) Provide a list of 12 variables and a scientific question. Students identify which variables are independent, dependent, and control.	**Extension**: Students make up their own questions based on variables given.	**Interactive**: Identifying variables

Homework		
Students write down variables linked to things they can investigate in everyday life, for example, boiling a kettle, kicking a football, or getting a seat on the tube.		

Planning investigations

Enquiry processes

- 2.9 Choose a suitable range and interval for the independent variable.
- 2.9 Test suitability of measuring instrument, and use it correctly.
- 2.9 Carry out the method carefully and consistently.
- 2.11 Decide how to vary the independent variable and to measure the dependent variable.
- 2.11 Identify and control the control variables.
- 2.13 Identify risks and hazards, and control measures.
- 2.13 Suggest how the question being investigated can be safely explored in a school science laboratory.

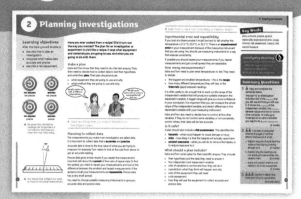

Band	Outcome	Checkpoint	
		Question	Activity
Know	State what should be included in the plan for an investigation.	A, 1	Main 1
	Identify different types of variable and experimental errors.		Main 1
	State what is meant by a risk assessment.	1	
Apply	Describe how to write a plan for an investigation.	1	Enq Proc
	Describe how to produce accurate and precise data, and reduce experimental error.	2	Main 1
	Describe a risk assessment.	C	Main 1
Extend	Write a detailed plan for a hypothetical investigation.		Enq Proc, Main 1
	Explain the effect of experimental error, and of not controlling all the variables adequately.	3	Main 1
	Identify risks in an experiment and write an appropriate risk assessment for an investigation and explain why the experiment can, or cannot, be conducted in a science laboratory.	C	Enq Proc, Main 1

Literacy

Students adopt the appropriate writing style when writing a plan for an investigation; presenting ideas in structured sentences, and in a coherent manner.

GCSE link

WS 1.5 Evaluate risks both in practical science and the wider societal context, including perception of risk in relation to data and consequences.

WS 2.2 Plan experiments or devise procedures to make observations, produce or characterise a substance, test hypotheses, check data or explore phenomena.

WS 2.3 Apply a knowledge of a range of techniques, instruments, apparatus, and materials to select those appropriate to the experiment.

WS 2.5 Recognise when to apply a knowledge of sampling techniques to ensure any samples collected are representative.

Key Words

plan, accurate, precise, spread, repeatable, **range, interval,** risk assessment, **risk, hazard, control measure**

Answers from the student book

In-text questions	**A** What equipment and method you are going to use and why.
	B Align the object for measurement with the zero mark on the ruler. Ensure the ruler is straight. Read the scale on the ruler by looking straight at it.
Activity	**Investigating dissolving**
	Independent: temperature of the water
	Dependent: mass of salt that dissolves
	Control: volume of water, time allowed for salt to dissolve, type of beaker, stirring or not stirring
	Plan to include: method of changing temperature, method of measuring mass of salt, variables to control, range of temperature, need to repeat measurements, risk assessment

Summary questions	**1** equipment, range, interval, risk assessment (6 marks)
	2a To get an accurate reading of the height and avoid parallax error. (2 marks)
	b There is an uncertainty in all measurements that produces a spread of results. (2 marks)
	c All experiments require a risk assessment for safety, for example, to reduce the chance of someone falling because of a rolling ball on the floor. (2 marks)
	3 Extended response question (6 marks). Example answers:
	Hypothesis shows scientific question that they are trying to answer.
	The independent and dependent variables will shows what they will change and what they will measure.
	A list of all the variables that they need to control and how they will do it will ensure a fair test.
	A prediction: what they think will happen and why will help to them to assess the reliability of their results.
	A list of the equipment they will need will help to carry out the method.
	A risk assessment will maximise safety.
	How they will use the equipment to collect precise, accurate, data and reduce experimental error will help to ensure accurate and precise results.

kerboodle

Starter	Support/Extension	Resources
Planning (5 min) Remind students of occasions when they had to plan, for example, packing their bags for school. Students state what they need to plan, consequences of not planning, and how they can tell their plan was good enough.	**Support:** Help students by asking questions, for example, 'What did you do next?' or 'What happens if you forget to bring something?'	
Risks (10 min) Students state different risks they took that day, for example, crossing the road or jumping the queue at lunch. Ask them to classify the consequences as minor and severe, and the likelihood as likely or unlikely. Discuss things that they did that could reduce the risk (control measures). Discuss whether a severe but unlikely risk is worth taking.	**Extension:** Students discuss why people are more worried about unfamiliar risks, for example, flying compared with familiar risks, for example, driving.	

Main	Support/Extension	Resources
Planning investigations (40 min) The activity sheet leads students through structured questions so they come across the main ideas and terminology used when planning. It is important to keep circulating around the groups to ask them why they are carrying out an activity in a certain way. You can help them compare their method or equipment at the time they carry out the activity.	**Support:** The support sheet includes a suggested table of results. The emphasis of the teacher should be to help students understand the ideas rather than worrying about remembering terminology.	**Activity:** Planning investigations **Skill sheet:** Accuracy and precision **Skill sheet:** Recording results

Plenary	Support/Extension	Resources
Accurate or precise? (10 min) Students are presented with four sets of data on the interactive resource and must decide whether each set of data is accurate, precise, or neither. Students can then suggest why these errors have occurred and suggest ways to improve data collection. They should make it clear how each way affects the precision and accuracy of the data.		**Interactive:** Accurate or precise?
Planning revisited (5 min) Students look again at their plans and suggest improvements based on what they have covered in the lesson.	**Support:** Demonstrate several ways to collect data, for example, measuring the volume of water using a beaker or a measuring cylinder. Students decide if the data is precise, accurate, or neither.	

Homework		
Students write a plan including a risk assessment for a simple activity, for example, preparing a meal or measuring how quickly a hot drink cools in different containers.		

EP3 Collecting, recording, and presenting data

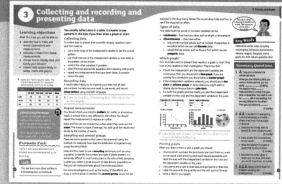

Enquiry processes

- 2.1 Calculate means from data.
- 2.4 Decide the type of chart or graph to draw based on its purpose or type of data.
- 2.4 Design a table for the data being gathered.
- 2.4 Draw line graphs to display relationships.
- 2.6 Record observations you want to explain.
- 2.9 Remove outliers and calculate mean of repeats.
- 2.11 Control the variables.

Band	Outcome	Checkpoint	
		Question	**Activity**
Know	State an example of how data can be recorded.	A	Starter 2
	With help, calculate a mean of two values.		Maths, Main 1, Plenary 2
	Add data to a graph or chart.		Main 1
Apply	Describe how to make and record observations and measurements.	1, 2	Starter 1, Starter 2, Main 1, Plenary 1
	Calculate a mean from three repeat measurements.		Maths, Main 1, Plenary 2
	Present data appropriately as tables and graphs.		Main 1
Extend	Explain how to collect and record accurate and precise data.	3	Main 1, Plenary 1
	Calculate a mean for repeat readings in a range of situations.	3	Maths, Main 1, Plenary 2
	Explain the choice of graph or chart for different types of data, and plot them.	2, B	Main 1

Maths

In the student-book activity students calculate arithmetic means based on data given from an experiment.

MyMaths
More support for the maths skills in this section can be found on MyMaths.

Literacy

Students are required to summarise what they have learnt in their approach to collecting and presenting data to a range of audiences.

GCSE link

WS 2.4 Carry out experiments appropriately having due regard for the correct manipulation of apparatus, the accuracy of measurements and health and safety considerations.

WS 2.5 Recognise when to apply a knowledge of sampling techniques to ensure any samples collected are representative.

WS 2.6 Make and record observations and measurements using a range of apparatus and methods.

WS 3.1 Presenting observations and other data using appropriate methods.

WS 3.2 Translating data from one form to another.

WS 3.3 Carrying out and represent mathematical and statistical analysis.

WS 3.4 Representing distributions of results and make estimations of uncertainty.

Key Words

outlier, mean, control group, line graph, pie chart, bar chart/column graph, sampling, **continuous variable**, **discontinuous variable**, discrete, categoric

Answers from the student book

In-text questions	**A** In a table with clearly labelled headings with units.
	B bar chart (or sometimes pie chart)
Activity	**Calculating the mean**
	3.5 cm

Summary questions	1 measuring instruments, repeat, outliers, mean (5 marks) 2a repeat his reading, use the thermometer correctly (2 marks) b (2 marks)

	Time to dissolve (s)			
Temperature of water (°C)	1st measurement	2nd measurement	3rd measurement	Mean

c A line graph, since both the variables are continuous. (2 marks)
d bar charts, column graphs - when the data is discontinuous
   scatter graphs - when you are looking for a correlation (2 marks)
3 Example answers (6 marks):
   Include the seven elements of a plan from the corresponding student-book spread.
   Draw a table for your results.
   Include columns for your repeat readings.
   Include a column for the mean.

kerboodle

Starter	Support/Extension	Resources
Equipment (5 min) Students describe how to use equipment to collect precise and accurate data. This reinforces the work in the previous lesson, for example, measuring volumes accurately using a measuring cylinder.	**Extension:** Students suggest the advantages of using different equipment, for example, ease of use and precision of reading.	
Using tables (5 min) Draw a table showing results from a mock investigation. Include incomplete headings. Ask students to identify what is missing and why the missing data is important, for example, missing units.	**Support:** Give students missing items to choose from. **Extension:** Give students a context and ask them to draw a results table from scratch.	

Main	Support/Extension	Resources
Collecting and presenting data (40 min) Remind students of the terminology (independent, dependent, and control variables). It is important at this stage to introduce ways to display data – line graphs for continuous data and bar charts or pie charts if data is discrete or categoric. Students carry out a straightforward experiment dropping different types of ball onto the floor from a vertical height of 1 metre. Students then measure how high the balls bounce. They prepare a suitable table to record the data and draw a graph to display their results.	**Support:** An access sheet is available with simplified questions. Tables and graph grids have also been partially filled in to help students with complex skills. **Extension:** Students can see if they can spot a pattern, attempt a conclusion, and explain why it is important to display data as graphs/charts (to display patterns).	**Practical:** Collecting and presenting data **Skill sheet:** Calculating means **Skill sheet:** Choosing scales **Skill sheet:** Recording results **Skill sheet:** Drawing graphs

Plenary	Support/Extension	Resources
'Good' data (10 min) Use examples from real-life to discuss issues raised by 'bad' use of data, for example, to compare different medical approaches including alternative medicine. The website Bad Science is a rich source of examples of misused data.	**Extension:** Students take a question, for example, 'Should doctors prescribe homeopathic medicine?' to suggest what data is needed to answer this question.	
Calculating means (10 min) Example data sets are provided in the interactive resource for students to calculate arithmetic means, given multiple choice answers.		**Interactive:** Calculating means

Homework		
Students collect data at home, for example, timing how long they take to do certain activities. They record the data in a suitable table for discussion in the next lesson.		

EP4 Analysing patterns in data

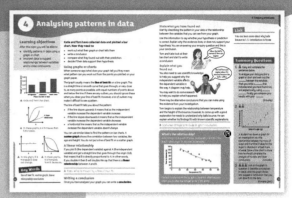

Enquiry processes

- 2.1 Identify a pattern in data from a results table or bar chart.
- 2.1 Interpret a sloping line on a graph to suggest the relationship between variables.
- 2.2 Suggest reasons for differences in repeat readings.
- 2.2 Comment on whether your findings fit with known scientific explanations.
- 2.3 Make conclusion and explain it.
- 2.3 Judge whether the conclusion is supported by the data.
- 2.3 Suggest other possible conclusions that could be drawn from your data.
- 2.6 Develop explanations.
- 2.12 Discuss whether the data support your hypothesis.

Band	Outcome	Checkpoint	
		Question	Activity
Know ↓	State what is meant by a line of best fit.	A	Plenary 1
	List what should be included in a conclusion.	B, 1	Main 1
Apply ↓	Find a pattern in data using a graph or chart, and draw a line of best fit on a line graph.	3	Enq Proc, Main 1
	Interpret data to draw conclusions using scientific explanations.	3	Enq Proc, Main 1
Extend ↓	Plot data on a graph and draw the line of best fit.		Main 1, Plenary 1
	Analyse data from an investigation to draw up a detailed conclusion, describe relationships, and suggest alternative explanations where appropriate.	3	Enq Proc, Main 1, Plenary 1

Maths
Students construct and interpret graphs to find a relationship between data.

MyMaths
More support for the maths skills in this section can be found on MyMaths.

Literacy
Students select and analyse information, presenting conclusions using scientific terms.

GCSE link
WS 3.5 Interpreting observations and other data (presented in verbal, diagrammatic, graphical, symbolic or numerical form), including identifying patterns and trends, making inferences and drawing conclusions.

WS 3.6 Presenting reasoned explanations including relating data to hypotheses.

WS 3.8 Communicating the scientific rationale for investigations, methods used, findings and reasoned conclusions through paper-based and electronic reports and presentations using verbal, diagrammatic, graphical, numerical and symbolic forms.

Key Words
line of best fit, linear relationship, repeatable, evidence, conclusion, **scatter graph**

Answers from the student book

In-text questions	A A line that goes through most of the points and has the same number of points above and below the line.
	B What you have found out, why you think this has happened.
Activity	**What's the relationship?** If you double the temperature of the water, the time it takes to dissolve does not halve, it is more than half.

Summary questions	1 relationship, conclusion, scientific, knowledge, prediction (5 marks)
	2 Draw a line of best fit, find the pattern on the graph, state what you have found out, explain what you have found out. (4 marks)
	3 Extended response question (6 marks). Example answers:
	The graph shows the relationship between mass of sugar and time taken to dissolve.
	There is an outlier when approximately half the maximum mass of sugar.
	The line shows that if there is more sugar it takes longer to dissolve.
	If you double the mass of sugar the time it takes to dissolve approximately doubles.
	Conclusion: There is a linear relationship between the mass of sugar and the time it takes to dissolve.
	If there is more mass of sugar there are more bonds between the particles in the sugar to break.
	It takes longer to break the bonds.

Starter	Support/Extension	Resources
Is there a relationship? (10 min) Students are presented with a range of statements on the interactive resource, for which they must decide whether the relationship in the statement is likely or unlikely.		**Interactive**: Is there a relationship?
What stages? (10 min) Show students data, for example, from a previous experiment stretching springs. Students will find it hard to state a relationship simply. Ask students to suggest the missing stages needed to analyse data.	**Support**: Provide a list of stages of analysis for students to put in order.	
Main	**Support/Extension**	**Resources**
Analysing data (35 min) Use the activity sheet to plot graphs showing different relationships. Part of this skill is choosing correct scales and drawing the axes. This is a written task, but students could use results from their own experiments. This will increase relevance and engagement for the students. Alternatively, graph axes could be drawn on the floor in chalk and students can demonstrate the shapes of their graphs by walking over the graph area. **Writing a conclusion** Students use data/graphs from the previous activity to write a conclusion, then peer assess them against the ideas in the book to check that they are complete.	**Support**: A support sheet is available where students are given pre-labelled graph grids to plot their data. An alternative source of support is to use the skill sheet for choosing scales instead of the accompanying support sheet. **Extension**: Encourage students to give numerical examples when describing patterns in graphs. Non-linear graphs are discussed in the extension.	**Activity**: Analysing data **Skill sheet:** Choosing scales **Skill sheet:** Drawing graphs
Plenary	**Support/Extension**	**Resources**
Line of best fit (10 min) Draw a graph with data plotted on it. Ask one student to draw a line of best fit. Other students decide if this is good enough or draw an improved line.	**Extension**: Describe the relationship shown by the graph in detail, encouraging students to give quantitative relationships.	
What's the conclusion? (10 min) Show graphs using ideas that the students will have met in KS2 (e.g., the temperature of water and the time it takes to dissolve a sugar lump, the thickness of a piece of plastic bag and the force needed to break it) and ask them to write a conclusion, including a scientific explanation.	**Support**: Students can use a writing frame/the beginnings of sentences to frame their conclusion.	
Homework		
Provide students with further data to practise drawing graphs and ask students to describe different relationships and write conclusions.		

EP5 Evaluating data and methods

Enquiry processes

- 2.2 Analyse strengths and weaknesses in your inquiry.
- 2.3 Comment on whether there is a real difference between data.
- 2.2 Identify potential sources of random and systematic error.
- 2.2 Suggest ways to improve the method, and to reduce measurement errors.
- 2.11 Explain why some variables are difficult to control.
- 2.3 Justify whether anomalous results can be explained or ignored.
- 2.2 Describe how the size of the error in an investigation affects the strength of the evidence.
- 2.2 Explain why having someone else repeat the experiment could increase confidence in the conclusion.

Band	Outcome	Checkpoint	
		Question	Activity
Know ↓	State how to evaluate data.	1	
	Suggest one improvement to an investigation.	2	Main 1
Apply ↓	Describe the stages in evaluating the data.	1	Main 1
	Suggest ways of improving a practical investigation.	B, 2	Main 1
Extend ↓	Compare and contrast data, suggesting reasons why the data may be different.	3	Main 1
	Explain ways of improving data in a practical investigation.	4	Main 1

Maths
Extract and interpret information from charts, graphs, and tables to evaluate the data.

MyMaths
More support for the maths skills in this section can be found on MyMaths.

Literacy
Students describe stages in evaluating data using scientific terminology and summarise information from scientific methods.

GCSE link
WS 3.7 Being objective, evaluating data in terms of accuracy, precision, repeatability and reproducibility and identifying potential sources of random and systematic error.

Key Words
evaluate, confidence, **random and systematic error, experimental error, real difference**

Answers from the student book

In-text questions	**A** Not stirring the liquid, pulling the thermometer out to read it. **B** wide range
Summary questions	**1** outliers, more, error, random, systematic, strengths, data (7 marks) **2a** Any two of the following: measure temperature using a thermometer, include a bigger range, take more readings, or use different apparatus to give smaller spread and fewer outliers. **b** Ask other people to do the experiment using their method to see if their results are reproducible. (3 marks) **3** Extended response question (6 marks). Example answers: A video camera takes lots of photographs in a short time period. If they put a ruler against the wall while they were bouncing the ball they could measure height. They could pause the video to see exactly which point where the ball reached the highest point of the bounce. They could take accurate readings (it is the height of the bounce). Repeat readings would have a much smaller spread that makes the data more precise. High-quality data is more precise than low-quality data.

10

Starter	Support/Extension	Resources
Do you believe it? (10 min) Provide students with examples of statistics, for example, 9 out of 10 cats prefer a certain brand of cat food. Encourage students to ask questions to judge whether to believe the data or not, for example, who prepared the data or how many cats were tested. Alternatively, students complete the interactive resource to select what information is needed to believe a claim.		**Interactive:** Patrick's claim
Improving data (10 min) Students look at data from previous experiments, or on the activity sheet Analysing data. They suggest ways to improve the quality of the data, for example, repeat experiments or measure a bigger range of the independent variable, use different measuring instruments, or the same instruments in a different way.	**Support**: Provide cloze suggestions for students to complete, for example, take fewer/more results, show data on a graph/in a table, take one/two sets of readings.	

Main	Support/Extension	Resources
Evaluating data (35 min) Students consider the collected data when they all measure one event, for example, you dropping a ball. Then complete the activity sheet to compare two different experiments and identify differences that make one experiment better than another. Suggest how to evaluate data, i.e., work out if there is a real difference between data points using the spread, consider the effect of experimental error, and the choice of range and interval. Discuss the effect of control variables and how some variables are difficult to control.	**Support**: The support sheet offers students a simplified text to summarise when considering differences between two experiments.	**Activity**: Evaluating data
Emphasise that students should differentiate between evaluating the data and evaluating the method. Display a range of measuring instruments that students regularly use and discuss/display/show images or video of alternative measuring instruments, such as video cameras, motion sensors, temperature sensors.		

Plenary	Support/Extension	Resources
Same experiment, different data (10 min) Give out two sets of data for the same experiment, one with a large spread, many outliers, not many repeats, and get students to suggest as many reasons as possible why they are different when the data is from the same experiment. Compare answers.		
What's wrong? What's right? (10 min) Students watch you doing an experiment, such as finding out the link between the height of a ramp and the stopping distance. You make lots of mistakes, such as measuring the height incorrectly, putting the car at different distances up the ramp) and make a list of improvements that you need to make to collect evidence that is more accurate, precise, repeatable etc. Ask students to consider the method and the type of measuring instruments that you can use.	**Extension:** Ask students to think about how scientists measure things that are difficult to measure, such as the global temperature or distance to the Moon.	

Homework		
Students investigate the measuring instruments they find at home (e.g., kitchen scales) and write a paragraph about the experimental errors that there can be when using them.		

① Forces

In this Big Idea students will learn:

- if the overall, resultant force on an object is non-zero, its motion changes and it slows down, speeds up, or changes direction
- mass and weight are different but related. Mass is a property of the object; weight depends upon mass but also on gravitational field strength
- every object exerts a gravitational force on every other object. The force increases with mass and decreases with distance. Gravity holds planets and moons in orbit around larger bodies.

AQA Enquiry process activities

Activity	Section
3.1.1 Investigate variables that affect the speed of a toy car rolling down a slope.	1.1.3 Speed
3.1.2 Explain the way in which an astronaut's weight varies on a journey to the moon.	1.2.1 Gravity

Preparing for Key Stage 4 success

Knowledge Underpinning knowledge is covered in this Big Idea for KS4 study of:	4.1.6.1/6.5.4.1 Describing motion along a line 4.1.6.2/6.5.4.2 Forces, acceleration, and Newton's Laws of motion 4.1.6.3/6.5.4.3 Forces and braking

Maths
 	
Skills developed in Big Idea 1
	1 Arithmetic and numerical computation
	   d Make estimates of the results of simple calculations (1.1.3)
	2 Handling data
	   a Use an appropriate number of significant figures (1.1.3, 1.1.4, 1.2.1)
	   b Find arithmetic means (1.1.3)
	3 Algebra
	   a Understand and use the symbols: $=, <, <<, >>, >, \propto, \sim$ (1.1.1, 1.1.3, 1.1.4, 1.2.1)
	   b Change the subject of an equation (1.1.3, 1.1.4, 1.2.1)
	   c Substitute numerical values into algebraic equations using appropriate units for physical quantities (1.1.3, 1.1.4, 1.2.1)
	4 Graphs
	   a Translate information between graphical and numeric form (1.1.4)
	   c Plot two variables from experimental or other data (1.1.4)

Literacy Skills developed in Big Idea 1	• Collaboration and exploratory talk. (1.1.1, 1.1.2, 1.1.3, 1.1.4, 1.2.1)		
	• Communicating ideas and information to a wide range of audiences and a variety of situations. (1.1.1, 1.1.2, 1.1.3, 1.1.4, 1.2.1)		
	• Predicting, making inferences, describing relationships. (1.2.1)		
	• Use of scientific terms. (1.1.1, 1.1.2, 1.1.3, 1.1.4, 1.2.1)		
	• Making connections within/across a range of texts/themes and from personal experience. (1.1.3, 1.2.1)		
	• Planning and adapting writing style to suit audience and purpose. (1.1.3, 1.2.1)		
	• Attention to the 'rules' of the particular form of writing (e.g., news article, scientific report). (1.1.3, 1.2.1)		
	• Organisation of ideas and information. (1.1.1, 1.1.2, 1.1.3, 1.1.4, 1.2.1)		
	• Identifying main ideas, events, and supporting details. (1.1.3, 1.2.1)		
	• Legibility, spelling, punctuation, grammar, and sentence structure. (1.1.3, 1.1.4, 1.2.1)		
	• Accessing information to ascertain meaning, using word skills and comprehension strategies. (1.1.3, 1.1.4, 1.2.1)		
Assessment Skills	• Extended response questions (1.1.1, 1.1.3, 1.1.4, 1.2.1) End-of-Big Idea questions, Q8.		
	• Quantitative problem solving (1.1.3, 1.1.4) End-of-Big Idea questions, Q4, Q5, Q7.		

KS2 Link	Check before	Checkpoint	Catch-up
Unsupported objects fall to the Earth because of the force of gravity acting between the Earth and the falling object.	1.1.1 Introduction to forces	Ask why dropped objects fall to the ground.	Demonstrate that dropped objects fall simultaneously, and name the force causing this effect as gravity.
Friction slows down moving objects.	1.1.3 Speed	Students describe motion of objects shown to them in a video clip.	Students label a force diagram of a moving object, explaining the effect of resultant forces.
Unsupported objects fall towards Earth because of the force of gravity.	1.1.4 Distance–time graphs	Students explain why a ball falls towards Earth when thrown in the air.	Use force arrows to label forces acting on supported and unsupported objects.

Key Stage 2 Quiz: Physics 1 Part 1 End-of-Big-Idea test (foundation) 1 Part 1 End-of-Big-Idea test (foundation) mark scheme 1 Part 1 End-of-Big-Idea test (higher) 1 Part 1 End-of-Big-Idea test (higher) mark scheme	

Answers to Picture Puzzler
Key Words
speaker, pull, eclipse, eye, dolphin
The key word is **speed**.
Close Up
a flea

MyMaths

You can find additional support for the maths skills covered in this Big Idea on **MyMaths**, including carrying out calculations, changing the subject of equations, calculating means, drawing graphs, and using ratios.

1.1.1 Introduction to forces

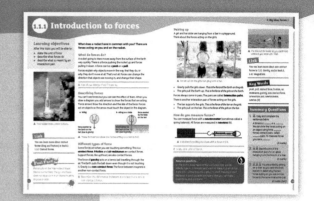

Securing Mastery Goals

- 3.1.2 Draw a force diagram for a problem involving gravity. (Pt 1/2)

Extending Mastery Goals

- 3.1.2 Compare and contrast gravity with other forces.

Enquiry processes

- 2.9 Use the measuring instrument correctly.
- 2.12 Make an experimental prediction.

Band	Outcome	Checkpoint	
		Question	**Activity**
Know	Describe what forces do.	A	Starter 1
	Identify a 'contact force', 'non-contact force', and 'newton'.	1	Starter 1/Starter 2
	Use a newtonmeter to make predictions about sizes of forces.	B	Main 1
Apply	Categorise everyday forces as 'contact' and 'non-contact' forces.	2	Starter 1
	Identify interaction pairs in a simple situation.		Main 2
	Interpret force diagrams used to illustrate problems involving gravity.	1	Main 2
	Describe what 'interaction pair' means.	B/C	Main 2
	Make predictions about forces in familiar situations.	3	Main 1
Extend	Identify interaction pairs in complex situations.		Main 2
	Explain the link between non-contact forces, contact forces, and interaction pairs.		Main 2
	Make predictions about pairs of forces acting in unfamiliar situations.		Main 1

Maths

In the student-book activity students use units for force.

Students can use size and scale and the quantitative relationship between units in the practical.

MyMaths More support for the maths skills in this section can be found on MyMaths.

Literacy

In the student-book activity students use scientific terms confidently and correctly in writing about forces.

Students can make clear descriptions of forces when using newtonmeters.

GCSE link

4.5.6.2.3/6.5.4.2.3 Newton's Third Law

Whenever two objects interact, the forces they exert on each other are equal and opposite.

Students should be able to apply Newton's Third Law to examples of equilibrium situations.

4.5.1.2/6.5.1.2 Contact and non-contact forces

Students should be able to describe the interaction between pairs of objects which produce a force on each object. The forces to be represented as vectors.

Key Words

push, pull, **contact force**, friction, air resistance, gravity, **non-contact force**, interaction pair, newtonmeter, **newton (N)**

Answers from the student book

In-text questions	**A** Forces change the shape, speed, or direction of motion.
	B For a contact force to act the objects have to be touching (e.g., the air and a car for air resistance) but non-contact forces act at a distance.
	C newtons

14

Summary questions	1 push, pull, arrows, interaction, newtonmeter (5 marks)
	2 The force of the Earth on the apple AND the force of the apple on the Earth OR the force of the tree on the apple AND the force of the apple on the tree. (2 marks)
	3 Extended response question. Example answers (6 marks):
	The Earth exerts a force on you.
	You exert a force on the Earth.
	The chair exerts a force on you.
	You exert a force on the chair.
	These are two interaction pairs.
	The two forces acting on you are from two different interaction pairs.
	This means one can be bigger than the other.

kerboodle

Starter	Support/Extension	Resources
What's the force? (10 min) Students recap on what forces are and what they do (from KS2), and individually name as many forces as possible. They then sort the forces into contact and non-contact forces.	**Support:** Show a picture as a prompt for listing forces, for example, forces acting on a cyclist.	
Who pulls harder? (10 min) Give groups of students a pair of newtonmeters, linking the hooks together. Ask them to predict the readings on each newtonmeter if one student holds their newtonmeter and the other student pulls theirs away.		

Main	Support/Extension	Resources
At this point it is important that students are clear on the effects and names of forces, as well as what interactive pairs are.		
Measuring forces (15 min) Introduce students to the idea of a newtonmeter and measuring forces in newtons.	**Support:** Make sure the forces are straightforward to measure. For example, objects with hooks or straps.	**Practical:** Measuring forces
Students measure the force needed to carry out different activities (e.g., to lift a pencil case) and record these in a table. Students should compare readings with each other, explaining differences. For accurate readings, the newtonmeter hook should be in line with its spring.	**Extension:** Students prepare their own table to record results. Students identify several forces acting on one object and explain why they chose these groups, for example, as pairs of interaction forces.	
Force arrows (20 min) Introduce students to force diagrams and force arrows. Give students three arrows of different lengths cut out of card. Students put arrows on objects in a forces circus and describe them as 'the force of the ... on the ...'		

Plenary	Support/Extension	Resources
Comparing the size of forces (10 min) Students list at least six situations involving forces and put these in order, ranked by size. This can be done using the list from the interactive resource or non-interactively on the board.	**Support:** Supply a list and ask students to rank these forces by size. **Extension:** Ask students to estimate the size of different forces in newtons.	**Interactive:** Comparing the size of forces
What's the difference? (10 min) If students have measured the same thing during the practical (for example, lifting a book) ask them to compare results. Students discuss the types of forces in the forces circus (contact or non-contact) and identify some interaction pairs.		

Homework	Support/Extension	
Provide students with a strong rubber band stapled to the top of a piece of stiff card, and tie one side of the top of a small sandwich plastic bag to the other end of the rubber band. Attach a piece of paper to the elastic band as a pointer. Students use this to measure forces at home calibrating the scale using their own units, depending on what is available to measure, by placing items in the plastic bag.	**Support:** Calibrate the newtonmeter in the classroom and ask students to use it to measure forces at home. **Extension:** Ask students to make their own newtonmeter using their own design.	

15

1.1.2 Balanced and unbalanced

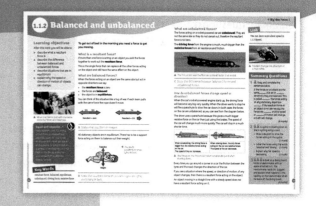

Securing Mastery Goals
- 3.1.2 Draw a force diagram for a problem involving gravity. (Pt 2/2)

Exceeding Mastery Goals
- 3.1.2 Predict changes in an object's speed when the forces on it change.

Enquiry processes
- 2.9 Gather sufficient data for the investigation and repeat if appropriate.
- 2.4 Select a good way to display data.

Band	Outcome	Checkpoint	
		Question	Activity
Know	Identify familiar situations of balanced and unbalanced forces.	1	
	Recognise equilibrium.	A	
	Identify a resultant force.	A	
	Identify when the speed or direction of motion of an object changes.		Main, Starter 1
	Present observations in a table with help.		Main
Apply	Draw a force diagram for a problem involving gravity.	B	Main
	Describe the difference between balanced and unbalanced forces.	C	Main, Plenary 1
	Describe situations that are in equilibrium.	B	
	Calculate resultant forces.	B	
	Explain why the speed or direction of motion of objects can change.	2	Starter 2
	Present observations in a table including force arrow drawings.	B	Main
Extend	Explain the difference between balanced and unbalanced forces.	2	
	Describe a range of situations that are in equilibrium.	B	Main
	Describe the link between the resultant force and the motion of an object.	B	Main
	Explain why the speed or direction of motion of objects can change using force arrows.		Main
	Predict and present changes in observations for unfamiliar situations.		Main

Maths
In the student-book activity students use proportion when estimating force arrows.

In the practical activity students can carry out calculations of resultant force involving $+$, $-$, $\times$, $\div$, either singly or in combination.

MyMaths More support for the maths skills in this section can be found on MyMaths.

Literacy
Students make connections within/across a range of texts when reading an account of Newton's work on forces.

GCSE link
4.5.1.4/6.5.1.4 Resultant forces

A number of forces acting on an object may be replaced by a single force that has the same effect as all the original forces acting together. This single force is called the resultant force.

Key Words
resultant force, balanced, **equilibrium**, unbalanced, driving force, resistive force

16

Answers from the student book

In-text questions	**A** An object is in equilibrium if the forces on it are balanced, or if the resultant force is zero. **B** Zero **C** Balanced forces cancel out/are equal in size and opposite in direction. Unbalanced forces are not of equal size/direction/do not cancel out.

Summary questions	**1** size, opposite/opposing, equilibrium, balanced, unbalanced, direction (6 marks)
	2a Force diagram with an arrow showing that the resistive force is smaller than the driving force. (1 mark)
	  b Arrow pointing backwards labelled resistive, arrow pointing forwards labelled driving. (1 mark)
	  c She continues to speed up but not as much, until she moves at a steady speed because the forces are balanced. (3 marks)
	3 The newtonmeter reads zero. (1 mark)
	The resultant force on the spring inside the newtonmeter is zero. (1 mark)
	For the reading to be bigger than zero, the Earth and the diver have to exert forces in opposite directions. (1 mark)

Starter	Support/Extension	Resources
Forces and sport (10 min) Show a short video of a sports activity. Students list what happens as the motion of a person or object changes, for example, the ball was kicked or the player swung a racket. **Changing speed** (10 min) Students describe their motion on a short car/bus journey, explaining how the driver changed the motion, for example, braked, accelerated, turned the steering wheel.	**Extension:** Students identify the type and direction of forces changing the motion.	
Main	**Support/Extension**	**Resources**
Force circus (40 min) Students identify forces acting on several experiments in a circus, deciding if they are balanced or not, and describing the different forces acting on the object. Students should make the link between the balanced forces, unbalanced forces, and the resultant forces. As part of the practical sheet, students sketch the force diagram for each experiment showing the size and direction of the forces acting on the object. They then identify situations where the resultant force is zero, and when it is not zero.	**Support:** The support sheet provides a pre-drawn table. **Extension:** Students identify the relative size and direction of unbalanced forces, linking this to the motion.	**Practical:** Force circus **Skill sheet:** Scientific apparatus
Plenary	**Support/Extension**	**Resources**
Riding a bicycle (5 min) Students describe and act out how to change motion when you ride a bicycle, linking the ideas to the forces. **Balanced and unbalanced forces** (5 min) Interactive resource where students sort statements describing the motion of a football being kicked into balanced or unbalanced forces.	**Support:** Name the forces and ask students to identify the direction, and if one force is larger or smaller than another. **Extension:** Students estimate the size of the different forces, and estimate the resultant force.	**Interactive:** Balanced and unbalanced forces
Homework	**Support/Extension**	
Students list different situations at home where forces are balanced or unbalanced, i.e., when the resultant force is zero or non-zero. Students name the forces involved in each case, identifying the direction and relative size.	**Support:** Students identify if the forces are balanced or unbalanced. **Extension:** Students name the forces involved and prepare force arrow diagrams.	

1.1.3 Speed

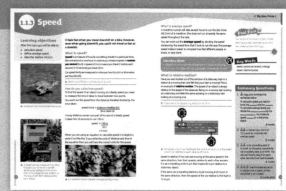

Securing Mastery Goals
- 3.1.1 Use the formula: speed = distance (m) ÷ time (s) or distance–time graphs, to calculate speed. (Pt 1/2)
- 3.1.1 The higher the speed of an object, the shorter the time taken for a journey.
- 3.1.1 Describe how the speed of an object varies when measured by observers who are not moving, or moving relative to the object.

Exceeding Mastery Goals
- 3.1.1 Suggest how the motion of two objects moving at different speeds in the same direction would appear to the other.

Enquiry processes
- 2.12 Make an experimental prediction.
- 2.9 Gather sufficient data for the investigation and repeat if appropriate.
- 2.12 Decide whether the conclusion of the experiment agrees with your prediction.
- 2.13 Identify risks and hazards.
- 2.11 Identify how to control each control variable.
- 2.13 dentify control measures.

Enquiry processes activity
- 3.1.1 Investigate variables that affect the speed of a toy car rolling down a slope.

Band	Outcome	Checkpoint	
		Question	Activity
Know	State the equation for speed and use it to calculate speed, with support.	A	Maths, Main
	Recognise relative motion.	C	Plenary 1
	Use appropriate techniques and equipment to measure times and distances.		Main
Apply	Calculate speed using the speed equation.	2	Maths, Starter 2, Main
	Describe relative motion.	3	Plenary 1
	Choose equipment to make appropriate measurements for time and distance to calculate speed.		Main
Extend	Use the speed equation to explain unfamiliar situations.		Main, Homework
	Describe and explain how a moving object appears to a stationary observer and to a moving observer.	4	Plenary 1
	Choose equipment to obtain data for speed calculations, justifying their choice based on accuracy and precision.		Main

Maths
Students carry out simple calculations to work out the average speed of objects given total distance and time taken.

Students must also use the correct units in their calculations, converting between various units of time and distance.

MyMaths More support for the maths skills in this section can be found on MyMaths.

Literacy
Students explain the concept of speed in their practical using scientific terminology, explaining how different factors affect reaction times, and in turn suggest why motorists should slow down at different places, for their homework.

Key Words
speed, metres per second, instantaneous speed, **average speed, relative motion**

GCSE link
4.5.6.1.2/6.5.4.1.2 Speed

Students should be able to make measurements of distance and time and then calculate speeds of objects.

For an object moving at constant speed the distance travelled in a specific time can be calculated using the equation:

distance travelled = speed × time

Answers from the student book

In-text questions	**A** How far something travels in a particular time. **B** It is less/shorter/decreases. **C** The movement of a body compared to another.
Activity	**Marathon times** distance in a marathon = 42.2 km; time taken to run marathon = 2.5 h average speed = distance ÷ time = 42.2 ÷ 2.5 = 16.88 km/h
Summary questions	1 distance, time, total distance, total time, relative (5 marks) 2 Average speed = total distance ÷ total time = 100 m ÷ 12.5 s = 8 m/s (2 marks) 3 Their relative motion is 70 km/h, either towards each other if they haven't passed yet, or away from each other if they have already passed. (2 marks) 4 Extended response question (6 marks). Example answers: Lines are painted on the road a set distance apart. The camera takes a photograph of the car on the road. The camera takes a photograph of the car a short time later. From the position of the car the camera can work out how far the car has travelled in the time between the two photographs were taken. The camera can use the time between the photographs to find the time using the equation speed = distance ÷ time. The speed camera uses the information obtained from the two photographs to calculate the speed of the car. If the car is travelling faster than the speed limit it will travel too far in the time between the photographs.

kerboodle

Starter	Support/Extension	Resources
How fast? (10 min) Students estimate speeds in different situations, for example, walking, running, driving, flying, speed of sound, and speed of light. Use tangible examples to begin with, for example, with speed limits on roads. **How quick was the ball?** (10 min) Students measure the time taken for a ball to fall from a vertical height of one metre. This can be done as a demonstration. Discuss where the ball travelled slowest and fastest in order to introduce the difference between average and instantaneous speed. Introduce the speed equation and calculate the average speed of the ball.	**Extension**: Ask students how they would convert a speed from kilometres per hour (km/h) to metres per second (m/s). **Extension**: Ask students to consider whether the average speed of the ball would change if the ball was dropped from a greater height.	

Main	Support/Extension	Resources
Rolling, Rolling (35 min) This activity is one of the AQA Enquiry process activities. Students investigate the effects of a selected variable on the average speed of a toy car as it rolls down a ramp. Students will have to calculate the speed of the car, as they vary the independent variable.	**Support**: The accompanying support sheet has a results table to help students set out their results and choose the number of repeats.	**Practical**: Rolling, rolling **Skill sheet:** Recording results

Plenary	Support/Extension	Resources
Talking about relative speed (10 min) Students choose the correct words on the interactive resource to summarise relative motion. This resource covers the definition, description, and an example of relative speed and motion. **What affects your reaction time?** (10 min) Students discuss who had the quickest reaction time, and factors that affect it. Discuss why a quick reaction time is important for athletes and drivers. This discussion can include drink driving, use of mobile phones while driving, and reasons why motorists should take regular breaks when driving long distances.		**Interactive**: Talking about relative speed

Homework	Support/Extension	
Produce a safety leaflet explaining when drivers should slow down (in built-up areas, during periods of poor visibility, and so on) and explain the physics behind this. An explanation of the speed equation should be included.	**Extension**: Students should be encouraged to give examples using the speed equation with numerical values.	

1.1.4 Distance–time graphs

Securing Mastery Goals

- 3.1.1 Use the formula: speed = distance (m) ÷ time (s) or distance–time graphs, to calculate speed.
- 3.1.1 A straight line on a distance–time graph shows constant speed, a curving line shows acceleration.
- 3.1.1 Illustrate a journey with changing speed on a distance–time graph, and label changes in motion.

Enquiry processes

- 2.1 Read values from a line graph.
- 2.4 Draw line graphs to display relationships.

Band	Outcome	Checkpoint	
		Question	**Activity**
Know	Describe simply what a distance–time graph shows.	A	Starter 2, Plenary 1
	Use a distance–time graph to describe a journey qualitatively.		Starter 1, Starter 2, Main, Plenary 2
	Present data given on a distance–time graph, with support.		Main
	Calculate speed from a distance–time graph, with support.		
Apply	Interpret distance–time graphs.	A, B, 1, 2	Starter 1, Starter 2, Main, Plenary 1, Plenary 2
	Calculate speed from a distance–time graph and convert between units.		Maths, Main, Homework
	Plot data on a distance–time graph accurately.		Main
Extend	Draw distance–time graphs for a range of journeys.	3	Main, Plenary 2, Homework
	Analyse journeys using distance–time graphs.	3	Starter 1, Starter 2, Main, Plenary 2
	Manipulate data appropriately to present in a distance–time graph.		Main

Maths

Students interpret and manipulate data from tables in order to draw and analyse distance–time graphs.

Students calculate speeds of moving objects using distance–time graphs.

MyMaths More support for the maths skills in this section can be found on MyMaths.

Literacy

Students describe journeys shown on distance–time graphs using scientific terminology, prepare a presentation to explain a distance–time graph they have drawn, and write a short story to accompany a new distance–time graph.

GCSE link

4.5.6.1.4/6.5.4.1.4 The distance–time relationship

Students should be able to draw distance–time graphs from measurements and extract and interpret lines and slopes of distance–time graphs, translating information between graphical and numerical form.

Students should be able to determine speed from a distance–time graph.

Key Words

distance–time graph, **acceleration**

Answers from the student book

In-text questions	A The distance that something travels in a certain time. B The speed of the object shown in the graph. C Acceleration tells you how quickly your speed increases or decreases.
Activity	**Working it out** speed = distance ÷ time = 60 ÷ 10 = 6 m/s

20

Summary questions	1 distance, time, slope, stationary, changing (5 marks)
	2a (2 marks) Two from:
	Journey is not as far/Speed for sections of the journey are different from each other/Journey took less time/In this graph the object was only stationary once
	b (2 marks) Corresponding reason:
	The scale only goes up to 1000m, not 4500/The gradients of the graph change, but for Lucy's journey the speeds are similar/stationary/The scale only goes up to 80s not 45 minutes/There is only one horizontal section of this graph, but there are two on the graph of Lucy's journey.
	3 Extended response (6 marks). Example answers:
	Both graphs start at a distance of zero and finish at a distance of 3 km. The graph for the car reaches 3 km faster than the graph for walking. Both graphs might have horizontal sections (e.g., the car may stop at a traffic light, or the person walking might stop at a shop). If the graph is horizontal the car or person has stopped. The slope of the graph for the car is much steeper. Cars travel faster than people walking. The car reaches school in a shorter time. The average speed of a car is much higher than that of a person. Both graphs should include curved lines. Curved lines show periods of changing speed.

Starter	Support/Extension	Resources
Using graphs (5 min) Sketch a distance–time graph on the board, explain what it shows, and demonstrate it to students by acting out each section of the graph. Draw a second graph for students to describe to one another in pairs.	**Support**: Label each section of the graph before acting it out. **Extension**: Students draw and interpret their own graphs.	
Comparing speeds (10 min) List typical speeds for different activities, for example, walking quickly (2 m/s) or running slowly (4 m/s). Students work out how long it will take to travel 10 m. Explain how a distance–time graph is used to compare speeds. Sketch a distance–time graph showing the three people travelling the same distance and point out the different slopes and times despite covering the same distance.	**Support**: Remind students of the speed equation. **Extension**: Students sketch and interpret their own graph.	

Main	Support/Extension	Resources
Using distance–time graphs (40 min) Introduce the idea of distance–time graphs, and explain how graphs can be used to interpret movement in detail. Demonstrate how the speed of a section of a journey can be found from the slope, and demonstrate this with two examples, in order to show that a steeper line shows the movement of a faster object. Students then interpret data on the activity sheet to plot a distance–time graph for a migrating bird, the Tour de France, or a sled dog race, and prepare a short summary of the graph they have drawn to present to the rest of the class.	**Support**: A support sheet is available where the breakdown of the times and distances during the ten-day sled dog race has been filled in for them to plot the information. **Extension**: Students write a short story and plot the graph of the journey described.	**Activity**: Using distance–time graphs

Plenary	Support/Extension	Resources
What can you tell from a distance–time graph? (5 min) Students match halves of sentences using the interactive resource to explain how distance–time graphs can be interpreted.	**Support**: Allow students to work in small groups.	**Interactive**: What can you tell from a distance–time graph?
Drawing distance–time graphs (10 min) Each pair of students should draw a distance–time graph on a mini-whiteboard. If a double-sided whiteboard is used, the other side can be used to write down the correct description of the sketch-graph drawn. Choose one side of the whiteboard to display, and allow students to walk around the classroom to find other whiteboards, giving descriptions of graphs shown, or imagining the shape of a graph if the description is shown.	**Support**: Choose pairs of students so that students in need of support are supported by extending students.	

Homework		
Students note down typical times and distances for their journey to or from school, a friend's house, or an after-school club. They produce a labelled distance–time graph, calculating the speed at different stages of the journey and explain what is shown on each section of the graph.		

1.2.1 Gravity

Securing Mastery Goals

- 3.1.2 Use the formula:
  weight (N) = mass (kg) × gravitational field strength (N/kg).
- 3.1.2 g on Earth = 10 N/kg. On the moon it is 1.6 N/kg.
- 3.1.2 Explain unfamiliar observations where weight changes.
- 3.1.2 Deduce how gravity varies for different masses and distances.
- 3.1.2 Compare your weight on Earth with your weight on different planets using the formula.

Exceeding Mastery Goals

- 3.1.2 Draw conclusions from data about orbits, based on how gravity varies with mass and distance.
- 3.1.2 Suggest implications of how gravity varies for a space mission.

Enquiry processes

- 2.9 Prepare a table with space to record all measurements.
- 2.9 Gather data, minimising errors.

Enquiry processes activity

- 3.1.2 Explain the way in which an astronaut's weight varies on a journey to the moon.

Band	Outcome	Checkpoint	
		Question	Activity
Know	Describe the difference between mass and weight.	1	Starter 1
	Describe simply how gravity varies with mass and distance.	3	Starter 1, Starter 2
	State the force that holds planets and moons in orbit around larger bodies.	1	Main 1
	State g on the Earth and the moon.	1	Plenary 1, Plenary 2
	Use the formula weight = mass × g, with support.	2	Main 1
Apply	Describe how gravity due to an object changes if the mass or the distance from the object changes.		Big Write
	Use a formula (weight = mass × g) to work out your weight on different planets, and compare it to your weight on Earth.	2	Main 1, Plenary 1
	Explain why your weight changes in unfamiliar circumstances.		Main 1, Big Write
Extend	Compare and contrast gravity with other forces.		Starter 1, Main 2, Plenary 1
	Explain how the effect of gravity changes moving away from Earth, and in keeping objects in orbit.		Main 1, Main 2
	Analyse data about orbits in terms of the variation of gravity with mass and distance.		Main 2
	Present results in a table, ensuring they are reliable.		Main 1

Maths

In the student book students use number size and scale, and the quantitative relationship between units of mass and weight.

In the practical students extract and interpret information from graphs and tables they have produced.

 MyMaths More support for the maths skills in this section can be found on MyMaths.

Literacy

Students communicate ideas and information to a wide range of audiences by writing holiday brochures for different planets for homework.

Students collaborate and use exploratory talk when they present ideas for the Olympics in Space.

Key Words

gravitational force **field**, **weight**, **mass**, kilogram (kg), **gravitational field strength**

GCSE link

4.5.1.3/6.5.1.3 Gravity

Weight is the force acting on an object due to gravity. The force of gravity close to the Earth is due to the gravitational field around the Earth.

The weight of an object depends on the gravitational field strength at the point where the object is.

The weight of an object can be calculated using the equation:

weight = mass × gravitational field strength

Answers from the student book

In-text questions	**A** masses of both bodies, distance between the bodies **B** A field is a region in which certain objects experience a force. The object does not need to be touching anything to experience this force. **C** The force on 1 kg in a gravitational field.
Activity	**Units of mass a** 2000 g **b** 3500 g **c** 400 g **d** 4.7 kg **e** 0.25 kg
Summary questions	**1** mass, force, newtons, mass, kilograms (5 marks) **2** weight = mass × gravitational field strength (1 mark) = 60 kg × 27 N/kg (1 mark) = 1620 N (1 mark) **3a** As the distance increases the force of gravity decreases. (1 mark) **b** As the mass increases the force of gravity increases. (1 mark) **4** Example answers (6 marks): Because the gravitational field strength is less, objects will travel further before they hit the ground. As such, events that involve throwing something a distance would produce new records; such as javelin/shot put/hammer throw. Because the gravitational field strength is less, events that involve lifting things would also produce new records as a mass would weigh less on the Moon than it did on Earth; such as weightlifting.

Starter	Support/Extension	Resources
Mass or weight? (10 min) Show students a video of astronauts on the Moon and discuss what is the same and what is different in terms of mass and weight.		
Contact and non-contact forces (10 min) Students group forces given on the interactive resource into contact and non-contact forces as a recap and introduction to this lesson.	**Extension**: Students make a list of similarities and differences between gravity and other non-contact forces, and gravity and contact forces.	**Interactive**: Contact and non-contact forces

Main	Support/Extension	Resources
Gravity cups (25 min) This activity is one of the AQA Enquiry process activities. Prepare sealed containers by placing different masses of sand in each to represent different celestial bodies. Students weigh the containers, and use $W = mg$. Students describe how their weight changes on a journey to the moon using values of weight on the surface of the Earth and on the surface on the Moon, and having worked out/been told that there is a point near the Moon where the force on them would be zero. **Gravity and orbits** (15 min) Give students a football and the task of rolling it on the floor and keeping it moving in a circle. Give them a list of objects that orbit other objects. They draw diagrams to show the force of gravity on each one keeping it in orbit. They compare and contrast making the ball move in a smaller or bigger circle, or using a ball with a bigger or a smaller mass.	**Support**: A support sheet is available with a pre-drawn table for results, and a step-by-step guide to work out the identity of each station. **Extension**: Students explain why the mass of the container varies. **Support**: Students explain why the ball moves in a circle. **Extension:** See the lesson player for an extension activity.	**Practical**: Gravity cups

Plenary	Support/Extension	Resources
Match the weight (5 min) Provide a list of five masses (and five equivalent weights) on the Earth and on the Moon. Students link the correct masses and weights. **Olympics in space** (5 min) Ask students to compare an astronaut doing sport on the Earth and on the Moon.	**Support**: Present data for one mass at a time. **Extension**: Students use the idea of gravity and weight to explain their answer.	

Homework	Support/Extension	
Write a holiday brochure for a trip to another planet. Explain what the conditions would be like, and how to prepare for the trip.	**Support**: Provide summary data about a specific planet. **Extension**: There is scope for a detailed discussion linking the conditions and preparations needed.	

Checkpoint lesson routes

The route through this lesson can be determined using the Checkpoint assessment.

Percentage pass marks are supplied in the Checkpoint teacher notes.

Route A (support)
Resource: 1 Part 1 Checkpoint revision

Students work through a selection of tasks that take students from achieving *Know* to *Apply* outcomes. Students have the opportunity to practise using distance–time graphs, calculate weight, and think about relative motion.

Route B (extension)
Resource: 1 Part 1 Checkpoint extension

Students create a poster about the Apollo 11 moon landings. Ensure students are clear about Apollo 11 being the rocket that launched the astronauts into space, but once they were in space it detached and they travelled to the Moon in the command module Columbia.

Progression to *Apply*

Know outcome	Apply outcome	Making progress
Know that mass and weight are different.	Compare weight on the Earth with weight on other planets.	For Task 1, remind students of the equation for calculating weight. When students have calculated the weights, discuss why an astronaut's weight changes on different planets but their mass stays the same.
Know that gravity holds planets and moons in orbit.	Draw a force diagram to show gravity acting between a planet and star.	Before they attempt Task 2, check that students understand that gravity acts from and towards the centre of mass of an object (in the case of planets and stars this will be the centre). Before attempting the task, ask students to draw the force arrows on diagrams of simple situations. They should use one colour for all the forces involving gravity and recognise that all situations involve gravity in terms of the weight of the object.
Know that observers judge speed differently if they are moving.	Describe how observers judge speed differently if they are moving too.	To help complete the sentences about relative motion in Task 3, ask students to walk in the classroom at different paces towards each other and in the same direction and observe relative motion for themselves.
Use speed = distance / time.	Illustrate a journey on a distance–time graph.	For Task 4, remind students which of the axes represents time and which distance, remind them how to rearrange speed = distance / time. To introduce distance–time graphs, have one student follow instructions to walk around the classroom (stopping, walking slowly, speeding up) and sketch a graph to represent their motion on the board.
Know that gravity changes with mass and distance.	Deduce how gravity changes for different masses and distances.	Use the data about the gravitational field strengths of the planets and what students know about the sizes of the planets (mercury and mars, saturn and earth) to help them see how the variables of distance and mass interplay with each other. They can then attempt Task 5 on the sheet.

Answers to End-of-Big Idea questions

1 m/s; m.p.h; km/s (3 marks)

2a B (1 mark) b gravity (1 mark)

3a Diagram of cyclist with weight acting downwards (1 mark) and normal reaction acting upwards (1 mark). b The normal reaction force (1 mark) of the ground on the cyclist acts upwards through the bicycle seat on the cyclist (1 mark) c non-zero (1 mark)

4a i B (1 mark) ii D (1 mark) iii C (1 mark)

 b $300 \div 60$ (1 mark) $= 5$ (1 mark) m/s (1 mark)

5a 20 m.p.h. (2 marks) b 0 m.p.h. (2 marks) c The car appears to be moving away from the lorry (1 mark) at 20 m.p.h. (1 mark).

6 Extended response (maximum 6 marks).

 All three snails travel the same distance of 30 cm.

 Cyril's average speed is highest, followed by Gertie, and then Harold.

 Cyril begins quickly then slows to a constant speed. He travels at constant speed for a time, then accelerates towards the end.

 Gertie travels at constant speed, then also accelerates towards the end.

 Harold accelerates slowly, stops for a while, then accelerates towards the end.

7 weight on Earth $= 5 \times 10 = 50$ N (1 mark)

 weight on Moon $= 5 \times 1.6 = 8$N (1 mark)

 difference $= 50 - 8 = 42$ N (1 mark)

8 Extended response (maximum 6 marks).

 The mass of the sun is far greater than the masses of Jupiter's moons. Hence, the gravitational force between Jupiter and the sun is much stronger than the gravitational force between Jupiter and its moons.

 However, the distance between Jupiter and the sun is much greater than the distance between Jupiter and its moons. This means that the force between Jupiter and the sun is much smaller than it would be if the sun were as close to Jupiter as its moons are.

Answer guide for Big Write

Know	Apply	Extend
1–2 marks	3–4 marks	5–6 marks
• Describes motion but with little explanation or attention to the text type (blog). • Example points made: Gravity acts on the Earth or the Moon. The force of gravity pulls the Earth/Moon into orbit. The force of gravity depends on mass and distance.	• Explains motion with some indication they have paid attention to the text type. • Example extra points made: The force of gravity due to the Sun is bigger than the force of gravity due to the Earth. The gravitational force of the Sun on the Earth keeps it in orbit because the mass of the Sun is bigger than that of the Earth. The gravitational force of the Earth on the Moon keeps it in orbit because the mass of the Earth is bigger than that of the Moon.	• Explains motion in detail, paying attention to the text type. • Example of extra points made: The gravitational force decreases with distance. The radius of orbit of the Earth, and the speed of the Earth, is such that the force exerted by the Sun keeps it moving in orbit. The radius of orbit of the Moon, and the speed of the Moon, is such that the force exerted by the Sun keeps it moving in orbit. If the Earth or Moon moved faster the force of gravity would not be great enough to keep them in orbit.

kerboodle

1 Part 1 Checkpoint assessment (automarked)
1 Part 1 Checkpoint: Revision
1 Part 1 Checkpoint: Extension
1.1 Progress task, 1.2 Progress task

② Electromagnets

National curriculum links for this unit	
Topic	**National Curriculum topic**
Potential difference and resistance	Potential difference and resistance
Current	Current electricity Static electricity

In this Big Idea students will learn:

- we can model potential difference as an electrical push from the battery, or the amount of energy per unit of charge transferred through the electrical pathway
- in a series circuit, potential difference is shared between each component
- in a parallel circuit, potential difference is the same across each loop
- components with resistance reduce the current flowing and shift energy to the surroundings

- current is a movement of electrons and is the same everywhere in a series circuit
- current flows in each loop of a parallel circuit, which makes the component in the loop work. The current in the loops add up to the total current
- around a charged object, the electric field affects other charged objects, causing them to be attracted or repelled. The field strength decreases with distance.

AQA Enquiry process activities

Activity	Section
3.2.1 Compare the potential difference drop across resistors connected in series in a circuit.	2.1.3 Series and parallel circuits
3.2.2 Compare and explain current flow in different parts of a parallel circuit.	2.2.1 Current

Preparing for Key Stage 4 success

Knowledge Underpinning knowledge is covered in this Big Idea for KS4 study of:	• 4.4.1/6.2.1 Current, potential difference, and resistance • 4.4.2/6.2.2 Series and parallel circuits • 4.4.5 Static electricity – forces and electric fields (*GCSE Physics only*)

Maths
 	
Skills developed in Big Idea 2
	1 Arithmetic and numerical computation
	  a Recognise and use expressions in decimal form (2.1.2, 2.2.1)
	  b Recognise and use expressions in standard form (2.1.2, 2.2.1)
	  c Use ratios, fractions and percentages (2.1.2, 2.2.1)
	  d Make estimates of the results of simple calculations (2.1.2, 2.2.1)
	2 Handling data
	  a Use an appropriate number of significant figures (2.1.2, 2.2.1)
	  b Find arithmetic means (2.2.1), (2.1.2, 2.2.1)
	  f Understand the terms mean, mode and median (2.1.2)
	  g Use a scatter diagram to identify a correlation between two variables (2.1.2)
	  h Make order of magnitude calculations (2.1.2)
	3 Algebra
	  a Understand and use the symbols: $=, <, <<, >>, >, \propto, \backsim$ (2.1.2, 2.2.1)
	  b Change the subject of an equation (2.1.2)
	  c Substitute numerical values into algebraic equations using appropriate units for physical quantities (2.1.2)
	  d Solve simple algebraic equations (2.1.2)

4 Graphs

    a Translate information between graphical and numeric form (2.1.2)

    b Understand that $y = mx + c$ represents a linear relationship (2.1.2)

    c Plot two variables from experimental or other data (2.1.2)

Literacy Skills developed in Big Idea 2	• Select, synthesise, and compare information from a variety of sources (2.1.1, 2.1.2, 2.1.3, 2.2.1). • Use scientific terms confidently and correctly in discussions and writing (all spreads). • Organise ideas and evidence (2.1.1, 2.2.2). • Use correct forms of writing styles and include information relevant to the audience (2.2.2). • Ideas are organised into well-developed, linked paragraphs (2.2.2, Big Write).
Assessment Skills	• Extended response questions (2.1.1, 2.1.2, 2.1.3, 2.2.1) (End-of-Big Idea questions Q7). • Quantitative problem solving (2.1.1, 2.1.2, 2.1.3, 2.2.1) (End-of-Big Idea questions Q5). • Application of Enquiry Processes (2.1.1, 2.1.2, 2.1.3, 2.2.1) (End-of-Big Idea questions Q4, Q6, Q7).

KS2 Link	Check before	Checkpoint	Catch-up
Names of the basic parts in simple series circuits, for example, bulb, cell, and switch.	2.1.1 Potential difference	Show circuit components and their symbols for students to name and match up.	Provide names of components for students to label on a circuit diagram.
A complete loop is required for a circuit to work.	2.2.1 Circuits and current	Show students a range of circuits with bulbs. Ask them to explain whether the bulbs will light up in each case.	Demonstrate building a simple series circuit with a bulb. Show students that the bulb does not light until the circuit is complete.
A switch opens and closes a circuit.	2.1.1 Potential difference	Students explain why bulbs light up depending on the position of the switch.	Students build a simple series circuit with a switch, a cell, and a bulb.
The brightness of a lamp depends on the number and potential difference of cells used in a circuit.	2.1.1 Potential difference	Students predict the brightness of bulbs in difference circuits.	Demonstrate a simple circuit making changes to the number of bulbs, cells, or potential difference of cells.
Metals are good conductors of electricity.	2.1.2 Resistance	Ask students what sorts of materials they would use to make wires.	Demonstrate a simple series circuit, adding conductors and insulators to the circuit to show the effect on a bulb in the circuit.

Key Stage 2 Quiz: Physics
2 Part 1 End-of-Big Idea test (foundation)
2 Part 1 End-of-Big Idea test (foundation) mark scheme
2 Part 1 End-of-Big Idea test (higher)
2 Part 1 End-of-Big Idea test (higher) mark scheme

Answers to Picture Puzzler

Key Words

comb, hair, athlete, remote control, gorilla, eye
The key word is **charge**.

Close Up

The broken filament of an incandescent lamp.

🞔 MyMaths

You can find additional support for the maths skills covered in this Big Idea on **MyMaths**, including carrying out calculations, changing the subject of equations, calculating means, drawing graphs, and using making estimates.

Potential difference

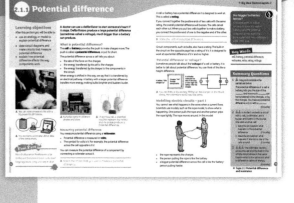

Securing Mastery Goals

- 3.2.1 Draw a circuit diagram to show how potential difference can be measured in a simple circuit.
- 3.2.1 Use the idea of energy to explain how potential difference and resistance affect the way components work. (Pt 1/2)
- 3.2.2 Turn circuit diagrams into real series and parallel circuits, and vice versa. (Pt 1/4)

Exceeding Mastery Goals

- 3.2.1 Justify the sizes of potential differences in a circuit, using arguments based on energy.
- 3.2.1 Draw conclusions about safety risks, from data on potential difference, resistance and current. (Pt 1/2)

Enquiry processes

- 2.9 Use the measuring instrument correctly.
- 2.9 Carry out the method carefully and consistently.
- 2.13 Identify features of an investigation which are hazardous.

Band	Outcome	Checkpoint	
		Question	Activity
Know	State the unit of potential difference.	B	Main, Starter 1
	Name the equipment used to measure potential difference.	A, 1	Main
	Describe the effect of a larger potential difference.	2	Main
	Use appropriate equipment to measure potential difference.		Main
Apply	Describe what is meant by potential difference.	1	Starter 1, Starter 2, Plenary 1
	Describe how to measure potential difference.	A, 1	Main
	Describe what is meant by the rating of a battery or bulb.		Starter 1
	Set up a simple circuit and use appropriate equipment to measure potential difference.		Main
Extend	Explain why potential difference is measured in parallel.	3	Starter 1, Starter 2, Main, Plenary 1
	Predict the effect of changing the rating of a battery or bulb in a circuit.	2	Plenary 1
	Set up and measure potential difference across various components in a circuit.		Main
	Explain the difference between potential difference and current.		Plenary 2

Maths

Students show understanding of number scales and relative sizes when ranking items in order of p.d. and when recording p.d. readings on analogue voltmeters.

They use the correct units when measuring in the practical activity.

MyMaths More support for the maths skills in this section can be found on MyMaths.

Literacy

Students use scientific key terms in the discussions of analogies, models, and their practical results.

GCSE link

4.2.1.2/6.2.1.2 Electrical charge and current

For electrical charge to flow through a closed circuit the circuit must include a source of potential difference.

4.2.1.3/6.2.1.3 Current, resistance and potential difference

Questions will be set using the term potential difference. Students will gain credit for the correct use of either potential difference or voltage.

Key Words

potential difference, voltmeter, volts, rating, battery, cell, **voltage**

Answers from the student book

In-text questions	**A** voltmeter **B** volt
Activity	**Are bigger batteries better?** Plan should include how to measure the size of the batteries, decision on diameter/weight/volume, use of voltmeter to measure the potential difference across the battery, collect a selection of different batteries, measure the 'size' and potential difference, record results in a table, plot the correct graph type.

Summary questions	**1** push, energy, voltmeter (3 marks)
	2a The potential difference is bigger because the extra cell supplies more energy. (2 marks)
	  b The buzzer would not work, the cells cancel out. (2 marks)
	3 Extended response question (6 marks). Example answers:
	  The p.d. across the bulb is the same as the p.d. across the battery.
	  The p.d. across the battery shows the work done by the battery on the charges/electrons.
	  The p.d. across the bulb shows the work done by the charges in the component.
	  They are the same because the energy transferred by the battery is the same as the energy transferred to the component.
	  They are different because one shows the work done on the charges, and the the other the work done by the charges.

Starter	Support/Extension	Resources
Comparing potential difference (10 min) Hand round five to six battery-powered items, or show images of appliances, including their operating potential difference (p.d.). Describe what is meant by the 'rating' of a battery or bulb, and discuss the ratings of different appliances or components. Explain that p.d. indicates energy transferred by the equipment, and is measured in volts. Group items as battery operated (mainly low p.d.) or mains operated (mainly high p.d.), and rank all items from the lowest to the highest p.d. Use the term potential difference, and not voltage, to avoid confusing students with additional terminology. **Looking at potential difference** (10 min) Introduce sources of p.d. (e.g., lightning, power lines, railway lines). Explain that in each case a different amount of energy is transferred, which is linked to p.d. The interactive resource can then be used to link the operating p.d. with objects.	**Support**: Provide cards with the p.d. written on the back of each item. Students place the images on a number line. **Extension**: Show students 'Danger of death' signs seen on substations. Discuss the difference between being in a circuit with a battery and being in a circuit with a high p.d. Students suggest dangers of high p.d., and understand that high current is the cause of fatalities.	**Interactive**: Looking at potential difference

Main	Support/Extension	Resources
Investigating potential difference (40 min) Set up a simple circuit to demonstrate the position of the voltmeter in a circuit. Students set up simple circuits to investigate p.d. in a range of different circuits, and answer the questions on their activity sheet. They should discuss the size of the potential difference across components using energy arguments. At the end of the experiment, ensure students understand the conclusions: p.d. is shared between components (depending on the component's resistance). The p.d. across the battery is the same as the sum of the p.d. across all the components in a series circuit.	**Support**: Provide enlarged circuit diagrams on A3 or A4 paper for students to place components on before linking them with wires. A support sheet is also available with suggested combinations of components to investigate in a results table.	**Activity**: Investigating potential difference **Skill sheet**: Recording results

Plenary	Support/Extension	Resources
Rope model for potential difference (10 min) Explain that as soon as the circuit is complete, charges transfer energy in all parts of the circuit at the same time. Discuss the rope model for p.d. Details can be found in the student book. **Comparing current and p.d.** (5 min) Students list similarities and differences between current and potential difference, for example, how they are measured, their value in different parts of a series circuit, and what they are.	**Extension**: Students can explain the effect of changing things in this circuit, offering limitations and improvements to this model.	

Homework	Support/Extension	
Students prepare a list of at least 10 pieces of electrical equipment used at home and the potential difference supplied, either from batteries or the mains (230 V). Students should get parental permission to move/unplug equipment.	**Extension**: Students should rank these in order of p.d., and suggest a reason for the order.	

2.1.2 Resistance

Securing Mastery Goals

- 3.2.1 Calculate resistance using the formula:
  resistance (Ω) = potential difference (V) ÷ current (A).
- 3.2.1 Use the idea of energy to explain how potential difference and resistance affect the way components work. (Pt 2/2)
- 3.2.1 Given a table of potential difference against current. Use the ratio of potential difference to current to determine the resistance.
- 3.2.1 Use an analogy like water in pipes to explain why part of a circuit has higher resistance.
- 3.2.1 Turn circuit diagrams into real series and parallel circuits, and vice versa. (Pt 2/4)

Enquiry processes

- 2.10 Identify a dependent variable.
- 2.10 Write a question linking variables in the form 'How does... affect...?'.
- 2.12 Suggest a hypothesis for the observation.
- 2.10 Identify an independent variable.
- 2.10 Explain which type of enquiry is best for answering a given scientific question.

Band	Outcome	Checkpoint	
		Question	Activity
Know	Calculate the resistance from values of p.d. and current with support.	2	Main
	Compare simply the resistance of conductors and insulators.	1	Main
	List examples of conductors and insulators.		Main
	Identify some of the variables in the investigation.		Main
Apply	Describe what is meant by resistance.	A, 1	Main
	Calculate resistance of a circuit.	2	Maths, Main, Plenary 1, Homework
	Describe the difference between conductors and insulators in terms of resistance.	1, 3	Main
	Identify independent, dependent, and control variables.		Main
Extend	Explain the causes of resistance.	1	Main
	Explain what factors affect the resistance of a resistor.		Starter 2, Main
	Compare the effect of resistance in different materials.	3	Starter 2, Main
	Independently select and control all the variables in the investigation, considering accuracy and precision.		Main, Plenary 2

Maths

Students calculate resistance using simple equations, giving units for their answers. Higher-ability students will be required to rearrange this equation.

They plot a graph of resistance against length of wire using experimental results.

MyMaths More support for the maths skills in this section can be found on MyMaths.

Literacy

Students use key words correctly when suggesting a conclusion for their experiment, and when discussing aspects of working scientifically.

GCSE link

4.2.13/6.2.1.3 Current, resistance and potential difference

The current (*I*) through a component depends on both the resistance (*R*) of the component and the potential difference (*V*) across the component. The greater the resistance of the component the smaller the current for a given potential difference (pd) across the component.

Current, potential difference or resistance can be calculated using the equation:
potential difference = current × resistance

Key Words

resistance,
ohms,
electrical conductor,
electrical insulator

Answers from the student book

In-text questions	**A** How easy or difficult it is for the charges to pass through a component in a circuit. **B** ohms **C** Use a pipe with a very small diameter.
Activity	**What's the resistance?** $\text{resistance} = \dfrac{\text{p.d.}}{\text{current}} = \dfrac{12\,\text{V}}{0.6\,\text{A}} = 20\,\Omega$
Summary questions	**1** potential difference, resistance, resistance, electrons, energy, conductors, insulators (7 marks) **2a** You calculate the resistance by dividing the p.d. by the current. (1 mark) **b** $\text{resistance} = \dfrac{2\text{V}}{0.4\text{A}}$ $\text{resistance} = \dfrac{4\text{V}}{0.8\text{A}}$ $\text{resistance} = \dfrac{6\text{V}}{1.2\text{A}}$ $= 5\Omega$ (1 mark) $= 5\Omega$ (1 mark) $= 5\Omega$ (1 mark) **c** The wires are like pipes with a wide diameter. The water flows easily through them, like a large current in a circuit. The resistor is like a narrow pipe. It produces a lower rate of flow, just like the lower current. (4 marks) **3** Extended response question (6 marks). Example answers: Both conductors and insulators have resistance. Conductors have many charges that can move readily. Conductors have low resistance. Insulators do not contain many charges that are free to move. Insulators have high resistance. Most conductors are metals that have electrons that are free to move. Current in an insulator would be smaller than the current through a conductor (for the same potential difference).

kerboodle

Starter	Support/Extension	Resources
What do you know already? (5 min) This interactive resource asks students to review what they know about circuits from KS2 and the previous lesson. **What affects resistance?** (10 min) Explain what resistance is in general, for example, resistance makes it harder for something to happen. Remind students that current is the flow of charge, so electrical resistance makes it harder for charge to flow. Discuss changes you could make in a circuit to increase resistance. This is a useful activity to highlight student misconceptions.	**Extension:** Students draw circuit symbols or diagrams to illustrate each key word or phrase. **Support:** Use the analogy of water flowing in a hosepipe. How can water flow be reduced? For example, it is harder for water to flow if the hosepipe is narrower.	**Interactive:** What do you know already?

Main	Support/Extension	Resources
Investigating the resistance of a wire (40 min) Introduce the idea of electrical resistance, including the equation to calculate resistance, and the difference in resistance between conductors and insulators. Students will investigate how changes in a wire affect its resistance. They should list the factors they can change, for example, length, diameter, material, and temperature. Students will then carry out an experiment to investigate the relationship between resistance and the length of a wire (or adapt the practical sheet for a different independent variable).	**Support:** The support sheet contains a partially filled results table. **Extension:** Students can use ammeters and voltmeters instead of a multimeter, in order to use their readings to calculate resistance for each length of wire.	**Practical:** Investigating the resistance of a wire **Skill sheet:** Recording results **Skill sheet:** Choosing scales

Plenary	Support/Extension	Resources
Calculating resistance (5 min) Draw a circuit diagram including an ammeter and voltmeter. Add sample readings for students to calculate the correct value of resistance. This can be a quiz dividing the class into three teams, and giving marks for correct calculations. **Evaluating my experiment** (10 min) Students individually list two things that went well, and two things they would change if they repeated their experiment.	**Support:** Provide a multiple-choice selection of resistance values. **Extension:** Provide circuit diagrams with resistance values but current or potential difference readings missing. Students should calculate the missing information.	**Skill sheet:** Evaluation

Homework	Support/Extension	
Provide students with further examples of resistance calculations for them to complete at home.	**Support:** Provide multiple-choice answers. **Extension:** Include calculations involving rearrangements.	

Securing Mastery Goals

- 3.2.2 Turn circuit diagrams into real series and parallel circuits, and vice versa. (Pt 3/4)

Exceeding Mastery Goals

- 3.2.1 Predict the effect of changing the rating of a battery or a bulb on other components in a series or parallel circuit.
- 3.2.1 Draw conclusions about safety risks, from data on potential difference, resistance and current. (Pt 2/2)
- 3.2.2 Compare the advantages of series and parallel circuits for particular uses.

Enquiry processes

- 2.1 Identify patterns in data.
- 2.3 Incorporate the pattern you found into an answer to the enquiry question.
- 2.3 Make a conclusion and explain it.

Enquiry processes activity:

- 3.2.1 Compare the potential difference drop across resistors connected in series in a circuit.

Band	Outcome	Checkpoint	
		Question	Activity
Know ↓	State one difference between series and parallel circuits.	1	Starter 2, Plenary 2
	State how potential difference varies in series and parallel circuits.	A, B	Main
Apply ↓	Describe the difference between series and parallel circuits.	1	Starter 2, Plenary 2
	Describe how potential difference varies in series and parallel circuits.	A, B	Main, Plenary 1
	Identify the pattern of potential difference in series and parallel circuits.	2, 3	Main
Extend ↓	Predict the effect of changing the resistance of a circuit component on the overall (net) resistance of the circuit.	3	Starter 2, Main, Homework
	Explain why potential difference varies in series and parallel circuits.	2, 3	Main, Plenary 1
	Explain the pattern in potential difference readings for series and parallel circuits, drawing conclusions.		Main

Maths

Students should identify numerical patterns in the data obtained for p.d. from their experiment.

MyMaths More support for the maths skills in this section can be found on MyMaths.

Literacy

Students should apply existing knowledge to explain the numerical patterns observed in their experiment using scientific key words.

GCSE link

4.2.2/6.2.2 Series and parallel circuits
For components connected in series:
- there is the same current through each component
- the total potential difference of the power supply is shared between the components
- the total resistance of two components is the sum of the resistance of each component.

For components connected in parallel:
- the potential difference across each component is the same
- the total current through the whole circuit is the sum of the currents through the separate components
- the total resistance of two resistors is less than the resistance of the smallest individual resistor.

Key Words

series, parallel

Answers from the student book

In-text questions	**A** The p.d. across each of the components in a series circuit add up to the p.d. across the battery. **B** 12V
Summary questions	**1** one, more than one, parallel, series (4 marks) **2** As you add more bulbs in a series circuit, the brightness of the bulbs decreases and the p.d. across each bulb decreases. (2 marks) **3a** The p.d. across the first bulb is the same as the p.d. across the battery, which has not changed (1 mark) **b** The resistance decreases (1 mark) adding another bulb increases the current (1 mark) the p.d. is the same (1 mark) so the resistance $= \frac{V}{I}$ is smaller (1 mark)

kerboodle

Starter	Support/Extension	Resources
What do you know? (10 min) Students write down what they already know about circuits, and then share their ideas. Identify misconceptions and correct mistakes at this stage.	**Support**: Prepare a short list of true/false statements about series circuits for students to categorise. **Extension**: Students should include explanations as well as descriptions.	
Series or parallel? (10 min) Ask students to list circuits where equipment or components can be controlled separately or together. For example, lighting circuits in the home or car, controls on a music system, cooker, or hairdryer. Explain how this can be done using series and parallel circuits. Students then apply this knowledge to group items into two categories: those that use series circuits, and those that use parallel circuits.	**Support**: Concentrate on whether components require separate controls. Introduce key words in the main activity. **Extension**: Students justify why a series or parallel circuit is required in each case.	**Interactive**: Series or parallel?

Main	Support/Extension	Resources
Series and parallel circuits (35 min) This activity is one of the AQA Enquiry process activities. Explain to students that the circuits they have been working with so far are series circuits, and introduce the idea of parallel circuits. Large diagrams of each type of circuit can be used to highlight similarities and differences, and will facilitate the tracing of electron paths around the circuits. Students then investigate circuit rules regarding p.d. in series and parallel circuits, by carrying out mini-experiments as part of an activity circus. Students must visit each station, each with a different circuit, and note down their observations. They then answer the questions that follow using their results.	**Support**: Diagrams of experimental setup are provided for students to add observations, and p.d. readings. **Extension**: Students should look for readings that are nearly the same, or that add up to roughly the same amount as another reading in the circuit.	**Practical**: Series and parallel circuits

Plenary	Support/Extension	Resources
Making predictions (10 min) Present students with circuit diagrams of simple series and parallel circuits. Each circuit will have partially filled data for p.d. Students must predict and complete the missing value for p.d. in each case.	**Support**: Provide multiple-choice answers for predictions.	
Rope model revisited (10 min) Revisit the rope model to demonstrate p.d. in a series circuit. Ask students to contribute ideas as to how this model can be used to demonstrate parallel circuits. This model shows that p.d. is supplied in all places of the circuit at the same time, and the same p.d. is supplied by the battery to both loops.	**Extension**: Once again, students can identify limitations and improvements to this model.	

Homework	Support/Extension	
Students consider what they have learned about series and parallel circuits, and use these ideas to draw a circuit for lighting in the home. This can be for several rooms in the home or for a staircase, for which the set-up for (two-way) switches should also be included.	**Support**: Students decide whether lights can be controlled independently or not, and draw a simple circuit diagram to explain their choice of circuit.	

Current

Securing Mastery Goals
- 3.2.2 Describe how current changes in series and parallel circuits when components are changed.
- 3.2.2 Turn circuit diagrams into real series and parallel circuits, and vice versa. (Pt 4/4)

Exceeding Mastery Goals
- Evaluate a model of current as electrons moving from the negative to the positive terminal of a battery, through the circuit.

Enquiry processes
- 2.9 Use the measuring instrument correctly.
- 2.9 Carry out the method carefully and consistently.
- 2.13 Identify features of an investigation which are hazardous.

Enquiry processes activity
- 3.2.2 Compare and explain current flow in different parts of a parallel circuit.

Band	Outcome	Checkpoint	
		Question	**Activity**
Know	State what current is.	A, 1	Lit, Main, Plenary 1
	Use an ammeter to measure current.		Main
	Identify the pattern of current in series and parallel circuits.	B, C	Main
Apply	Describe how current changes in series and parallel circuits when components are changed.	B, C	Maths, Main, Plenary 1
	Describe how to measure current.	1	Main, Plenary 2
	Set up a circuit including an ammeter to measure current.		Main
Extend	Use a model to explain how current flows in a circuit.	3	Plenary 1
	Predict the current in different circuits.		Maths, Main
	Measure current accurately in a number of places in a series circuit.		Main
	Explain the pattern in current readings for series and parallel circuits, drawing conclusions.	3	Main

Maths

Students must demonstrate their understanding of the number scale if reading current in a circuit using an analogue ammeter.

Students will also use the appropriate units for current values.

MyMaths More support for the maths skills in this section can be found on MyMaths.

Literacy

In the student-book activity students must explain key words using scientific understanding, and relate this to how the key words may be used differently in everyday life.

Key Words
current, ammeter, amps

GCSE link
4.2.1.2/6.2.1.2 Electrical charge and current

Electric current is a flow of electrical charge. The size of the electric current is the rate of flow of electrical charge.

4.2.2/6.2.2 Series and parallel circuits

For components connected in series there is the same current through each component. For components connected in parallel the total current through the whole circuit is the sum of the currents through the separate components.

Answers from the student book

In-text questions	A charge flowing per second	B it decreases	C it increases
Activity	**Current issues** 0.2 ÷ 2 = 0.1 A If you double the number of bulbs but keep the p.d. the same, the current will halve. **Confusing words** charge: the electron has a negative charge; there is a charge to go into a theme park current: current is the amount of charge flowing per second; there can be a strong current in the river cell: component that pushes charge around a circuit; the smallest functional unit in an organism/American term for a mobile phone; a police or prison cell		
Summary questions	**1** charge, second, electrons, ammeter, amps, A (6 marks) **2a** Series circuit with battery of cells, motor, and switch. Students should annotate the switch, and explain how this can be switched on and off to control the circuit. (2 marks) **b** The electrons move/a current flows. (1 mark) **3** Extended response question (6 marks). Example answers: Start with a small series circuit with a switch, lamp, and cell. Show that the light comes on as soon as you press the switch. Make the leads longer, and show that this has no effect. Make a really big circuit, and show that the lamp comes on straight away. Use the rope model to show that the bulb comes on straight away if the charges are already in the wires. It does not matter how long the wire is, the bulb still comes on straight away. If the charges were in the battery, there would be a time delay.		

kerboodle

Starter	Support/Extension	Resources
Comparing currents (10 min) Recap current and that some appliances use larger currents than others. Explain that larger currents flow in more powerful equipment and equipment that heats things. List appliances that plug into the mains. Students to rank these in order of the current they use. If a current meter is available, the current drawn by different appliances can be demonstrated.	**Support**: Group equipment as mains and battery-operated. **Extension**: Students explain their rank order in terms of the function of the appliance.	

Main	Support/Extension	Resources
Investigating current (40 min) This activity is one of the AQA Enquiry process activities. Introduce students to current as a flow of charge. The water pipe analogy can be used to facilitate understanding. Students carry out a practical to measure current using simple series and parallel circuits and answer the questions that follow on the practical sheet. Ensure that at the end of the experiment, students are aware of the effect of adding more cell, or adding more components in series and parallel.	**Support**: A partially filled results table is available on the support sheet that gives combinations students should test in their series circuit. **Extension**: Students predict changes in current if the number of components in a circuit is changed. This links to resistance, which is covered later.	**Practical:** Investigating current

Plenary	Support/Extension	Resources
Rope model (10 min) Explain that charge is spread throughout the circuit, and as soon as it turns on, the charge moves at the same time, transferring energy. Use the rope model, as described in the student book, to show this phenomenon. Students should discuss what each part of the model represents in a circuit. Model a parallel circuit with two separate loops. You need to use separate hands to work each loop so the current in the loops can be different. **Bigger or smaller?** (5 min) In this interactive students predict the change to the reading on an ammeter when changes are made to a circuit.	**Extension**: Students should suggest limitations and improvements to this model.	**Interactive:** Bigger or smaller?

Homework		
Students draw the circuit diagrams for simple pieces of equipment, for example, a torch, a handheld fan, or a hairdryer.		

2.2.2 Charging up

Securing Mastery Goals
- 3.2.2 Two similarly charged objects repel, two differently charged objects attract.
- 3.2.2 Describe what happens when charged objects are placed near to each other or touching.
- 3.2.2 Use a sketch to describe how an object charged positively or negatively became charged up.

Exceeding Mastery Goals
3.2.2 Suggest ways to reduce the risk of getting electrostatic shocks.

Enquiry processes
- 2.1 Identify patterns in data.
- 2.3 Incorporate the pattern you found into an answer to the enquiry question.
- 2.3 Make a conclusion and explain it.

Band	Outcome	Checkpoint	
		Question	Activity
Know	Describe how to charge insulators.	1	Starter 1, Plenary 1
	State the two types of charge.	1	Main
	State what surrounds charged objects.	C	Main
	Describe what happens when you bring similarly charged object together, and when you bring differently charged objects together.	1	Starter 1, Main
Apply	Use a sketch to explain how objects can become charged.	1, B	Main, Starter 1, Plenary 1
	Describe how charged objects interact.	1	Main, Starter 1, Plenary 1, Plenary 2
	Describe what is meant by an electric field.	3	Main
	Interpret observations, identifying patterns linked to charge.		Main
Extend	Explain, in terms of electrons, why something becomes charged.	1, 2	Main, Starter 1, Plenary 1, Plenary 2
	Predict how charged objects will interact.	2	Main
	Suggest ways to reduce the risk of getting electrostatic shocks.	2, 3	Homework
	Use observations to make predictions.		Main

Maths
Students use the relative positions of materials in the triboelectric series to predict whether friction will cause an object to become positively or negatively charged.

MyMaths More support for the maths skills in this section can be found on MyMaths.

GCSE link
4.4.1.1/6.4.1.1 The structure of an atom

The basic structure of an atom is a positively charged nucleus composed of both protons and neutrons surrounded by negatively charged electrons.

4.2.5.1 Static charge (*GCSE Physics*)

When certain insulating materials are rubbed against each other they become electrically charged.

4.2.5.2 Electric fields (*GCSE Physics*)

A charged object creates an electric field around itself.

Key Words
charged up, **positively charged**, **negatively charged**, attract, repel, **electron**, neutral, electric field, **electrostatic force**

Answers from the student book

In-text questions	**A** a tiny (sub-atomic) particle with a negative charge **B** Suitable diagrams showing the transfer of electrons from the rod to the cloth. **C** If there is an electric field then a charged object experiences a force.

36

Summary questions	1 positive, negative, electrons, repel, attract, decreases (6 marks)
	2a Electrons are transferred between the balloon and the jumper. The balloon is charged, but the wall is neutral. The charge of the balloon repels like charges from the surface of the wall. (3 marks)
	b The electrons on the charged object flow through the wire and not through you. (1 mark)
	3 Extended response question (6 marks). Example answers:
	Gravitational and electric fields produce forces. You cannot see or feel a gravitational or electric field. They produce non-contact forces. Gravitational fields are produced by masses. Electric fields are produced by charges. Gravitational fields produce forces that only attract. Electric fields produce forces that attract and repel.

Starter	Support/Extension	Resources
Charges on a balloon (15 min) Rub a balloon (or a plastic straw) on cloth and hold it near some hair. For the best results, hair should be clean, fine, and not too long. Ask students to describe what they observe (the hairs are attracted to the balloon; when the balloon is removed, the hair strands remain repelling each other). Discuss why this is happening as a class.	**Extension:** Demonstrate the effect of a charged object on a stream of water. Students should apply their existing ideas.	
Non-contact forces (10 min) Students list as many non-contact forces as possible, describing their effects in terms of attraction/repulsion (gravitational, magnetic, electrostatic). Discuss their ideas and explain that electrostatic forces are between charged objects, and they will be investigating these forces during this lesson.	**Support:** Give examples that students group by the non-contact force they experience. Note that some objects experience more than one non-contact force. **Extension:** Students identify common features of non-contact forces.	

Main	Support/Extension	Resources
Electrostatics (35 min) Demonstrate several effects of electrostatics, for example, repulsion between charged balloons and the attraction between scraps of paper and a charged balloon. Students should see that a non-contact force exists between charged objects. Explain why the balloon becomes charged (electric charge moves from hair to the balloon in the example in Starter 1) and use the idea of an electric field creating forces to explain each demonstration. Ask students for their own suggestions of effects they have already seen. Students then complete the tasks on the activity sheet.	**Support:** A support sheet is available with a partially filled table for observations. **Extension:** Introduce the triboelectric series. This lists materials and their tendency to lose or gain charge. It can be used to predict which becomes negatively charged, which becomes positively charged, and which will not gain a charge.	**Activity:** Electrostatics **Skill sheet:** Recording results

Plenary	Support/Extension	Resources
What happens with the balloon? (5 min) Students use the interactive resource to re-order sentences to explain the effect of a charged balloon on hair.		**Interactive:** What happens with the balloon?
Draw it (10 min) Students make labelled drawings showing what they think happens when something is charged. Use their drawings to explain any remaining misconceptions.	**Support:** Students should focus on illustrating key words from this lesson. **Extension:** This activity can be extended to electric fields.	

Homework		
Students research the uses of static electricity, at home or in industry, and write a short summary paragraph.	**Extension:** Students should include information on how to reduce the risk of getting electrostatic shocks.	

Checkpoint lesson routes

The route through this lesson can be determined using the Checkpoint assessment.

Percentage pass marks are supplied in the Checkpoint teacher notes.

Route A (support)
Students complete a range of tasks on the revision sheet. The questions are broken down into steps and the grid below provides guidance for how to support students.

Route B (extension)
Students design and describe circuits for a range of electrical appliances in the home.

Progression to *Apply*

Know outcome	Apply outcome	Making progress
Recognise the symbol for a voltmeter and that it is used for measuring potential difference.	Draw a circuit diagram to show how potential difference can be measured in a simple circuit.	Task 1 asks students to identify what the symbol for a voltmeter is and draw a circuit. They can use their student book to look this up or you could set up the circuit described for them to draw as a circuit diagram.
Calculate the resistance using the formula resistance = potential difference ÷ current. Describe potential difference as the amount of energy shifted from the battery to the moving charge, or from the moving charge to the circuit components.	Use the ratio of potential difference against current to calculate resistance (without access to the equation). Use the idea of energy to explain how potential difference and resistance affect the way that components work.	Before starting Task 2, remind students of the analogies of raising and lowering to model potential difference and energy transfer in circuits. For question 1, remind students that they are expected to remember the formula for resistance. They can create a flashcard and/or mnemonic to help them remember. A worked example is provided on the student sheet – you may wish to remove this depending on the level of the students.
Define resistance as a property of a component, making it difficult for charge to pass through.	Use the idea of energy to explain how potential difference and resistance affect the way that components work.	For questions 2 and 3 of Task 2, demonstrate how conductors allow current to flow and insulators do not using the analogy of electrons rolling down a slope with pegs on to model resistance. Explain that collisions will cause energy to be transferred as heat.
Know that components with resistance reduce the current flowing and shift energy to the surroundings.	Use an analogy like water in pipes to explain why parts of a circuit have higher resistance.	For Task 3, you may have a demonstration of the water model of electricity you can show to students. Generate a discussion about how the width of pipes would affect the current flowing through the pipe and how this could model electricity. Also demonstrate the rope model with students and ask questions about how increased resistance can be modelled.
Know that in a series circuit potential difference is shared between each component but in a parallel circuit potential difference is the same across each loop.	Use the idea of energy to explain how potential difference and resistance affect the way that components work.	For Task 4, set up series circuits and show how the potential difference of the battery is equal to the sum of the potential differences. Use the model of raising and lowering to explain why the potential difference must be shared between components. Set up parallel circuits and show how the potential difference in each loop is the same.
Know that current is the same everywhere in a series circuit but divides between loops in a parallel circuit.	Describe how current changes in series and parallel circuits when components are changed.	For Task 5, set up a series circuit with ammeters to demonstrate that the current is the same throughout. Set up a parallel circuit with ammeters to demonstrate that the current is split into the different loops.
Know that two similarly charged objects repel, two differently charged objects attract.	Use a sketch to describe how an object charged positively or negatively became charged up.	For Task 6, demonstrate a balloon being rubbed on hair and how it will attract the hair afterwards. Remind students that atoms are made from positive protons and negative electrons, and that electrons move between objects to make them charged. Students may also find section 2.2.2 in the student book useful.

Answers to End-of-Big Idea questions

1a B (1 mark)

 b Circuit A: connect a lead from the bulb to the battery. Circuit C: turn one of the cells around. (2 marks)

2a repel (1 mark)   **b** attract (1 mark)   **c** field, force (2 marks)

3a The quantity that tells you how much a component reduces the current flowing through it (1 mark)

 b An insulator has a high resistance (1 mark), a conductor has a low resistance (1 mark)

4a Credit suitable parallel circuits with two cells on one branch, with a bulb and a switch on each of the two other branches. (2 marks)

 b parallel (1 mark)   **c** A, B, A, and B (3 marks)   **d** Attach an ammeter between the bulbs and the switches. (2 marks)

5a The push of the battery/energy transferred in a component. (1 mark)

 b The potential difference that the lamp is designed to work at. (1 mark)

 c resistance $= \dfrac{\text{p.d.}}{\text{current}} = \dfrac{3\,\text{V}}{0.4\,\text{A}} = 7.5\,\Omega$ (2 marks)

 d The current increases (1 mark) and the bulb is brighter (1 mark).

6a Reading on the ammeter is halved, because there is twice the resistance. (2 marks)

 b The voltmeter reading is halved, there is less energy transferred to the lamp because the current is less. (2 marks)

7 This is an extended response question. Students should be marked on the use of good English, organisation of information, spellingand grammar, and correct use of specialist scientific terms. The best answers will explain in detail how the rod becomes charged and is able to attract the small pieces of paper (maximum of 6 marks).

Examples of correct scientific points:

Both the rod and cloth contain atoms.

Atoms contain electrons, protons, and neutrons.

Electrons are negatively charged.

Protons are positively charged.

When you rub the rod, electrons move from the cloth to the rod (or vice versa).

The rod becomes negatively charged/cloth becomes positively charged (or vice versa, as above)

The rod repels the electrons on the top of the pieces of paper.

The top of the pieces of paper become positively charged.

The paper is attracted to the rod.

8 It incorporates a high resistance (1 mark) that reduces the current to a safer level (1 mark).

Answer guide for Big Write

Know	Apply	Extend
1–2 marks	3–4 marks	5–6 marks
• At least one storyboard produced • Some text that explains current, p.d. or resistance • A page that describes a simple series circuit	• A story board for a battery/cell, bulb, switch, ammeter, or more • Correct text for each component • A page that describes a simple series circuit, and a page that describes a parallel circuit	• A story board for a battery/cell, bulb, switch, ammeter, voltmeter, and possibly buzzer, resistor. • Correct text for each component • A page that describes a simple series circuit, and a page that describes a parallel circuit • Further pages explaining how to make more complicated circuits e.g. staircase lighting

kerboodle

2 Part 1 Checkpoint assessment (automarked)

2 Part 1 Checkpoint: Revision

2 Part 1 Checkpoint: Extension

2.1 Progress task, 2.2 Progress task

③ Energy

In this Big Idea students will learn:

- we pay for our domestic electricity usage based on the amount of energy transferred
- electricity is generated by a combination of resources which each have advantages and disadvantages
- how to calculate the cost of home energy usage, using the formula: power (kW) × time (hours) × price (per kWh)
- that we can describe how jobs get done using an energy model where energy is transferred from one store at the start to another at the end
- when energy is transferred, the total is conserved, but some energy is dissipated, reducing the useful energy.

AQA Enquiry process activities

Activity	Section
3.3.1 Compare the running costs of fluorescent and filament light bulbs.	3.1.3 Energy and power
3.3.2 Explain the energy transfers in a hand-crank torch.	3.2.1 Energy adds up

Preparing for Key Stage 4 success

Knowledge Underpinning knowledge is covered in this Big Idea for KS4 study of:	• 4.1.1/6.1.1 Energy changes in a system, and the ways energy is stored before and after such changes • 4.1.2/6.1.2 Conservation and dissipation of energy • 4.1.3/6.1.3 National and global energy sources

Maths
 	
Skills developed in Big Idea 3
	1 Arithmetic and numerical computation
	  a Recognise and use expressions in decimal form (3.1.3, 3.2.1)
	  c Use ratios, fractions and percentages (3.1.3, 3.2.1)
	  d Make estimates of the results of simple calculations (3.1.3, 3.2.1)
	2 Handling data
	  a Use an appropriate number of significant figures (3.1.3, 3.2.1)
	  b Find arithmetic means (3.2.1)
	3 Algebra
	  a Understand and use the symbols: $=, <, \ll, \gg, >, \propto, \sim$ (3.1.3, 3.2.1)
	  b Change the subject of an equation (3.1.3, 3.2.1)
	  c Substitute numerical values into algebraic equations using appropriate units for physical quantities (3.1.3, 3.2.1)
	  d Solve simple algebraic equations (3.1.3, 3.2.1)
	4 Graphs
	  a Translate information between graphical and numeric form (3.1.2)
	  c Plot two variables from experimental or other data

Literacy	• Select, synthesise, and compare information from a variety of sources (3.1.1, 3.1.2, 3.1.3, 3.2.2).
Skills developed in Big Idea 3	• Use scientific terms confidently and correctly in discussions and writing (all spreads).
	• Organisation of ideas and evidence (3.1.1, 3.1.2, 3.2.1, 3.2.2).
	• Identify ideas and supporting evidence in text (3.1.2, 3.1.3, 3.2.2).
	• Use correct forms of writing styles and include information relevant to the audience (3.1.2, 3.1.3, 3.2.2).
	• Ideas are organised into well-developed, linked paragraphs (3.1.1, 3.1.2, 3.1.3, 3.2.1, 3.2.2, Big Write).
Assessment Skills	• Extended response questions (3.1.1, 3.1.3, 3.2.1, 3.2.2,) (End-of-Big Idea questions Q8, Q10).
	• Quantitative problem solving (3.1.1, 3.1.2, 3.1.3, 3.2.1, 3.2.2, (End-of-Big Idea questions Q5, 6, 7, 8).
	• Application of Enquiry Processes (3.1.1, 3.1.2, 3.1.3, 3.2.1, 3.2.2) (End-of-Big Idea questions Q4, Q8).

Energy is not taught explicitly at KS2. Students will have used the word 'energy' in everyday life and will have lots of different ideas about what it means.

It is useful to elicit these prior conceptions during the suggested activities and emphasise that:

• energy does not make things happen
• energy is not a 'thing'
• energy does not explain why one thing happens and another does not.

It is helpful to emphasise that:

• energy is quantifiable, a number you can calculate
• energy is a property of an object or a system
• energy is conserved.

It is useful to avoid the use of types or forms of energy (thermal energy, light energy) and talk about energy associated with an energy store, and pathways that transfer energy between stores.

Key Stage 2 Quiz: Physics
3 Part 1 End-of-Big Idea test (foundation)
3 Part 1 End-of-Big Idea test (foundation) mark scheme
3 Part 1 End-of-Big Idea test (higher)
3 Part 1 End-of-Big Idea test (higher) mark scheme

Answers to Picture Puzzler
Key Words
kettle, icicle, night, ear, tug of war, iron, chocolate
The key word is **kinetic**.
Close Up
a smooth metal surface

MyMaths

You can find additional support for the maths skills covered in this Big Idea on **MyMaths**, including carrying out calculations, changing the subject of equations, calculating means, drawing graphs, and using making estimates.

3.1.1 Food and fuels

Securing Mastery Goals

- 3.3.1 Food labels list the energy content of food in kilojoules (kJ).
- 3.3.1 Compare the amounts of energy transferred by different foods and activities.

Enquiry processes

- 2.6 Describe the evidence for your idea.
- 2.6 Explain why the evidence supports your idea.
- 2.12 Suggest a hypothesis for the observation.
- 2.12 Conclude if hypothesis is correct.

Band	Outcome	Checkpoint	
		Question	Activity
Know	Identify energy values for food and fuels.	A, 1	Main
	Describe energy requirements in different situations.	1, 2	Maths, Starter 2, Main, Plenary 1
	Interpret data on food intake for some activities.		Main
Apply	Compare the energy values of food and fuels.	2	Starter 1, Main, Plenary 2
	Compare the energy in food and fuels with the energy needed for different activities.	2, 3	Maths, Starter 2, Main, Plenary 1, Plenary 2
	Explain data on food intake and energy requirements for a range of activities.		Main
Extend	Calculate energy requirements for various situations, considering diet and exercise.	2, 3	Maths, Starter 2, Main, Plenary 1
	Suggest different foods needed in unusual situations, for example, training for the Olympics.	3	Starter 2, Main
	Explain why an athlete needs more energy from food using data provided.		Main

Maths
In the student-book activity students carry out simple calculations involving multiplication and division to deduce the energy expenditure per minute for different activities.

Students are also required to convert between joules and kilojoules in this lesson.

MyMaths More support for the maths skills in this section can be found on MyMaths.

Literacy
Students extract and use information from different resources to describe situations where food and activities need to be matched.

Key Words
energy, joule, kilojoule

Answers from the student book

In-text questions	**A** joules **B** Three from: wood, oil, coal, gas
Activity	**How far?** 50 g of chocolate contains: 0.5 × 1500 = 750 kJ You would need to run for: 750 ÷ 60 = 12.5 minutes This means you will need to run: 12.5 × 150 = 1875 m

Summary questions	
	1 food, fuels, joules, breathing, bones/muscles/brains (6 marks)
	2 200g chips contains 2000kJ (1 mark), so you need to cycle for 2000kJ/25kJ/min = 80 minutes (1 mark)
	3 Example answers (6 marks):
	Identifies a range of activities.
	Identifies the time that he/she spends doing each activity.
	Identifies the energy used per minute for the activities using the table.
	Calculates the energy for each activity by multiplying the time by the energy per minute.
	Identifies the energy stored in bananas, peas, chips, and chocolate from the table.
	Works out the mass of each that would be needed for the daily activities.
	Comments on the contrast in mass between fruit and chips/chocolate.

kerboodle

Starter	Support/Extension	Resources
Energy stored in foods (5 min) A list of statements relating to the energy stored in foods is given on the interactive resource. Students must categorise these statements according to whether they are true or false.	**Extension**: Students correct the statements that are false, and prepare three more statements (true or false) to share with the class.	**Interactive**: Energy stored in foods
Food and activity (10 min) Students consider how the food requirements change for different people engaged in different activities. These can be ranked in order of energy used.	**Extension**: Students suggest how energy requirements change for different people or activity levels. They predict the effect of keeping the amount of food eaten constant.	

Main	Support/Extension	Resources
Food and fuels (35 min) This activity uses props to demonstrate the size of a joule to students. Students extract information from food labels about energy intake per portion, suggest foods that could be eaten to provide their daily amount of energy, and rank energy requirements for carrying out different activities in order.	**Support**: The accompanying access sheet has simplified questions. **Extension**: Students can suggest similar activities that use the same amount of energy (or 10 times the amount of energy).	**Activity**: Food and fuels **Skill sheet:** Converting units

Plenary	Support/Extension	Resources
What used the most energy today? (10 min) Students decide which of the activities they do during a typical school day has the greatest energy requirement, and give a justification for their answer. Students compare their choices. Ask students 'Do you adjust your food intake to allow for an active school day?'	**Support**: Provide a data sheet listing approximate energy requirements by activity for a fixed duration, which students can refer to.	
Energy in fuel (10 min) Provide students with information about the energy supplied by burning fuels. Students compare the amount of energy supplied by fuel with the amount of energy supplied by food. Explain that fuels are often a more concentrated form of energy than food.	**Extension**: Students compare reasons for using fuels in different situations (e.g., coal is not used in cars because it leaves ash).	

Homework	Support/Extension	
Students keep track of what they do during a 24-hour period (activity and duration), and estimate their energy requirements for that day.	**Support**: Provide a table listing approximate energy requirements by activity and duration, which students can complete based on their own activity.	

Securing Mastery Goals

- 3.3.1 Explain the advantages and disadvantages of different energy resources.
- 3.3.1 Represent the energy transfers from a renewable or non-renewable resource to an electrical device in the home. (Pt 1/2)

Exceeding Mastery Goals

- 3.3.1 Evaluate the social, economic and environmental consequences of using a resource to generate electricity, from data.
- 3.3.1 Suggest actions a government or communities could take in response to rising energy demand. (Pt 1/2)

Enquiry processes

- 2.1 Select relevant data and do calculations. 2.1 Identify patterns in data.
- 2.3 Judge whether the conclusion is supported by the data.
- 2.7 Identify the claim; check the claim; check the evidence; check the reasoning.
- 2.8 List all the facts, scientific ideas, data, or conclusions that support your opinion.
- 2.14 Consider people; consider the environment; consider money.
- 2.14 Describe how each group could benefit or be harmed.

Band	Outcome	Checkpoint	
		Questions	Activities
Know	Name renewable and non-renewable energy resources.	A, C, 1	Main, Plenary 1
	State one advantage and one disadvantage of fossil fuels.	B, 1	Main, Plenary 1
	Use one source of information.		Main
	Name a renewable resource used to generate electricity.	3	Main, Plenary 1
Apply	Describe the difference between a renewable and a non-renewable energy resource.	1	Main, Plenary 1
	Describe how electricity is generated using a fossil fuel or a renewable resource.	2	Main
	Choose an appropriate source of secondary information.		Main
	Explain the advantages and disadvantages of different energy resources.	3	Main
Extend	Compare renewable and non-renewable resources.	3	Main, Homework
	Explain how a range of resources generate electricity, drawing on scientific concepts.	2	Main, Homework
	Justify the choice of secondary information.		Main
	Suggest actions a government or communities could take in response to rising energy demand.		Main, Homework

Literacy

Students collate information from a number of different sources to prepare a poster or leaflet to summarise information appropriately to their target audience.

Key words

energy resource, fossil fuel, non-renewable, renewable

GCSE link

4.1.3/6.1.3 National and global energy resources

The main energy resources available for use on Earth include: fossil fuels (coal, oil and gas), nuclear fuel, bio-fuel, wind, hydroelectricity, geothermal, the tides, the Sun and water waves.

A renewable energy resource is one that is being (or can be) replenished as it is used.

The uses of energy resources include: transport, electricity generation and heating.

Answers from the student book

In-text questions	A A fuel like coal, oil, or gas that took millions of years to form. B carbon dioxide
Summary Questions	1 non-renewable, fossil fuel, renewable, pollution, reliable (6 marks)
	2 Burning coal produces steam. Steam drives a turbine. The turbine drives a generator. The generator generates electricity. (4 marks)
	3 Credit any suitable board game, for example, snakes and ladders or collecting cards/tokens relating to different types.
	Points/board relates to ways fuels are formed or ways electricity is generated.
	Point system includes ideas about climate change/pollution.
	Board game must have a suitable scoring method relating to advantages and disadvantages of each method of electricity generation. (6 marks)

Starter	Support/Extension	Resources
Sorting fuels (10 min) Provide samples of fuels (e.g., wood, coal, oil, ethanol, and candle) for students to put into two groups. Students should justify how they have categorised their fuels during the class discussion. Introduce the idea of energy release during combustion of fuels, and the difference between renewable and non-renewable energy resources.	**Support:** Offer suggestions on how fuels can be grouped. **Extension:** Students compare different ways of categorising fuels.	
Life without electricity (5 min) Students describe how their lives would be different without electricity, identifying activities that rely on electricity and activities that use other fuel sources.	**Support:** Students identify activities in everyday life that rely on electricity.	

Main	Support/Extension	Resources
Energy resources (40 min) Provide a range of research stations, including various levels of textbooks, information posters, leaflets, and if possible, computers with Internet access. Students carry out research, in groups or independently, in order to cover the topics posed in the research activity regarding the generation of electricity. Students produce a poster or leaflet to answer these questions, and if students work in small groups, they should present their findings to each other. An animation to show how electricity is generated in thermal power stations can be shown at the end of student presentations for recap. A second animation that illustrates how electricity can be generated using renewables can be shown for comparison. These animations are readily available on the Internet.	**Support:** A support sheet is available that gives students a much more structured approach to their research task. **Extension:** Students identify the advantages and disadvantages of using different energy resources, linking waste products from burning fossil fuels to risks, and considering the social, economic and environmental issues.	**Activity:** Energy resources

Plenary	Support/Extension	Resources
Fossil fuels vs renewables (5 min) Students complete the gaps on the interactive resource to explain the formation and uses of fossil fuels, including the advantages and disadvantages of using fossil fuels to generate electricity. Students should then produce a similar summary for renewable energy sources. **Ranking key points** (10 min) List different methods of electricity generation on the board, with help from students. Students should diamond rank these ways in order of importance, and justify their answers in small groups.		**Interactive:** Fossil fuels

Homework	Support/Extension	
Students write a short newspaper article explaining the opening of a fossil fuel power station in their neighbourhood. This should explain how the power station benefits the community, include some effects it has on local surroundings, and discuss the views of locals regarding this new power station.	**Extension:** Students should suggest actions that a government or the community could take in response to rising energy demand.	

3.1.3 Energy and power

Securing Mastery Goals
- 3.3.1 Compare the energy usage and cost of running different home devices.

Exceeding Mastery Goals
- 3.3.1 Suggest actions a government or communities could take in response to rising energy demand. (Pt 2/2)
- 3.3.1 Suggest ways to reduce costs, by examining data on a home energy bill.

Enquiry processes
- 2.1.2 Make an experimental prediction.

Enquiry processes activity:
- 3.3.1 Compare the running costs of fluorescent and filament light bulbs.

Band	Outcome	Checkpoint	
		Question	Activities
Know	State the definitions of energy and power.	1	Main
	State that power, fuel used, and cost are linked.	1, 3	Main, Plenary 1, Homework
	Predict which equipment is more powerful when given a selection of appliances.		Starter 1, Starter 2, Main
Apply	Explain the difference between energy and power.	1	Main
	Describe the link between power, fuel use, and cost of using domestic appliances.	2	Main, Plenary 1, Homework
	Predict the power requirements of different home devices, and compare their energy usage and how much they cost to run.		Maths, Starter 2, Main, Plenary 1
Extend	Compare the power consumption of different appliances.	2	Starter 1, Main, Plenary 2, Homework
	Calculate and compare energy costs in different scenarios.	2	Main, Homework
	Predict the effect on energy bills of changing the power of equipment.	3	Main, Plenary 1

Maths
Students carry out simple calculations for energy, power, and energy costs.

Students also demonstrate their understanding of the number scale and an appreciation of J, kJ, W, kW, and kWh in their calculations.

MyMaths More support for the maths skills in this section can be found on MyMaths.

Literacy
Students use scientific terminology when explaining the link between power, energy, and cost.

GCSE link
4.2.4.2/6.2.4.2 Energy transfers in everyday appliances

Everyday electrical appliances are designed to bring about energy transfers. The amount of energy an appliance transfers depends on how long the appliance is switched on for and the power of the appliance.

Work is done when charge flows in a circuit.

The amount of energy transferred by electrical work can be calculated using the equation:
energy transferred = power × time

Key Words
power, watt, kilowatt, kilowatt hour

Answers from the student book

In-text questions	A watt (W)
	B kilowatt hour (kWh)

46

Activity	**What's the cost?**	
	a energy = 10 kW × 1 h × 7 days = 70 kWh	**b** cost = 70 kWh × 10 p ÷ 100 = £7
Summary Questions	**1** joules, watts, second, kWh, lower, less (6 marks)	
	2 Extended response question (6 marks). Example answers:	
	The power rating tells you the energy that each kettle can transfer per second.	
	The higher the power, the quicker the element will transfer energy to the water.	
	The higher the power, the quicker the temperature of the water will rise.	
	A power of 1200 W is the same as 1.2 kW (or 2 kW is the same as 2000 W).	
	The 2 kW kettle will heat water faster than the 1.2 kW kettle.	
	The energy that you pay for is measured in kilowatt hours (kWh).	
	The energy that you pay for depends on the power and the time that you use it for.	
	3a One from: Run a campaign to raise awareness/raise taxes on energy use/require the use of lower power devices. (1 mark)	
	b People like to save money/care about the environment. (1 mark)	

Starter	Support/Extension	Resources
What's the power? (10 min) Show students a range of light bulbs of different power ratings (including energy-saving and incandescent light bulbs), and ask students to choose from everyday observations the bulb that will produce the brightest light, before offering the definition of power (amount of energy transferred per second).	**Extension**: Students link power to the energy transferred from a chemical store to a thermal store via electricity.	
	Support: Allow students to work in small groups.	
Power appliances (10 min) Explain what is meant by power. Students list 10 appliances they used yesterday, and rank these according to power. Keep the list to reassess at the end of the lesson.	**Extension**: Students justify why they have ranked the appliances this way.	

Main	Support/Extension	Resources
Power (35 min) This activity is one of the AQA Enquiry process activities. Introduce the difference between energy and power, and check students know the units for each.	**Support**: Remind students that power is measured in watts (W) or kilowatts (kW), and that these are the only letters they should look for when reading appliance labels.	**Activity**: Power **Skill sheet**: Converting units
Demonstrate an energy monitor or joulemeter to show that the energy transferred depends on the power and time that the equipment is used.		
Compare the power of two light bulbs (an energy-saving and an incandescent light bulb), leave them on for a minute and compare their temperatures.	**Extension**: Introduce kilowatt hours (kWh) in general terms, and allow students to read the corresponding section in the student book.	
Students carry out the task on the activity sheet, examining different items found around the home, and answer the questions that follow.		

Plenary	Support/Extension	Resources
Reducing energy bills (10 min) Students use ideas gained from this lesson to summarise ways to reduce energy bills. They choose the correct words to complete sentences in the interactive resource.	**Extension**: Students suggest the relative importance of each energy-saving measure.	**Interactive**: Reducing energy bills
Power appliances (revisited) (10 min) Students check their order of the 10 appliances from the start of the lesson, and decide if they still agree with their original ranking based on what they have learnt this lesson. Ask students to justify any changes made.	**Support**: Allow students to work in small groups.	
	Extension: Ask students to answer summary question 3.	

Homework	Support/Extension
Students check appliances at home to find out the power rating of each. Students **must** check with their parents before unplugging or moving appliances, or else carry out this task under adult supervision. They then list these appliances in order of power, starting from the lowest power rating, and state the relevance power rating has on an energy bill.	**Extension**: Students should estimate the time and cost of using each appliance per month.

3.2.1 Energy adds up

Securing Mastery Goals

- 3.3.2 Describe how the energy of an object depends on its speed, temperature, height or whether it is stretched or compressed.
- 3.3.1 Show how energy is transferred between energy stores in a range of real-life examples.

Exceeding Mastery Goals

- 3.3.2 Explain why processes such as swinging pendulums or bouncing balls cannot go on forever, in terms of energy. (Pt 1/2)
- 3.3.2 Evaluate analogies and explanations for the transfer of energy. (Pt 1/2)

Enquiry processes

- 2.9 Choose range, interval, readings.
- 2.9 Gather data, minimising errors.
- 2.9 Test suitability of measuring instrument.

Enquiry processes activity

- 3.3.2 Explain the energy transfers in a hand-crank torch.

Band	Outcome	Checkpoint	
		Question	Activity
Know	State the definition of the conservation of energy.	A, 1	Starter 2, Main
↓	State how energy is transferred.	C	Starter 2, Main, Plenary 2
	Present simple observations of energy transfers.		Main, Homework
Apply	Describe energy stores before and after a change, including stores relating to an object's speed, temperature, height or shape.	2, 3	Starter 1, Main, Plenary 2
	Explain what brings about transfers in energy between stores.	2, 4	Starter 2, Main, Plenary 2, Homework
↓	Present observations of energy transfers in a table.		Main
Extend	Apply ideas about stores and transfers to a range of unfamiliar situations.	2, 3, 4	Starter 2, Main, Plenary 2
	Compare energy transfers to energy conservation.	4	Starter 2, Main, Plenary 2
↓	Present detailed observations of energy transfers in a table, explaining changes to the physical system, and how that relates to the ways in which energy is stored.		Main

Literacy

Students use scientific terminology to explain the Law of conservation of energy, describing energy transfers in different situations.

Students are also required to create their own mnemonics for remembering the names of energy stores in the student-book activity.

Key Words

law of conservation of energy, **chemical energy store, thermal energy store, kinetic energy store, gravitational potential energy store, elastic energy store**

GCSE link

4.1.1.1/6.1.1.1 Energy stores and systems

Students should be able to describe all the changes involved in the way energy is stored when a system changes, for common situations. For example:

- an object projected upwards
- a moving object hitting an obstacle
- an object accelerated by a constant force
- a vehicle slowing down
- bringing water to a boil in an electric kettle.

4.1.2.1/6.1.2.1 Energy transfers in a system

Energy can be transferred usefully, stored or dissipated, but cannot be created or destroyed.

Answers from the student book

In-text questions	**A** Energy cannot be created or destroyed. It can only be transferred.
	B kinetic, thermal, gravitational, chemical, elastic **C** Three from: radiation, waves, forces, electricity
Activity	**Remember those stores!** Credit suitable mnemonics using the letters C, T, K, G, and E.

Summary Questions	**1** created, destroyed, chemical, thermal, cannot (5 marks)
	2a Energy is transferred from a chemical store of a battery to a thermal store of the surroundings (1 mark) by an electric current and heating. (1 mark)
	   b Energy is transferred from the chemical store of the coal to thermal stores of the food and the surroundings (1 mark) using an electric current. (1 mark)
	   c Energy is transferred from the kinetic store of the wind to kinetic and thermal stores of the motor and the surroundings (1 mark) using an electric current. (1 mark)
	3 Kinetic – speed increases (1 mark), thermal – temperature increases (1 mark), gravitational potential – height increases (1 mark), elastic – extension/deformation increases (1 mark).
	4 Extended response question (6 marks). Example answers.
	There is a chemical store associated with the wood (and oxygen). The wood burns in the oxygen. Energy is transferred to the sausages. Because the fire heats the sausages. There is more energy in the thermal store associated with the sausages. There is more energy in the thermal store associated with the air. There is less energy in the chemical store associated with the wood.

kerboodle

Starter	Support/Extend	Resources
Energy stores (10 min) Introduce energy stores (chemical, thermal, kinetic, gravitational potential, and elastic) to students giving examples of each type. Students suggest another example of each type of energy store by trying to use examples in the room. **Energy changes** (10 min) Show some examples of energy changes and ask students to describe in words what is happening, for example, an antacid rocket, burning an indoor sparkler, and dropping a ball. Introduce the idea of energy stores and that energy is transferred from a store when anything happens. Explain that all energy must be accounted for (law of conservation of energy).	**Support**: Provide sort cards with named energy sources to match against types of energy stores. **Extension**: Students should point out unwanted energy transfers during each activity, and discuss the differences between electricity, light, sound, and energy stores.	

Main	Support/Extend	Resources
The conservation of energy (35 min) This activity is one of the AQA Enquiry process activities. It is extremely important to introduce/recap the types of energy store and transfer, as well as the law of conservation of energy first. Students will then carry out a circus activity where they identify energy stores before and after an energy transfer, in addition to the energy transfers taking place during the experiment. The circus should include the energy transfers in a hand-crank torch. Students then answer questions that follow.	**Support**: The support sheet allows students to choose the type of energy store each time from two possible answers.	**Practical**: The conservation of energy

Plenary	Support/Extend	Resources
Energy stores and transfers (10 min) Students sort a list of items and scenarios into energy stores or energy transfers using the interactive resource. **Is it conserved?** (10 min) Ask students to write the law of conservation of energy on their mini-whiteboards. Students should then use an example from the practical and account for all the energy during the transfer. Demonstrate how you can model a change in energy in stores using liquid in beakers (beaker = store, liquid = energy), or with money (money = energy).	**Extension**: Students should match each energy store to a corresponding energy transfer, offering the energy transfer in full for each example. **Extension**: Write down a pro and a con of the two methods of representing energy transfers.	**Interactive**: Energy stores and transfers

Homework		
Students describe five energy changes that take place during a normal school day, including the changes in the energy content of corresponding energy stores.		

Securing Mastery Goals
- 3.3.2 Calculate the useful energy and the amount dissipated, given values of input and output energy.
- 3.3.2 Explain how energy is dissipated in a range of situations.

Exceeding Mastery Goals
- 3.3.2 Explain why processes such as swinging pendulums or bouncing balls cannot go on forever, in terms of energy. (Pt 2/2)
- 3.3.2 Compare the percentages of energy wasted by renewable energy sources.
- 3.3.2 Evaluate analogies and explanations for the transfer of energy. (Pt2/2)

Enquiry processes
- 2.4 Present findings of research into cost and efficiency.
- 2.9 Prepare a table with space to record all measurements.
- 2.9 Gather data, minimising errors.

Band	Outcome	Checkpoint	
		Question	Activity
Know	State what dissipation means.	A, 1	Starter 2
	Do simple calculations of wasted energy from input and useful energies.	2	Main 1
	State what lubrication and streamlining mean.	B	Main 1
Apply	Explain how energy is dissipated in a range of situations.	1, 2	Starter 1 and 2, Plenary 2
	Calculate useful energy and wasted energy from input and output energies.	2	Main 2
	Describe how dissipated energy can be reduced.	B	Main 1, Plenary 1 and 2
Extend	Account for all energy transfers in a range of situations.	2	Starter 1
	Calculated a useful energy and wasted energy, and efficiency.	2	Main 2
	Evaluate methods of reducing energy dissipation.		Homework

Maths
Student use fractions and percentages in calculations of energy efficiency.

MyMaths More support for the maths skills in this section can be found on MyMaths.

Literacy
Students use scientific terminology to explain dissipation, and methods of reducing it such as lubrication and streamlining. They describe situations where dissipation takes place.

GCSE link
4.1.2.1/6.1.2.1 Energy transfers in a system

Students should be able to describe, with examples, how in all system changes energy is dissipated, so that it is stored in less useful ways. This energy is often described as being 'wasted'.

Students should be able to explain ways of reducing unwanted energy transfers, for example through lubrication and the use of thermal insulation.

4.1.2.2/6.1.2.2 Efficiency

The energy efficiency for any energy transfer can be calculated using the equation:

$$\text{efficiency} = \frac{\text{useful output energy transfer}}{\text{total input energy transfer}}$$

Key Words
dissipation, lubrication, streamlining

Answers from the student book

In-text questions	A	The transfer of energy to a store, usually the thermal store of the surroundings, so that it is no longer useful.
	B	Two suitable suggestions e.g., reducing air resistance by streamlining, reducing friction in the engine by lubrication.

Summary questions	**1** friction, heating, dissipated (3 marks)
	2a wasted energy $= 500J - 200J = 300J$ (2 marks)
	b efficiency $= \dfrac{\text{useful energy} \times 100\%}{\text{total energy}} = \dfrac{200J \times 100\%}{500J} = 40\%$ (2 marks)
	3 Extended response question (6 marks) Example answers:
	Conservation of energy says energy cannot be created or destroyed, just transferred
	Energy dissipation is when energy is transferred to a store so that it is no longer useful/spread out
	All processes dissipate energy (usually to the thermal store of the surroundings)
	In any process there is a useful energy transfer, and a wasted energy transfer (dissipation)
	You can calculate the energy dissipated if you know the useful energy transferred and the total energy transferred
	Using the conservation of energy, the energy dissipated = total energy transferred − useful energy transferred.

Starter	Support/Extend	Resources
Watts the difference? (10 min) Show three different types of light bulb of the same output power (incandescent, CFL, and LED) and discuss the difference in their appearance. Use an energy meter to show that the power being transferred electrically is different. Students discuss what is happening in terms of energy stores and how they could represent what is happening. Students rank the bulbs in terms of least to most wasted energy.	**Support**: Students get cards with values of useful and total input energies/powers. **Extension**: Students can discuss which bulb is the most 'efficient' and why.	
What happens to the wasted energy? (5 min) Show thermal images of houses/cars, and discuss what we mean by 'dissipation'. Students discuss ways to reduce dissipation in each case. Alternatively, students complete the statements about energy dissipation in the interactive activity.		**Interactive:** Efficiency statements

Main	Support/Extend	Resources
Lubrication (20 min) Introduce lubrication as a way of reducing dissipation due to friction. Show close up photos of smooth surfaces, such as metals, and show that they are not really smooth.		
Students use a block, newtonmeter and different fluids to find the best lubricant. They put a set amount of each lubricant on the bottom of a tray. They place the block on the bottom of the tray, and measure the height to which they need to raise one end of the tray to make the block move.		
Bulbs and efficiency (15 min) Revisit the comparison of light bulbs from 3.1.3 Energy and power. Give out data for input and useful energy and get students to calculate the wasted energy. Introduce 'efficiency' and ask students to rank bulbs in terms of efficiency.	**Extension**: Given data, make a bar chart of energy wasted.	**Practical:** Investigating the efficiency of lightbulbs

Plenary	Support/Extend	Resources
Which is the best? (10 min) Students report back on their finding and the class ranks the lubricants in order of best to worse. Discuss any differences in methods and results, and the situations where the choice of lubricant is important (cars/bikes) and less important (hinges).	**Extension**: Students make a table to show how ideas about energy (stores, transfers, conservation, dissipation) are explained using different analogies.	
'Saving' energy (10 min) Show a range of situations that involve energy dissipation (bouncing ball, pendulum, streamlined cars, bike chains etc), and ask the same two questions about each for students to answer on whiteboards: ● How is the energy dissipated? ● How do you reduce energy dissipation?		

Homework	Support/Extension	
Students research the history of efficiency labels on appliances and what they mean. They could conduct a survey in a shop selling washing machines etc, and see if there is a link between cost and efficiency. They present their findings in a leaflet.	**Extension**: Students plot the data on a suitable graph.	

Checkpoint lesson routes

The route through this lesson can be determined using the Checkpoint assessment.

Percentage pass marks are supplied in the Checkpoint teacher notes.

Route A (support)
Students can work through the revision activity, with support from the rest of the group and the teacher. The tasks cover the outcomes listed below.

Route B (extension)
Students compile a report about the most appropriate energy resources to use for supplying energy to a coastal town.

Progression to *Apply*

Know outcome	Apply outcome	Making progress
Know that food labels list the energy content of food in kilojoules (kJ).	Compare the amounts of energy transferred by different foods and activities.	Remind students about the units of energy. Show students food labels so they may see example of how this information is presented. In Task 1, students compare the values of energy for certain masses of food with different activities. To give an idea of 1 J students can lift 1 N (100 g) by 1 m.
Know that electricity is generated by a combination of resources which each have advantages and disadvantages.	Explain the advantages and disadvantages of different energy resources.	Ask the students about the difference between renewable and non-renewable energy resources. In Task 2, students match the advantages and disadvantages with the most appropriate energy resource. Show photos or video clips of different methods of generating electricity.
	Represent energy transfers from a renewable or non-renewable resource to an electric device in the home.	Show students a diagram or animation of the steps involved in getting electricity into the home. You could provide diagrams of each stage and ask students to order them. In Task 2, students complete a paragraph about the energy transfers involved.
Calculate the cost of home energy usage, using the formula: cost = power (kW) × time (hours) × price (per kWh).	Compare the energy usage and cost of running different home devices.	Remind students of the difference between energy and power and how to calculate the cost of using a device. Students need to remember the formula so could think of ways to help them remember, such as a mnemonic or flash card. In Task 3, students calculate the cost of running a series of devices.
Describe how jobs get done using an energy model where energy is transferred from one store at the start to another at the end.	Show how energy is transferred between energy stores in a range of real-life examples.	Task 4 covers how energy is transferred between energy stores. Have examples of activities where energy is transferred, for example a ball on a slope, a pull-back car, a candle, and a hand-held fan. Ask students to: • identify the start and end points • identify the energy store(s) that has more energy at the start and less at the end • identify the store(s) that has less energy at the start and more at the end • identify the physical process involved. Use a model, such a liquid in beakers or coins, to show the difference between start and end points. Demonstrate dropping a tennis ball that is on top of a basketball. Ask students to use the model to work out what is happening. (You may need to point out that the basketball does not bounce to the same height as it would on its own.)
Know that when energy is transferred, the total is conserved, but some energy is dissipated, reducing the useful energy.	Calculate the useful energy and the amount dissipated, given values of input and output energy and explain how energy is dissipated in a range of situations.	For Task 5, illustrate the law of conservation of energy by explaining that the energy put into the device is equal to the useful energy out and the dissipated energy. Revisit the model used in Task 4 and extend it to dissipation. This can be done by putting the liquid somewhere it cannot be poured, such as into a tray of sand. Students describe the physical process that dissipates energy.

Answers to End-of-Big Idea questions

1 wind, solar, geothermal (1 mark)   **2a** C (1 mark)   **b** kW, watts, kilowatts, W (1 mark)

3a Energy is transferred to the surroundings (1 mark) So the energy in the gravity store decreases over time (1 mark)

  b Any suitable situation where energy is dissipated by friction e.g. braking (1 mark)

4a Any one from coal, oil, gas. (1 mark)

  b Fossil fuels are formed from the remains of plants and animals that died millions of years ago. (1 mark)

  c When all fossil fuels are burnt there will not be any more as they take millions of years to form. (2 marks)

5a 100W = 0.1kW (1 mark)

  b cost = power × time × cost of 1kWh

$$= 0.1\text{kW} \times 3 \text{ hours} \times \frac{10\text{p}}{\text{kWh}}$$

$$= 3\text{p (2 marks)}$$

  c Sensible suggestion, e.g., use appliances for less time, use more efficient appliances. (1 mark)

    Because this will reduce the number of kWh, and hence the cost. (1 mark)

6a power = energy ÷ time = 6000 J ÷ 60 s = 100 W (2 marks)

  b Lightbulbs transfer energy by light and by heating. (1 mark)

    Lightbulb B transfers more energy usefully (as light)/Lightbulb A transfers less energy usefully (as light). (1 mark)

    Lightbulb A has a greater heating effect/lightbulb B has less of a heating effect. (1 mark)

  c Any sensible suggestion and reason for how it will reduce cost. (2 marks)

7a gravitational potential (1 mark)

  b i Energy is conserved/cannot be lost. (1 mark)   **ii** Some energy is transferred/dissipated to the thermal store as the ball falls through the air. (1 mark)

  c There is a force (of gravity) acting on the ball. (2 marks)

8a

Kettle	Energy input (kJ)	Useful energy output (kJ)	Wasted energy (kJ)
BoilFast	600	540	60 (1 mark)
KettlePro	800	720 (1 mark)	80

  b efficiency = useful energy out in kWh/total energy in

$$= \frac{540\text{kJ} \times 100\%}{600\text{J}} \text{ (1 mark)}$$

$$= 90\% \text{ (1 mark)}$$

    efficiency = useful energy out in kWh/total energy in

$$= \frac{720\text{kJ} \times 100\%}{900\text{kJ}} \text{ (1 mark)}$$

$$= 80\% \text{ (1 mark)}$$

  c It is not about the amount of wasted energy but the fraction of wasted energy (1 mark)

    The Boilfast wastes a smaller fraction so is more efficient (1 mark)

Answer guide for Big Write

Know	Apply	Extend
1–2 marks	**3–4 marks**	**5–6 marks**
• Design a simple diary that students could use to log what they eat/the activities that they do. • State that closing doors will save money/energy. • State that burning fossil fuels is needed to keep houses warm.	• Describe some foods and their energy content. • Describe the energy used in some activities. • Design a diary that students could use to log what they eat/the activities that they do. • Describe how we burn fossil fuels to maintain the temperature in our houses. • Link the closing of doors with reduced fossil fuel use and cost.	• Describe in detail foods and their energy content. • Describe the energy used in many activities. • Design a detailed diary that students could use to log what they eat/the activities that they do. • Describe how we use a range of fossil fuels to heat homes, including the burning of fossil fuels in power stations to provide electricity. • Explain how leaving a door open leads to an increase use of fossil fuels. • Make a clear link between the burning of fossil fuels and the cost of energy bills.

3 Part 1 Checkpoint assessment (automarked)	3 Part 1 Checkpoint: Extension
3 Part 1 Checkpoint: Revision	3.1 Progress task, 3.2 Progress task

(4) Waves

National curriculum links for this unit	
Topic	**National Curriculum topic**
4.1 Sound	Energy and waves. Sound waves
4.2 Light	Light waves

In this Big Idea students will learn:

- sound consists of vibrations which travel as a longitudinal wave through substances
- the denser the medium, the faster sound travels
- the greater the amplitude of the waveform, the louder the sound
- the greater the frequency (and therefore the shorter the wavelength), the higher the pitch
- when a light ray meets a different medium, some of it is absorbed and some reflected

- for a mirror, the angle of incidence equals the angle of reflection
- the ray model can describe the formation of an image in a mirror and how objects appear different colours
- when light enters a denser medium it bends towards the normal
- when light enters a less dense medium it bends away from the normal
- refraction through lenses and prisms can be describe using a ray diagram as a model.

AQA Enquiry process activities

Activity	Section
3.4.1 Relate changes in the shape of an oscilloscope trace to changes in pitch and volume	4.1.3 Frequency and pitch
3.4.2 Use ray diagrams to model how light passes through lenses and transparent materials	4.2.4 The eye and vision

Preparing for Key Stage 4 Success

Knowledge	4.6.1.1/6.6.1.1 Transverse and longitudinal waves
Underpinning knowledge is covered in this Big Idea for KS4 study of:	4.6.1.2/6.6.1.2 Properties of waves
	4.6.1.3 Reflection of waves (*GCSE Physics only*)
	4.6.1.4 Sound waves (*GCSE Physics only*)

Maths	**1** Arithmetic and numerical computation
Skills developed in Big Idea 4	**a** Recognise and use expressions in decimal form (4.1.1, 4.1.2, 4.1.3)
	b Recognise and use expressions in standard form (4.2.1)
	c Use ratios, fractions and percentages (4.1.1, 4.1.2, 4.1.3)
	d Make estimates of the results of simple calculations (4.1.1, 4.1.2, 4.1.3)
	2 Handling data
	a Use an appropriate number of significant figures (4.1.1, 4.1.2, 4.1.3)

3 Algebra

    a Understand and use the symbols: $=, <, \ll, \gg, >, \propto, \sim$ (4.1.1, 4.1.2, 4.1.3).

    b Change the subject of an equation (4.1.1, 4.1.2, 4.1.3).

    c Substitute numerical values into algebraic equations using appropriate units for physical quantities (4.1.1, 4.1.2, 4.1.3).

    d Solve simple algebraic equations (4.1.1, 4.1.2, 4.1.3).

4 Graphs

    a Translate information between graphical and numeric form (4.1.4).

Literacy Sills developed in Big Idea 4	• Select, synthesise, and compare information from a variety of sources (4.1.1, 4.1.2, 4.1.3, 4.1.4, 4.2.4, 4.2.5). • Use scientific terms confidently and correctly in discussions and writing (all spreads). • Organisation of ideas and evidence (4.1.1, 4.1.2, 4.1.3). • Identify ideas and supporting evidence in text (4.1.1, 4.1.2, 4.1.3). • Use correct forms of writing styles and include information relevant to the audience (4.1.3, 4.1.4, 4.2.4, 4.2.5). • Ideas are organised into well-developed, linked paragraphs (4.1.1, 4.1.4 4.2.4, 4.2.5, end-of-topic 4 Big Write).
Assessment Skills	• Extended response questions (4.1.1, 4.1.2, 4.1.3, 4.2.1). • Quantitative problem solving (4.1.1, 4.1.2, 4.1.3), (End-of-Big Idea questions Q8). • Application of Enquiry Processes (3.1.1, 3.1.2, 3.1.3, 3.2.1, 3.2.2) (End-of-Big Idea questions Q6, Q9).

KS2 Link	Check before	Checkpoint	Catch-up
Vibrating objects make sound, which varies in pitch and loudness, travels through a medium to your ear, and gets fainter as you move away.	4.1.1 Sound waves and speed 4.1.2 Loudness and amplitude 4.1.3 Frequency and pitch 4.1.5 The ear and hearing	Ask students how sounds are made.	Demonstrate this using a vibrating ruler at the end of a table, or by placing a vibrating tuning fork in water.
Light travels in straight lines, which explains the size and shape of shadows.	4.2.1 Light	Students sketch how light travels from a torch to a book.	Shine light through sheets of cardboard spaced apart, each with a small central hole. Show that the holes must be lined up for light to travel through.
Objects are seen because they give out or reflect light into the eye.	4.2.1 Light	Students sketch how light travels from a torch to a book to our eyes.	Students group objects as ones that give out light (lit torch bulb, candle) and ones that reflect light (book, mirror).

Key Stage 2 Quiz: Physics
4 Part 1 End-of-Big Idea test (foundation)
4 Part 1 End-of-Big Idea test (foundation) mark scheme
4 Part 1 End-of-Big Idea test (higher)
4 Part 1 End-of-Big Idea test (higher) mark scheme

Answers to Picture Puzzler
Key Words
dam, eclipse, car, ice, bungee jumper, earth mover, LED
The key word is **decibel**.
Close Up
Hairs in the cochlea

⊕ **MyMaths**

You can find additional support for the maths skills covered in this Big Idea on **MyMaths**, including carrying out calculations, changing the subject of equations, calculating means, drawing graphs, and using making estimates.

4.1.1 Sound waves and speed

Securing Mastery Goals

- 3.4.1 Sound does not travel through a vacuum.
- 3.4.1 The speed of sound in air is 330 m/s, a million times slower than light.
- 3.4.1 Explain observations where sound is reflected, transmitted or absorbed by different media. (Pt 1/2)

Enquiry processes

- 2.6 Develop an explanation.
- 2.6 Decide if a diagram might help the explanation.
- 2.6 Suggest a scientific idea that might explain the observation.
- 2.6 Communicate your idea, evidence and reasoning.

Band	Outcome	Checkpoint	
		Question	**Activity**
Know	Name some sources of sound.	1	Starter 1, Starter 2
	Name materials that sound can travel through.	B, 1	Main
	State that sound travels at 330 m/s in air, a million times more slowly than light.	1	Main
	Use data to compare the speed of sound in different materials.		Main
Apply	Describe how sound is produced and travels.	A, 1	Starter 1, Starter 2, Main
	Explain observations where sound is transmitted by different media.	1, 2	Main
	Contrast the speed of sound and the speed of light.	3	Maths
	Compare the time for sound to travel in different materials using data given.		Main
Extend	Explain what is meant by supersonic travel.		Plenary 2, Homework
	Describe sound as the transfer of energy through vibrations and explain why sound cannot travel through a vacuum.	2	Main
	Compare the time taken for sound and light to travel the same distance.	3	Maths
	Explain whether sound waves from the Sun can reach the Earth.	3	Main

Maths

Students calculate speeds of light and sound using simple calculations of distance and time.

MyMaths More support for the maths skills in this section can be found on MyMaths.

Literacy

For homework, students write about supersonic travel, linking key concepts and scientific terminology gained from the lesson.

GCSE link

4.5.6.1.2/6.5.4.1.2 Speed
A typical value for the speed of sound in air is 330 m/s.

4.6.1.1/6.6.1.1 Transverse and longitudinal waves
Longitudinal waves show areas of compression and rarefaction. Sound waves travelling through air are longitudinal.

Key Words

vibration,
medium,
vacuum,
speed of sound,
speed of light

Answers from the student book

In-text questions	A vibrations
	B solids, liquids, gases
	C 330 m/s

Activity	How fast?
	a Table should have two columns, with headings 'material' and 'speed (m/s)'.
	b A bar chart because one of the variables is categoric.
	Stormy night
	a distance = 330m/s × 4 = 1320 m = 1.32 km
	b There would be no time difference between seeing the lightning and hearing the thunder.
Summary questions	**1** vibrating, vibrate, solids, gases, vacuum (5 marks)
	2a The particles in a gas are further apart than the particles in a liquid.
	The vibration is not passed on so quickly. (1 mark)
	b There are no particles in a vacuum to transmit the sound/through which a sound wave can travel. (1 mark)
	3 Example answers (6 marks):
	Light travels much faster than sound.
	So the light reaches you first.
	It takes about 0.03 seconds for the sound to reach you.
	The speed of sound is about 300 m/s.
	It would take 0.000 000 03 seconds for light to reach you.
	The speed of light is 300 million m/s.
	So light is about 1 million times faster than sound.
	The time it takes light to reach you is about a millionth of the time it takes sound to reach you.

Starter	Support/Extension	Resources
Sources of sound (5 min) Students list five sources of sound, explaining how the sounds are caused. They should identify the source of the vibration (which is not always obvious, for example, in the loudspeaker).	**Extension:** Students describe how the sound can be controlled.	
Good vibrations (5–10 min) Students hum with their hand resting on their throat to feel the larynx vibrating. When students are quiet, hit a tuning fork on the bench so it vibrates and produces a sound, then dip the tips of its prongs just under the surface of water to show it is vibrating. Explain that all sounds are caused by vibrations and travel through a medium.	**Extension:** Use several tuning forks and ask students for the link with pitch and size, or as a recap on superposition of waves.	

Main	Support/Extension	Resources
The speed of sound (40 min) Explain that sound travels at different speeds in different materials. Review the particle arrangement in solids, liquids, and gases. You should emphasise the need for particles in sound vibrations (and so sound cannot travel through a vacuum). Students predict whether sound travels fastest in solids, liquids, or gases, then complete the questions on the activity sheet.	**Support:** Sketch diagrams of particle arrangements for students to identify as solid, liquids, or gases. **Extension:** Students make clear links with the arrangement of particles and the transfer of energy by sound waves.	**Activity:** The speed of sound

Plenary	Support/Extension	Resources
Faster than the speed of sound (10 min) Explain that *supersonic* means faster than the speed of sound. Show video clips of supersonic objects, for example, Concorde, rockets, Thrust SSC (land speed world record holder), and remind students how fast these objects are travelling (the speed of sound in air is 330 m/s).	**Support:** Pause the video at points where features of supersonic travel can be emphasised.	
Vibrations and energy (10 min) The interactive resource involves students linking up sentences to consolidate the ideas of the lesson.		**Interactive:** Vibrations and energy

Homework		
Students explain what is meant by supersonic travel, and how the objects are designed to travel faster than the speed of sound. Students suggest what the implications of supersonic travel are, and present their ideas on the benefits and drawbacks of supersonic travel.		

4.1.2 Loudness and amplitude

Securing Mastery Goals

- 3.4.1 Explain observations of how sound travels using the idea of a longitudinal wave.
- 3.4.1 Explain observations where sound is reflected, transmitted or absorbed by different media. (Pt 2/2)
- 3.4.1 Describe the amplitude and frequency of a wave from a diagram or oscilloscope picture. (Pt 1/2)
- 3.4.1 Use drawings of waves to describe how sound waves change with volume or pitch. (Pt 1/2)

Exceeding Mastery Goals

- 3.4.1 Evaluate the data behind a claim for a sound creation or blocking device, using the properties of sound waves. (Pt 1/2)

Enquiry processes

- 2.9 Choose range, interval, readings.
- 2.9 Use the measuring instrument correctly.
- 2.9 Carry out the method carefully and consistently.
- 2.9 Gather data, minimising errors.

Band	Outcome	Checkpoint	
		Question	Activity
Know	Define amplitude, frequency, and wavelength.	1	Main 1, Plenary 1
	State the link between loudness and amplitude.	1	Starter 1, Starter 2
	State two things that can happen when sound goes through matter or hits a boundary.		Homework
	Label amplitude on a diagram of an oscilloscope trace of a wave.		Main 1
Apply	Explain observations of how sound travels using the idea of a longitudinal wave.	A	Starter 1
	Describe the link between loudness and amplitude, using diagrams.	1	Starter 2, Main 1
	Explain what happens when sound goes through matter or hits a boundary.	3	Homework
	Describe how to find the amplitude of a wave from an oscilloscope trace.	2	Main 2, Plenary 1
Extend	Explain how you can make measurements of the amplitude of a sound wave.		Main 2, Plenary 1
	Compare and contrast waves of different loudness using a diagram.		Main 1, Plenary 1
	Describe in detail the behaviour of sound as it travels in matter or hits a boundary.	3	Homework
	Use an oscilloscope on a variety of settings of p.d./division to find the amplitude of a sound wave.	2	Main 2

Maths

In the student book, students use scales to work out the amplitude of sound waves.

MyMaths More support for the maths skills in this section can be found on MyMaths.

Literacy

Students write clear, coherent, well-developed sentences to describe various volume reduction measures for their homework.

Key Words
amplitude, frequency, wavelength, longitudinal wave, volume, echo, oscilloscope, absorption

GCSE link

4.6.1.2/6.6.1.2 Properties of waves
Students should be able to describe wave motion in terms of their amplitude, wavelength, frequency and period.

They should be able to define amplitude, frequency, and wavelength.

Answers from the student book

In-text questions	**A** Three from: amplitude, frequency, wavelength, speed
	B It shows a changing p.d. produced from a sound wave by a microphone.
Summary questions	**1** energy, amplitude, wavelength, amplitude, longitudinal, the same (6 marks)
	2 amplitude = 3 divisions $\times \dfrac{4V}{\text{division}} = 12V$ (1 mark)
	3 Extended response question. Example answer (6 marks):
	In a cave you hear an echo/multiple echoes because sound is reflected once/many times. The echoes get quieter because the sound spreads out and is eventually absorbed. You hear the sound through the door because some is transmitted, but it is quieter than the shout because some is absorbed.

Starter	Support/Extension	Resources
Loudness (5 min) The interactive resource asks students to categorise ways to change the loudness of sounds based on everyday observations and musical instruments. Demonstrate how the amplitude of a sound made by a ruler overhanging the bench depends on the force applied.	**Extension**: Students supply their own suggestions to add to the lists.	**Interactive**: Loudness
Longitudinal waves (5–10 min) Introduce the idea of a longitudinal waves, and show a speaker moving in and out. Show an appropriate video/animation to show how air molecules move when a sound wave travels. Ask students to consider the waves produced by a ruler/tuning fork.	**Extension**: Students investigate sound from rulers independently and state a clear relationship between the variables.	

Main	Support/Extension	Resources
Wave diagrams (20 min) Students find drawing wave diagrams difficult so a lot of practice of this skill is essential. Use simple examples, changing one factor at a time to begin with. Make sure students keep wavelengths and amplitudes consistent. Connect the signal generator and loudspeaker to the output of an oscilloscope. Show the shape of the wave for a frequency of about 400–600 Hz. Change the volume to demonstrate how the amplitude changes. Students then complete the activity sheet.	**Support**: A support sheet is available as a reference for key terms used during this activity.	**Activity**: Wave diagrams
Measuring amplitude (15–20 min) When students have worked with the oscilloscope traces qualitatively, introduce the idea of measuring the amplitude using the oscilloscope.		
Explain that the oscilloscope is showing a p.d. vs time graph. Show waves of two different amplitudes and ask the students to calculate the amplitude of each wave in volts.		

Plenary	Support/Extension	Resources
Changing waves (10 min) Students sketch a wave on a mini-whiteboard and then draw a louder wave. Check answers. Show diagrams of waves from an oscilloscope screen with the V/div for each and the amplitude stated. Students use whiteboards to identify the correct/incorrect diagrams.	**Support**: Present a choice of waves for students to choose the loudest.	
What do you know? (10 min) Students write down three things they have learned this lesson. This is a useful chance to check misconceptions, for example, confusing amplitude with wavelength.		

Homework		
Students investigate methods for reducing the volume of sound in areas where it could cause problems. They can use observations (e.g., double glazing, trees), or research. They write a short paragraph explaining how the different methods work.		

4.1.3 Frequency and pitch

[An image of the student book spread "4.1.3 Frequency and pitch" appears here]

Securing Mastery Goals

- 3.4.1 Use drawings of waves to describe how sound waves change with volume or pitch. (Pt 2/2)
- 3.4.1 Describe the amplitude and frequency of a wave from a diagram or oscilloscope picture. (Pt 2/2)

Exceeding Mastery Goals

- 3.4.1 Use diagrams to compare the waveforms a musical instrument makes when playing different pitches or volumes.

Enquiry process activity

- 3.4.1 Relate changes in the shape of an oscilloscope trace to changes in pitch and volume.

Band	Outcome	Checkpoint	
		Question	Activity
Know	Define auditory range.	B, 1	Starter 1
	State the difference between frequency and pitch.	A	Main
↓	Label time period on a diagram of a sound wave on an oscilloscope.		Main, Plenary 1
Apply	Describe the auditory range of humans.	B	Starter 1
	Describe the link between frequency and pitch.	A	Main
↓	Describe how to find the frequency of a wave from an oscilloscope trace.	2	Main, Plenary 2
Extend	Present a reasoned prediction using data of how sounds will be differently heard by different animals.	B	Starter 1
	Compare and contrast waves of different frequency using a diagram.		Main, Plenary 1
↓	Use an oscilloscope on a variety of settings of s/div to find the period and frequency of a sound wave.	2	Main, Plenary 2

Maths

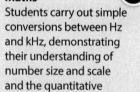

Students carry out simple conversions between Hz and kHz, demonstrating their understanding of number size and scale and the quantitative relationship between units.

MyMaths More support for the maths skills in this section can be found on MyMaths.

Literacy

In the homework activity students explain in writing how mosquito alarms are used.

GCSE link

4.6.1.2/6.6.1.2 Properties of waves

The frequency of a wave is the number of waves passing a point each second.

$$period = \frac{1}{frequency}$$

wave speed = frequency × wavelength

The wave speed is the speed at which the energy is transferred (or the wave moves) through the medium.

Key Words

pitch, auditory range, hertz, kilohertz, infrasound, ultrasound

Answers from the student book

In-text questions	**A** frequency	**B** whale
Activity	**Conversions** a 0.02 kHz–20 kHz b 1 kHz–123 kHz	

Summary questions	1 hertz, frequency, time period, auditory, narrower (5 marks)
	2 frequency $= \dfrac{1}{\text{period}}$
	$= \dfrac{1}{4}$
	$= 0.25$ Hz (2 marks)
	3 Extended response question. Example answers (6 marks):
	Vocal chords vibrate to produce sound. Sound waves are made when air is squashed and stretched. Pitch depends on frequency. To make a higher note her vocal chords vibrate more times per second. That makes the frequency of a sound wave higher. Loudness depends on amplitude. To make a louder note her vocal chords vibrate with a bigger amplitude. That makes the amplitude of a sound wave bigger.

kerboodle

Starter	Support/Extension	Resources
What's the range of hearing? (10 min) Show images of different animals and ask what is different about their hearing (dogs, bats, dolphins etc.).		
Loudness and pitch (5 min) The interactive resource asks students to categorise ways to change the pitch or loudness of sounds based on everyday observations and musical instruments.		**Interactive:** Loudness and pitch

Main	Support/Extension	Resources
What's the frequency? (30 minutes) This activity is one of the AQA Enquiry process activities. Use a signal generator, loudspeaker, and oscilloscope to display a trace on the screen at the same time as listening to the sound. Ask students to look at the screen while listening to the sound and note the difference between high-pitched and low-pitched sounds. Students draw waveforms in their books or on mini-whiteboards. Explain that the trace on the screen shows how the displacement of air molecules changes with time. Define period and amplitude. The activity sheet contains a diagram of the screen. Students to label the axes and sketch a particular waveform. The sheet takes them through the process of: - finding the period from the time between two peaks - finding the frequency using $f = 1 \div T$. Care will need to be taken with the units of period, which will be in milliseconds. Use this as an opportunity to develop maths skills to convert between units.		**Activity:** What's the frequency?

Plenary	Support/Extension	Resources
Making music (10 min) Show waveforms of the same note played on different musical instruments and discuss the differences. Show soft and loud sound, and high and low frequencies. Give out waveforms and descriptions of what they sound like and ask students to match the description to the wave.	**Extension:** Give out waveforms for a range of instruments playing middle C and ask students to draw the wave with the fundamental frequency (512Hz) on the diagram, then use the time base setting to calculate the frequency. They could calculate the frequency of a higher frequency within one of the traces (a harmonic).	
High notes (10 min) A volunteer, or you, can try whistling the highest note possible. Another student takes a measurement of the number of waves in a certain number of divisions and students work out the frequency of the note.	**Support:** Students can use a structured worksheet to do the calculation.	

Homework	Support/Extension	Resources
Students write a short paragraph explaining how high-pitched 'mosquito' alarms can be used to deter anti-social teens from loitering outside shops.		

4.1.4 The ear and hearing

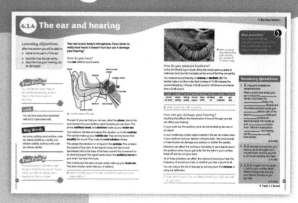

Exceeding Mastery Goals

- 3.4.1 Suggest the effects of particular ear problems on a person's hearing.
- 3.4.1 Evaluate the data behind a claim for a sound creation or blocking device, using the properties of sound waves. (Pt 2/2)

Enquiry processes

- 2.13 Identify risks and hazards.
- 2.13 Identify ways of reducing the risk.

Band	Outcome	Checkpoint	
		Question	**Activity**
Know	Name some parts of the ear.	A, 1	Starter 2, Main 2
	State some ways that hearing can be damaged.	2	Main 2
	Describe some risks of loud music.		Main 2, Homework
Apply	Describe how the ear works.	1	Main 2, Plenary 1
	Describe how your hearing can be damaged.	2	Main 2
	Explain some risks of loud music.		Main 2, Plenary 2, Homework
Extend	Evaluate the data behind a claim for a sound creation or blocking device, using the properties of sound waves.	1, 3	Homework
	Suggest the effects of particular ear problems on a person's hearing.	2, 3	Main 2, Plenary 2
	Explain, in detail, risks of hearing damage linked to sound level and time of exposure.		Main 2, Plenary 2

Literacy

For homework, students summarise information from this lesson in a leaflet on the dangers of loud music.

Students extract information from text, and use this information when answering comprehension questions in the activity.

Key Words

ear, pinna, auditory canal, eardrum, outer ear, ossicles, middle ear, amplify, oval window, cochlea, auditory nerve, inner ear, decibel

Answers from the student book

In-text questions	**A** ear drum **B** decibel **C** ear drum
Activity	**What protection?** Example: somebody wears the ear defenders, another person reduces a loud sound until the person with the ear defenders cannot hear it. Change ear defenders and repeat. The independent variable is the ear defenders. The control variables are person, distance to loudspeaker, frequency of sound. Repeat with different people and compare the results.
Summary questions	**1** ear drum, ossicles, oval window, cochlea, hairs, cochlea, auditory nerve, decibels, damaged, (9 marks) **2** Not permanent: ear wax, perforated ear drum, ear infection. Permanent: listening to loud music, head injury. (2 marks) **3** Shorter hairs in your cochlea detect higher frequencies. Longer hairs detect lower frequencies. As you get older the shorter hairs break off/are damaged. So you cannot hear such high frequencies. (4 marks)

Starter	Support/Extension	Resources
Measuring loudness (10 min) Display a decibel scale, which indicates safe sound levels and everyday examples. Discuss the display, explaining how loudness is measured in decibels and suggest ways to reduce harm. **Parts of the ear** (10 min) As a class, play hangman using the names of the different parts of the ear (e.g., pinna, eardrum, cochlea). As students guess each part, identify where it is within the ear, and how vibrations pass through the different parts of the ear.	**Extension**: Discuss whether the link between decibels and exposure-time is as clear-cut as diagrams suggest. **Support**: Students describe parts of the ear rather than naming them. **Extension**: Students consider different ways to categorise the parts of the ear (where they are found, what they are made of).	
Main	**Support/Extension**	**Resources**
Detecting sounds (20 min) Connect the microphone to the input of the oscilloscope. Demonstrate sound waves produced when a noise is made. Recap the parts of the ear and how sounds are measured in decibels. **Hearing and how it is damaged** (20 min) If a sound level meter is available, measure sound levels during the lesson. Students complete the activity sheet identifying parts of the ear and then extract information from text to identify ways the ear can be damaged, suggesting methods to reduce harm.	**Extension**: Students may choose to add descriptions to their diagram explaining the function of each part of the ear.	**Activity**: Hearing and how it is damaged
Plenary	**Support/Extension**	**Resources**
Hearing (5 min) Students rearrange sentences to explain how sounds travel from the pinna to the brain in the interactive resource. **How loud was the lesson?** (20 min) Display sound levels during the lesson against a decibel scale. Discuss implications, for example, duration and levels, impact on concentration, the need to reduce levels so instructions can be heard, and so on. Depending on the location of the school, also give out a table showing sound levels in the neighbourhood (near roads with heavy traffic, airports, building works).	**Extension**: Ask students to give additional details. **Extension**: Discuss implications in more detail (e.g., varied impact on people, factors beyond control).	**Interactive**: Hearing
Homework		
Students write a leaflet for primary students on the dangers of loud music and list ways to reduce the harm. An alternative WebQuest homework activity is also available on Kerboodle where students research the science of music.	**Extension**: Students research a sound creation device (e.g., ear bud headphones) and a blocking device (e.g., noise reduction headphones) and evaluate the claims about them using the properties of sound waves.	**WebQuest**: The science of music

4.2.1 Light

Securing Mastery Goals

- 3.4.2 Light travels at 300 million metres per second in a vacuum.
- 3.4.2 ray diagrams of eclipses to describe what is seen by observers in different places.

Enquiry processes

- 2.2 Analyse strengths and weaknesses in your inquiry.

Band	Outcome	Checkpoint	
		Question	Activity
Know	Describe some ways that light interacts with materials.	A, 1	Lit, Starter 2
	State the speed of light.		Starter 1
	State the positions of the Earth, Moon, and Sun during a solar eclipse.	C, 1, 3	Main
Apply	Describe what happens when light interacts with materials.	1, 2	Lit, Starter 1, Starter 2, Homework
	Explain how ray diagrams can explain the formation of shadows.	3	Starter 1
	Use ray diagrams to describe what observers see during an eclipse.		Main, Plenary 1
Extend	Predict how light will interact with different materials.		Starter 2, Plenary 2, Homework
	Use ray diagrams to explain what observers see during an eclipse.	3	Main, Plenary 1

Literacy

The literacy activity in the student book requires students to use scientific terms accurately in a given context.

GCSE link

4.6.2.1/6.6.2.1 Types of electromagnetic waves

Electromagnetic waves form a continuous spectrum and all types of electromagnetic wave travel at the same velocity through a vacuum (space) or air.

4.6.2.2/6.6.2.2 Properties of electromagnetic waves 1

Different substances may absorb, transmit, refract or reflect electromagnetic waves in ways that vary with wavelength.

Key Words

luminous, non-luminous, **absorption, transparent, translucent, opaque,** eclipse

Answers from the student book

In-text questions	A You can see clearly through a transparent material but not through a translucent material, even though light travels through both.
	B 300 million m/s
	C In a solar eclipse the moon is between the Earth and the Sun. In a lunar eclipse the Earth is between the Sun and the moon.
Activity	**Sort those words**
	For example, the light bulb emits light because it is luminous.
	The flower reflects light because it is non-luminous and opaque. This light is then absorbed by your eye.
	The water transmits light and is transparent.

Summary questions	
	1 luminous, emits, reflects, non-luminous, opaque (5 marks)
	2 Light is absorbed by water even though you can see through it.
	Only a small amount is absorbed, so you need a lot of water for it to become dark. (2 marks)
	3 Extended response question (6 marks). Example answers:
	Light from all parts of the Sun reaches the Earth
	So the Sun appears as a disc
	As the Moon passes in front of the Earth you see a section of the Sun is now black/a partial eclipse
	Light from part of the Sun no longer reaches the Earth at that point
	If you are in the right place on the Earth's surface you will see the Sun as a black disc with a halo/corona around it/total eclipse
	The Moon blocks the light from all of the Sun.

kerboodle

Starter	Support/Extension	Resources
Sun's light (5 min) Discuss how the Sun's light travels into the classroom and how we see it. Key points: It travels through a vacuum, air, and glass; it takes about 8 minutes to reach us; it reflects off surfaces into our eyes. (Students may not realise there is a vacuum between the Earth and the Sun.) Remind students of the speed of light (300 million km/s).	**Support**: Make sure key terms are understood (e.g., vacuum). **Extension**: Discuss how we can see the Moon, planets, and stars other than the Sun.	
Types of material (5 min) Students use the interactive resource to classify different objects using the terms translucent, opaque, and transparent. Discuss answers to check understanding.	**Extension**: Students can offer further examples of materials in each category.	**Interactive**: Types of material

Main	Support/Extension	Resources
The Moon and eclipses (20 min) Students model a solar eclipse using the instructions on the practical sheet. The lunar eclipse model is shown as a teacher-led demonstration. Students then answer the questions on the practical sheet.	**Support**: Clarify these concepts using animations and diagrams. A support sheet is available with partially drawn diagrams for students to complete.	**Practical**: The Moon and eclipses
How bright is the light? (20 min) Measure the light transmitted through different materials using a light dependent resistor (LDR) and multimeter to measure resistance, or a light meter. Many light meters give readings in lux. An LDR is a resistor with lower resistance for higher light levels. Set the multimeter to read resistance and aim the LDR towards the light source. Resistance is not directly proportional to light levels, so this is best for ranking materials rather than quantitative comparisons. Students check equipment by seeing how light levels vary in the room first. Place samples of different materials between the light and LDR/light meter and use measurements to rank materials on a scale from transparent to opaque.	**Extension**: Students suggest why we don't see eclipses every day/month.	

Plenary	Support/Extension	Resources
Explaining eclipses (10 min) Students draw diagrams on A4 whiteboards to explain a solar eclipse. They compare diagrams, and peer assess them. They repeat this for lunar eclipses.	**Extension**: Students compare and contrast the diagrams, suggest why lunar eclipses are more frequent than solar eclipses.	
Comparing materials (5–10 min) Students compare materials that light or sound travels easily through. These may not be the same (e.g., double glazing does not transmit sound well but does transmit light well).	**Support**: Students have a list of materials and they have to decide whether the material will let light or sound through.	

Homework		
Students list 10 materials used at home, classifying them as opaque, transparent, and translucent. They write a sentence for each material, explaining why being opaque, transparent, or translucent makes it suitable for its purpose.		

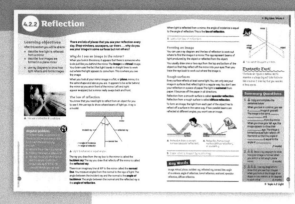

Securing Mastery Goals

- 3.4.2 Construct ray diagrams to show how light reflects off mirrors, forms images and refracts. (Pt 1/2)
- 3.4.2 Use ray diagrams to describe how light passes through lenses and transparent materials. (Pt 1/3)

Exceeding Mastery Goals

- 3.4.2 Use a ray diagram to predict how an image will change in different situations. (Pt 1/2)
- 3.4.2 Predict whether light will reflect, refract or scatter when it hits the surface of a given material. (Pt 1/2)
- 3.4.2 Use ray diagrams to explain how a device with multiple mirrors works.

Enquiry processes

- 2.9 Use the measuring instrument correctly.
- 2.9 Carry out the method carefully and consistently.
- 2.13 Identify features of an investigation which are hazardous.

Band	Outcome	Checkpoint	
		Question	Activity
Know	With guidance, construct ray diagrams to show how light reflects off mirrors and forms images.	1	Starter 1
	Identify examples of specular and diffuse reflection.	B, 2	Starter 2
↓	Use appropriate equipment safely with guidance.		Main
Apply	Explain how images are formed in a plane mirror using a ray diagram.	1	Plenary 2
	Explain the difference between specular and diffuse reflection.	2	Main
↓	Use appropriate equipment and take readings safely without help.		Main
Extend	Use a ray diagram to explain how an image in a mirror changes as you move the mirror/object, or to explain the formation of images in multiple mirrors.		Plenary 2, Homework
	Predict how light will reflect from different types of surface.	3	Main
↓	Take accurate readings using appropriate equipment and working safely.		Main

Maths

Students carry out simple calculations with angles in the student-book activity, applying existing knowledge of geometry.

MyMaths More support for the maths skills in this section can be found on MyMaths.

Literacy

Students use scientific terminology in explaining their reflection experiment and when answering corresponding questions.

GCSE link

4.6.2.2/6.6.2.2 Properties of electromagnetic waves 1

Different substances may absorb, transmit, refract or reflect electromagnetic waves in ways that vary with wavelength.

Key Words

image, virtual, plane, **incident ray, reflected ray, normal line, angle of incidence, angle of reflection,** law of reflection, specular reflection, diffuse reflection, **scattered**

Answers from the student book

In-text questions	**A** When light is reflected from a mirror, the angle of incidence is equal to the angle of reflection. **B** When light reflects from a surface in all directions it is scattered.
Activity	**Angular problem** **a** 50° **b** 50° **c** No, the angle of incidence is equal to the angle of reflection and the angle between them can be anything from nearly 180° to 0°.
Summary questions	**1** virtual, size, shape, distance, right, incidence, reflection (7 marks) **2** Ray from top of head to mirror and then to the eye. (1 mark) Ray from the feet to the mirror and then to the eye. (1 mark) Rays traced back to show virtual image. (1 mark) **3** See the teacher notes in the Kerboodle lesson player for this section. (4 marks)

Starter	Support/Extension	Resources
Mirror images (5 min) Hand students mirrors and ask them to describe the image of an object, for example, which way up, which way round, its size.	**Support**: Ask structured questions, for example, which way up is it? **Extension**: Students explain why the image is the same size, right way up, and laterally inverted.	
Different reflections (10 min) Explain the difference between specular reflection (as in mirrors) and diffuse reflection (as from rougher surfaces). Students classify examples, for example, specular reflection from surface of still water, from mirrors, or from glass surfaces. Diffuse reflection from painted walls, from clothes, from whiteboards, or pages in a book.	**Support**: Show images that students can classify as specular reflection or diffuse reflection.	

Main	Support/Extension	Resources
Investigating reflection (40 min) This works best if black out blinds are used. Start by demonstrating the law of reflection using a mirror. Students predict and explain results. Students follow this by investigating specular reflection and diffuse reflection. They shine a torch onto a selection of different flat surfaces and observe the reflected light on a nearby white surface. The experiment shows that a clear image will form from a mirror (specular reflection) and that coloured surfaces reflect their own colour of light, while dull, dark surfaces absorb light.	**Support**: Students are given a choice of reflected rays on the practical sheet when considering specular reflection. Demonstrate the practical procedure for diffuse reflection beforehand to ensure students understand the task fully.	**Practical**: Investigating reflection

Plenary	Support/Extension	Resources
Reflection experiment (5 min) Interactive resource where student choose words to complete a paragraph on the reflection experiment.		**Interactive**: Reflection experiment
Forming images in mirrors (10 min) Demonstrate how mirror images are formed. Draw a triangle on one half of an OHP sheet. Fold the plastic down the centre (the fold represents the mirror). Trace the triangle on the other half of the sheet. Unfold the sheet to compare the image's position, size, and so on with the object. Add lines to represent the path of the rays of light. Students copy down the ray diagram.	**Extension**: Students apply this concept to explain how a kaleidoscope works.	

Homework	Support/Extension	
Set questions showing the position of an object and the position of a mirror. Students draw the position they expect to see the images formed in the mirror, and check their answers using a mirror if possible.	**Extension**: Students should add light rays to their diagrams. They should explain what happens to your mirror image as you move towards the mirror using ideas about rays, mirrors and images.	

4.2.3 Refraction

Securing Mastery Goals

- 3.4.2 Construct ray diagrams to show how light reflects off mirrors, forms images and refracts. (Pt 2/2)
- 3.4.2 Use ray diagrams to describe how light passes through lenses and transparent materials. (Pt 2.2)

Exceeding Mastery Goals

- 3.4.2 Use a ray diagram to predict how an image will change in different situations. (Pt 2/2)
- 3.4.2 Predict whether light will reflect, refract or scatter when it hits the surface of a given material. (Pt 2/2)

Enquiry processes

- 2.4 Decide the type of chart or graph to draw based on its purpose or type of data.

Band	Outcome	Checkpoint	
		Question	Activity
Know	Describe what happens when light is refracted.	1	Starter 1, Main, Plenary 1
	State a difference between what happens to light when it goes through a convex lens and a concave lens.	2	Plenary 1, Plenary 2
	Record some observations as a diagram with help.		Main
Apply	Use a ray diagram to describe how light travels through a transparent block.	2	Main
	Use a ray diagram to describe what happens when light travels through a convex or concave lens.	B	Starter 2, Plenary 1
	Record observations using a labelled diagram.		Main
Extend	Predict whether light will refract when it hits a surface.	2, 3	Main
	Draw ray diagrams to show what happens when light goes through a convex or concave lens.	2	Plenary 1
	Record observations using labelled diagrams, and apply this to other situations.		Main

Literacy
Students identify the correct spellings of key words in the student-book activity.

GCSE link
4.6.2.2/6.6.2.2 Properties of electromagnetic waves 1

Some effects, for example refraction, are due to the difference in velocity of the waves in different substances.

Students should be able to construct ray diagrams to illustrate the refraction of a wave at the boundary between two different media.

Key Words
refraction, medium, lens, **convex lens**, **concave lens**, diverging, converging, focus, focal point

Answers from the student book

In-text questions	**A** In reflection light bounces off something, in refraction it changes direction.
	B A lens focuses or bends the rays of light to a focal point.
Activity	**Watch that spelling!**
	a lens
	b parallel

Summary questions	**1** towards, away from, ray (3 marks)

2a Ray diagrams that show: A convex lens is thicker in the middle than at the edges
A concave lens it thicker at the edges than in the middle
A convex lens focuses light
A concave lens spreads light out. (4 marks)

b Ray diagrams that show: Light travelling through a block is refracted, and so is light through a convex lens. (1 mark)
Light travelling through a block continues in a direction parallel to the initial direction, but light through a lens comes to a focus. (1 mark)

3a Light is scattered from the building towards your eye (1 mark)
It refracts towards the normal going into the glass (1 mark)
And away from the normal as it comes out (1 mark)
Some of it is reflected. (1 mark)

b Diagram as on page 68 (1 mark) showing bending towards/away from labelled normal (1 mark).

Starter	Support/Extension	Resources
Becoming invisible (5 min) We can only see transparent objects if light changes direction (refracts) when it passes through them. Place a test tube in a beaker. Pour glycerol in the beaker. Then pour glycerol inside the test tube – the test tube becomes invisible. Explain light doesn't refract (change direction) when it travels between the test tube and the glycerol, so we cannot detect the test tube. Students complete the interactive activity to check their understanding of the key words for this topic. **Lenses** (5 min) Show a range of objects that use convex and concave lenses (spyholes, microscope, glasses etc). Give out some convex and concave lenses. Student look at the physical difference between the lenses, and how writing on a page appears when you look through the lens.	**Extension:** Show that the test tube is not invisible if water is used, even though both the test tube and the water are transparent. Ask for suggestions why (light refracts when travelling from one medium to another).	**Interactive**: Key words in light

Main	Support/Extension	Resources
Investigating refraction (40 min) Students investigate the path of light through a glass or perspex block, changing the angle of incidence. For accuracy, students mark the path of each emerging ray using dots, then remove the block and draw the rays using a ruler. Students then complete the practical sheet questions. The ray of light arriving along the normal (at right angles to the block) goes straight through; light arriving at an angle changes direction at the boundary. It moves towards the normal. It emerges parallel to the original ray.	**Support:** An access sheet is available where students are required to carry out the experiment along pre-drawn incident rays, then answer a series of multiple-choice statements. **Extension:** Use the ideas about refraction to explain why a swimming pool looks shallower than it actually is.	**Practical**: Investigating refraction

Plenary	Support/Extension	Resources
Lens action (10 min) Students use cylindrical convex and concave lenses to look at what happens to light as it travels through each lens. As an alternative, show an animation or several images. Discuss how the refraction of light explains the path of the light through the lens. **Water lenses** (5 min) Place a drop of water on an image drawn on a shiny surface (e.g., mini-whiteboard with a small picture on it). The water magnifies the image. Explain that this is due to refraction through the lens. Additionally, draw three parallel arrows on a piece of paper and ask students to view them through a beaker of water (they change direction). Discuss what happens to the light.	**Extension**: Students explain why the lens magnifies the image, and why the image of the picture changes with the size of the drop.	

Homework		
Students identify items that use lenses (or refraction) at home. They write a sentence explaining what the job of the lens is in each example.		

Securing Mastery Goals

- 3.4.2 Use ray diagrams to describe how light passes through lenses and transparent materials. (Further examples)
- 3.4.2 Describe how lenses may be used to correct vision.

Enquiry processes

- 2.5 Use scientific vocabulary accurately, showing that you know its meaning and use appropriate units and correct chemical nomenclature.

Enquiry processes activity

- 3.4.2 Use ray diagrams to model how light passes through lenses and transparent materials.

Band	Outcome	Checkpoint	
		Question	Activity
Know	Name parts of the eye.	A, 1	Starter 2, Main
	Name two problems that people can have with their vision.	2	Main
	Describe problems people have with their eyesight.	2	Main, Plenary 2
Apply	Describe how the eye works.	A, B, 1	Main, Plenary 2, Homework
	Name the lens used to correct short sight, and the lens used to correct long sight.	C, D, 2	Main
	Describe how lenses correct short-sight and long-sight.		Main, Plenary 1
Extend	Explain how the eye forms an image.	1	Plenary 1, Homework
	Explain how lenses correct vision.	3	Main, Plenary 1
	Use ideas about refraction to explain the action of lenses in glasses and contact lenses.	3	Main

Literacy
In the student-book activity students use scientific terminology to explain the difference between real and virtual images. Students describe how lenses can be used to correct vision. Students research the eyes of other animals and write a short summary with a labelled diagram.

GCSE link
4.6.2.5 Lenses (*GCSE Physics*)

Students should produce ray diagrams for convex and concave lenses, and describe the type of images produced by lenses.

Key Words
iris, **retina,** pupil, cornea, inverted, photoreceptors, optic nerve, brain

Answers from the student book

In-text questions	A the cornea and the lens
	B chemical reaction
	C concave
	D long sight
Activity	**Real or virtual**
	A real image is an image that you can put on a screen whereas a virtual image is one that you see in a mirror.

Summary questions	
	1 reflects, pupil, cornea, lens, retina, real, electrical, optic nerve (9 marks)
	2 If you are short sighted you cannot see distant objects You correct this with a concave lens If you are long sighted you cannot see nearby objects You correct this with a convex lens (4 marks)
	3 In long-sight light from a distant object is focused behind the retina The convex lenses in glasses refract the light inwards so that the light focuses on the retina The contact lens is closer to your eye than glasses So can be thinner because it needs to refract light less to focus the image on the retina. (4 marks)

kerboodle

Starter	Support/Extension	Resources
An alternative question-led lesson is also available. **What do lenses do?** (10 min) Students look through convex lenses and describe the images seen when objects are varying distances away. Nearby objects are magnified, distant objects are smaller. If they are focused on a screen, images are upside down.	**Support:** Target students with easier questions. **Extension:** Link shape of lens (thickness) with focal length.	**Question-led lesson:** The camera and the eye
What's in your eye? (5 min) Students list as many parts of the eye as they can, and what that part does. In the interactive activity, students match the parts of the eye to their functions.	**Support:** Allow students to use the image in the student book. **Extension:** Students match parts of the eye to their function.	**Interactive:** What's in your eye?

Main	Support/Extension	Resources
Correcting vision (40 min) This activity is one of the AQA Enquiry process activities. Show an opticians chart and discuss problems with the vision (long/short-sight, colour blindness, astigmatism), being sensitive to the issues around this topic. Demonstrate what happens in the eye with short and long-sight using a model eye (large spherical flask filled with fluorescein with lenses attached to the front with blu-tak). Demonstrate how to correct the problems with convex and concave lenses. Alternatively use a suitable video or animation from the Internet. Students complete the ray diagrams on a worksheet. They answer questions about short-sight and long-sight.	**Support:** Students use the textbook to complete the worksheet.	**Activity:** Short sight and long sight

Plenary	Support/Extension	Resources
The journey through the eye (5 min) Students describe how light travels from an object to the retina using scientific terminology. The description should be for short sight or for long sight. They swap stories with a partner who guesses whether the story describes short sight or long sight.	**Support:** Use the list on the support sheet provided for the main activity.	
Why we have two eyes (10 min) Students view an object across the room using each eye in turn, then both eyes. Ask how the image seemed to change, for example, if it seemed to change position, appear 2D rather than 3D, and so on. Discuss why we need two eyes, for example, to judge the speed of approaching objects.	**Extension:** Students discuss why predators have eyes at the front of their heads and prey have eyes at the side of their heads.	

Homework		
Students research eyes of another animal to write a short article with a labelled diagram. The article should include a ray diagram for the eye.		

4.2.5 Colour

Securing Mastery Goals

- 3.4.1 Different colours of light have different frequencies.
- 3.4.2 Explain observations where coloured lights are mixed or objects are viewed in different lights.

Enquiry processes

- 2.12 Make an experimental prediction.
- 2.12 Decide whether the conclusion of the experiment agrees with your prediction.

Band	Outcome	Checkpoint	
		Question	**Activity**
Know	State what happens to light when it passes through a prism.	A, 1	Starter 1, Starter 2
	State the difference between colours of light in terms of frequency.	B	Main, Plenary 2
	State the effect of coloured filters on light.	1	Main
	Predict how red light will appear on a white surface.		Main
Apply	Explain what happens when light passes through a prism.	1	Starter 1, Starter 2
	Describe how primary colours add to make secondary colours.		Main, Plenary 2
	Explain how filters and coloured materials subtract light.	1	Main, Plenary 1
	Predict the colour of objects in red light and the colour of light through different filters.		Main, Plenary 1
Extend	Explain why a prism forms a spectrum.	1, 2	Starter 1, Starter 2
	Explain the formation of secondary colours.		Main, Plenary 1
	Predict how coloured objects will appear given different coloured lights and filters.	1	Main, Plenary 1
	Predict the colour of objects in lights of secondary colours, giving a reason for the prediction.		Main, Plenary 1

Literacy
Students use scientific terminology to explain how filters work in the summary questions, on their practical sheet, and in their homework.

GCSE link
4.6.2.1/6.6.2.1 Types of electromagnetic waves

The waves that form the electromagnetic spectrum are grouped in terms of their wavelength and their frequency. Going from long to short wavelength (or from low to high frequency) the groups are: radio, microwave, infrared, visible light (red to violet), ultraviolet, X-rays and gamma rays.

Our eyes only detect visible light and so detect a limited range of electromagnetic waves.

Key Words
prism, spectrum, dispersion, continuous, frequency, primary colour, secondary colour, filter

Answers from the student book

In-text questions	A Splits white light into a spectrum. B cyan, yellow, magenta
	C A black object absorbs all colours of light.
Activity	**What table?**

	Colour of material	Appearance in red light	Appearance in green light	Appearance in blue light	Appearance in cyan light	Appearance in magenta light

Summary questions	1 refracted, least, most, dispersion, transmits, absorbs, absorbs, reflects, reflects, green (10 marks)
	2 Diagram shows white light hitting a prism at a glancing angle (1 mark)
	Refracted at both surfaces (1 mark)
	Violet refracted more than red. (1 mark)
	3 A white light sources emits all the frequencies of light (1 mark)
	The filter absorbs most frequencies but transmits a narrow range of frequencies (1 mark)
	If these some of the frequencies that pass through the green and red filters are the same you will see some light. (1 mark)

kerboodle

Starter	Support/Extension	Resources
Big prism (10 min) Use a very bright light source (e.g., the Sun, an OHP) to project a spectrum using a prism. This is dispersion. Ask why the colours appeared (white light travelling through the prism is a mixture of coloured light). The prism does not create coloured light – it splits white light into a spectrum. Explain that different colours have different frequencies.	**Support**: Prompt students towards the colours seen (and link to a rainbow). **Extension**: Students give examples of other spectra, for example, rainbows in waterfalls.	
Rainbows (10 min) Class discussion: Where do we see rainbows? Why do they occur? This can be used as a consolidation of refraction as well as a short introduction to dispersion.	**Support**: Prompt students with 'Under what circumstances do you see rainbows?' to help students make the link between water, light, and refraction.	

Main	Support/Extension	Resources
Colour mixing (40 min) Introduce the concept by asking students to look around the room using coloured filters. They should see that objects appear different colours. Students then carry out the experiment on the practical sheet. This works best if black out blinds are used. If these are not available, place the experiments in boxes.	**Support**: The support sheet includes a suggested table of results, guiding students through a simpler experimental procedure. **Extension**: Some students may be able to predict a pattern based on the preliminary experiment.	**Practical**: Colour mixing
Remind students we see light reflecting off objects. Explain black is not a colour – black objects absorb all light.		
Students predict the colour of a red object in different coloured light and predict the colour of light through two coloured filters. They then test their predictions. Students then move on to testing colours of objects by shining different coloured lights onto them, against a black background.		

Plenary	Support/Extension	Resources
How can you see colours? (5 min) Students suggest ways to make an object appear red (e.g., it is red so it reflects red light, a red light source shines on a red or white object, or white light passes through a red filter onto a red or white object).		
Types of colours (5 min) Interactive resource where students sort colours into primary, secondary, or neither.	**Extension**: Students suggest additional ways to make something appear yellow (combining two primary colours).	**Interactive**: Types of colours

Homework		
Students write a guide telling police how to collect accurate witness statements for crimes committed in yellow street light, suggesting mistakes witnesses may make describing colours.		
An alternative WebQuest homework activity is also available on Kerboodle where students research how lights can be used during concerts on stage.		**WebQuest**: Stage lighting

4 Waves: Checkpoint

Checkpoint lesson routes

The route through this lesson can be determined using the Checkpoint assessment.

Percentage pass marks are supplied in the Checkpoint teacher notes.

Route A (support)

Students can work through the revision activity, with support from the rest of the group and the teacher. The tasks cover the outcomes listed below.

Route B (extension)

Students need two plane mirrors, a ray box, and a protractor to complete the activity.

Students begin by drawing ray diagrams to show how two mirrors can be used to turn a ray through 90°, 180° and alter its course up or down by a few centimetres. Students then investigate how the angle between to mirrors affects the number of images seen.

Progression to *Apply*

Know outcome	Apply outcome	Making progress
Know that sound consists of vibrations which travel as a longitudinal wave through substances. The denser the material the faster the wave travels.	Explain observations of how sound travels using the idea of a longitudinal wave.	For Task 1, demonstrate to students a longitudinal wave and a bell in a vacuum to show that as the air is withdrawn the loudness decreases. Students then complete an activity looking at the speed of sound in different materials. Students use ideas about the particle arrangements in solids, liquids, and gases to explain the differences in the speeds.
Know that the greater the amplitude of the waveform the louder the sound. The greater the frequency (and therefore the shorter the wavelength) the higher the pitch.	Use drawings of waves to describe how sound waves change with volume or pitch.	For Task 2, show students how the trace on an oscilloscope changes with loudness. Then ask students to draw traces which represent loud and quiet sounds. Show students how the trace on an oscilloscope changes with pitch. Remind students that the higher the pitch the higher the frequency. Then ask students to draw traces which represent high and low sounds. Challenge students to produce traces that combine ideas of frequency and amplitude, for example, high, soft sound, and low, loud sounds.
Know that when a light ray meets a different medium some of it is absorbed and some is reflected.	Use ray diagrams of eclipse to describe what is seen by observers in different places.	Ask students questions about how shadows are formed. Demonstrate how the Moon will cast a shadow over the Earth during an eclipse. Task 3 asks the students to add lines to the diagram to show how shadows are formed on the Earth and Moon during eclipses.
Recall that for a mirror the angle of incidence is equal to the angle of reflection.	Construct ray diagrams to show how light reflects from mirrors. (Skill)	Use a ray box and a mirror to show that the angle of incidence is equal to the angle of reflection. Ask students why you cannot do the same thing with a piece of paper instead of the mirror. Students can complete the diagram in Task 4 showing specular reflection and diffuse scattering.
Recall that when light enters a denser material it bends towards the normal, when it enters a less dense medium it bends away from the normal.	Use ray diagrams to describe how light passes through lenses and transparent materials.	Demonstrate refraction using a pencil in a glass and ask students to explain. Use a ray box to demonstrate what happens to rays passing through glass blocks of different shapes. In Task 5, students complete ray diagrams for light travelling through a variety of shaped glass blocks.
Recall that the retina is a layer at the back of the eye that detects light and where the image is formed.	Describe how lenses may be used to correct vision.	Demonstrate what happens to three parallel rays travelling through concave and convex lenses. Show (using a model eye or suitable animation) how light is focussed by the cornea and lens on to the retina. Show what happens in short-sighted and long-sighted eyes. In Task 6, students complete ray diagrams to show how lenses can be used to correct long and short sightedness.
Know that different colours of light have different frequencies.	Explain observations where coloured lights are mixed or objects are viewed in different lights.	Use filters or different coloured lights to demonstrate the effect of adding coloured light and reflect white light from different coloured objects. In Task 7, students summarise the addition of the primary colours and how different coloured objects appear in different coloured lights, using the ideas of transmission, reflection, and absorption.

Answers to End-of-Big Idea questions

1 Diagram with correct label of amplitude and correct label of wavelength. (2 marks)

2 A, H, I, M, O, T, U, V, W, X, Y (1 mark)

3a Diagram with the same wavelength but larger amplitude. (1 mark)

 b Diagram with the same amplitude but smaller wavelength. (1 mark)

 c Amplitude correctly labelled on diagrams from part **a** and **b**. (2 marks)

4a Blue jacket and red trousers. All colours are in white light, the blue jacket reflects blue and the red trousers reflect red. (2 marks)

 b Black jacket and black trousers. The blue jacket and red trousers would absorb green light so no light is reflected. (2 marks)

5a The light is refracted so the image of the fish is below where it really is. (2 marks)

 b The light does not change direction so the fish is below the bird. (2 marks)

6 Credit a sensible situation where ear defenders might be needed, such as on a building site. (1 mark)

7a C (1 mark)

 b B (1 mark)

 c The particles in C are closer together than the particles in A. The particles in A are closer together than the particles in B. Sound travels better through materials where the particles are closer together. (3 marks)

8a 10 divisions means a time of 10 divisions $\times \dfrac{2\,\text{ms}}{\text{division}} = 20\,\text{ms}$

  $= 20 \times 10^{-3}\text{s}$, or 0.02s (1 mark)

  There are 5 waves in 0.02s

  So frequency $= \dfrac{5\,\text{waves}}{0.02\text{s}}$ (1 mark)

  $= 250\,\text{Hz}$ (1 mark)

 b p.d $= 5$ divisions $\times \dfrac{2\text{V}}{\text{division}}$ (1 mark)

  $= 10\text{V}$ (1 mark)

9a How does the intensity of a sound vary with distance from the source? (1 mark)

 b Independent – distance from sound source; dependent – loudness of sound; controls – frequency and loudness of sound from source (1 mark)

 c line graph (1 mark)

Answer guide for the Big write

Know	Apply	Extend
1–2 marks	3–4 marks	5–6 marks
<ul><li>Uses coloured lights to 'change' the colours of clothing, writing on posters, and writing on programmes.</li><li>Shows an understanding of how mirrors reflect light.</li><li>Plan lacks detail and organisation.</li></ul>	<ul><li>Uses simple ideas about reflection to suggest ways to use mirrors to produce images that the audience could see.</li><li>Produce examples of materials that could be used on a programme/poster that would change colour.</li><li>Plan lacks organisation of ideas.</li></ul>	<ul><li>Uses ideas of partial reflection in glass to explain how to produce a ghostly image e.g., pepper's ghost where you could have an image and a person in the same place.</li><li>Describes in detail how it could be done practically.</li><li>Plan is clearly organised and has sufficient detail.</li></ul>

kerboodle

4 Part 1 Checkpoint assessment (automarked)
4 Part 1 Checkpoint: Revision
4 Part 1 Checkpoint: Extension
4.1 Progress task, 4.2 Progress task

5 Matter

National curriculum links for this unit

Topic	National Curriculum topic
5.1 Particle model	The particulate nature of matter
5.2 Separating mixtures	Pure and impure substances

In this Big Idea students will learn:

- properties of solids, liquids, and gases can be described in terms of particles in motion but with differences in the arrangement and movement of these same particles: closely spaced and vibrating (solid), in random motion but in contact (liquid), or in random motion and widely spaced (gas)
- observations where substances change temperature or state can be described in terms of particles gaining or losing energy

- a pure substance consists of only one type of element or compound and has a fixed melting and boiling point. Mixtures may be separated due to differences in their physical properties
- the method chosen to separate a mixture depends on which physical properties of the individual substance are different.

AQA Enquiry process activities

Activity	Section
3.5.1 Relate the features of the particle model to the properties of materials in different states.	5.1.1 The particle model
3.5.2 Devise ways to separate mixtures, based on their properties.	5.2.1 Mixtures

Preparing for Key Stage 4 success

Knowledge	
Underpinning knowledge is covered in this Big Idea for KS4 study of:	• 4.3.3/6.3.3 Particle model and pressure (GCSE Physics and GCSE Physics for Combined Science) • 4.1.1.1/5.1.1.1 Atoms, elements, and compounds • 4.8.1/5.8.1 Purity, formulations and chromatography • 4.1.1.2/5.1.1.2 Mixtures • 4.8.1.3/5.8.1.3 Chromatography

Maths
Skills developed in Big Idea 5:
	1 Arithmetic and numerical computation
	  d Make estimates of the results of simple calculations (5.1.2)
	2 Handling data
	  c Construct and interpret frequency tables and diagrams, bar charts and histograms (5.1.3)
	  h Make order of magnitude calculations (5.1.2, 5.1.4, 5.1.6)
	3 Algebra
	  c Substitute numerical values into algebraic equations using appropriate units for physical quantities (5.2.2, 5.2.4)
	  d Solve simple algebraic equations (5.2.2, 5.2.4)
	4 Graphs
	  a Translate information between graphical and numeric form (5.1.3, 5.2.1, 5.2.2, 5.2.3)
	  c Plot two variables from experimental or other data (5.1.3)

Literacy Skills developed in Big Idea 5:	• Predicting, making inferences, describing relationships. (5.1.4, 5.1.5) • Accessing information to ascertain meaning, using word skills and comprehension strategies. (5.1.5, 5.1.7) • Communicating ideas and information to a wide range of audiences and a variety of situations. (5.1.3, 5.1.7, 5.2.2) • Use of scientific terms. (5.1.1, 5.2.2, 5.2.4, 5.2.6) • Organisation of ideas and information. (5.1.1, 5.1.2, 5.1.3, 5.1.4, 5.1.5, 5.1.6, 5.2.1, 5.2.6)

- Collaboration and exploratory talk. (5.1.2, 5.2.3, 5.2.5, 5.2.6)
- Making connections within/across a range of texts/themes and from personal experience. (5.2.2)
- Identifying main ideas, events, and supporting details. (5.2.2, 5.2.3)
- Attention to the 'rules' of the particular form of writing (e.g., news article, scientific report). (5.2.2, 5.2.3)

Assessment Skills
- Extended response questions (5.1.3, 5.1.5, 5.1.6, 5.2.1, 5.2.5) (End-of-Big Idea questions, Q7)
- Quantitative problem solving (5.1.2, 5.1.4, 5.1.6, 5.2.1, 5.2.2, 5.2.4) (End-of-Big Idea questions, Q5)
- Application of Enquiry processes (5.1.1, 5.1.3, 5.1.4, 5.1.6, 5.2.1, 5.2.2, 5.2.4, 5.2.5, 5.2.6) (End-of-Big Idea questions, Q3, Q5, Q6, Q7)

KS2 Link	Check before:	Checkpoint	Catch-up
Many materials can exist in the solid, liquid, and gas states.	5.1.1 The particle model	Ask students to name two materials they know for each of solids, liquids, and gases.	Give simple materials to hold and classify, such as chocolate and water. This can be linked to the properties below.
Different materials have different properties.	5.1.2 States of matter	Ask students to write a list of different properties materials can possess.	Card sort activity where students need to match the correct definition to property key words, such as 'hardness'.
The different properties of different materials make them suitable for different uses.	5.1.2 States of matter	Ask students to suggest suitable materials for making a saucepan and a tent. Ask them to explain their choices.	Provide a selection of materials, with descriptions of their properties and uses, for students to observe.
The state of a material depends on the temperature.	5.1.3 Melting and freezing	Ask students what will happen to a snowman when the temperature increases.	Allow students to observe an ice cube placed in a warm location.
Changes of state are reversible.	5.1.3 Melting and freezing	Ask students what will happen to water in an ice cube tray when it is placed in a freezer.	Place an ice cube tray filled with water into a freezer – allow students to observe before and after.
Melting, freezing, evaporating, boiling, and condensing are changes of state.	5.1.3 Melting and freezing	Ask students to label a diagram of water boiling in a kettle to show their understanding of the key terms.	Demonstrate a kettle boiling, with discussion of what is happening. Include what happens when you place a cold surface in the path of steam.
All materials are made up of one or more elements.	5.2.1 Pure substances and mixtures	Students discuss the differences between elements, compounds, and mixtures.	Students use beads, models, or particle diagrams to show the differences between elements, compounds, and mixtures.
Mixtures can be separated through filtering, sieving, and evaporating.	5.2.4 Filtration	Students explain how they would separate named mixtures.	Use diagrams, animations, and simulations to demonstrate the difference between basic separation techniques.

Key Stage 2 Quiz: Chemistry
5 Part 1 End-of-Big-Idea test (foundation)
5 Part 1 End-of-Big-Idea test (foundation) mark scheme
5 Part 1 End-of-Big-Idea test (higher)
5 Part 1 End-of-Big-Idea test (higher) mark scheme

Answers to Picture Puzzler
Key Words
perfume, acid, ring, thermometer, ice, copper, liquid, egg
The key word is **particle**
Close Up
frost on a window

MyMaths

You can find additional support for the maths skills covered in this Big Idea on **MyMaths**, including carrying out calculations, drawing graphs, and using ratios.

5.1.1 The particle model

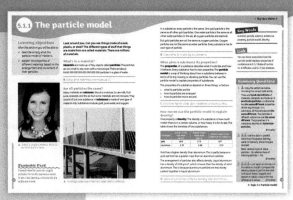

Securing Mastery Goals

- 3.5.1 Explain the properties of solids, liquids and gases based on the arrangement and movement of their particles. (Pt 1/2)

Enquiry processes

- 2.6 Suggest a scientific idea that might explain an observation.

Enquiry processes activity

- 3.5.1 Relate the features of the particle model to the properties of materials in different states.

Band	Outcome	Checkpoint	
		Question	Activity
Know	State that materials are made up of particles.	A, 1	Main 1, Main 2
	State that the properties of substances can be described in terms of particles in motion.		Main 3
	State what toy building bricks are representing when they are used to model substances.		Main 1
Apply	Explain, in terms of particles, why different substances have different properties.	C	
	Explain properties, such as density, based on the arrangement and mass of particles.	3	
	Use models to investigate the relationship between the properties of a material and the arrangement of its particles.		Main 3
Extend	Evaluate particle models that explain the properties of substances.		Plenary 1, Plenary 2
	Use data about particles to predict and explain differences in properties such as density.	D, 2, 3	
	Design and explain a new representation for the particle model.		Main 2

Maths

The Summary Questions ask students to interpret data and use ideas of direct proportion to make predictions about the relative mass of elements.

MyMaths More support for the maths skills in this section can be found on MyMaths.

GCSE link

4.2.2.1/5.2.2.1 The three states of matter

The three states of matter can be be represented by a simple model. In this model, particles are represented by small solid spheres.

Key Words

material, **particle**, **mixture**, substance, property, **particle model, density**

Answers from the student book

In-text questions	A tiny particles
	B A material that has the same properties all the way through.
	C What its particles are like, how its particles are arranged, and how its particles move.
	D The relative mass of a gold particle is greater than the relative mass of an aluminium particle, so gold has the higher density.

Summary questions	1 millions, particles, the same, the same, different, behaviour (6 marks)
	2 Mercury has the greater density because its particles have a greater mass. (2 marks)
	3 The density of gold in the liquid state is slightly less than its density in the solid state. The difference results from the arrangement of particles - in the liquid state, the particles are a little less closely packed. The particles in the two states are identical, so the difference in density cannot be explained in terms of any difference in mass of the particles. (4 marks)

Starter	Support/Extension	Resources
What do these key words mean? (5 min) Ask students to decide what each of the key words displayed in the corresponding student-book spread mean. Asking students to explain key words will gauge prior knowledge students have from KS2, and provide indications of which terms need revisiting.		
Who can identify the most materials? (10 min) Ask students to make a list of all the different materials they can see in the classroom – see who has the longest list. Can students group the materials in their lists at all?	**Extension:** Students could be asked to see if there are any similarities or differences in the materials they identify.	

Main	Support/Extension	Resources
Introducing the particle model (25 min) This activity is one of the AQA Enquiry process activities. Use toy building bricks to demonstrate individual particles within a larger amount of substance – start with a large group all connected and then break them down into the individual particles. It is important to stress that each building brick is the same if you have a single substance. Use different coloured bricks to demonstrate different substances and discuss how these would have different properties. Students complete the activity sheet, introducing them to the particle model. Students will need to complete a written section about particles and discuss the particle model.	**Support:** All students should be shown other models that can be used to represent particles, for example, different coloured paperclips. **Extension:** Students will be able to suggest their own representations of the particle model and suggest possible weaknesses of these representations.	**Activity:** Introducing the particle model
Particles and properties (20 min) Students should complete the questions provided in the corresponding student-book spread to check their understanding of how the properties of materials depend on the type of particle present, and the way these particles are arranged.		
In pairs, students discuss how the toy building bricks model could be used to show the relationship between the properties of a material and the arrangement of its particles. For example, if the particles have a greater mass, the substance might have a greater density.		
Take feedback and discuss as a class.		

Plenary	Support/Extension	Resources
Considering models (10 min) Students will see a picture that represents particles within a material. Students need to think about how this model is representing particles. They must then decide if the reasons given in the resource make the model a good or a bad one.	**Extension:** Ask students to describe how they could improve the model given.	**Interactive:** Considering models
Particle sentences (5 min) Ask students to use the key words from the student book to write sentences that summarise what they have learnt about materials and particles.	**Support:** Display the key words during the activity.	

Homework		
Students research a material of their choice and write a summary of its properties and uses.		

5.1.2 States of matter

Securing Mastery Goals
● 3.5.1 Explain the properties of solids, liquids and gases based on the arrangement and movement of their particles. (Pt 2/2)

Exceeding Mastery Goals
● 3.5.1 Argue for how to classify substances which behave unusually as solids, liquids or gases.

Enquiry processes
● 2.3 Make a conclusion and explain it.

Band	Outcome	Checkpoint	
		Question	**Activity**
Know	Describe the properties of a substance in its three states.	B, 1, 2	Main 1, Plenary 1
	State that the properties of substances can be described in terms of the arrangement and movement of its particles.	C	Main 1
	Make relevant observations in order to decide is a substance is in its solid, liquid or gas state.		Starter 2
Apply	Compare the properties of a substance in its three states.		Main 1
	Explain the properties of solids, liquids, and gases based on the arrangement and movement of their particles.	C, 2	Main 1 Main 2
	Use observations to decide if a substance is in its solid, liquid or gas state.		Starter 1, Starter 2, Main 3, Plenary 2
Extend	Argue for how to classify substances which behave unusually as solids, liquids, or gases.	3	Main 3
	Justify whether a given property of a substance in a given state can be explained by the arrangement, or by the movement, of its particles.		Main 1
	Evaluate a representation of the particle model.		Main 2

Maths
The activity asks students to use number size and scale to convert between km/s and m/s to apply these to real-life situations.

Ask students to estimate how many particles are in tiny objects such as a pin head and then find out the answer.

MyMaths More support for the maths skills in this section can be found on MyMaths.

Literacy
Students pay close attention to what others say in discussions, ask questions to develop ideas and make contributions that take account of others' views, by discussing and planning a flow chart of questions to help them decide if a substance is solid, liquid, or gas.

GCSE link
4.2.2.1/5.2.2.1 The three states of matter

The three states of matter can be be represented by a simple model. In this model, particles are represented by small solid spheres.

Key Words
solid, liquid, gas, states of matter

Answers from the student book

In-text questions	**A** solid, liquid, gas **B** Solids cannot flow, liquids can flow. A Solid's shape is fixed; a liquid takes the shape of its container. A given substance exists as a solid at lower temperatures than it exists as a liquid. **C** You cannot compress a liquid because its particles touch their neighbours.
Activity	**Express particle?** The train travels at 0.135 km/s. This is (0.135 × 1000) = 135 m/s. So the oxygen particles travel faster.

Summary questions	1 There are **three** states of matter. You **cannot** compress a substance in the solid state because the particles touch each other. In the liquid and gas states, a substance flows because the particles **can** move from place to place. You **can** compress a gas because the particles are spread out. (4 marks)
	2 Extended response question (6 marks). Example answer:
	Water flows in the liquid and gas state, but it does not flow in the solid state. This is because in the liquid and gas states particles move from place to place, but in the solid state the particles are in fixed positions.
	In the solid and liquid states you cannot compress water, but you can compress water in the gas state. This is because the particles touch their neighbours in the solid and liquid state, but in the gas state the particles do not touch their neighbours. In the solid state the shape is fixed, in the liquid state water takes the shape of the bottom of its container, and in the gas state water takes the shape of the whole container. This is because in the solid shape the particles are in fixed positions but in the liquid and gas states the particles move around from place to place.
	3 Example answers (accept well-argued alternatives):
	a Toothpaste behaves as a liquid because it can flow, its shape is not fixed, and you cannot compress it. However, you can feel tiny 'grains' in it. You cannot compress these grains, and they appear to have a fixed shape, so the grains are in the solid state. This shows that toothpaste is a mixture of substances in the liquid and solid state. (6 marks)
	b A cake has bubbles of air in the gas state, but between the air bubbles the shape of the cake is fixed unless you apply a force. For these reasons Daisy is correct. (3 marks)

Starter	Support/Extension	Resources
An alternative question-led lesson is also available.		**Question-led lesson**: States of matter
Solid, liquid, or gas? (5 min) Display interactive activity of various objects that students can drag into the correct columns for solids, liquids, or gases. Discussion should take place of how small particles are. For example, there are over 300 000 000 000 000 000 000 000 particles in a teaspoon of water.		**Interactive**: Solid, liquid, or gas?
What state is this? (10 min) Provide students with an array of simple objects and substances to classify as solids, liquids, or gases.	**Support**: Students will often prefer to touch/see objects to aid their decision making.	

Main	Support/Extension	Resources
Defining states of matter (10 min) Display interactive particle model animations (found on the Internet) for solids, liquids, and gases. Draw up a table of properties for each state, including, density, particle motion, and shape (an example is available on the corresponding student-book spread). Explain these properties using information about the arrangement and movement of the particles in each state.	**Extension**: Ask students to explain a given property in terms of the arrangement, or by the movement, of its particles, and to justify their choice.	
Students as particles (5 min) Use a group of students to represent particles. Arrange them as a solid, liquid, and gas. Discuss the arrangement and movement of the particles in each state. Ask observing students to explain different properties of solids, liquids and gases based on the model. Evaluate this representation of the particle model.	**Support**: The support sheet contains an observation table with questions to help students identify the state of matter.	
Properties of solids, liquids, and gases (20 min) Students complete the practical allowing them to make observations on the properties of materials, and conclude whether they are in the solid, liquid, gas, or more than one of these states.	**Extension**: Give students substances that are harder to define (e.g., sand, hair gel, jelly).	**Practical**: Properties of solids, liquids, and gases **Skill sheet**: Recording results

Plenary	Support/Extension	Resources
Quick-fire identification (5 min) Call out properties of solids, liquids, and gases. Students should correctly identify solid, liquid, or gas, displaying their answer on mini-whiteboards.	**Extension**: Ask students to explain their choices.	
States of matter taboo (10 min) One student describes a material in terms of its properties, without identifying its state at room temperature. Another student tries to identify what it is and its state of matter.		

Homework		
Students design a detailed poster with explanatory notes on the three states of matter, discussing the properties of each and giving examples for each state.		

5.1.3 Melting and freezing

Securing Mastery Goals

- 3.5.1 A substance is a solid below its melting point, a liquid between its melting and boiling points, and a gas above its boiling point.
- 3.5.1 Explain changes in states in terms of changes to the energy of particles. (Pt 1/3)
- Draw before and after diagrams of particles to explain observations about changes of state, gas pressure, and diffusion. (Pt 1/5)

Enquiry processes

- 2.4 Select a good way to display data.
- 2.4 Draw line graphs to display relationships.

Band	Outcome	Checkpoint	
		Question	Activity
Know	Describe how the properties of a substance change as it melts or freezes.	1	Starter 1, Starter 2
	Recognise an energy transfer during a change of state.		Main 2
	Describe the observations as stearic acid cools in terms of states of matter.		Main 1
Apply	Draw annotated before and after diagrams of particles, and use words, to explain observations about melting and freezing.	B	Plenary 1
	Explain melting and freezing in terms of changes to the energy of particles.	3	Main 2
	Use cooling data to identify the melting point of stearic acid.		Main 1
Extend	Explain why there is a period of constant temperature during melting and freezing based on the arrangement and movement of particles, and energy transfers.		Main 2
	Explain in detail the differences between melting and freezing.	3	
	Suggest reasons for the different melting points of different substances based on the arrangement, movement, and energy of their particles.		Plenary 2

Maths

Record temperatures of stearic acid as it cools, using this to plot a cooling curve and to identify the melting point.

MyMaths More support for the maths skills in this section can be found on MyMaths.

Literacy

Students can present and explain their results to the rest of the class.

Key Words
melt, change of state, freeze, melting point

GCSE link
4.2.2.1/5.2.2.1 The three states of matter

The amount of energy needed to change state from solid to liquid depends on the strength of the forces between the particles of the substance.

Students should be able to:

predict the states of substances at different temperatures given appropriate data.

explain the different temperatures at which changes of state occur in terms of energy transfers and types of bonding.

Answers from the student book

In-text questions	A liquid and solid
	B The particles first gain more energy and vibrate more in their fixed positions. The particles then begin to break the bonds that hold them together and move about freely.
	C oxygen, water, gallium, gold

Activity	**Using melting points to identify substances**
	Since the painkiller must be one of the three listed, and the melting points are widely spaced, it is reasonable to be very confident that this answer is correct.
Summary questions	**1** melting, faster, around, liquid, temperature (5 marks)
	2 Ben is correct. If the melting point is −7 °C then the substance must be in either the liquid or gas state at 20 °C. You cannot know which of these two states it is in unless you also know its boiling point. (3 marks)
	3 Extended response question (6 marks). Example answers:
	Melting is the change from the solid to the liquid state.
	On melting, energy is transferred from the surroundings to the particles as the particles vibrate faster and move away from their places in the pattern. More and more particles start moving around. When all the particles are moving around from place to place, the substance has melted.
	Freezing is the change from the liquid to the solid state.
	On freezing, energy is transferred from the substance to the surroundings as the particles start to move more slowly. Particles become arranged in a pattern, and vibrate on the spot.
	4 In the solid the particles vibrate on the spot, but in the gas they move around randomly throughout the container. In the solid the particles are arranged in a regular pattern, but in the gas they are arranged randomly. The total energy stored by the particles in the solid is less than the total energy stored by the particles in the gas. (3 marks)

Starter	Support/Extension	Resources
How does water become ice? (5 min) Ask students to name the processes that occur when water is placed into an ice cube tray and placed into the freezer, and then when an ice cube is left in a warm place. Introduce the terms reversible and irreversible.	**Extension:** To extend the starter activities, students should be asked to consider the energy transfers involved in the processes.	**Interactive**: What happens as water freezes?
What happens as water freezes? (10 min) Students reorder the descriptions of freezing on the interactive resource to check their understanding.		

Main	Support/Extension	Resources
Observing the cooling of stearic acid (20 min) Students make predictions before they observe the temperature of stearic acid over time as it cools and then plot their data to produce a cooling curve for stearic acid.	**Support:** Students should be provided with pre-drawn axes. **Extension:** Students will be able to choose their own scales for each axis.	**Practical**: Observing the cooling of stearic acid **Skill sheet**: Choosing scales
Presentation and discussion of results (20 min) Introduce students to cooling curves and how these can be interpreted to find the melting point. In groups, students should plan a two-minute presentation to the class to explain their results. Students should describe and explain the energy transfers during this phase change. As a class, discuss where the melting point would be found on the graph. Discuss how melting points can be used to identify substances.	**Extension:** Students should explain why the graph 'levels off' and has a period with no temperature change.	**Skill sheet**: Recording results **Skill sheet**: Drawing graphs

Plenary	Support/Extension	Resources
What is happening to the particles in the stearic acid? (5 min) Ask students to sketch the cooling curve for stearic acid on a mini-whiteboard. Then ask students to draw particle diagrams for each stage in the curve and name the state for each significant section of the graph.	**Extend:** Ask students to suggest reasons for the different melting points of different substances based on the arrangement, movement, and energy transfers of their particles.	
Melting points (5 min) Ask students to refer to the table of melting points on the corresponding student-book spread. Name a temperature and ask students which state each substance would be in.		

Homework		
Give students the melting point of iron (1538 °C) and ask them to suggest why steel does not have one specific melting temperature. An alternative WebQuest homework activity is also available on Kerboodle where students research how roads are made safer in adverse weather conditions.		**WebQuest**: Safer roads

5.1.4 Boiling

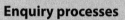

Securing Mastery Goals

- 3.5.1 A substance is a solid below its melting point, a liquid between its melting and boiling points, and a gas above its boiling point.
- 3.5.2 Liquids have different boiling points.
- 3.5.1 Explain changes in states in terms of changes to the energy of particles. (Pt 2/3)
- 3.5.1 Draw before and after diagrams of particles to explain observations about changes of state, gas pressure, and diffusion. (Pt 2/5)

Enquiry processes

- 2.4 Draw line graphs to display relationships.
- 2.6 Suggest a scientific idea that might explain the observation.

Band	Outcome	Checkpoint	
		Question	Activity
Know	Describe how the properties of a substance change as it boils.	1	
	Recognise an energy transfer during a change of state.		Starter 1
↓	Draw straightforward conclusions from boiling point data presented in tables and graphs.	D	Main 1 Main 2
Apply	Draw annotated before and after diagrams of particles, and use words, to explain observations about boiling.	A, B	Starter 2
	Explain why different substances boil at different temperatures in terms of changes to the energy of particles.	3	Main 1 Plenary 1
↓	Select data and information about boiling points and use them to contribute to conclusions.	D, 2	Main 1 Main 2
Extend	Explain why there is a period of constant temperature during boiling based on the arrangement and movement of particles, and energy transfers.		Main 1
	Suggest reasons for the different boiling points of different substances based on the arrangement, movement, and energy transfers of their particles.	3	Plenary 1
↓	Assess the strength of evidence from boiling point data, deciding whether it is sufficient to support a conclusion.		Main 1

Maths

Order, add, and subtract negative numbers in the context of boiling and melting point data.

MyMaths More support for the maths skills in this section can be found on MyMaths.

Literacy

In the Heating water activity students construct clear and coherent sentences to summarise points made in a class discussion.

GCSE link
4.2.2.1/5.2.2.1 The three states of matter

The amount of energy needed to change state from solid to liquid depends on the strength of the forces between the particles of the substance.

Students should be able to:

predict the states of substances at different temperatures given appropriate data.

explain the different temperatures at which changes of state occur in terms of energy transfers and types of bonding.

Key Words
boil, boiling point

In-text questions	**A** Drawing of particles that are spread out, not touching each other, in a random arrangement.
	B steam OR water in the gas state OR water vapour
	C The temperature at which a substance boils. **D** Silver is in the liquid state at 1000 °C.
Activity	The substance is likely to be ethanol.
Summary questions	**1** liquid, gas, all the way through, a certain (4 marks) **2** Copper is in the liquid state at 2000 °C. (1 mark)
	3 Answer to include (6 marks):
	Diagrams of particles in two substances in the liquid state indicating stronger forces of attraction between particles in one of the substances.
	Example included, such as the boiling points of water and ethanol.
	The forces of attraction between water particles in the liquid state are stronger than those between ethanol particles in the liquid state, so water has the higher boiling point.
	Table or similar listing how the diagrams are like, and are not like, liquids in reality.

Starter	Support/Extension	Resources
Describing boiling (5 min) Boil a beaker of water. Ask students to describe why they see bubbles forming, and where the energy is transferred from.	**Support:** Students could be asked to focus on observations only.	
What happens when water boils? (10 min) Students use the interactive resource to reorder descriptions of boiling to check their understanding of the sequence of events.	**Extension:** Students could be asked to suggest explanations for what is happening.	**Interactive:** What happens when water boils?

Main	Support/Extension	Resources
Heating water (25 min) Students use the supplied data to plot a heating curve for water. Students then need to consider what is happening to the particles at each stage of the process, together with the energy transfers that occur. Discuss where the boiling point is found on the curve, and why there are periods with constant temperatures. Students then write a few sentences to summarise the discussion. Students should discuss the reversibility of boiling at this stage.	**Support:** A support sheet is available with pre-drawn axes for drawing the graph.	**Activity:** Heating water **Skill sheet:** Choosing scales **Skill sheet:** Drawing graphs
Consolidating states (15 min) Students should complete the questions provided on the corresponding student-book spread to check their understanding of boiling and to gain practice at predicting the state of a substance at certain temperatures, given its melting point and boiling point.		

Plenary	Support/Extension	Resources
Which boiling point is which? (5 min) Display a list of substances on the board (e.g., oxygen, water, iron, mercury) with a jumbled up list of their boiling points. Ask students to guess which boiling point belongs to which substance using their everyday knowledge of them. (Substances selected will need to have boiling points that are not close to one another and will need to have well known properties.)	**Support:** Extra information can be added about the chosen substances, such as the state it is in at room temperature. **Extend:** Ask students to justify their answers and to suggest reasons for the different boiling points based on the arrangement, movement, and energy transfers of their particles.	
How can substances be identified using boiling points? (5 min) Students write a paragraph to explain how to do an experiment to use boiling point data to identify a substance.		

Homework	Support/Extension	
Students prepare a fact sheet on different ways the boiling point of water can be changed. They should explain why being able to change the boiling point of water may be useful.	**Support:** This can be given in the form of hints. For example, ask students to answer questions such as 'Why do we add salt to icy roads?'	

5.1.5 More changes of state

Securing Mastery Goals
- 3.5.1 Explain changes in states in terms of changes to the energy of particles. (Pt 3/3)
- 3.5.1 Draw before and after diagrams of particles to explain observations about changes of state, gas pressure and diffusion. (Pt 3/5)

Exceeding Mastery Goals
- 3.5.1 Make predictions about what will happen during unfamiliar physical processes, in terms of particles and their energy.

Enquiry processes
- 2.9 Prepare a table with space to record all measurements.
- 2.11 Identify control variables.
- 2.11 Describe how controlling variables is important in providing evidence for a conclusion.
- 2.10 Write a fair test enquiry question.
- 2.11 Control the variables.

Band	Outcome	Checkpoint	
		Question	Activity
Know	State the names of changes of state involving gases.	C, D, 1	Starter 1, Starter 2
	Describe one difference between evaporation and boiling.	A	Plenary 1
	Write a fair test enquiry question on evaporation, and plan the method and how to control the variables.		Main
Apply	Draw annotated before and after diagrams of particles, and use words, to explain observations about evaporating, condensing and subliming.	2	
	Explain differences between evaporation, sublimation and boiling based on the arrangement and movement of particles.	2	Plenary 2
	Explain why it is important to control variables to provide evidence for a conclusion in an evaporation investigation.		Main
Extend	Make predictions about what will happen during an unfamiliar physical process – deposition – in terms of particles and their energy.	3	
	Compare evaporation, boiling and sublimation based on the arrangement, movement, and energy transfers of particles.		Plenary 2
	Justify the procedure and evaluate the results in an evaporation investigation.		Main

Literacy
Students can answer extended questions describing the differences in the crystals they have produced and why these have arisen, applying their knowledge to the answers.

GCSE link
4.2.2.1/5.2.2.1 The three states of matter

The three states of matter can be be represented by a simple model. In this model, particles are represented by small solid spheres. Particle theory can help to explain melting, boiling, freezing and condensing.

Students should be able to:

predict the states of substances at different temperatures given appropriate data.

explain the different temperatures at which changes of state occur in terms of energy transfers and types of bonding.

Key Words
evaporate, evaporation, **condense**, condensation, **sublime**, sublimation

Answers from the student book

In-text questions	A In evaporation, particles escape from the surface of the liquid, but in boiling, bubbles of the substance in the gas state form throughout the liquid, rise to the surface, and escape. Evaporation happens at any temperature, but boiling happens only at the boiling point.
	B A hairdryer heats the substance in its liquid state, and supplies moving air to move just evaporated particles away. C On condensing, a substance in the liquid state is formed. D subliming

Activity	**Evaluating evaporation** Make the test fair by soaking the same type of material in water and having equal-sized pieces of this material. It is not possible to know whether the evidence supports the conclusion because the investigation is not fair.
Summary questions	**1** In boiling, substances change from the liquid to the gas state. In boiling, particles leave from all parts of the liquid. In condensing, substances change from the gas state to the liquid state. In evaporating particles leave from the surface of the liquid. In evaporating, substances change from the liquid to the gas state. (5 marks) **2** On condensing, particles in the gas state move closer together until they touch each other. The particles stop moving around throughout the whole container, and instead they move around each other in the bottom part of the container. Answers include annotated diagrams to illustrate this process. (4 marks) **3** Extended response question (6 marks). Example answers: Before deposition the particles are moving from place to place. They are arranged randomly and are not touching each other. After deposition the particles are arranged in a regular pattern. They are touching each other. They are vibrating on the spot. During deposition, energy is transferred from the substance to the surroundings. Answers should include diagrams to show particle arrangements.

Starter	Support/Extension	Resources
Iodine sublimation (10 min) Demonstrate the sublimation of iodine in a fume cupboard. If available, solid carbon dioxide ('dry ice') could also be shown. Demonstrate how the solid that has sublimed can be recollected (see RSC Practical Chemistry) as a solid again without the liquid being seen. As with the previous changes of states, students should consider the energy transfers involved in sublimation and condensation, and discuss the reversibility of this change. **Observing condensation** (5 min) Ask students to breathe on a cold surface such as a mirror. Discuss what is happening to the particles as the gas turns into a liquid. Ask students to explain whether this change is reversible or irreversible.	**Support:** Evaporation and condensation will need to be revisited. **Extension:** Students can be told that the process of gases being collected back as a solid is called deposition.	

Main	Support/Extension	Resources
Who can make the biggest crystals? (40 min) Explain to students that copper sulfate crystals will form from copper sulfate solution as the solution evaporates, and that the speed of evaporation affects crystal size. Students write a fair test question, plan the method and how to control the variables, then explain why it is important to control variables to provide evidence for a conclusion in this investigation. Students then carry out the investigation. Students should read the corresponding student-book spread and answer the summary questions to check their understanding of the processes met. The crystals made will need to be revisited in another lesson.	**Support:** Issue students with the access sheet, which gives instructions for making copper sulfate crystals. **Extension:** Students suggest why slower evaporation may result in larger crystals. They also justify the procedure and evaluate the results in their investigation.	**Practical:** Who can make the biggest crystals?

Plenary	Support/Extension	Resources
Identifying evaporation, condensation, and sublimation (5 min) An interactive resource where students match state changes to pictures of evaporation, condensation, and sublimation. **What's the difference between evaporation and boiling?** (5 min) Ask students to explain the differences between evaporation, boiling and sublimation based on the arrangement and movement of particles.	**Extension:** Ask students to draw particle diagrams to illustrate the processes. **Extension:** Students compare evaporation, boiling and sublimation based on the arrangement, movement, and energy transfers of particles.	**Interactive:** Identifying evaporation, condensation, and sublimation

Homework		
Students use their knowledge of evaporation to prepare a leaflet for householders on how they can dry their washing most efficiently.		

5.1.6 Diffusion

Securing Mastery Goals

- 3.5.1 Draw before and after diagrams of particles to explain observations about changes of state, gas pressure, and diffusion. (Pt 4/5)

Exceeding Mastery Goals

- 3.5.1 Evaluate observations that provide evidence for the existence of particles.

Enquiry processes

- 2.9 Prepare a table with space to record all measurements.
- 2.10 Write a fair test enquiry question.
- 2.11 Decide how to vary the independent variable between planned values.
- 2.11 Decide how to measure the dependent variable.
- 2.11 Identify control variables.
- 2.11 Control the variables.
- 2.11 Describe how controlling variables is important in providing evidence for a conclusion.

Band	Outcome	Checkpoint	
		Question	Activity
Know	Describe examples of diffusion.		Starter 1
	State that observations about diffusion can be explained in terms of particles in motion.	1	Starter 2
	Write a fair test enquiry question on diffusion, identify the independent and dependent variables, and plan the method and how to control the variables.		Main 1
Apply	Describe evidence for diffusion.	2	Starter 1
	Draw annotated before and after diagrams of particles, and use words, to explain diffusion.	A	Starter 2
	Explain why it is important to control variables to provide evidence for a conclusion in a diffusion investigation.		Main 1
Extend	Evaluate observations that provide evidence for the existence of particles.	4	Main 2
	Draw annotated before and after diagrams of particles, and use words, to predict the relative speed of diffusion when the value of a given independent variable is changed.	B,3	Plenary 1
	Justify the procedure and evaluate the results in a diffusion investigation.		Main 1

Maths

In the practical activity students use the quantitative relationship between units to convert the times they record between the units of seconds and minutes.

MyMaths More support for the maths skills in this section can be found on MyMaths.

Literacy

In the Summary Questions, students construct a clear, structured argument to present the evidence for diffusion.

Key Word
diffusion

GCSE link

4.1.3.1 Transport in cells: diffusion (*GCSE Biology and GCSE Combined Science: Trilogy*)

Students should be able to explain how different factors affect the rate of diffusion.

Answers from the student book

In-text questions	
	A In the first diagram the particles of the diffusing substance are close together. In the second diagram they are spread out, randomly, to fill the whole container.
	B temperature, particle size and mass, state

Summary questions	1 randomly, spread, many, diffusion (4 marks)
	2 You might be able to see particles of a coloured substance moving through the air. You might be able to see particles of a coloured substance moving through a liquid. (2 marks)
	3 Nitrogen particles diffuse faster because their particles have a smaller mass. (2 marks)
	4 Extended response question (6 marks). Example answers:
	Diffusion (the movement of particles from an region where there are many particles, to a region where there are fewer) is evidence for the existence of particles.
	Further evidence for the existence of particles is that gases spread out to fill their containers, and that liquids and gases can flow.

kerboodle

Starter	Support/Extension	Resources
Bromine diffusion (5 min) In a fume cupboard, place one drop of bromine liquid in a gas jar. Put a lid on the gas jar, and place an inverted gas jar of air on top. Remove the lid between the two gas jars. Gradually, bromine fills the upper gas jar. Use the particle model to explain this observation, and identify the phenomenon as diffusion.		
Modelling diffusion (10 min) Have five students acting as diffusing particles. Ask them to make their way across the room. Put more and more other students in their way to demonstrate diffusion through the different states, and hence the relative speeds. Asking students to travel in pairs with arms interlinked will allow modelling of how greater particle mass affects diffusion speed.		

Main	Support/Extension	Resources
Which factors affect the rate of diffusion? (30 min) Ask students to suggest factors that affect the rate of diffusion, then use the suggestions to write a fair test question to investigate the effect of temperature on diffusion speed. Students plan the method and how to control the variables, explaining why this is important. Students then carry out the investigation, using the diffusion of potassium manganate(VII) in test tubes of water at different temperature. **Checking understanding of diffusion and evidence for particles** (10 min) Students should complete the questions provided in the corresponding student-book spread to check their understanding of diffusion and how it provides evidence for the existence of particles.	**Support**: The support sheet contains a table of results for students to fill in. Support students in order to make their investigations as fair as possible, for example, by discussing the size of particles chosen or how they are placed in the water to minimise early diffusion. **Extension**: Students justify their chosen procedure and evaluate their results. **Extension**: Students discuss in pairs the strength of the evidence for the existence of particles provided by observations of diffusion.	**Practical**: What affects the rate of diffusion? **Skill sheet**: Choosing scales **Skill sheet**: Recording results **Skill sheet**: Drawing graphs

Plenary	Support/Extension	Resources
Describing diffusion (5 min) Students complete a passage on diffusion from the interactive resource.		**Interactive**: Describing diffusion
Diffusion true or false statements (5 min) Assign one corner of the room to 'true' and one to 'false'. Call out statements about diffusion, for example, 'it is faster when the temperature is colder'. Students decide if the statement is true or false and move to the appropriate corner of the room.	**Extension**: Ask students to explain their decisions.	

Homework		
Students write a short paragraph explaining why hot water is best for making cups of tea.		

5.1.7 Gas pressure

Securing Mastery Goals

- 3.5.1 Explain unfamiliar observations about gas pressure in terms of particles.
- 3.5.1 Draw before and after diagrams of particles to explain observations about changes of state, gas pressure, and diffusion. (Pt 5/5)
- 3.5.1 Make predictions about what will happen during unfamiliar physical processes, in terms of particles and their energy.

Enquiry processes

- 2.3 Make a conclusion and explain it.
- 2.3 Judge whether the conclusion is supported by the data.

Band	Outcome	Checkpoint	
		Question	Activity
Know	Describe examples of gas pressure.		Starter 1, Plenary 2
	Use words to explain gas pressure simply.	A, 1	Main 1
	Collect and interpret simple primary data to provide evidence for gas pressure.		Main 1
Apply	Draw annotated particle diagrams, and use words, to explain gas pressure.	2	Main 2, Plenary 1
	Explain unfamiliar observations about gas pressure in terms of particles.	B, C, 2	Main 1, Main 2
	Collect, analyse and draw a conclusion from primary data providing evidence for gas pressure.		Main 1
Extend	Draw annotated before and after particle diagrams, and use words, to explain what happens to gas pressure as conditions are changed.	3	Main 1
	Predict what will happen to gas pressure as conditions are changed in terms of particles and their energy.	3	
	Evaluate the extent to which a conclusion made from primary data about gas pressure is justified by the evidence collected.		Main 2

Literacy

In the student book students identify main ideas, events, and supporting details when writing and performing a script.

GCSE link

4.3.3.1 (*GCSE Physics*) 6.3.3.1 Particle motion in gases (*GCSE Combined Science: Trilogy*)

Changing the temperature of a gas, held at constant volume, changes the pressure exerted by the gas.

Students should be able to:

- explain how the motion of the molecules in a gas is related to both its temperature and its pressure
- explain qualitatively the relation between the temperature of a gas and its pressure at constant volume.

Key Word

gas pressure

Answers from the student book

In-text questions	
	A The force per unit area caused by particles colliding with the walls of their container.
	B There are more particles causing more frequent collisions with the walls inside the container.
	C The air particles inside the bottle transfer energy to the freezer and the air cools down. The particles move more slowly. They collide with the plastic less often, so the pressure in the bottle decreases.

Activity	**Particle performance** Script to indicate that particles move faster as the air gets hotter, leading to more frequent collisions with the rubber tyres, and so increased pressure.
Summary questions	**1** Gas particles collide with the walls of their container. Colliding gas particles exert pressure on the inside of their container. The more particles in a container, the **higher** the pressure. The higher the temperature, the **higher** the pressure. (4 marks) **2** There are air particles in the closed can, above the baked beans. On heating, the gas particles move faster. They collide with the walls of the container more frequently, so the pressure increases. Eventually the pressure is so high that the container isn't strong enough to withstand this pressure, and the container explodes. (3 marks) **3** Example points. Students should also include before and after particle diagrams in their answer. (6 marks): In a warm room, the particles inside the balloon are moving more quickly. The particles collide with the walls of the rubber more often. The air pressure inside the balloon increases. The rubber will stretch and the balloon expand. In the freezer the particles inside the balloon transfer energy to the freezer, and the air cools down. The particles move more slowly and collide with the rubber less often. The pressure inside the balloon decreases. The rubber stretches out less and the balloon shrinks.

Starter	Support/Extension	Resources
What happens when gas pressure builds up? (5 min) Demonstrate gas pressure by placing a small amount of water in an empty camera film cartridge case along with an effervescent indigestion tablet, placing the lid on and turning it upside down. (Ensure there is plenty of space around the experiment and that students wear eye protection.) **What are gases like?** (10 min) Discuss the statements with students to ensure that they all have a good recall of the behaviour of gases from previous lessons and from KS2. The interactive resource will allow you to find out how confident students are with the behaviour of gases. Any weaknesses will need to be revisited before the concept of gas pressure can be taught.	**Support:** Students can also be given a blown-up balloon in order to feel the pressure inside. Alternatively, this can be done over the end of a plastic gas syringe, with students trying to compress it. This will help them to visualise what is happening to the particles within a gas.	**Interactive:** What are gases like?
Main	**Support/Extension**	**Resources**
What affects gas pressure? (25 min) Students carry out a practical in which they consider the factors that affect how much gas pressure is generated. A recap at the end of the practical can make use of animations that are readily available on the internet. Students then draw annotated particle diagrams, and use words to explain their observations. **Drawing particle diagrams** (15 min) Ask students to draw a storyboard of particle diagrams to show what happens as you blow a balloon up, giving in-depth explanations for each picture on their storyboard.	**Support:** Provide key words and phrases on which to base drawings. **Extension:** Students evaluate the extent to which their conclusions are justified by the data collected.	**Practical:** What affects gas pressure?
Plenary	**Support/Extension**	**Resources**
Gas pressure explanations (5 min) Without referring to their books or class notes, students should explain to a partner what causes gas pressure. **When do we need pressure?** (5 min) Ask students to come up with three situations where pressure is helpful or essential, and three situations where it is unhelpful or even dangerous.	**Extension:** Students should use particle diagrams when discussing how pressure builds up.	
Homework		
Students use their knowledge of gas pressure to explain why fizzy drinks sometimes spray out when they are opened.		

This lesson covers prerequisite knowledge, key words, and facts for AQA KS3 science Topic 6.1 Metals and non-metals and Topic 6.2 Acids and alkalis.

Band	Outcome	Checkpoint	
		Question	**Activity**
Know ↓	State definitions of atoms, elements, molecules and compounds.	A, B, C, 1	Plenary 2
	Name one element and one compound.		Main 1
Apply ↓	Represent atoms, molecules and elements using models.		Main 1, Main 2, Main 3
	Use diagrams to represent atoms and molecules of elements and compounds.	2, 3	Plenary 1
Extend ↓	Compare atoms, molecules and elements using models.		Main 2, Main 3
	Use diagrams to compare molecules of an element and a compound.	4	

Maths
Students make models containing specific numbers of atoms of different elements.

Literacy
In Question 4 students compare two particles in writing.

GCSE link
4.1.1.1/5.1.1.1 Students should know that all substances are made of atoms. An atom is the smallest part of an element that can exist. There are about 100 different elements.

Key Words
element, atom, molecule, compound

Answers from the student book

In-text questions	**A** An element is a substance that contains just one type of atom. All materials are made up of one or more elements.
	B A molecule is a group of two or more atoms, strongly joined together.
	C A compound is a substances that is made up of atoms of two or more elements, strongly joined together.
Summary questions	**1** The smallest particle of an element that can exist. (1 mark)
	2 Diagram showing two identical spheres touching each other. (2 marks)
	3 Diagram showing one atom in one colour joined to two atoms in another colour. (2 marks)
	4 Similarities – both include one or more oxygen atoms, and both are made up of atoms that are strongly joined together. Differences – an oxygen molecule is made up of two oxygen atoms only, but a water molecule is made up of one oxygen atom joined to two hydrogen atoms. (2 marks)

Starter	Support/Extension	Resources
Different particles (10 min) Show students a copper water pipe (or similar) and pour water through it. Elicit differences in properties between the two substances, and ask student pairs to use the particle model to discuss reasons for these differences. Then show students some ice, and ask if it is possible to use the particle model to explain the differences in properties between copper and ice – it is not. Point out that the differences in properties must be because ice and copper particles are different from each other.	**Extension**: Students suggest differences in water and copper particles (for example a piece of copper is heavier than ice of the same size, so copper particles are heavier.)	
Particle reminder (5 min) Students remind themselves of the arrangements of particles in liquid and solid water by drawing these on mini-whiteboards. They then peer assess by comparing their own diagrams with those of another student.	**Support**: Draw the particle diagrams on the board, and ask students which is which.	

Main	Support/Extension	Resources
Elements and atoms (10 min) Tell students that pure substances can be classified as elements or compounds. Display samples of elements, including copper and sulfur, and state that there are about 100 elements. Tell students that elements are made up of atoms, and that every element has its own type of atom. Students use plasticine to make a few 2 cm diameter spheres to represent copper atoms, and a few 1 cm diameter spheres to represent oxygen atoms.		**Activity:** Atoms and molecules
Molecules (10 min) Collect in all the model copper atoms, and use them to show the arrangement of atoms in solid copper. Students then join their oxygen atoms in pairs to represent oxygen molecules.	**Extension**: Students model a greater number of molecules, such as ozone (O_3) and carbon dioxide (CO_2) and sulfur trioxide (SO_3). They then compare these models.	
Compounds (20 min) Show a video clip of a hydrogen-oxygen explosion, and point out the differences in properties between this mixture and water, a compound made from atoms of the same elements. Students use modelling clay or other materials to make model water molecules for classroom display.		

Plenary	Support/Extension	Resources
Drawing challenge (10 min) On mini-whiteboards, ask students to draw the following: an element that exists as single atoms, molecules made up of three atoms of the same element, and so on.		
Defining key words (5 min) Students write definitions of the key words in their books, and peer assess.	**Support**: Provide a list of words and definitions for students to match.	**Interactive:** Defining key words
Alternatively, use the interactive resource to check students' understanding of the key words from this section.		

Homework	Support/Extension	
Make an illustrated A4 poster explaining the meanings of the key words element, atom, molecule, compound	**Support**: Provide an outline poster for students to complete.	

5.2.1 Pure substances and mixtures

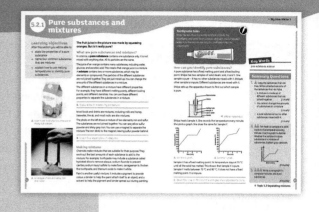

Securing Mastery Goals

- 3.5.2 Air, fruit juice, sea water and milk are mixtures.
- 3.5.2 Choose the most suitable technique to separate out a mixture of substances. (Pt 1/3)

Enquiry processes

- 2.9 Carry out the method carefully and consistently.

Enquiry processes activity

- 3.5.2 Devise ways to separate mixtures, based on their properties.

Band	Outcome	Checkpoint	
		Question	Activity
Know ↓	State what a mixture is and give examples of mixtures.	A, B, 1	Starter 1, Starter 2
	State that a mixture can be separated as a result of the different melting points of its components.		Main 1
	With help, choose a simple technique to separate the substances in a mixture.		Main 2
Apply ↓	Explain what a mixture is using the particle model.		Plenary 1
	Explain how to use melting temperatures to distinguish mixtures from pure substances.	C, 2	Main 1 Plenary 2
	Devise suitable techniques to separate mixtures, based on their properties.		Main 2
Extend ↓	Use particle models to compare mixtures and pure substances.	3	Plenary 1
	Comment on the purity of a substance by interpreting temperature change data.		Main 1 Plenary 2
	Justify the suitability of separation techniques in terms of the properties of constituent substances.		Main 2

Maths

Students interpret numerical data in graphs in order to determine whether substances are pure or impure.

MyMaths More support for the maths skills in this section can be found on MyMaths.

Literacy

Students explain the terms mixtures, pure, and impure, using these words when describing and explaining experimental observations.

GCSE link

4.1.1.2/5.1.1.2 Mixtures

Students should be able to:

- describe, explain and give examples of the specified processes of separation

- suggest suitable separation and purification techniques for mixtures when given appropriate information.

Key Words

mixture, **pure substance**

Answers from the student book

In-text questions	A Two or more different substances not chemically joined together.
	B Any four examples of mixtures.
	C Substances with clearly-defined melting (or boiling) points are pure. If the melting or boiling of a substance occurs over a temperature range then it is impure.
Activity	**Toothpaste tales**
	Ingredients list and uses should include hydrated silica (removes plaque), sodium fluoride (prevents cavities), sodium lauryl sulfate (makes foam), carrageenan (thickens toothpaste), and titanium oxide (whitener).

Summary Questions	**1a** A mixture is made up of different substances that are **not** joined together.
	b You **can** change the amounts of substances in a mixture.
	c A pure substance has no other substances mixed with it. (3 marks)
	2 Substance is pure because the change of state takes place at a clearly-defined temperature. (2 marks)
	3 Extended response question (6 marks). Example answers:
	A pure substance contains one substance only, but a mixture contains more than one substance.
	In a pure substance, all the particles are the same. A mixture contains different types of particles, which are not joined together.
	You can change the amounts of substances in a mixture so that the proportions of the substances are different.

kerboodle

Starter	Support/Extension	Resources
An alternative question-led lesson is also available. **What is a mixture?** (5 min) Students describe what they think a mixture is and give examples of any everyday mixtures they can think of. A common misconception is that mixtures cannot contain substances that appear to remain together, and students will often assume if a substance looks the same throughout (such as white toothpaste) then it cannot be a mixture, so this can cause confusion.	**Support**: Remind students of the definitions of atom, element, and compound before they proceed. **Extension**: Students recall and use the words pure and impure.	**Question-led lesson**: Pure substances and mixtures
Spot the mixtures (10 min) Students sort a list of common substances according to whether they are mixtures or not using the interactive resource. Students should justify their suggestions. Check their answers and ask students if there are any substances that they have found surprising in its category.	**Extension**: Students should suggest how mixtures are related to elements and compounds.	**Interactive**: Spot the mixtures

Main	Support/Extension	Resources
Identifying mixtures (15 min) Discuss the definition of a mixture, explaining that a mixture contains parts that can easily be separated, and that they would be classified as impure. Explain that pure substances will have sharp melting points, whereas impure substances melt over a range of temperatures since each component of a mixture has its own melting point. Students answer questions C, 2 and 3 in the student-book to consolidate these ideas.	**Extension**: Ask students to sketch a temperature-time graph for heating chocolate, which is an impure substance, showing that its melting range is 30 – 37 °C.	
Separating mixtures (25 min) This activity is one of the AQA Enquiry process activities. Students devise ways to separate different mixtures, choosing appropriate techniques based on the properties of the constituent substances, justifying their choice of techniques, and answer the questions that follow. Emphasise that separation techniques rely on the different properties of the constituents of a mixture.	**Support**: The accompanying support sheet lists possible separation techniques and how they work.	**Practical**: Separating mixtures **Skill sheet**: Scientific apparatus

Plenary	Support/Extension	Resources
Defining mixtures (10 min) Draw particle diagrams of pure substances and mixtures on the board. Students use their knowledge to decide on the category and use mini-whiteboards to display their answer.	**Extension**: Students draw other examples of their own, particularly if double-sided whiteboards are available.	
Pure or impure? (10 min) Draw sketch graphs for phase changes of hypothetical substances. Students use mini-whiteboards to say whether the graph shows a pure or impure substance. Select students to justify their answer.	**Extension**: Students should be able to suggest, using the direction of the line graph, whether the graph is showing the melting/boiling or freezing/ condensing of a substance.	

Homework	Support/Extension	
Students write a list of five mixtures from around the home and local environment. Students explain how they decided the substances were mixtures.	**Extension**: Encourage students to offer suggestions on how to separate mixtures into individual substances.	

5.2.2 Solutions

Securing Mastery Goals
- 3.5.2 Air, fruit juice, sea water and milk are mixtures.
- 3.5.2 Explain how substances dissolve using the particle model.

Enquiry process
- 2.3 Make a conclusion and explain it.
- 2.3 Judge whether the conclusion is supported by the data.

Band	Outcome	Checkpoint	
		Question	Activity
Know	When provided with key words, describe solutions using key words.	A, B, 1, 3	
	Describe observations when a substance dissolves.	3	Starter 1
	Use observations or data to draw a conclusion to distinguish a solution from a pure liquid.		Starter 2
Apply	Explain how substances dissolve using the particle model.	3	Plenary 2
	Draw annotated before and after particle diagrams to represent dissolving.	C, 3	Main 1
	Use data to draw a conclusion about the mass of solute dissolved in a solution.	2	Main 2
Extend	Explain the relationship between solutes, solvents, and solutions.	3	Plenary 1
	Justify whether a given particle diagram represents a solution or a pure substance.		
	Explain the applications of solution chemistry to different contexts.		Main 2

Maths
Students carry out subtractions to determine the mass of solutes in solution.

Students also interpret numerical data from a table to draw a line graph and answer questions.

MyMaths More support for the maths skills in this section can be found on MyMaths.

Literacy
Students plan ways to explain dissolving to a KS2 audience in the student-book activity, using scientific terminology in the explanation.

GCSE link
4.3.2.5/5.3.2.5 Concentration of solutions

Students should be able to:
calculate the mass of solute in a given volume of solution of known concentration in terms of mass per given volume of solution

Key Words
solution, dissolve, solvent, solute

Answers from the student book

In-text questions	A A mixture of a liquid with a solid or gas dissolved in it.
	B coffee powder
	C Solvent particles surround solute particles. The particles are arranged randomly and can move around.
Activity	**Solution masses**
	mass of solution = 3 g + 100 g = 103 g
	Modelling dissolving
	Credit sensible suggestions for how a model for dissolving can be set up. For example, small handfuls of beans can be placed carefully at different intervals throughout a container of rice. The rice represents solvent particles and the beans represent solute particles. When mixed, the content is shaken until the beans are scattered throughout the rice.

Summary Questions	1 solution, solute, solvent, water, salt, completely (6 marks)
	2 Since pure water has a density of 1 g/cm³, Laura should find the masses of each liquid on a mass balance. The liquid with a mass of 200 g will be pure water and the other two liquids will be solutions. (3 marks)
	3 Visual summary example answers (6 marks):
	Definitions of the key words solute, solvent, and solution.
	How dissolving requires solvent particles to surround the solute particles.
	All particles are freely moving in a solution.
	Use of mass to identify solvents from solutions.
	Examples of different solutions, stating the solutes and solvents used.
	Particle diagrams to illustrate the points above.

Starter	Support/Extension	Resources
When does dissolving occur? (5 min) Ask students to make a list of times when they dissolve something, and to describe in their own words what happens when substances are dissolved. This is a useful starting point to gauge student preconceptions.	**Extension:** Encourage students to explain their observations using scientific terminology and in terms of particles.	
Do all substances dissolve? (5 min) Demonstrate salt dissolving in water in a beaker and ask the question 'Has the salt gone away?'. This is a common misconception as the salt can no longer be seen. Some students should be able to point out that salt must still be present since the water would taste salty.	**Extension:** Encourage students to explain observations using particles.	

Main	Support/Extension	Resources
Introducing solutions (15 min) Using an everyday example such as adding coffee powder to water, define solute as the substance being dissolved (coffee powder), solvent as the substance doing the dissolving (water), and the resulting mixture as the solution (coffee). Demonstrate the conservation of mass by dissolving a known mass of coffee powder in a known mass of water (mass of coffee solution = mass of coffee powder + mass of water). Ask students to suggest possible applications of the conservation of mass (to distinguish pure solvents from solutions). Students draw annotated before and after particle diagrams to represent dissolving.	**Support:** A support sheet is available with a graph grid for students to plot numerical data. **Extension:** Students should consider the advantages and disadvantages of the method investigated in deciding if an unknown sample is a solvent or a solution. Students draw particle diagrams representing solutions and pure substances, and justify which diagrams represent which.	**Practical:** Solution of not? **Skill sheet:** Recording results **Skill sheet:** Drawing graphs
Solution or not? (30 min) Students watch a demonstration (which can be turned into a student-led investigation if time) on whether or not different solutes dissolve in a range of solvents, recording observations in a results table. Students then carry out a short task about the conservation of mass, plotting a graph, and identifying unknown substances as solvents or solutions given their volumes and masses.		

Plenary	Support/Extension	Resources
Solutes, solvents, and solutions (5 min) Students match the key words solute, solvent, and solution to images on the interactive resource. Students should then explain how the key words relate to one another.	**Extension:** Encourage students to link the three terms using the particle model.	**Interactive:** Solutes, solvents, and solutions
Modelling dissolving (10 min) Students design and perform role plays to describe what happens to particles when a solute dissolves. Students should ensure that their role plays illustrate the difference between solutes, solvents, and solutions.	**Extension:** Students should evaluate the strengths and weaknesses of each role play.	

Homework		
Students identify one example of dissolving that happens in the home, and draw particle diagrams to illustrate this process. They write a description of their observations and identify the solute, solvent, and solution.		

5.2.3 Solubility

Securing Mastery Goals
- 3.5.2 Use the solubility curve of a solute to explain observations about solutions.

Exceeding Mastery Goals
- 3.5.2 Analyse and interpret solubility curves.

Enquiry processes
- 2.9 Prepare a table with space to record all measurements.
- 2.9 Identify the independent variable.
- 2.9 Identify control variables.
- 2.9 Decide how to measure the dependent variable.
- 2.9 Control the variables.
- 2.9 Describe how controlling variables is important in providing evidence for a conclusion.
- 2.10 Write a fair test enquiry question.
- 2.10 Make a conclusion and explain it. (2.10)

Band	Outcome	Checkpoint	
		Question	Activity
Know	Use key words about dissolving.	A, 1	Starter 1
	Interpret solubility data shown on a bar chart.	B	Main 1, Plenary 2
	Write a fair test enquiry question on solubility, and plan the method and how to control the variables.		Main 2
Apply	Explain observations about dissolving.	2	Starter 2, Plenary 1
	Use the solubility curve of a solute to describe and explain simply observations about solutions.	2, 3	Main 1
	Explain why it is important to control variables to provide evidence for a conclusion in a solubility investigation.		Main 2
Extend	Suggest a reason for the effect of temperature on solubility for a given solute.		Plenary 2
	Analyse and interpret solubility curves.	3	Main 1, Plenary 2
	Justify the procedure and evaluate the results in a solubility investigation.		Main 2

Maths

Students will extract and interpret information from tables and graphs when completing the student-book activity and summary questions, describing trends shown in graphs and extrapolating data beyond the regions shown.

MyMaths More support for the maths skills in this section can be found on MyMaths.

Literacy

Students use scientific terminology to explain the relationship between solubility of different solutes, and how solubility differs with changing temperatures.

Key Words
saturated solution, **solubility**, **soluble (insoluble)**, **solubility curve**

GCSE link
4.3.2.5/5.3.2.5 Concentration of solutions

Students should be able to: calculate the mass of solute in a given volume of solution of known concentration in terms of mass per given volume of solution.

Answers from the student book

In-text questions	**A** A solution where no more solute will dissolve. **B** lithium chloride (most), sodium chloride (least)
Activity	**Solubility curves** Solubility increases with temperature for each straight-line graph (sodium nitrate, lead nitrate, potassium chloride, and sodium chloride). Lead nitrate has the steepest gradient (solubility increases the most for each degree of temperature increase) while sodium chloride has the smallest gradient. Curves for calcium chloride, potassium nitrate, and potassium chlorate (VII) show a slow increase in solubility with temperature at first, before a rapid increase after a certain temperature. Credit inclusion of correct temperature values. The curve for cerium(III) sulfate is the only one to show a decrease in solubility with temperature, to a constant solubility of 3 g/100 g of water from 30 °C onwards.

Summary Questions	**1** A saturated solution is a solution that contains the greatest mass of solid that can dissolve. A saturated solution contains undissolved solid. An insoluble substance does not dissolve. Solubility is the mass of substance that dissolves in 100 g of water. (4 marks)
	2 Graph should show an upward curve of decreasing gradient. This shows that solubility increases with temperature but up to a limit of approximately 700 g per 100 g of water. (4 marks)
	3a When the student adds 20 g of potassium chloride to 100 g of water, he would see that all the solid dissolved to make a solution. (3 marks)
	b When the student adds 200 g of cerium(III) sulfate to 100 g of water, he would see that some of the solid would dissolve, but most would remain undissolved at the bottom of the container. (3 marks)

kerboodle

Starter	Support/Extension	Resources
Describing dissolving (5 min) Ask students to write a simple description of what happens when sugar dissolves in water. The idea of particles should be used in the explanation. This activity will serve to dispel any remaining misconceptions about dissolving from the previous lesson.	**Extension:** Students may draw particle diagrams to explain the process of dissolving a particular solute.	
Dissolving substances (10 min) Demonstrate the differences in solubility in 20 cm³ of water for salt, calcium carbonate, and potassium manganate(VII). Explain that calcium carbonate is insoluble and hence all falls to the bottom, whilst the other two are both soluble, but a different amount of each can be added before some solid remains undissolved and falls to the bottom. Explain that when this happens a saturated solution has been made and that different substances have different solubility values.	**Extension:** Ask students to suggest the relative solubilities of everyday substances, for example, sugar.	

Main	Support/Extension	Resources
Solubility graphs (10 min) Introduce the term solubility, and how this relates to saturated solutions. Explain that solubility graphs are used to compare solubility of different solutes, or to compare solubility at different temperatures. Discuss the solubility graphs on the corresponding student-book spread to ensure students are able to extract information and to quote solubility at given temperatures in the units g/100 g water.	**Support:** Discuss the relevance of the units g/100 g water to facilitate students' understanding of solubility graphs and what the numbers mean.	**Practical:** Seawater solubility **Skill sheet:** Planning investigations
Seawater solubility (30 min) Students will plan a practical investigation to find out whether the solubility of salt in seawater differs according to the temperature of the region. Students carry out the investigation and record observations.	**Support:** Step-by-step guidance on writing a method and a partially filled results table are available on the support sheet.	**Skill sheet:** Recording results **Skill sheet:** Scientific apparatus

Plenary	Support/Extension	Resources
Understanding solubility (5 min) Students fill in the gaps in a short paragraph summarising solubility using the interactive resource.		**Interactive:** Understanding solubility
Solubility graphs (10 min) Discuss the solubility graphs shown in the corresponding student-book spread. Ask students to describe the trends shown in the graphs. Students should then use the graphs to state the solubility of particular solutes at given temperatures.	**Extension:** Students should suggest an explanation for why the solubility of different substances varies with temperature.	

Homework		
Students complete the questions on the practical sheet, and write a short paragraph to explain why sugar crystals can sometimes be found at the bottom of a teacup after the tea has been drunk.		

5.2.4 Filtration

Securing Mastery Goals
- 3.5.2 Use techniques to separate mixtures. (Pt 1/2)
- 3.5.2 Choose the most suitable technique to separate out a mixture of substances. (Pt 2/3)

Exceeding Mastery Goals
- 3.5.2 Suggest a combination of methods to separate a complex mixture and justify the choices. (Pt 1/2)

Enquiry processes
- 2.9 Carry out the method carefully and consistently.

Band	Outcome	Checkpoint	
		Question	Activity
Know	State that mixtures may be separated due to differences in their physical properties.		Starter 1
	State that the method chosen to separate a mixture depends on which physical properties of the individual substances are different.		Starter 1
	With support, use the correct techniques to filter a mixture.	1	Starter 1, Plenary 1, Main 2
Apply	Identify a physical property that must be different in order for given separation technique to work.	D	Main 2
	Choose the most suitable technique(s) to separate a mixture of substances.		Main 2
	Use annotated before and after particle diagrams, and words, to explain how filtration works.		Main 2, Plenary 1
Extend	Explain why a stated physical property must be different in order for a given separation technique to work.		Main 2
	Justify a chosen technique for separating a mixture of substances.		Main 2
	Design a model to explain filtering, and identify advantages and disadvantages of the model.	3	Starter 2

Maths
Students carry out simple calculations and apply the concept of ratios when working through the student-book activity and summary questions.

MyMaths More support for the maths skills in this section can be found on MyMaths.

Literacy
Students use scientific terminology to explain their experiment and in answering questions.

Key Words
filtration, filtrate, residue

GCSE link
4.1.1.2/5.1.1.2 Mixtures

Students should be able to:

describe, explain and give examples of the specified processes of separation.

suggest suitable separation and purification techniques for mixtures when given appropriate information.

Answers from the student book

In-text questions	**A** A liquid from an insoluble solid, or solution from an insoluble solid. **B** glitter = residue, water = filtrate **C** Removing coffee from ground-up coffee beans, removing solid impurities from oil, making water safe to drink. **D** Salt is soluble in water and sand is not.
Activity	**Solubility puzzle** Remove undissolved solid solute by filtering the solution into a pre-weighed beaker. Find the mass of the filtrate by: final mass of beaker – initial mass of beaker Pour the filtrate into a measuring cylinder to measure volume; volume of solution = volume of solvent Convert volume of solvent to mass by using 1 cm³ of water = 1 g Solubility of zinc sulfate in the volume of solvent used can be found by: mass of solution – mass of solvent Scale up or down to give solubility in g per 100 g of water

Summary Questions	1 insoluble residue (top), liquid filtrate (bottom) (2 marks)
	2 Amount of solute dissolved in 100 g of water: calcium chloride = 100 − 25 = 75 g calcium hydrogencarbonate = 100 − 84 = 16 g (least soluble) calcium bromide = 100 g (most soluble) calcium iodide = 100 − 33 = 67 g (4 marks)
	3 Students design a suitable model and identify at least one advantage and one disadvantage of their model. They also include relevant diagrams that help describe their model. (6 marks)

Starter	Support/Extension	Resources
Filtration demonstration (10 min) Demonstrate the filtration of a mixture of sand and water. Explain that filter paper contains tiny holes, large enough for water molecules to pass through but not grains of sand. Identify the apparatus names and introduce the terms filtrate and residue. Point out that this method of separation (filtration) relies on a difference in physical properties between the two substances in the mixture.	**Extension**: Ask students whether the residue is always discarded after filtration. Discuss that sometimes the residue is important (production of aspirin) and sometimes it can be discarded (ground coffee beans).	
Filter paper model (10 min) Introduce filtration apparatus and the terms filtrate and residue. Stretch a badminton net across the classroom, or arrange chairs with tiny gaps between them. Line up students on one side of the room and give them coloured balls. Ask students to approach the net (or chairs) and to pass the balls through the gaps. Ask students to explain this model of filtration (students = residue, coloured balls = filtrate).	**Extension**: Students should offer strengths and weaknesses of this model.	

Main	Support/Extension	Resources
Uses of filtration (15 min) Students work in pairs or small groups to gather as many ideas as possible on what filtration may be used for. Students then share these ideas as a class, before noting down two important uses of filtration in society (oil filters in cars and sand filters for drinking water).	**Extension**: Students should attempt the maths activity on the corresponding student-book spread to test their understanding and application of the concepts from this lesson and the last.	
Investigating filtration (25 min) Students solve a problem of separating salt from a mixture of rock and salt by filtration and evaporation. Students start by planning the investigation, using the particle model and drawing a particle diagram to explain why their plan works. They then answer the questions that follow about filtration.	**Support**: The support sheet includes diagrams of apparatus that can be used during filtration to help students draw their own labelled diagrams. **Extension**: Students explain why this separation technique relies on differences in solubility.	**Practical**: Investigating filtration **Skill sheet**: Planning investigations **Skill sheet**: Scientific apparatus

Plenary	Support/Extension	Resources
How does filtering work? (5 min) Students summarise key concepts and terminology from this lesson using a gap-fill exercise on the interactive resource.		**Interactive**: How does filtering work?
Filtering apparatus (5 min) Students draw a labelled diagram showing the apparatus for filtering on mini-whiteboards and define what the residue and filtrate are. Students should also give a brief description about how filter paper works in separating the filtrate from the residue.	**Extension**: Students should offer detailed explanations that involve a discussion of relative particle sizes and solubility.	

Homework	Support/Extension	
Students research six uses of filtration. They should include three examples where the residue is useful, and three examples where the filtrate is useful. An explanation of how filtration works is required.	**Extension**: Students may use particle diagrams to explain this process.	

5.2.5 Evaporation and distillation

Securing Mastery Goals
- 3.5.2 Use techniques to separate mixtures.
- 3.5.2 Choose the most suitable technique to separate out a mixture of substances. (Pt 3/3)

Exceeding Mastery Goals
- 3.5.2 Suggest a combination of methods to separate a complex mixture and justify the choices. (Pt 2/2)

Enquiry processes
- 2.9 Carry out the method carefully and consistently.

Band	Outcome	Checkpoint	
		Question	Activity
Know	State that mixtures may be separated owing to differences in their physical properties.	A, B	Main
	State that the method chosen to separate a mixture depends on which physical properties of the individual substances are different.	C	Main
↓	Label distillation apparatus and describe what happens in distillation.	1	Main
Apply	Identify the physical property that must be different in order to separate a mixture by evaporation or distillation.	2	Main
	Draw annotated before and after particle diagrams, and use words, to explain how evaporation and distillation work.		Starter 2
↓	Use the particle model to explain observations made during the distillation of inky water.		Main
Extend	Compare evaporation and distillation.	3	Starter 2
	Justify whether evaporation or distillation would be suitable for obtaining given substances from solution.	2	Plenary 2
↓	Suggest a combination of methods to separate a complex mixture and justify the choices made.	EoBI 6	Main

Literacy
Students discuss early scientific ideas and principles when suggesting possible ways the alembic could work.

Students also write an article explaining salt flats for a science magazine.

Key Words
distillation, evaporation

GCSE link
4.1.1.2/5.1.1.2 Mixtures

Mixtures can be separated by physical processes such as filtration, crystallisation, simple distillation, fractional distillation and chromatography.

Students should be able to:

describe, explain and give examples of the specified processes of separation.

suggest suitable separation and purification techniques for mixtures when given appropriate information.

Answers from the student book

In-text questions	A Pour some seawater into an evaporating dish. Heat over a water bath until some of the water has evaporated. Leave in a warm place for the rest of the water to evaporate.
	B making copper sulfate crystals, drying of glue, obtaining lithium compounds from solution
	C Salt has a much higher boiling point than water.
Activity	**Ancient distillation**
	Credit sensible suggestions for how the alembic might work. Answers should include evaporation of the mixture and condensation once vapours reach the curved lid.

Summary Questions	1 differences, physical, properties (3 marks)
	2a Evaporation because water has a lower boiling point than copper chloride, so on heating the water evaporates, leaving copper chloride in the container. (1 mark)
	b Distillation because propanone has a lower boiling point than water, so on heating the propanone evaporates first. It then condenses and is collected as a liquid. (1 mark)
	c Distillation (same reasoning as for **b**). (1 mark)
	d Evaporation because water has a lower boiling point than potassium chloride, so on heating the water evaporates, leaving potassium chloride in the container. (1 mark)
	3 Extended response question (6 marks). Example answers:
	Evaporation separates solute from a solution. The solvent evaporates and enters the atmosphere. The solvent cannot be obtained from evaporation. Distillation uses evaporation and condensation to obtain a solvent from a solution. Solids (main solute and other soluble impurities) remain. Only distillation can be used to obtain a solvent from solution. Both distillation and evaporation can be used to obtain solutes from solution, but evaporation uses much simpler apparatus and is therefore easier to set up, and to carry out.

Starter	Support/Extension	Resources
How do we get salt? (5 min) Ask students to suggest how salt can be obtained from seawater and why this may be a useful thing to be able to do.		
Evaporation apparatus (10 min) Show students the apparatus used for evaporation. Ask students what this is used for before demonstrating the evaporation of salty water. Students should be able to see the presence of small salt crystals, but ask students where the water particles have gone and if there is any way to get them back. On mini-whiteboards, students draw annotated particle diagrams to explain how evaporation separates salt from its solution. This activity is useful to highlight any misconceptions, such as the water particles 'disappearing'.	**Extension**: Students should compare evaporation to filtration.	

Main	Support/Extension	Resources
Distillation of inky water (40 min) Students carry out (or observe as a demonstration) how pure water is extracted from inky water. Point out that the substances can be separated by distillation as a result of a difference in one physical property - the two substances have different boiling points. Students draw a labelled diagram and answer the questions that follow. They also draw annotated before and after particle diagrams to explain how distillation works. If the distillation of inky water is carried out as a demonstration, time will be left over to attempt questions from the corresponding student-book spread, or to demonstrate distillation in separating mixtures using the extraction of limonene experiment. Further details of this experiment can be found on the RSC Learn Chemistry website.	**Support**: The accompanying support sheet contains labels students can use for their distillation diagram, as well as a suggested results table for their observations.	**Practical:** Distillation of inky water **Skill sheet:** Scientific apparatus **Skill sheet:** Recording results

Plenary	Support/Extension	Resources
Describing evaporation and distillation (5 min) Students summarise the key stages in distillation, explaining when evaporation and distillation are used, using the gap-fill exercise on the interactive resource. This activity can also be used as a consolidation of the terms solute, solvent, and solution.		**Interactive**: Describing evaporation and distillation
Evaporation or distillation (10 min) Call out mixtures or solutions and ask students to decide if they would be suitable for separation by evaporation, distillation, or both. Students display their answers using mini-whiteboards. They should be able to justify their answers by explaining the distillation and evaporation processes.	**Extension**: Students offer an extensive comparison between the two processes.	

Homework		
Students write an article for a science magazine about why geographic areas called salt flats (huge expanses of salt) arise. Students should include scientific terminology wherever possible.		

Securing Mastery Goals

- 3.5.2 Use evidence from chromatography to identify unknown substances in mixtures.

Enquiry processes

- 2.9 Gather data, minimising errors.
- 2.9 Decide whether the conclusion of the experiment agrees with your prediction.

Band	Outcome	Checkpoint	
		Question	Activity
Know	Describe what happens to a mixture when it undergoes chromatography.	A, 1	Lit, Main 2, Plenary
	Describe what a chromatogram looks like.	B	Main 1, Plenary
	Use evidence from chromatography to identify unknown substances in mixtures, and to identify the pen or plant a sample is from.		Main 1
Apply	Explain how chromatography separates mixtures.	2	Lit, Main 2, Plenary 1, Plenary 2
	Identify one physical property which must be different, and one physical property which must be the same, in order to separate a mixture by chromatography.		Main 2
	Use evidence from chromatography to explain how to identify unknown substances in mixtures, and to identify the pen or plant a sample is from.	3	Main 1
Extend	Justify the use of chromatography in different scenarios.	4	Lit
	Consider how chromatography can be used to monitor the progress of reactions.		Main 1, Plenary 2
	Suggest possible issues to consider when using chromatography to identify unknown substances.	4	Main 1

Literacy
Students use scientific terminology when explaining what happens during chromatography, and in relation to how it can be used to aid crime-solving in the practical.

Students must also decide on the appropriate level to pitch their explanation of chromatography when writing to the general public for homework.

Key Words
chromatography, chromatogram

GCSE link
4.8.1.3/5.8.1.3 Chromatography

Students should be able to:

explain how paper chromatography separates mixtures

suggest how chromatographic methods can be used for distinguishing pure substances from impure substances.

Interpret chromatograms and determine R_f values from chromatograms

Answers from the student book

In-text questions	**A** Chromatography separates substances in a mixture that are soluble in the same solvent. **B** The result from a chromatography experiment, where different colours have travelled up the chromatography paper by different amounts.
Activity	**Clever chromatography** Answers must include three uses of chromatography, for example, separating mixtures in solution, identifying coloured dyes, identifying the presence of vitamins and minerals, matching an unknown sample to a known specimen, and checking the progress of a reaction against a known product. Credit detailed descriptions of how chromatography is used, and check that scientific terminology has been used correctly.
Summary Questions	**1** a mixture, solvent, chromatogram (3 marks) **2** Some substances are more soluble than others, and some stick to the chromatography paper more/better than others. (3 marks)

3 Plant C – all the pigments in the unknown plant match all the constituent pigments in plant C. The pattern of spots for plant C is exactly the same as that for the unknown sample, so it is reasonable to be fairly confident that the answer is correct. However, there could be more than one plant producing identical chromatograms, so it is not possible to be 100% certain. (4 marks)

4 Example answers (6 marks):
Place a sample of the unknown ink onto chromatography paper. Obtain samples from the three possible pens. Place dots of sample inks along a line with the unknown sample on the same piece of chromatography paper. Carry out the chromatography procedure to obtain a chromatogram. Compare chromatograms obtained and one of the samples will match the unknown ink.

Possible issues:

Obtaining the sample of the unknown ink from the note.

If more than one person uses the same ink (same brand) then their chromatograms will look the same.

Chromatography tests the ink for the soluble substances inside it, not the pen itself.

Starter	Support/Extension	Resources
How are different colours made? (5 min) Ask students to recall the primary colours and use these to explain how other colours can be made. Discuss how coloured felt-tip pens are made from a combination of dyes, and ask students to suggest ways in which we can separate the different coloured dyes. Students will most likely suggest methods they have met, such as filtration, evaporation, and distillation.	**Extension:** Students should explain why each of filtration, evaporation, and distillation, will not work for this problem.	
Colourful sweets (10 min) Place a coloured sugar-coated chocolate in the middle of a piece of filter paper. Place one drop of water on it very slowly using a pipette. Show students how the dyes in the sugar coating separate out. Discuss that the shell contains a mixture of colours and they dissolve in the water and travel outwards with the water. Discuss what this method of separation can be used for.	**Extension:** Students should predict colours they expect to see on the chromatogram based on previous knowledge about primary and secondary colours.	

Main	Support/Extension	Resources
Who stole the money? (25 min) Students carry out a short investigation using chromatography to solve a mystery involving a fraudulent cheque, before answering questions that follow.		**Practical:** Who stole the money?
Modelling chromatography (15 min) Give each student a different coloured ball or coloured piece of paper. Working in small groups, ask students to make a role play to model chromatography, which they will perform and explain to the rest of the class.	**Extension:** Students should offer strengths and weaknesses of the models demonstrated.	

Plenary	Support/Extension	Resources
Colourful sweets – part two (10 min) Students explain chromatography in terms of what they saw with the sugar-coated chocolate, using key ideas and scientific terminology from this lesson. This can be done as a game of pair-share consequences, where each pair adds the next step in the chromatography procedure or explanation.		
Describing chromatography (5 min) Students re-order sentences on the interactive resource to explain what happens during chromatography.	**Extension:** Students share how chromatography is useful in determining whether a reaction has gone to completion or not.	**Interactive:** Describing chromatography

Homework		
Students prepare a newspaper article on how chromatography was used to catch the practical fraudster.		
An alternative WebQuest homework activity is also available on Kerboodle where students research the use of chromatography in forensic science.		**WebQuest:** Chromatography and crime

Checkpoint lesson routes

The route through this lesson can be determined using the Checkpoint assessment.

Percentage pass marks are supplied in the Checkpoint teacher notes.

Route A (support)
Resource: 5 Part 1 Checkpoint revision

A guided worksheet where students draw diagrams and add descriptions to demonstrate that they can securely use the particle model to describe state changes, diffusion, and gas pressure.

Route B (extension)
Resource: 5 Part 1 Checkpoint extension

A series of independent tasks that are designed to improve and extend student's scientific literacy and explanations using the particle model.

Progression to *Apply*

Know outcome	Apply outcome	Making progress
Describe how substances are made up of particles.	Use the particle model to explain why different substances have different properties	In Task 1 students fill in change-of-state diagrams. Provide the key words to students if they are struggling to fill in all the changes of state.
Describe the properties of a substance in its three states.	Use the particle model to explain the properties of substance in its three states.	In Task 2 students describe how the particles behave in a solid, liquid, and gas. Encourage students to use the particle diagrams they have drawn. Students could also look at animations of particles in the solid, liquid and gas states, or use beads or beans to model the particles.
Use the particle model, and ideas about energy transfer, to explain changes of state involving solids and liquids.	Draw particle diagrams to explain observations about melting and freezing.	In Task 3 students use the particle model, and ideas about energy transfer, to explain changes of state in their own words. Remind students that energy is transferred from the surroundings to the substance in melting, and the reverse for freezing. Encourage them to work out how to remember this – for example, you have to heat chocolate to make it melt. This means that energy is being transferred from the surroundings to the chocolate.
Draw particle diagrams to explain observations about boiling.	Use the particle model, and ideas about energy transfer, to explain boiling. Interpret melting point and boiling point data to predict the state of a substance.	In Task 3 students use the particle model to explain boiling in their own words. Provide a particle diagram of boiling as a starting point. Using the diagram, point out that in the liquid part of a boiling substance, the particles touch their neighbours and are sliding past each other. Ask students what is different about the spacing and movement of the particles in the bubbles.
Draw particle diagrams to explain observations about changes of state involving gases.	Use the particle model to make and explain predictions.	In Task 4 students describe differences between boiling and evaporation. Demonstrate the evaporation of a drop of ethoxyethane from a watch glass – students will soon smell the substance. Then demonstrate boiling water. Ask students to start by describing the observable differences between evaporation and boiling, and then to use the particle model to explain these differences.
Use the particle model to explain diffusion.	Draw particle diagrams to explain diffusion observations. Evaluate observations that provide evidence for the existence of particles.	In Task 5 students draw a particle diagram and explain observations. Start by placing a solid air freshener in the room. Ask students to indicate when they can smell it. Then get a few students to play the role of air freshener particles moving randomly in the room, from an area where there are many to an area where there are fewer.
Describe the factors that affect gas pressure.	Use the particle model, including diagrams, to explain observations about gas pressure.	In Tasks 6 and 7 students focus on the particles and the explanation for gas pressure. Demonstrate a model of gas pressure by shaking beads or dried beans in a plastic bottle. Ask students to explain how the model represents particles exerting pressure on the bottle. Then ask students how they could represent the increase in pressure that results when more particles are added. Students draw and annotate a particle diagram to show what happens. Point out the major shortcoming of the model – that, in the real situation, the container does not need to be shaken for the particles to move and hit the walls.

Answers to End-of-Big Idea questions

1 The particles are identical, touching each other, and arranged in a regular pattern. (2 marks)

2a Before and after particle diagrams as follows:

Before: particles touching each other and randomly arranged.

After: particles separate from each other and randomly arranged.

The particles in both diagrams should be identical, and there should be the same number of particles in each diagram. (2 marks)

 b Energy transferred from the surroundings is needed to separate the particles from each other, and to make them move faster. (2 marks)

3a Filtration – Set up a filter paper cone in a funnel with a flask underneath. Pour the mixture into the filter paper cone. Sand remains in the filter paper cone and water goes through the filter paper to the flask beneath. (2 marks)

 b Evaporation – Heat the salty water with a Bunsen burner in an evaporating basin until its volume halves. Then leave the remaining mixture in a warm, dry place for a day or so. Salt crystals form in the evaporating basin. Water evaporates and mixes with the air. (2 marks)

 c Chromatography – Draw a pencil line 1 cm from the bottom of a strip of chromatography paper. Draw and colour in a circle (0.5 cm diameter) with the felt tip pen at the centre of the pencil line. Place the filter paper in a beaker containing water to a depth of 0.5 cm, with the pencil line near the bottom. Allow water to move up the chromatography paper until it is near the top. The different coloured dyes of the pen will have travelled different distances up the filter paper. (2 marks)

4a C (1 mark)

 b Credit a sensible explanation of why statements A, B, or D do not explain why solids cannot be poured. (1 mark)

5a Distillation. (1 mark)

 b The technique makes use of the different boiling points of the two substances. The substance with the lower boiling point (propanone) is collected first, and that with the higher boiling point is collected next. (1 mark)

6a Use a magnet to remove iron filings from the mixture. Add water to the remaining mixture of potassium chloride and sand. The potassium chloride dissolves. Filter the mixture of sand and potassium chloride solution. The sand remains in the filter paper. Then heat the potassium chloride solution in an evaporating basin until its volume halves. Leave the remaining mixture in a warm, dry place for a day or so. Potassium chloride crystals form in the evaporating basin. (4 marks)

 b Magnet – the iron filings are attracted to the magnet, none of the other substances in the mixture is.

Adding water – sand is insoluble in water, but potassium chloride is soluble in water.

Filtration – separates the insoluble solid (sand) from the solution it is mixed with.

Evaporation – water boils and evaporates but potassium chloride does not. (2 marks)

7a Sophie's evidence – fast-moving air particles collide with the dust particles at random times and from different directions. This causes the random movement of the dust particles.

Amie's evidence – as you blow in more air, you are adding more air particles. These collide with the rubber of the balloon. Eventually, the increased frequency of collisions resulting from the increased number of particles makes the balloon burst.

Javier's evidence – the blackcurrant juice particles mix with the water particles. (6 marks)

 b Any one piece of evidence, with clear justification given. (2 marks)

Answer guide for the Maths challenge

Know	Apply	Extend
1–2 marks	3–4 marks	5–6 marks
● The student has drawn one of the three charts/graphs correctly, with suitable scales and correctly labelled axes and segments **OR** the student has drawn all three charts/graphs but the scales are unsuitable and/or the axes or segments are incorrectly or incompletely labelled. ● Some points, bars, and angles are plotted correctly but there are many mistakes. ● The student has not stated which type of chart or graph is most suitable.	● The bar chart, scatter graph, and pie chart are all drawn but their scales may not be suitable, and some of the axes or segments may be incorrectly or incompletely labelled. ● Most points, bars, and angles are plotted correctly but there are some mistakes. ● The student has stated that the bar chart or the pie chart are suitable ways of displaying the data but has not given a convincing reason.	● The bar chart, scatter graph, and pie chart have suitable scales, and all axes and segments are labelled. ● Points, bars, and angles are plotted correctly. ● The student has explained that the pie chart is the best way to display the data because it shows the different proportions of each gas that are in the air.

kerboodle

5 Part 1 Checkpoint assessment (automarked)
5 Part 1 Checkpoint: Revision
5 Part 1 Checkpoint: Extension
5.1 Progress task, 5.2 Progress task

6 Reactions

National curriculum links for this unit	
Topic	**National Curriculum topic**
Metals and non-metals	Chemical reactions
Acids and alkalis	Energetics

In this Big Idea students will learn:

- metals and non-metals react with oxygen to form oxides, which are either bases or acids
- metals can be arranged as a reactivity series in order of how readily they react with other substances
- some metals react with acids to produce salts and hydrogen
- to describe an oxidation, displacement, or metal–acid reaction with a word equation

- to use particle diagrams to represent oxidation, displacement, and metal–acid reactions
- to identify an unknown element from its physical and chemical properties
- to place an unfamiliar element into the reactivity series based on information about its reactants.

AQA Enquiry process activities

Activity	Section
3.6.1 Use experimental results to suggest an order of reactivity of various metals.	6.2.5 Metals and water
3.6.2 Devise an enquiry to compare how well indigestion remedies work.	6.1.5 Neutralisation

Preparing for Key Stage 4 Success

Knowledge Underpinning knowledge is covered in this Big Idea for KS4 study of:	• 4.4.1.1/5.4.1.1 Metal oxides • 4.4.1.2/5.4.1.2 The reactivity series • 4.4.2.1/5.4.2.1 Reactions of acids with metals • 4.4.2.2/5.4.2.2 Neutralisation of acids and salt production • 4.4.2.6/5.4.2.6 Strong and weak acids (Higher-tier only)
Maths Skills developed in Big Idea 2	**2** Handling data **c** Construct and interpret frequency tables and diagrams, bar charts and histograms. (6.1.3, 6.1.4, 6.1.5) **3** Algebra **a** Understand and use the symbols: $=, <, <<, >>, >, \propto, \sim$ (6.1.5) **4** Graphs **a** Translate information between graphical and numeric form (6.1.5) **5** Geometry and trigonometry **b** Visualise and represent 2D and 3D forms including two dimensional representations of 3D objects (6.1.4, 6.2.2, 6.2.3, 6.2.6)
Literacy Skills developed in Big Idea 2	• Identify meaning in scientific text, taking into account potential bias (6.1.1) • Summarise a range of information from different sources (6.1.5) • Use scientific terms confidently and correctly in discussions and writing (all sections) • Collaboration and contribution to group discussions (6.2.4, 6.2.5) • Identify main ideas and supporting evidence in text (6.1.1, 6.2.6) • Use largely correct form in a range of writing styles and text, and include information relevant to the audience (6.1.5, 6.1.6, 6.2.1, 6.2.6) • Ideas are organised into well-developed, linked paragraphs. (6.1.1, 6.1.2, 6.1.6, 6.2.6)
Assessment Skills	• Extended response questions (6.1.1, 6.1.2, 6.1.5, 6.2.1) (End-of-Big Idea questions Q4). • Application of Enquiry Processes (6.1.2, 6.1.3, 6.1.4, 6.1.5, 6.1.6, 6.2.4, 6.2.5) (End-of-Big Idea questions Q2, 3).

KS2 Link	Check before:	Checkpoint	Catch-up
Some changes result in the formation of new materials.	6.1.1 Chemical reactions	Ask students to describe what happens when a cake is baked, in terms of the starting materials and the end product.	Use students to model the individual ingredients. Model them reacting. Discuss what has happened to the ingredients and that the new product has different properties to the original.
Changes that form new materials are not reversible.	6.1.1 Chemical reactions	Ask students to describe differences between bread and toast, and raw and cooked eggs, and to decide if the original material can be obtained from the product.	Demonstrate cooking an egg in a tin lid over a Bunsen burner. Allow students to make observations that will allow them to conclude that the original material has been changed irreversibly.
All materials are made up of one or more elements.	6.2.1 More about elements	Students discuss the differences between elements and compounds.	Students use beads, models, or particle diagrams to show the differences between elements and compounds.
Changes that are not reversible include burning, oxidation, and reactions of acids.	6.2.2 Chemical reactions of metals and non-metals	Ask students if lighting a match is a reaction that can be reversed or what happens when bread is toasted.	Demonstrate lighting a match. Show how it looks before and after the reaction. Discuss the new substances that have been formed.
Changes that are not reversible include burning, oxidation, and reactions of acids.	6.2.3 Metals and acids	Demonstrate bicarbonate of soda reacting with vinegar. Students list the signs of reaction observed and explain whether this is a reversible or irreversible change.	Students compare bread being toasted with chocolate being melted and cooled.

Key Stage 2 Quiz: Chemistry .
6 Part 1 End-of-Big Idea test (foundation)
6 Part 1 End-of-Big Idea test (foundation) mark scheme
6 Part 1 End-of-Big Idea test (higher)
6 Part 1 End-of-Big Idea test (higher) mark scheme

Answers to Picture Puzzler
Key Words
mercury, explosion, test tube, acid, lava
The key word is metal.
Close up
Close up image of atoms in gold.

You can find additional support for the maths skills covered in this Big Idea on **MyMaths**, including drawing and interpreting graphs.

6.1.1 Chemical reactions

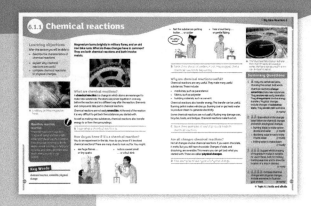

This section covers prerequisite knowledge for AQA KS3 Science topic 3.6.2 Acids and alkalis.

Enquiry processes

- 2.6 Suggest a scientific idea that might explain the observation.
- 2.6 Describe the evidence for your idea.
- 2.6 Explain why the evidence supports your idea.

Band	Outcome	Checkpoint	
		Question	Activity
Know	Describe some features of chemical reactions.	B, 1	Lit, Main 1, Plenary 1, Homework
	Give examples of chemical reactions and physical changes.	C, D	Main 1
↓	Record simple observations from practical work.		Main 1
Apply	Explain what a chemical reaction is, giving examples.	A	Starter 1, Plenary 2
	Deduce whether described change is a physical change or a chemical reaction.	2	Main 2
↓	Record detailed observations from practical work.		Main 1
Extend	Justify the use of specific metals and non-metals for different applications.	3	
	Compare chemical reactions to physical changes.	4	Main 2, Plenary 1
↓	Deduce whether an observed or described change is a physical change or a chemical reaction.		Main 1

Maths

Students use ideas of the number scale when measuring different quantities of reactants in the practical, as well as measuring temperature changes using a thermometer.

MyMaths More support for the maths skills in this section can be found on MyMaths.

Literacy

Students will use scientific terminology, apply their understanding, and organise ideas and information when completing the student-book activity.

GCSE link

4.1.1.1/5.1.1.1 Atoms, elements and compounds

Compounds are formed from elements by chemical reactions.

Chemical reactions always involve the formation of one or more new substances, and often involve a detectable energy change.

Compounds contain two or more elements chemically combined in fixed proportions and can be represented by formulae using the symbols of the atoms from which they were formed. Compounds can only be separated into elements by chemical reactions.

Chemical reactions can be represented by word equations or equations using symbols and formulae.

Key Words

chemical reaction, reversible, physical change

Answers from the student book

In-text questions	
	A A change that makes new substances and that is not easily reversible.
	B Any three from: flames/sparks, smells, chemicals getting hotter or colder, bubbles, fizzing.
	C paracetamol, polyester, cement
	D dissolving and changes of state

Activity	**Reaction, reaction, reaction** Possible points include: • Some reactions cause bangs. • Some reactions produce gases with bad smells. • Many reactions do not cause bangs or produce gases with bad smells, for example, cooking foods, reactions in humans, burning gas in cooking.
Summary questions	1 always, are not, always, state, are (5 marks) 2 **a** chemical (1 mark) **b** physical (1 mark) **c** physical (1 mark) 3 Magnesium burns with a very bright flame. (1 mark) 4 Extended response question (6 marks). Example answers: Chemical changes make new substances. Physical changes do not make new substances. Chemical changes are not reversible. Physical changes are reversible. Chemical changes include burning reactions. Physical changes include changes of state, dissolving, and mixing.

Starter	Support/Extension	Resources
An alternative question-led lesson is also available. These starter activities are designed to gauge preconceptions within the class. **What is a reaction?** (5 min) Ask students to discuss what they think a reaction is, and to give some examples of reactions they know about, for example, burning methane in a Bunsen burner or frying an egg. **Greedy teacher!** (10 min) Set up a Bunsen burner and use this to boil a beaker of water, add a teabag and then, using tongs, toast a piece of bread. Ask students to guess why you may be doing this, and how it relates to the lesson.	**Extension:** Some students may be able to spot a difference between the physical and chemical changes taking place.	**Question-led lesson:** Chemical reactions
Main	**Support/Extension**	**Resources**
Finding out about reactions (30 min) Students carry out a series of reactions to observe what happens and find the signs that can be used to show reactions are occurring. Students then use their observations to answer questions based on chemical reactions and physical changes. **Consolidation** (10 min) Ask groups of students to feed back what they observed during the practical. Discuss the key differences between chemical and physical changes. Students can complete questions in the student book to check their understanding.	**Support:** The support sheet allows students to record their observations in a suggested table of results.	**Practical:** Finding out about reactions **Skill sheet:** Recording results
Plenary	**Support/Extension**	**Resources**
Signs of reactions (5 min) Ask students to write down on a mini-whiteboard the signs of a chemical reaction, and explain the differences between a physical and a chemical change. **Reactions crossword** (10 min) Students use the clues given on the interactive resource to complete a crossword of key words in this topic.	**Extension:** Students should be asked to describe how physical reactions can be seen to be occurring.	**Interactive:** Reactions crossword
Homework	**Support/Extension**	
Students make a poster showing the signs of a chemical reaction. An alternative WebQuest homework activity is also available on Kerboodle where students research how chemicals and chemical reactions are involved in cooking.	**Extension:** Students can dedicate a section on their poster to the differences between physical changes and chemical reactions.	**WebQuest:** Kitchen chemistry

6.1.2 Acids and alkalis

This section covers prerequisite knowledge and facts for AQA KS3 Science topic 3.6.2 Acids and alkalis.

Securing Mastery Goals

- 3.6.2 Acids and alkalis can be corrosive or irritant and require safe handling.

Enquiry processes

- 2.13 Identify risks and hazards.
- 2.13 Identify control measures.

Band	Outcome	Checkpoint	
		Question	Activity
Know	Name some common properties of acids and alkalis.	1, 3	Main 1
	Describe, in simple terms, what the key words 'concentrated' and 'dilute' mean.	C, 1	Main 1, Main 3
	Label hazard symbols and describe the hazards relating to them.		Main 2, Homework
Apply	Compare the properties of acids and alkalis.	1, 3	Main 1, Main 3
	Describe differences between concentrated and dilute solutions of an acid.	C, 1	Main 1, Main 3
	Identify and describe the meaning of hazard symbols and offer suitable safety precautions.		Main 2, Homework
Extend	Compare the different particles found in acids and alkalis.	1, 3	Main 1, Main 3
	Explain what 'concentrated' and 'dilute' mean, in terms of the numbers of particles present.	C, 1, 2	Main 1, Main 3
	Offer suitable safety precautions when given a hazard symbol, and give a reason for the suggestion.		Main 2, Homework

Maths
Students carry out simple calculations when comparing concentrations of acids.

MyMaths More support for the maths skills in this section can be found on MyMaths.

Literacy
Students use scientific terms correctly when labelling and describing hazards associated with substances.

Students summarise information about the properties of acids and alkalis when designing their posters.

GCSE link
4.4.2.6/5.4.2.5 Strong and weak acids (HT only)

Students should be able to use and explain the terms dilute and concentrated (in terms of amount of substance), and weak and strong (in terms of the degree of ionisation) in relation to acids.

Key Words
acid, alkali, corrosive, concentrated, dilute, irritant

Answers from the student book

In-text questions	A hydrochloric acid, ethanoic acid, citric acid
	B Corrosive solutions can burn your skin, and they can burn your eyes.
	C A concentrated solution has more acid particles per litre than a dilute solution. Alternatively, credit suitable hazards. For example, concentrated acids burn skin and eyes but dilute acids only hurt if they make contact with open cuts.
Activity	**Safe handling**
	Control risks by wearing eye protection and avoiding contact with skin, perhaps by wearing gloves. Mop up spills immediately.
	Credit any reasonable decision, supported by a suitable reason.

Summary questions	
	1 taste sour, corrosive, more, more (4 marks)
	2 20 g of alkali in 250 cm³ of solution is equivalent to (20 × 2 = 40 g) of alkali in 500 cm³ of solution. The other solution has 10 g of alkali in 500 cm³ of solution. So the first solution is more concentrated. (3 marks)
	3 Extended response question (6 marks). Example answers: Both acids and alkalis can be corrosive, depending on the concentration. This means that both acids and alkalis can, at certain concentrations, burn the skin and eyes. In both acids and alkalis, the more acid or alkali particles there are in a certain volume of solution, the more concentrated the solution. Acids taste sour. Alkalis feel soapy.

kerboodle

Starter	Support/Extension	Resources
Looking at acids and alkalis (10 min) Display a selection of acids and alkalis around the classroom, including household substances such as soap, vinegar, and drain cleaner. Make sure any household containers are empty and thoroughly clean and sealed. Ask students to make a list of the precautions noted on each item and the types of uses seen. **Common acids and alkalis** (5 min) The interactive resource contains a word search where students can familiarise themselves with the chemical names of common acids and alkalis.	**Support**: Students should concentrate on recalling the meaning of each hazard symbol. **Extension**: Students should deduce whether each of the substances contains an acid or an alkali.	**Interactive**: Common acids and alkalis

Main	Support/Extension	Resources
Introducing acids and alkalis (10 min) Ask students to give their understanding of what acids and alkalis are and where they may have heard of them. Discuss the chemical nature of acids and alkalis and the properties they each have. Discuss that acids and alkalis can have different concentrations, which means that there are different numbers of acid/alkali particles in a given volume of their solutions. If Starter 1 was not chosen, introduce the fact that some acids and alkalis are safe to ingest and use whereas others are dangerous and can cause serious burns. **Acids and alkalis** (10 min) In this activity students are required to match each hazard symbol to its name and description. Students are then asked to apply this to a laboratory situation, and are asked to identify suitable precautions for risks and hazards. **Whiz bang!** (20 min) Students often think that acids and alkalis react together to make an explosion. Demonstrate to them that this is not the case. Then give students 15 minutes to design a poster to summarise the properties of acids and alkalis.	**Extension**: Students can be introduced to H^+ for acid particles and OH^- for (most) alkali particles. **Extension**: Students should discuss the presence of H^+ and OH^- ions in acids and alkalis.	**Activity**: Acids and alkalis

Plenary	Support/Extension	Resources
Memory game (10 min) Go through a list of common acids and alkalis on the board. Students must decide on their mini-whiteboards if the substance concerned is an acid or an alkali. Remove the list and ask students to recall from memory as many acids and alkalis as possible. **Acid and alkali safety** (5 min) Call out the hazard names associated with most acids and alkalis (corrosive and irritant) and ask students to sketch the symbol from memory on a mini-whiteboard.		

Homework	Support/Extension	
Students write a short report on the hazard symbols that can be found around the home. For each hazard symbol found, students must sketch the symbol, give a brief description of the hazard, and suggest a precaution for the risk. Ensure students know to do this under adult supervision, that they must not open any containers, and that they must handle all containers carefully.	**Support**: Guide students towards looking at containers in the kitchen or the garden shed.	

6.1.3 Indicators and pH

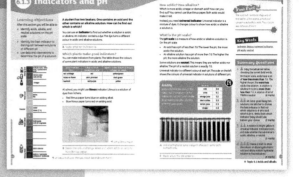

Securing Mastery Goals

- 3.6.2 Acids have a pH below 7, neutral solutions have a pH of 7, alkalis have a pH above 7.
- 3.6.2 Identify the best indicator to distinguish between solutions of different pH, using data provided.
- 3.6.2 Use data and observations to determine the pH of a solution and explain what this shows.

Enquiry processes

- 2.12 Make an experimental prediction.
- 2.9 Gather data, minimising errors.
- 2.12 Decide whether the conclusion of the experiment agrees with your prediction.
- 2.12 State whether or not the hypothesis is correct.

Band	Outcome	Checkpoint	
		Question	**Activity**
Know	State that acids have a pH below 7, neutral solutions have a pH of 7, alkalis have a pH above 7.	1, 3	Main 1, Plenary 1
	State that indicators will be different colours in acids, alkalis, and neutral solutions.	A, B, 2, 3, 4	Starter 2, Main 1, Plenary 1, Plenary 2
	Identify the pH of a solution using experimental observations.	3	Main 1
Apply	Use the pH scale to measure acidity and alkalinity.	C, 1, 3	Main 1, Plenary 2
	Describe how indicators categorise solutions as acidic, alkaline, or neutral.	A, B, 2, 4	Starter 2, Main 1, Plenary 1
	Identify the best indicator to distinguish between solutions of different pH, using data provided.	2	
Extend	Compare the use of a variety of indicators and a pH probe to measure acidity and alkalinity.	2, 3, 4	Starter 2, Main 1, Main 2
	Deduce the hazards of different acids and alkalis using data about their pH.		Main 3
	Evaluate the accuracy of the pH values chosen through the experimental observations.		Main 1

Literacy
Students summarise their knowledge using scientific terms to explain the application and importance of pH testing in farming for their homework.

Key Words
indicator, litmus, universal indicator, **pH scale,** neutral

GCSE link
4.4.2.4/5.4.2.4 The pH scale and neutralisation

The pH scale, from 0 to 14, is a measure of the acidity or alkalinity of a solution, and can be measured using universal indicator or a pH probe.

A solution with pH 7 is neutral. Aqueous solutions of acids have pH values of less than 7 and aqueous solutions of alkalis have pH values greater than 7.

Answers from the student book

In-text questions	A An indicator is a solution that contains a dye that changes colour to show whether a solution is acidic or alkaline.
	B The colour of the litmus paper changes from blue to red.
	C The pH scale is a measure of how acidic or alkaline a solution is.

Activity	**Acidity**
	milk, urine, black coffee, orange juice, vinegar, lemon juice
Summary questions	**1** less than, less, more than, 7.0 (4 marks)
	2 Universal indicator, since it is a different colour in solutions of pH 4 and pH 6. (2 marks)
	3 Its pH is 6, and the substance is acidic. (2 marks)
	4 The chart should correctly show the colours of dilute hydrochloric acid and dilute sodium hydroxide solution in five indicators, for example universal indicator, litmus, red cabbage, hibiscus flowers, and beetroot. (6 marks)

Starter	Support/Extension	Resources
Properties of acids and alkalis (5 min) Ask students to list as many properties of acids and alkalis as they can recall from the previous lesson. This can be done on mini-whiteboards and can be run as a competition.	**Support**: A list of properties can be provided for students to categorise.	
Indicator demonstration (10 min) Discuss with students the uses of indicators in everyday life, and that chemical indicators such as litmus paper can be used to identify acids and alkalis. Demonstrate red litmus paper turning blue when alkali is added and blue litmus paper turning red when acid is added. Discuss the term 'indicator' and why these substances are useful to chemists.	**Support**: Although the use of red and blue litmus paper is useful to see the colour change between acids and alkalis, it may be useful to keep to one type of litmus paper to avoid confusing students.	

Main	Support/Extension	Resources
Using universal indicator (20 min) Students carry out a simple practical using universal indicator (in both paper and solution form) to find the pH of mystery solutions. They then answer questions that follow.	**Support**: A support sheet is available for students to record their observations. **Extension**: Students could be provided with a pH probe during the practical to allow them to consider the difference in accuracy between the two techniques. Also, ask students to justify the use of universal indicator in this practical rather than litmus.	**Practical**: Using universal indicator **Skill sheet**: Recording results
Applications of pH testing (10 min) Discuss applications of pH testing, for example, soil testing or determining urine pH. Show students a pH probe and explain why these can provide a more accurate pH value for solutions. **pH and hazards** (10 min) Tell students that the lower the pH of an acidic solution, or the higher the pH of an alkaline solution, the more corrosive the solution is likely to be. Read out pairs of pH values of solutions (for example pH 1 and pH 4) and ask students to predict which solution in each pair is more corrosive.		

Plenary	Support/Extension	Resources
pH values (10 min) Call out pH values between 1 and 14 randomly and ask students to display acid, alkali, or neutral on a mini-whiteboard. Then ask students to call out the colours of universal indicator expected for these pH values.		
Indicator colours (5 min) The interactive resource includes pictures of solutions after universal indicator has been added. Students must match the correct pH value to each picture.		**Interactive**: Indicator colours

Homework	Support/Extension	
Students produce leaflets explaining why pH testing is important for farmers.	**Support**: A hint can be given to students, asking them to consider the type of soil in which a plant will thrive, in order to focus them onto soil acidity/alkalinity.	

6.1.4 Acid strength

Securing Mastery Goals
- 3.6.2 Hydrochloric, sulfuric and nitric acid are strong acids.
- 3.6.2 Ethanoic (acetic) and citric acid are weak acids.

Exceeding Mastery Goals
- 3.6.2 Deduce the hazards of different alkalis and acids using data about their concentration and pH.

Enquiry processes
- 2.3 Make a conclusion and explain it.

Band	Outcome	Checkpoint	
		Question	**Activity**
Know ↓	State examples of strong and weak acids.	A, 1	Main 1
	State the pH range for acidic solutions.		Starter 2
Apply ↓	Explain the difference between a strong acid and a weak acid.	1	Main 1, Main 2, Plenary 1, Plenary 2
	Compare pH values of concentrated and dilute solutions of the same acid.	B, C, 2	Main 1, Main 2
	Use models to show the difference between a strong acid and a weak acid.		Main 2
Extend ↓	Explain the difference between acid strength and acid concentration.		Main 1, Plenary 1
	Deduce the hazards of different acids using data about their concentration and pH.	3	Main 1
	Evaluate models for strong and weak acids, and suggest improvements.		Main 2

Maths
Use pH data to compare the concentrations of acidic solutions and the strengths of different acids.

MyMaths More support for the maths skills in this section can be found on MyMaths.

Literacy
Students write a paragraph to explain clearly the difference between a strong acid and a weak acid.

GCSE link
4.4.2.6/5.4.2.5 Strong and weak acids (HT only)

Students should be able to use and explain the terms dilute and concentrated (in terms of amounts of substance), and weak and strong (in terms of the degree of ionisation) in relation to acids.

Key Words
strong acid, weak acid, **concentration**

Answers from the student book

In-text questions	**A** Strong acids: hydrochloric, sulfuric, and nitric. Weak acids: ethanoic acid and citric acid. **B** Jordan **C** The solution of pH 1.
Summary questions	**1** Strong, weak, all, only some of (4 marks) **2** Sulfuric acid because it is a strong acid and ethanoic acid is a weak acid. All the molecules have split up in sulfuric acid, but only some of those in ethanoic acid have split up. (2 marks) **3a** Wear eye protection and avoid splashing onto skin. (2 marks) **b** On dilution the pH increases. Do not change the safety precautions, even though the hazards are slightly reduced, since it is better to take too many precautions than too few. (3 marks)

Starter	Support/Extension	Resources
Food acid (5 min) Show students some citric acid in a packet, an orange, and a bottle of hydrochloric acid. Point out that citric acid is used to make drinks taste sour, and is the natural acid in citrus fruits, but that hydrochloric acid is not used in food or drink. Ask students to suggest why.		
pH (5 min) Read out pairs of pH values for acidic solutions, e.g., pH 4 and pH 5. For each pair, students write the pH of the more acidic solution on mini-whiteboards.	**Extension**: Students make up similar questions for each other and peer assess in pairs.	

Main	Support/Extension	Resources
Investigating strong and weak acids (30 min) Students add magnesium ribbon to strong and weak acids and – by observing the vigour of the reactions that occur – judge which acids are strong and which are weak. They then estimate the pH of each acid used and suggest a suitable substance for checking their estimates. During this activity, remind students about dilute and concentrated solutions, as studied in 6.1.2. Point out that the terms 'concentrated' and 'strong' have different meanings in chemistry, as do the terms 'weak' and 'dilute'.	**Extension**: Students deduce the relative hazards associated with using the different acids. **Support**: Provide diagrams for students to annotate to help them write their explanations. **Extension**: Students evaluate their models and suggest improvements.	**Practical**: Investigating strong and weak acids
Modelling strong and weak acids (10 min) Students use a molecular model kit to model hydrochloric acid particles by joining green and white spheres in pairs. They then add these to beans representing water particles in a beaker, breaking up the hydrochloric acid particles as they enter the 'water'. This represents a strong acid.		
Next, students join white and yellow spheres in pairs to model particles of a weak acid. They add these to beans representing water particles in a beaker, breaking up only some of the acid particles as they enter the 'water'.		
Students then write a short paragraph explaining the difference between a strong and weak acid.		

Plenary	Support/Extension	Resources
Definitions (5 min) Read out definitions of the terms listed below, without stating which term is being defined. Students write which term is being defined on mini-whiteboards. Terms: strong acid, weak acid, dilute acid solution, concentrated acid solution. Alternatively, students use the interactive activity to check their understanding of the key terms.		**Interactive**: Definitions
Stronger or weaker? (10 min) Ask students to identify the stronger acid when given the pH values of solutions of two different acids, each of the same concentration. For example, which is stronger – an acid solution of pH3 or a solution of a different acid of pH2?		

Homework	Support/Extension	
Students use the Internet to research the properties and uses of a weak acid, for example ethanoic acid, ascorbic acid (vitamin C), or citric acid.		

6.1.5 Neutralisation

Securing Mastery Goals
- 3.6.2 Explain how neutralisation reactions are used in a range of situations.
- 3.6.2 Describe a method for how to make a neutral solution from an acid and alkali.

Enquiry processes
- 2.3 Make a conclusion and explain it.
- 2.10 Write a fair test enquiry question.
- 2.11 Identify control variables.

Enquiry processes activity
- 3.6.2 Devise an enquiry to compare how well indigestion remedies work.

Band	Outcome	Checkpoint	
		Question	**Activity**
Know	State simply what happens during a neutralisation reaction.	1	Starter 1, Starter 2, Main, Plenary 1, Plenary 2
	Give one example of a neutralisation reaction.	3	Starter 1, Starter 2, Main
	Identify independent, dependent, and control variables in an investigation.		Main
Apply	Describe a method for making a neutral solution from an acid and an alkali.	B, 3	Main
	Explain how neutralisation reactions are used in a range of situations.	C, 4	Starter 2, Main, Plenary 1, Homework
	Design an investigation to find out which indigestion remedy is 'better'.		Main
Extend	Interpret a graph of pH changes during a neutralisation reaction.		Enq proc
	Justify the method chosen to investigate which indigestion remedy is 'better'.		Main

Maths
Students can interpret pH from a graph of pH against volume of acid added to a solution in the student-book activity.

MyMaths More support for the maths skills in this section can be found on MyMaths.

Literacy
Students can summarise information using scientific terminology on neutralisation to explain to gardeners the importance of monitoring soil pH.

Students will also be tested on their spelling of key words in the interactive resource.

GCSE link
4.4.2.2/5.4.2.2 Neutralisation of acids and salt production

Acids are neutralised by alkalis (eg soluble metal hydroxides) and bases (eg insoluble metal hydroxides and metal oxides) to produce salts and water, and by metal carbonates to produce salts, water and carbon dioxide.

The particular salt produced in any reaction between an acid and a base or alkali depends on:
- the acid used (hydrochloric acid produces chlorides, nitric acid produces nitrates, sulfuric acid produces sulfates)
- the positive ions in the base, alkali or carbonate.

Key Words
neutralisation, **base**

Answers from the student book

In-text questions	
	A A base is any substance that neutralises an acid. An alkali is a base that is soluble in water.
	B 7 cm³
	C Neutralisation reactions are useful for adjusting soil pH to make the soil suitable for particular crops, and for increasing the pH of lakes whose pH is low as a result of acid rain.

Activity	**Data logger details**
	The pH decreases gradually at first until, when 7 cm³ of acid has been added, the pH is 13. Then the pH decreases rapidly to pH 5 on the addition of just 2 cm³ of acid. Then the pH decreases gradually on addition of more acid solution until the pH value is 1.
Summary questions	**1** neutralisation, base, indicator, data (4 marks)
	2 Agriculture – to ensure soil pH is correct for desired crops. (2 marks)
	Acidic lakes – adding a base to neutralise excess acid. (2 marks)
	3 Example answer: Pour some dilute acid into a flask. Add a few drops of universal indicator.
	Add the alkaline solution until the universal indicator shows that the pH of the mixture is 7. (3 marks)
	4 Extended response question (6 marks). Example answers:
	Different crops grow well in soils of different pH.
	It is useful to measure soil pH to know which plants are more likely to grow well in the soil.
	Farmers can add acid to a soil to make it more acidic (reduce the pH).
	Farmers can add bases to a soil to make it less acidic (increase the pH).

Starter	Support/Extension	Resources
Rainbow fizz (10 min) Add universal indicator to a beaker of dilute NaHCO₃ and a beaker of dilute HCl. Pour the bicarbonate solution into a clamped burette. Slowly add acid into the burette, and point out the colour changes that occur where the two solutions meet. The fizzing is for added effect and students should be made aware of this. (A large amount of universal indicator will be required for obvious colour changes to be seen; boiling tubes can be used instead of a burette.)		
How do indigestion remedies work? (5 min) Dissolve an indigestion remedy in a beaker of water and use red litmus paper to show the solution is alkaline. Ask students to consider what happens when this is taken for indigestion (it neutralises excess stomach acid).		

Main	Support/Extension	Resources
Neutralisation (40 min) This activity is one of the AQA Enquiry process activities. Students decide what is meant by a 'better' indigestion remedy. They follow tips provided to plan an experiment to test two indigestion remedies, including writing a fair test question and identifying control variables. They then carry out their investigation and use their results to draw conclusions. Students then answer the questions that follow.	**Support**: An access sheet is available where students are not required to plan the method for this investigation. **Extension**: Students justify their chosen method for the investigation.	**Practical**: Neutralisation **Skill sheet**: Planning investigations **Skill sheet**: Recording results

Plenary	Support/Extension	Resources
Neutralisation conclusion (10 min) Ask students to explain which indigestion remedy they decided would be 'better' at neutralising stomach acid. How did they decide the criteria for 'better'?		
Neutralisation key words (5 min) The interactive resource consolidates student understanding of acids and alkalis, the pH scale, and neutralisation reactions by asking students to type in key words and figures.		**Interactive**: Neutralisation key words

Homework	Support/Extension	
Students make an A4 poster to describe and explain some uses of neutralisation reactions.		
An alternative WebQuest homework activity is also available on Kerboodle where students research soil pH.		**WebQuest**: Soil pH

6.1.6 Making salts

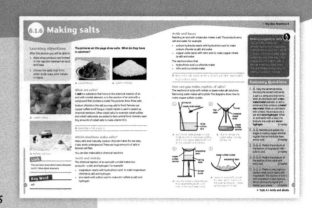

Exceeding Mastery Goals

- 3.6.2 Estimate the pH of an acid based on information from reactions.
- 3.6.2 Given the names of an acid and an alkali, work out the name of the salt produced when they react.

Know and Apply students need to know that neutralisation reactions produce a salt and water.

Enquiry processes

- 2.12 Identify and record key features of an observation.

Band	Outcome	Checkpoint	
		Question	**Activity**
Know	State the type of substances made when an acid and alkali react.	1	Main 1
↓	Match the type of salt that will form from the type of acid used.		Main 1, Plenary 2, Homework
	Describe observations during an experiment.		Main 2
Apply	Describe what a salt is.	A, 1	Main 1
↓	Choose the correct name of the salt formed in a neutralisation reaction from a list of possible salts.		Main 1, Plenary 2
	Describe the steps in making a salt in a neutralisation reaction.	2	Main 2
Extend	Explain what salt formation displaces from the acid.		Main 1
↓	Predict the names of salts formed when acids react with metals or bases and write word equations to represent the reactions.	B, 3, 4	Main 1, Main 2, Plenary 2, Homework
	Describe and explain the steps involved in making a salt in a neutralisation reaction.	2	Main 2
↓	Estimate the pH value of an acid based on information about its reactions.	5	

Literacy

Students organise ideas and information to write a clear and concise scientific method for preparing magnesium chloride crystals.

Students use scientific terms, including the spelling of chemical names correctly, to identify reactants and products, and name the missing substances in word and formula equations.

GCSE link

4.4.2.2/5.4.2.2 Neutralisation of acids and salt production

The particular salt produced in any reaction between an acid and a base or alkali depends on:

- the acid used (hydrochloric acid produces chlorides, nitric acid produces nitrates, sulfuric acid produces sulfates)
- the positive ions in the base, alkali or carbonate.

4.4.2.3/5.4.2.3 Soluble salts

Salt solutions can be crystallised to produce solid salts.

Key Word

salt

Answers from the student book

In-text questions	**A** Substance in which hydrogen atoms of an acid are replaced by atoms of a metal element. **B** sodium chloride
Activity	**Making magnesium salts** Add small pieces of magnesium (ribbon) to dilute hydrochloric acid in beaker. Continue adding Mg until some remains unreacted in the mixture. Filter mixture to remove excess Mg ribbon, keeping solution. Pour the solution (MgCl) into an evaporating dish. Place dish over a water bath on a tripod and gauze. Heat with a Bunsen burner until half of the water has evaporated. Leave dish and its contents in a warm, dry place for the rest of the water to evaporate, leaving magnesium chloride crystals in the dish.

Summary questions	
	1 metal, metal, hydrogen, water (4 marks)
	2 Example answers (6 marks): Add copper oxide (credit hydroxide) to dilute hydrochloric acid in a beaker, one spatula measure at a time. Continue to add copper oxide until some remains unreacted in the mixture. Filter the mixture to remove the excess copper oxide. Keep the solution (filtrate). This has separated excess reactant (copper oxide) from a solution of the product (copper chloride). Pour the filtrate into an evaporating dish. Place the evaporating dish over a water bath on a tripod and gauze, and heat with a Bunsen burner until about half the water has evaporated. Leave the evaporating dish and its contents in a warm, dry place for the rest of the water to evaporate. Copper chloride crystals remain in the evaporating dish.
	3 magnesium sulfate and hydrogen (2 marks)
	4 zinc nitrate and water (2 marks)
	5 The acid with the higher pH is the one that reacts less vigorously, so acid Y has the higher pH. (2 marks)

Starter	Support/Extension	Resources
An alternative question-led lesson is also available.		**Question-led lesson**: Making salts
Salt facts (10 min) Ask students to list facts they know about the everyday usage of the word 'salt', for example, table salt or bath salts. Students should consider where they come from as well as their uses, risks, and benefits. Build up a list as a class and discuss why, in particular, table salt is of huge importance globally and biologically (e.g., preservation of food, cooking, chemical industry, nerve conduction in the body).		
Why is salt safe to eat? (5 min) Show students some hydrochloric acid and sodium hydroxide and discuss the hazards of each. Ask students to decide if it would be safe to consume these. Then display sodium chloride (from a table salt container). Explain that it is made from the previous two substances – ask students to consider why it is safe to consume in small quantities.	**Support**: Students may need a reminder of reactions forming new products, with different properties to the reactants.	

Main	Support/Extension	Resources
How are salts made? (15 min) Discuss with students how the reaction between an acid and a base will produce a salt and water, and the reaction between an acid and a metal will produce a salt and hydrogen gas. Students should write down the definition of a salt. Show examples of word equations. Discuss the names of salts – the metal involved followed by the name derived from the type of acid used, for example, chlorides from hydrochloric acid.		
Making salts (25 min) Students carry out the reaction between HCl and NaOH to make table salt crystals. Students note down their observations throughout the reaction and answer the questions that follow, including a question on writing the word equation for this reaction.		**Practical**: Making salts

Plenary	Support/Extension	Resources
Salt definition (5 min) Ask students to recall from memory the definition of a salt, and write this on their mini-whiteboard.	**Extension**: Students can be asked to give examples of salts.	
Name the substances (10 min) Interactive resource in which students complete word equations of reactions between acids and metals.	**Support**: Give students alternative salts to choose from.	**Interactive**: Name the substances

Homework	Support/Extension	
Students find out the name of a base that can be used to neutralise acids in soils (for example calcium hydroxide). Then they find out names of acids present in soils and predict the names of the salts that would form during these reactions, as well as the secondary products of the reactions.		

6.2.1 More about elements

Securing Mastery Goals
- 3.6.1 Iron, nickel and cobalt are magnetic elements.
- 3.6.1 Mercury is a metal that is liquid at room temperature.
- 3.6.1 Bromine is a non-metal that is liquid at room temperature.
- 3.6.1 Identify an unknown element from its physical and chemical properties. (Pt 1/2)

Exceeding Mastery Goals
- 3.6.1 Justify the use of specific metals and non-metals for different applications, using data provided.

Enquiry processes
- 2.4 Select a good way to display data.

Band	Outcome	Checkpoint	
		Question	Activity
Know	State what an element is.	A	Starter 2, Main
	State examples of elements.	1, 2	Starter 1, Main 1
	Present some simple facts about an element.	3	Lit, Main 1, Main 2, Homework
Apply	Identify an unknown element from its physical and chemical properties.	4	
	Compare the properties of typical metals and non-metals.	C, 2, 3	Main 2, Plenary 1, Plenary 2
	Record observations and data on elements.		Main 1
Extend	Justify the use of specific metals and non-metals for different applications, using data provided.	5	Lit, Main 1
	Deduce the relationship between the position of an element in the periodic table and its properties.		Main 2
	Use observations and data obtained to form conclusions about given elements.	4	

Maths
Students can use the data from the Fantastic Fact! box to calculate simple percentages of different elements found in the human body.

MyMaths More support for the maths skills in this section can be found on MyMaths.

Literacy
In the student-book activity students write a leaflet to persuade car scrapyard owners to recycle platinum.

Students summarise ideas about elements into a leaflet during the activity, and as a dating profile for homework.

GCSE link
4.1.1.1/5.1.1.1 Atoms, elements and compounds

Atoms of each element are represented by a chemical symbol, e.g., O represents an atom of oxygen, Na represents an atom of sodium.

There are about 100 different elements. Elements are shown in the periodic table.

Key Words
element,
periodic table,
chemical
symbol **metal,
non-metal**

Answers from the student book

In-text questions	
	A A substance that cannot be broken down into simpler substances.
	B The Periodic Table lists the elements. In the Periodic Table, elements with similar properties are grouped together.
	C Six from: low melting point, poor conductor of electricity, poor conductor of heat, dull, brittle, not sonorous, low density

Activity	**Platinum propaganda**
	Points to include: Platinum has many uses. Platinum is rare. For these reasons, platinum is expensive. Recycling platinum can make money for car scrapyard owners. Recycling platinum increases the likelihood of there being enough platinum to meet future demand for important uses, such as heart pacemakers and catalytic converters.
Summary questions	**1a** iron, nickel, cobalt (or any other three magnetic elements) (3 marks) **b** mercury, bromine (2 marks)
	2 iron – metal; oxygen – non-metal; chlorine – non-metal; mercury – metal. (4 marks)
	3 A typical metal has high boiling and melting points, but the boiling and melting points of non-metals are low.
	Metals are good conductors of heat and electricity, but non-metals are not.
	Most metals are shiny, but most non-metals are dull.
	Metals tend to have high densities and non-metals have low densities.
	A typical metal is malleable and ductile, but a non-metal is brittle.
	Many metals are sonorous, but non-metals are not. (6 marks)
	4 Mercury (1 mark)
	5 Extended response question (6 marks). Example answers:
	Uses of platinum include jewellery, catalytic converters, hard disks, making heart pacemakers.
	Jewellery – platinum suitable because it is shiny, not damaged by air or water, can be made into different shapes. Heart pacemaker – platinum suitable because it is not damaged by air and water and can be made into different shapes.

Starter	Support/Extension	Resources
Elements wordsearch (5 min) Students locate names of different elements from the interactive resource using the list provided.		**Interactive:** Elements wordsearch
Looking at elements (5 min) Display samples of several different elements. Ask students to consider how they are the same. Point out that an element is a substance that cannot be broken down into other substances, and that everything is made up of one or more elements.		
Main	**Support/Extension**	**Resources**
The elements (40 min) Students work in small groups to research the properties and uses of several elements assigned to them, and then produce small (A5) information posters that can be placed together to produce a large scale, class periodic table. Indicate the metals and non-metals.	**Support:** Students should research familiar elements. **Extension:** Students should research more obscure or reactive elements, considering why some elements are known about but can be isolated only briefly.	**Activity:** The elements **Skill sheet:** Calculating percentages
Comparing metals and non-metals (10 min) Students work in pairs to reflect on their findings from the previous activity, and to list properties that are typical of metal elements and those that are typical of non-metal elements.	**Extension:** Students deduce the relationship between the position of an element in the periodic table and its properties.	
Plenary	**Support/Extension**	**Resources**
Metal or non-metal? (5 min) Read out a list of properties, for example high melting point, sonorous, poor conductor of heat and so on. For each property, students indicate whether it is typical of a metal or non-metal element.		
Comparing properties (5 min) Ask students to write five sentences with 'but' in the middle, for example *Most metals have high melting points but most non-metals do not.* Students then compare their answers in pairs.		
Homework		
Students make a 'dating profile' for a particular element, imagining it is a person. The dating profile should outline all the element's wonderful qualities, where it is useful, and whether it is a metal or a non-metal.		

Chemical reactions of metals and non-metals

Securing Mastery Goals

- 3.6.1 Describe an oxidation, displacement, or metal–acid reaction with a word equation. (Pt 1/4)
- 3.6.1 Use particle diagrams to represent oxidation, displacement and metal-acid reactions. (Pt 1/3)
- 3.6.1 Identify an unknown element from its physical and chemical properties. (Pt 2/2)

Exceeding Mastery Goals

- 3.6.1 Deduce the physical or chemical changes a metal has undergone from its appearance. (Pt 1/2)

Enquiry processes

- 2.4 Design a table for the data being gathered.
- 2.9 Gather sufficient data for the investigation.

Band	Outcome	Checkpoint	
		Question	Activity
Know	State that many elements react with oxygen to form oxides.		Starter 1, TBC
	State what the arrow means in a word equation.		TBC, Plenary 1
	Describe a difference in physical properties between typical metal and non-metal oxides.	B, 1	Starter 2, TBC
Apply	Use particle diagrams to represent oxidation reactions.	3	
	Describe an oxidation reaction with a word equation.	2	TBC, Plenary 1
	Classify the products obtained when typical metal and non-metal elements react with oxygen.	B, 1, 2	TBC
Extend	Decide whether a word equation represents an oxidation reaction.		TBC, Plenary 1
	Interpret a word equation to name reactants and products.	C	TBC
	Deduce the physical or chemical changes a metal has undergone from its appearance.	4	TBC

Maths
Students explain how a maths equation is different from a word equation in chemistry.

Literacy
In question 4 students write a justification for their decision about the type of change a pictured metal has undergone.

GCSE link
4.1.1.1/5.1.1.1 Atoms, elements and compounds

Students should be able to write word equations for the reactions in the specification.

4.1.1.1/5.4.1.1 Metal oxides

Metals react with oxygen to produce metal oxides. The reactions are oxidation reactions because the metals gain oxygen.

Key Words
physical property, chemical property, oxide, reactant, product, word equation

Answers from the student book

In-text questions	A Any three from: shiny, malleable, ductile, high melting point, high boiling point, good conductor of heat, good conductor of electricity.
	B A typical metal oxide is solid at 20 °C and is a base. A typical non-metal oxide is a gas at 20 °C and is an acid.
	C Sulfur and oxygen.
	D A reaction in which a substance reacts with oxygen to make one or more oxides.

Summary questions	1 Metal properties: high melting point, forms oxides that are bases. Non-metal properties: brittle, forms oxides that are acids. (4 marks)
	2a copper + oxygen → copper oxide
	carbon + oxygen → carbon dioxide (2 marks)
	b Product in first reaction is a base, and product in second reaction is an acid. (2 marks)
	3 Diagram showing a number of spheres (for example eight) arranged in two or more rows to represent magnesium, as well as four pairs of spheres to represent oxygen atoms. Product showing magnesium and oxygen atoms arranged alternately in rows. The total number of atoms of each element in the reactant and product should be the same. (3 marks)
	4 The change is a physical change. In the first picture gallium is in the solid state, and in the second picture it is in the liquid state. This means that the process that has occurred is melting, which is a physical change. (4 marks)

Starter	Support/Extension	Resources
Elements in oxygen (10 min) Sprinkle iron filings into a Bunsen burner and ask students what is happening. Elicit that there is a chemical reaction in which iron reacts with oxygen from the air to make iron oxide. Then demonstrate cutting a sample of sodium, and point out that the cut face quickly goes dull as a result of its reaction with oxygen to form sodium oxide.	**Extension:** Students predict the names of the products formed when other elements react with oxygen.	
Metals and non-metals (5 min) Students remind themselves of typical metal and non-metal properties by listing as many of these properties as possible.	**Support:** Give examples of a typical metal (copper) and non-metal (oxygen) to help students to remember typical properties.	

Main	Support/Extension	Resources
Examining oxides (25 min) Demonstrate burning charcoal (carbon) in a gas jar. Tell students that the reaction makes a gas, carbon dioxide. Add damp blue litmus paper to the gas jar. Its colour change to red indicates that carbon dioxide forms an acidic solution on dissolving in water. Next, students burn magnesium in oxygen, without looking directly at the flame. They place the white substance formed into a test tube of distilled water and shake. They dip red litmus into the resultant mixture. The litmus goes blue. Tell students that the white substance is magnesium oxide. The litmus colour change shows that magnesium oxide is a base. Tell students that a typical metal reacts with oxygen to form an oxide that is a base, and a typical non-metal reacts with oxygen to form an oxide that is an acid.	**Extension:** Give students the names of several metals and non-metals. They should use the Periodic Table to help them predict whether the products formed when they react with oxygen are acids or bases.	**Practical:** Examining oxides

Plenary	Support/Extension	Resources
Completing equations (10 min) Students read about word equations in the Student book, and complete word equations for oxidation reactions. Emphasise the meaning of the arrow in an equation in chemistry. Alternatively, set the interactive activity in which students complete word equations, paying particular attention to correct spelling.		**Interactive:** Completing equations
Defining key words (5 min) Students use mini-whiteboards to write the key word when you give them a definition based on the work in this lesson.		

Homework	Support/Extension	Resources
Students research how different elements produce different coloured flames when burned in oxygen, and how this is useful for making fireworks.	**Support:** Guide students to the fact that it is the metal compound that affects the colour of the flame.	

Securing Mastery Goals

- 3.6.1 Describe an oxidation, displacement, or metal–acid reaction with a word equation. (Pt 2/4)
- 3.6.1 Use particle diagrams to represent oxidation, displacement and metal–acid reactions. (Pt 2/3)

Enquiry processes

- 2.3 Make a conclusion and explain it.

Band	Outcome	Checkpoint	
		Question	**Activity**
Know	Describe what happens when metals react with acids.	1	Enq, Starter 1, Main, Plenary 2
	State that when a metal reacts with an acid the products are a salt and hydrogen gas.	A, 1	Enq, Starter 2, Main, Plenary 2
↓	State which metals produce bubbles when reacting with acid.		Starter 1, Main
Apply	Compare the reactions of different metals with dilute acids.	4	Enq, Main
	Predict the names of the products formed in a metal-acid reaction, and describe the reaction with a word equation or represent it with a particle diagram.	B, 2, 4	Main, Plenary 1, Plenary 2, Homework
↓	Decide which metals react more vigorously from practical observations.		Main
Extend	Suggest how temperature changes may be linked with differences in reactivity between metals with acid.		Main

Literacy

Students use scientific terminology to explain observations in metal–acid reactions, suggesting relative reactivity between different metals.

Students also explain the naming convention of metal salts in their tutorial sheet that they write for homework.

GCSE link

4.4.2.1/5.4.2.1 Reactions of acids with metals

Acids react with some metals to produce salts and hydrogen.

Key Word

salt

Answers from the student book

In-text questions	**A** metal salt and hydrogen gas
	B magnesium sulfate
Activity	**Sulfuric similarities**
	Plan should include appropriate apparatus list, method, risk assessment, and consideration for different variables.
	An example method would be to place different metals that are known to react vigorously with HCl in H_2SO_4 to see if bubbles are produced at a similar rate.

Summary questions	1	a salt, hydrogen, lead, magnesium, silver (5 marks)
	2	Iron chloride and hydrogen. This is because all metal–acid reactions result in a salt and hydrogen being made. Hydrochloric acid forms chloride salts. (3 marks)
	3	Reactants: diagram showing iron particles arranged in rows; diagram showing hydrochloric acid, with hydrogen and chloride particles in water.
		Products: diagram of iron chloride, with iron and chloride particles arranged alternately in rows; diagram of pairs of hydrogen particles.
		There should be the same number of atoms of each element in the reactants and products. (3 marks)
	4a	magnesium + nitric acid → magnesium nitrate + hydrogen (1 mark)
	b	tin + hydrochloric acid → tin chloride + hydrogen (1 mark)
	c	zinc + sulfuric acid → zinc sulfate + hydrogen (1 mark)

Starter	Support/Extension	Resources
Do acids and metals react? (10 min) Show a strip of magnesium ribbon and a test tube containing dilute hydrochloric acid. Students predict if the two will react and recall the signs of a chemical reaction. Discuss the observations. **Testing for hydrogen gas** (10 min) Demonstrate the reaction between magnesium and hydrochloric acid, collecting the hydrogen gas produced using an empty, inverted test tube. Hold a lit splint to the test tube containing the collected gas to demonstrate the characteristic squeaky pop as a test for hydrogen gas.	**Support**: Recap the differences between physical and chemical reactions. **Extension**: Students suggest what may have happened to the hydrogen gas to produce the squeaky pop.	

Main	Support/Extension	Resources
Reacting metals with acids (40 min) Students add four different metals (zinc, lead, iron, magnesium) to dilute hydrochloric acid, one at a time, ensuring that a fair test is carried out. They test the gas produced with a lighted splint to show that it is hydrogen. Students observe the reactions that occur and list the metals in order of increasing reactivity. They then write word equations for the reactions.		**Practical:** Reacting metals with acids

Plenary	Support/Extension	Resources
Spot the salt (5 min) Students match reactants to products of different metal–acid reactions using the interactive resource. Ask students for the other product formed in all these reactions (hydrogen). **Metal and acid facts** (5 min) Students write the general equation for the metal–acid reaction on mini-whiteboards. Students then write down the signs of chemical reactions that would show the metal was reacting, and explain the test for hydrogen gas.		**Interactive:** Spot the salt

Homework		
Students produce a tutorial sheet that teaches other students how to name the salts made when metals react with acids.		

6.2.4 Metals and oxygen

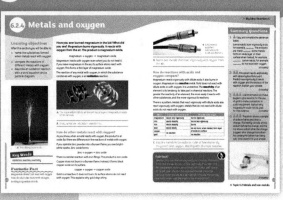

Securing Mastery Goals
- 3.6.1 Describe an oxidation, displacement, or metal–acid reaction with a word equation. (Pt 3/4)

Exceeding Mastery Goals
- 3.6.1 Deduce the physical or chemical changes a metal has undergone from its appearance. (Pt 2/2)
- 3.6.1 Justify the use of specific metals and non-metals for different applications, using data provided. (Pt 2/2)

Enquiry processes
- 2.3 Make a conclusion and explain it.

Band	Outcome	Checkpoint	
		Question	Activity
Know	State the product of a reaction between a metal and oxygen.	1	Starter 1, Main 1, Plenary 1, Plenary 2, Homework
	Name one metal that reacts vigorously with oxygen and one metal that does not react with oxygen.	B, 1	Starter 1, Main 1
	Make observations about how different metals react with oxygen.		Starter 1, Main 1
Apply	Compare the reactions of different metals with oxygen.	B, C	Enq, Starter 1, Main 1, Plenary 2, Homework
	Describe an oxidation reaction with a word equation.		Main 1, Plenary 2, Homework
	Rank metals in order of how vigorously they react with oxygen.	C	Main 1, Homework
Extend	Explain the reactivity of metals according to how they react with oxygen.		Starter 1, Main 1, Homework
	Justify the use of specific metals for different applications, using data provided.	3	Main 2
	Deduce the physical or chemical changes a metal has undergone from its appearance.	4	

Literacy
Students use scientific terminology when explaining fair tests in the student-book activity, and when explaining experimental observations.

GCSE link
4.4.1.1/5.4.1.1 Metal oxides

Metals react with oxygen to produce metal oxides. The reactions are oxidation reactions because the metals gain oxygen.

Key Words
oxidation, reactive, **reactivity**

Answers from the student book

In-text questions	A The reaction of any substance with oxygen, in which the substance combines with oxygen.
	B Two from: magnesium, zinc, and iron
	C magnesium, zinc, iron, lead, copper, and gold
Activity	**Fair test?**
	Jamilla should hold each metal sample using tongs over the Bunsen flame and take note of how long it takes for the metal to ignite.
	The metal that burns most vigorously is the most reactive, whilst the one that does not burn will be the least reactive.
	Some metals may not burn but may gain oxide coating. These metals are less reactive than those that burn.
	Possible improvements:
	Use the same mass of metal with the same surface area.
	Testing reactivity with acid as well, since metals demonstrate the same reactivity trends whether burning in oxygen or reacting with acid.

128

Summary questions	1 magnesium, oxides, copper, gold (4 marks)
	2 Potassium oxide will be made in an explosive/very vigorous reaction. This is because the reactivity trends of metals are the same whether burning in oxygen or reacting with acid. (4 marks)
	3 Gold is an unreactive element. It does not burn and its surface atoms do not react with oxygen. This means that its ability to conduct electricity is never compromised by a layer of oxide on its surface. The surface atoms of magnesium react with oxygen from the air to form a layer of magnesium oxide. Magnesium oxide does not conduct electricity. (4 marks)
	4 The surface atoms of sodium have reacted with oxygen from the air to make sodium oxide. This happens because sodium is a very reactive element. (2 marks)

Starter	Support/Extension	Resources
What is happening to these metals? (10 min) Demonstrate cutting a piece of lithium on a white tile. Show the shiny surface rapidly becoming dull. Also show a new iron nail and a rusty iron nail. Ask students to suggest what has happened to the metals in both examples. Discuss and lead to metals reacting with oxygen to produce metal oxides. Clarify that rusting only refers to the formation of iron (III) oxide; rusting is an example of corrosion. **What is in these compounds?** (5 min) Give the names of several metal oxides and ask students to identify which elements the compounds are made from. This task will serve as good revision of naming of compounds, such as the ending '–ide' for compounds containing only two elements.	**Extension:** Students consider the relative speeds of the oxidation reaction and how this is linked to reactivity. Explain that most metals require heating before tarnishing.	

Main	Support/Extension	Resources
How do metals react with oxygen? (30 min) Students carry out the reactions of four different metals with oxygen using a Bunsen flame, record their observations in a suitable results table, and write a word equation to represent each reaction. Students then answer the questions that follow based on reactivity. **Using metals** (15 min) Discuss how the uses of metals depend on their properties, for example the use of gold, which does not tarnish, as electrical connectors in audio equipment. Students answer the questions in the student book to check their understanding of the concepts covered in the lesson.		**Practical:** How do metals react with oxygen? **Skill sheet:** Recording results

Plenary	Support/Extension	Resources
Can this be true? (5 min) Interactive resource where students categorise statements on the reactions of metals and oxygen, according to whether they are true or false. **Revisiting lithium and iron** (10 min) Revisit the starter demonstration involving the oxidation of lithium and iron. Students should now be able to explain what has happened to both metals and write word equations on mini-whiteboards.	**Extension:** Students justify their answers by applying their scientific knowledge and understanding.	**Interactive:** Can this be true?

Homework		
Students write a paragraph to explain why some metals lose their shine over time but why gold does not. Students should include examples of other metals and word equations.		

6.2.5 Metals and water

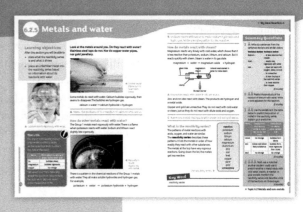

Securing Mastery Goals
- 3.6.1 Place an unfamiliar metal into the reactivity series based on information about its reactions.

Exceeding Mastery Goals
- 3.6.1 Deduce a rule from data about which reactions will occur or not, based on the reactivity series.

Enquiry processes
- 2.10 Write a fair test enquiry question.
- 2.11 Identify control variables.

Enquiry processes activity
- 3.6.1 Use experimental results to suggest an order of reactivity of various metals.

Band	Outcome	Checkpoint	
		Question	Activity
Know	State the products of the reaction between metals and water.	A, 2	Plenary 2
	State whether a metal is more or less reactive than another metal.	1	Lit, Starter 2, Main, Plenary 1, Plenary 2
↓	Write a simple method to find out how easily metals react with acids or water.		Main
Apply	Compare the reactions of different metals with water.	C, 1	Lit, Starter 2, Main, Plenary 2
	Use the reactivity series to predict reactions, and place an unfamiliar metal into the reactivity series based on information about its reactions.	3	Main
↓	Plan a practical to compare the reactivity of three metals, including identifying control variables and planning how to control them.		Main
Extend	Link a metal's reactions with its place in the reactivity series.	1, 3, 4	Lit, Starter 2, Main, Plenary 2
	Deduce a rule from data about which reactions will occur or not, based on the reactivity series.	4	Main
↓	Write a suitable fair test question and plan in detail which variables to control and how to control them.		Main

Literacy
Students use scientific terminology when explaining experimental observations and the uses of the reactivity series.

Students will also write a mnemonic for their homework to help them remember the order of metals in the reactivity series.

Key Words
reactivity series

GCSE link
4.4.1.2/5.4.1.2 The reactivity series

When metals react with other substances the metal atoms form positive ions. The reactivity of a metal is related to its tendency to form positive ions. Metals can be arranged in order of their reactivity in a reactivity series. The metals potassium, sodium, lithium, calcium, magnesium, zinc, iron and copper can be put in order of their reactivity from their reactions with water and dilute acids.

Answers from the student book

In-text questions	**A** calcium hydroxide and hydrogen gas **B** sodium + water → sodium hydroxide + hydrogen **C** zinc
Activity	**Tim's tin** From Tim's data, tin is less reactive than magnesium but more reactive than copper. In order to learn more about the reactivity of tin, Tim should repeat the reaction with hydrochloric acid using other metals. He should also carry out the reactions of metals with water and metals with oxygen for all metals tested. This is because metals follow similar reactivity trends for all these reactions.

Summary questions	**1** (6 marks) Any six from: Sodium reacts very vigorously with water. Sodium is near the top of the reactivity series. Sodium is more reactive than copper. Iron is more reactive than copper. Gold is less reactive than copper. Gold does not react with oxygen, water, or acid. Gold is unreactive. **2** Products: lithium hydroxide and hydrogen Word equation: lithium + water → lithium hydroxide + hydrogen (2 marks) **3** Extended response question (6 marks). Example answers: Nickel is less reactive than iron. Iron reacts with water and air but nickel does not. Iron reacts more vigorously with acid than nickel. Nickel is more reactive than lead. Neither nickel nor lead react with water and air, but nickel reacts with acid whereas lead does not. **4** Calcium and metals above it in the reactivity series react vigorously with cold water. Copper and metals below it in the reactivity series do not react with cold water or steam. The metals between calcium and copper react with steam but not cold water. (4 marks)

kerboodle

Starter	Support/Extension	Resources
How do different metals react with water? (10 min) Remind students that some metals react with water to produce metal hydroxides and hydrogen gas. This can be done by demonstrating the reactions of Group 1 metals in water again. This time the vigour of the reaction can be linked to reactivity. Show what happens when magnesium in placed in water, to show that some metals (less reactive than calcium) react only very slowly with cold water. Magnesium and zinc, though, do react with steam. **Comparing metals** (5 min) Ask students to predict the relative reactivity of gold compared to iron based on daily observations.	**Extension:** Students may suggest reasons why steam triggers a reaction when water does not. This can lead to a gentle introduction of activation energy. **Support:** Students may require hints, for example, why is jewellery made from gold, or why do we need to oil bike chains?	

Main	Support/Extension	Resources
Comparing the reactivity of metals (40 min) This activity is one of the AQA Enquiry process activities. Students plan an investigation to test the reactivity of three metals (sodium, magnesium, and copper) in water and in acid. In their planning, they will need to write a fair test enquiry question and decide how to control variables so that the investigation is fair. They then carry out this experiment, note down observations in a results table, and answer the questions that follow. There should be a class discussion after the experiment to go through experimental observations and conclusions regarding the order of reactivity. Students should also be encouraged to offer their experimental methods for peer assessment during the class discussion.	**Support:** The accompanying support sheet provides students with prompts when planning the investigation, as well as a suggested results table to fill in observations. **Extension:** Students use their observations and knowledge of the reactivity series to deduce a rule about which metals will react with cold water.	**Practical:** Comparing the reactivity of metals **Skill sheet:** Planning investigations **Skill sheet:** Recording results

Plenary	Support/Extension	Resources
Ordering metals (10 min) Students explain what the reactivity series is and what it can tell you about the reactions of elements. Students then re-order the metals given on the interactive resource according to their position in the reactivity series. **Guess who** (5 min) Students make up a 'Guess Who'-style game about the identity of different metals using their existing knowledge about the reactions each metal can undergo as clues to their identities.	**Extension:** Students should give further details on each metal, for example, by giving word equations.	**Interactive:** Ordering metals

Homework
Students write a mnemonic to help them remember the order of metals in the reactivity series.

6.2.6 Metal displacement reactions

Securing Mastery Goals

- 3.6.1 Describe an oxidation, displacement, or metal–acid reaction with a word equation. (Pt 4/4)
- 3.6.1 Use particle diagrams to represent oxidation, displacement and metal-acid reactions. (Pt 3/3)

Enquiry processes

- 2.12 Make an experimental prediction.

Band	Outcome	Checkpoint	
		Question	Activity
Know	State which metal is more reactive in a pair of named metals.	B, 1	Starter 1, Main, Plenary 1, Plenary 2
	State where different metals are found in the reactivity series.		Lit, Starter 1, Plenary 1, Plenary 2
	Use observations from experiment to state whether or not a displacement reaction has occurred.		Main
Apply	Predict if a given pair of substances will react in displacement reactions.	1, 2	Main
	Use the reactivity series to explain displacement reactions.	B	Main
	Use word equations and particle diagrams to represent displacement reactions.	3	Main, Plenary 1
Extend	Explain predictions about displacement reactions.	2	Main, Plenary 1, Plenary 2
	Devise a model to explain displacement reactions.		Homework
	Suggest the identity of unknown metals, given information about their reactions.	4	

Maths

Students use the mathematical symbol > when stating the order of reactivity of metals from their experiment.

MyMaths More support for the maths skills in this section can be found on MyMaths.

Literacy

Students organise ideas and information in a coherent manner when completing the student-book activity.

Students use scientific terminology when explaining key concepts demonstrated in their experimental observations.

GCSE link

4.4.1.2/5.4.1.2 The reactivity series

A more reactive metal can displace a less reactive metal from a compound.

Key Words

displace, **displacement**, thermite reaction

Answers from the student book

In-text questions	**A** A reaction where a more reactive element displaces a less reactive element from a compound. **B** Copper is less reactive than magnesium (lower in the reactivity series).
Activity	**Planning paragraphs** Credit suitable prose to explain displacement reactions. Possible information to include in each paragraph: What a displacement reaction is. Displacement of metal salts. Displacement of metal oxides. Using the reactivity series to predict displacements.

Summary questions	1 In a displacement reaction, a **more** reactive metal pushes out a **less** reactive metal from its compound. For example, **aluminium** displaces **iron** from **iron** oxide. (5 marks)
	2 Reactions a, c, and d will occur, since the element on its own is more reactive (positioned higher in the reactivity series) than the metal found in the compound. (8 marks)
	3 Diagram showing a number of spheres (for example eight) arranged in two or more rows to represent magnesium, as well as eight spheres of copper and eight spheres of oxygen arranged alternately in rows to represent copper oxide. Two products – one showing magnesium and oxygen atoms arranged alternately in rows, the other showing copper atoms only, arranged in rows. The total number of atoms of each element in the reactant and product should be the same. (3 marks)
	4 Metal X is above lead in the reactivity series, since it displaces lead from lead oxide. It is below aluminium because it does not displace aluminium from aluminium oxide. Metal X could be iron or zinc. (3 marks)

Starter	Support/Extension	Resources
Demonstrating displacement (10 min) Set up a boiling tube containing silver nitrate solution and a coiled-up piece of copper wire, hooked over the edge of the boiling tube. Ask students to find silver and copper in the reactivity series, and to predict what may happen in the boiling tube. Introduce the concept of displacement, and ask students to suggest what they will see in the boiling tube by the end of the lesson.	**Extension:** Students should offer the word equation for this reaction based on the definition of displacement.	
The thermite reaction (10 min) Demonstrate the thermite reaction. (Use video clips from the Internet as an alternative.) Explain that aluminium displaces iron from iron oxide, forming aluminium oxide and iron. Introduce this as a displacement reaction based on the positions of iron and aluminium in the reactivity series.	**Extension:** Encourage students to list the signs of a chemical reaction here (including the fact that this is a useful exothermic reaction that produces molten iron).	

Main	Support/Extension	Resources
Will a displacement reaction occur? (35 min) Students predict whether displacement reactions will occur between combinations of four metals and their nitrates (Mg, Zn, Cu, and Pb). Students then carry out the experiment, record their observations, and answer questions that follow.	**Support:** An access sheet is provided where students are not required to use the reactivity series to predict the possibility of reactions. Students carry out the experiment for only copper, magnesium, and their nitrates.	**Practical:** Will a displacement reaction occur? **Skill sheet:** Recording results

Plenary	Support/Extension	Resources
Revisiting the displacement demonstration (10 min) Look back at the demonstration of copper wire in silver nitrate, set up at the start of the lesson. Ask students to describe what they can see (they should see silver solid on the coiled wire or in the bottom of the boiling tube). Ask students to explain in their own words what has happened to the particles and why. Students should use the reactivity series, the word displacement, and a word equation in their explanation.	**Extension:** Students should suggest how silver can be separated from copper nitrate solution.	**Interactive:** True or false?
True or false? (10 min) Students use their knowledge of metal displacement to decide if statements given on the interactive resource are true or false. Mini-whiteboards may be used at this stage to encourage whole-class participation. Students should be asked to justify their answers using the reactivity series, and write word equations for the displacement reactions that occur.	**Extension:** Students may be able to suggest other sentences to add to the interactive resource, with the rest of the class deciding if the statement is true or false, and correcting if necessary.	

Homework	Support/Extension	
Students draw a cartoon to show and explain what happens during a displacement reaction.	**Extension:** Students should write a short paragraph to explain the strengths and weaknesses of their cartoon model.	

6 Reactions: Checkpoint

Checkpoint lesson routes

The route through this lesson can be determined using the Checkpoint assessment.

Percentage pass marks are supplied in the Checkpoint teacher notes.

Route A (support)
Students can work through the revision activity, with support from teacher-led demonstrations and explanations. The tasks cover the outcomes listed below.

Route B (extension)
Students produce a leaflet about displacement reactions and the reactivity series.

Progression to *Apply*

Know outcome	Apply outcome	Making progress
Describe the physical and chemical properties of metals and non-metals.	Identify an unknown element from its chemical and physical properties.	Show students examples of a metal, such as a sheet of copper, and a non-metal, such as a lump of sulfur. Ask students to compare their easily observable properties. Then demonstrate adding universal indicator to samples of metal oxide solutions (e.g., sodium oxide – use NaOH) and non-metal oxide solutions (e.g., nitrogen dioxide – use HNO_3). Students then tackle Task 1.
Know the pH of acid, alkali and neutral.	Describe a method for how to make a neutral solution.	Demonstrate adding universal indicator solution to solutions of different pH. Elicit from students the pH range of acidic and alkaline solutions, and the pH of a neutral solution. Then demonstrate how to make a neutral solution by adding copper oxide powder to dilute hydrochloric acid. Students then complete Task 2.
State that mixing an acid and an alkali is a chemical reaction known as neutralisation. Indicators are substances used to identify whether unknown solutions are acidic or alkaline.	Explain how neutralisation reactions are used in a range of situations. Identify the best indicator to distinguish between solutions of different pH.	Students should be able to use Task 2 to help them with the first part of Task 3. You could also use universal indicator solution to demonstrate the change in pH as an acid is added to an alkaline solution. Demonstrate using red litmus, blue litmus, and universal indicator to test samples of acidic and alkaline solutions. Encourage students to realise that only universal indicator can show you if a substance is neutral.
Name the strong and weak acids.	Link strong and weak acids to pH values. Describe the difference between acid strength and acid concentration.	Show students samples of hydrochloric, sulfuric, and nitric acid in lab bottles. Then show them a packet of citric acid for food use and a bottle of vinegar. Students state which acids are strong and which are weak. Then use molecular models to demonstrate the difference between strong and weak acids, as shown in the Student Book. Students then complete Task 4.
Know some metals reaction with acids to make hydrogen.	Use word equations to describe oxidation and displacement reactions.	For Task 5, demonstrate burning iron filings by sprinkling them into a Bunsen burner flame. Help students name the product of the reaction (iron oxide) and write a word equation for the general reaction of a metal with oxygen. Repeat the procedure with zinc and hydrochloric acid, and with copper and silver nitrate solution (the latter reaction needs to be left for at least 39 minutes).
State that metals can be arranged in a reactivity series of how readily they react with other substances.	Place an unfamiliar metal into the reactivity series when given information about its reactions.	Demonstrate adding magnesium and copper to dilute hydrochloric acid. Ask which metal is higher in the reactivity series, and how students know this. Students then tackle Task 6.

134

Answers to End-of-Big Idea questions

1 Sweat – acidic, blood – alkaline, urine – acidic (3 marks)

2a Two from: same sized pieces of metal, same volume of acid, same concentration of acid. (2 marks)

b Wear eye protection to prevent corrosive acid entering his eye and causing damage. (2 marks)

c Zinc – closest to the top of the reactivity series. (1 mark)

d Hydrogen (1 mark)

3a sweet cherry (1 mark)

b blueberry (1 mark)

c sweet cherry, pineapple, strawberry (3 marks)

d Add an acidic substance to neutralise some of the alkaline substances in the soil (making the pH suitable for growing strawberries). (2 marks)

4 Points to include:

Pour dilute hydrochloric acid into a conical flask/beaker.

Add a few drops of universal indicator solution from a teat pipette.

Slowly add sodium hydroxide solution from a beaker, a little at a time, to the flask/beaker, whilst stirring with a stirring rod.

When the colour of the mixture shows that the mixture is neutral, stop adding the sodium hydroxide solution. (6 marks)

5a lithium hydroxide, hydrogen (2 marks)

b magnesium, oxygen (2 marks)

c zinc chloride, hydrogen (2 marks)

d sulfuric acid, hydrogen (2 marks)

6a X and Z – because the metal elements are more reactive than the metals in the compounds. In each case the metal element can displace the metal in the compound. (4 marks)

b iron + copper oxide → iron oxide + copper

OR iron + lead oxide → iron oxide + lead (2 marks)

Case study

Know	Apply	Extend
1–2 marks	3–4 marks	5–6 marks
• Instructions are given for one test, such as adding the metals to water, to acid, or heating the metal in air.	• The instructions include two tests such as adding the metals to water, to acid, or heating the metal in air.	• The instructions include three tests such as adding the metals to water, to acid, and heating the metal in air.
• The instructions do not state how the test results show the order of reactivity.	• The instructions state that the metals that react most vigorously with these reagents are the most reactive.	• The instructions state that the metals that react most vigorously with these reagents are the most reactive.
• The instructions give one way of making the test fair, for example, using similarly-sized pieces of metal, or acid samples of the same concentration.	• The instructions give two ways of making the tests fair, for example, by using similarly-sized pieces of metal or samples of acid of the same concentration.	• The instructions state that the tests can be made fair by using similarly-sized pieces of metal, samples of acid of the same concentration, Bunsen flames of the same temperature, and so on.
• The instructions are not clear, and would be difficult to follow.	• The instructions lack detail, but overall are clear and easy to follow.	• The instructions are detailed, clear, and easy to follow.
• There is no results table, or one that is poorly laid out. Some variables may be missing from the results table.	• The results table is clearly laid out with all variables involved. Some units may be missing.	• The results table is clearly set out with all variables involved including their units.

kerboodle

6 Part 1 Checkpoint assessment (automarked)
6 Part 1 Checkpoint: Revision
6 Part 1 Checkpoint: Extension
6.1 Progress task, 6.2 Progress task

National curriculum links for this unit	
Topic	**National Curriculum topic**
Space	Space physics
Earth structure	Earth and atmosphere

In this Big Idea students will learn:

- sedimentary, igneous and metamorphic rocks can be interconverted over millions of years through weathering and erosion, heat and pressure, and melting and cooling
- the three layers that make up the Earth are the crust, the mantle, and the core
- how to explain the properties of rocks based on how they were formed and how to construct a rock cycle
- how to identify the causes of weathering and erosion
- how to model the planets rotating on tilted axes and orbiting the Sun, and moons orbiting planets, which helps to explain the appearance of planets and moons
- we see some objects, like stars, because they emit light and others, like planets and moons, because they reflect light

- light from the Sun spreads out, and this helps to explain the intensity of the Sun
- seasons happen because of the tilted axis of the Earth, which affects day length, visibility of objects from Earth, and the amount of sunlight during the year
- our Solar system is a tiny part of a galaxy, and there are billions of galaxies in the Universe
- light takes minutes to reach us from the Sun, years to reach us from our nearest star, and billions of years to reach us from other galaxies, and we use light years as a convenient unit of distance
- space exploration is affected by the scale of the universe
- ideas about the universe have changed as new evidence has been collected.

AQA Enquiry process activities

Activity	Section
3.7.1 Model the processes that are responsible for rock formation and link these to the rock features.	7.1.4 The rock cycle
3.7.2 Relate observations of changing day length to an appropriate model of the solar system.	7.2.3 The Earth

Preparing for Key Stage 4 Success

Knowledge Underpinning knowledge is covered in this Big Idea for KS4 study of:	• 4.9.1.4/5.9.1.4 How carbon dioxide increased • 4.9.1.1/5.9.1.1 Our solar system • 4.9.1.2/5.9.1.2 The life cycle of a star • 4.9.1.3/5.9.1.3 Orbital motion, natural and artificial satellites • 4.9.2/5.9.2 Red shift

Maths
 	
Skills developed in Big Idea 2
	1 Arithmetic and numerical computation: **a** Recognise and use expressions in decimal form (7.2.1)
	   b Recognise and use expressions in standard form (7.2.1)
	   c Use ratios, fractions and percentages (7.2.1)
	2 Handling data: **a** Use an appropriate number of significant figures (7.2.1)
	   b Find arithmetic means (7.1.3)
	   c Construct and interpret frequency tables and diagrams, bar charts and histograms (7.1.1 and 7.1.5)
	   h Make order of magnitude calculations (7.2.1)
	3 Algebra: **a** Understand and use the symbols: $=, <, <<, >>, >, \propto, \sim$ (7.2.1)
	4 Graphs: **a** Translate information between graphical and numeric form (7.2.2)
	5 Geometry and trigonometry: **b** visualise and represent 2D and 3D forms including two dimensional representations of 3D objects (7.1.1 and 7.1.4)

Literacy Skills developed in Big Idea 2	• Identify meaning in scientific text, taking into account potential bias (7.4.4)		
	• Summarise a range of information from different sources (7.2.1, 7.2.2, 7.2.3, 7.2.4)		
	• Use scientific terms confidently and correctly in discussions and writing (all sections)		
	• Collaboration and contribution to group discussions (7.1.1, 7.1.2)		
	• Identify main ideas and supporting evidence in text (7.2.1, 7.2.2, 7.2.3, 7.2.4)		
	• Use largely correct form in a range of writing styles and text, and include information relevant to the audience (7.1.5, 7.2.1, 7.2.2, 7.2.3, 7.2.4)		
	• Ideas are organised into well-developed, linked paragraphs. (7.1.1, 7.1.4, 7.1.5, 7.2.1, 7.2.2, 7.2.3)		
Assessment Skills	• Extended response questions (7.1.1, 7.1.2, 7.2.1, 7.2.2, 7.2.3, 7.2.4) (End-of-Big Idea questions Q6).		
	• Application of Enquiry Processes (7.1.1, 7.1.3, 7.1.4, 7.2.1, 7.2.2, 7.2.3, 7.2.4) (End-of-Big Idea questions Q2).		

KS2 Link	Check before	Checkpoint	Catch-up
Simple descriptions of the three states of matter.	7.1.1 The structure of the Earth	Students name two materials for each state, giving the characteristics of each state of matter.	Give simple materials to classify, such as chocolate and water.
Rocks can be grouped according to their appearance and properties.	7.1.2 Sedimentary rocks	Students use hand lenses to group rocks according to their appearance.	Provide students with a list of possible properties to look out for when observing rocks and repeat the exercise.
The properties of everyday materials, for example hardness and solubility.	7.1.5 Ceramics	Ask students to write a list of different properties a material can possess.	Students use a card sort activity to match the properties of substances to their definitions.
Properties of materials that make them suitable for particular uses.	7.1.5 Ceramics	Students explain why they wouldn't use lead to make a shopping bag.	Compare items with their uses, for example, a strong iron nail compared with silk used in clothing.
The Sun, Earth, and Moon are roughly spherical bodies.	7.2.1 The night sky	Students describe the Sun, Moon, and Earth using three words for each.	Students group objects as ones that give out light and ones that reflect light.
The Earth orbits the Sun.	7.2.2 The solar system 7.2.3 The Earth	Students sketch the Sun and Earth using arrows to show how they move relative to each other.	Show photographs of the Sun, Moon, and Earth.
Earth spins on its axis to create day and night. This causes day length and temperature change during the year.	7.2.3 The Earth	Students explain in words why we have day and night.	Demonstrate using a globe and lamp.
The Moon orbits the Earth.	7.2.4 The Moon and changing ideas	Students sketch the Moon and Earth using arrows to show how they move relative to each other.	Two students act out the relative motion for the class, or demonstrate using a globe and a tennis ball.

Key Stage 2 Quiz: Physics, Key Stage 2 Quiz: Chemistry
7 Part 1 End-of-Big Idea test (foundation)
7 Part 1 End-of-Big Idea test (foundation) mark scheme
7 Part 1 End-of-Big Idea test (higher)
7 Part 1 End-of-Big Idea test (higher) mark scheme

Answers to Picture Puzzler
Key Words
golf club, astronaut, lightning, ant, x-ray, yawn
The key word is **galaxy**.
Close up
Image of Neil Armstrong's footprint on the Moon.

MyMaths

You can find additional support for the maths skills covered in this Big Idea on **MyMaths**,
including drawing and interpreting graphs.

7.1.1 The structure of the Earth

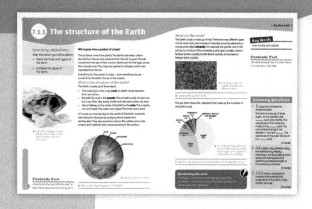

This spread covers prerequisite knowledge, key words and facts for AQA KS3 Science topic 3.7.1 Earth structure.

Securing Mastery Goals
- 3.7.1 The three rock layers inside Earth are the crust, the mantle and the core.

Enquiry processes
- 2.4 Select a good way to display data.

Band	Outcome	Checkpoint	
		Question	**Activity**
Know	Name the layers of the Earth.	A, 1	Starter 2, Main 2, Plenary 1, Plenary 2
	State what a mineral is.	B	Main 1
	Design a simple model of the Earth using information about its structure.		Main 2
Apply	Describe properties of the different layers of the Earth's structure.	1, 3	Starter 2, Main 2, Plenary 1, Plenary 2
	Explain that most rocks are mixtures of minerals.	3	Main 1
	Describe advantages and disadvantages of a given model of the Earth's structure.		Starter 2, Main 2
Extend	Compare the different layers of the Earth in terms of their properties.	3	Starter 2, Main 2, Plenary 1, Plenary 2
	Interpret data about the elements that make up the Earth's crust.	C	Lit
	Explain why models are good or poor representations of the Earth's structure in terms of materials used.		Starter 2, Main 2

Maths
Students interpret numerical data in tables and charts to extract information, draw conclusions, and ask questions.

MyMaths More support for the maths skills in this section can be found on MyMaths.

Literacy
Students use scientific terminology when describing the composition and properties of the Earth.

GCSE link
4.10.1.1 (GCSE Chemistry)/ 5.10.1.1 Using the Earth's resources and sustainable development

Finite resources from the Earth, oceans and atmosphere are processed to provide energy and materials.

Key Words
crust, mantle, core

Answers from the student book

In-text questions	A From the outer layer: crust, mantle, core
	B naturally occurring elements or compounds
	C oxygen, silicon, aluminium, iron, calcium, sodium
Activity	**Questioning the crust**
	Questions should be linked to the data in the pie chart, ideally asking for quantitative comparisons.

Summary questions	1 crust, solid, nickel, liquid (4 marks)
	2 It is not possible to observe the mantle directly, since it is not technically possible to gather samples of the mantle in normal circumstances, nor to dig through the crust to reach the mantle. For this reason, indirect methods, such as studying shock waves from earthquakes and examining materials brought to the surface by volcanoes, are used instead. (2 marks)
	3 Extended response question (6 marks). Example answers:
	The crust and mantle are both made up of solid rock.
	The mantle can flow and the crust cannot flow.
	Like the crust, the inner core is solid.
	The outer core is the only liquid layer of the Earth.
	It can flow, as can the mantle.
	The core is mainly iron and nickel.

kerboodle

Starter	Support/Extension	Resources
Imagining the scale of the Earth (10 min) Display pictures of mountain ranges and ocean trenches from the internet and tell students that these landforms can be around the height of 140 double-decker buses for mountains, and over 380 double-decker buses deep for ocean trenches. Ask students to consider how big these are in comparison to the size of the Earth. Explain that these structures are part of a small layer on the outside of the Earth called the crust, and would account for less than 0.5% of the overall planet.	**Extension:** Students should suggest what they think lies beneath the crust, justifying their suggestions.	
In what ways is the Earth like an apple or a Scotch egg? (5 min) Show students an apple cut in half, and a Scotch egg cut in half. Ask students to give ideas about how these are similar to Earth (if the Earth were also cut in half). Some students may be able to offer suggestions before the cross-section of the Earth is shown.	**Extension:** Students should give advantages and weaknesses of the models shown. For example, a weakness of the apple model is that the flesh of the apple (the mantle) does not flow.	

Main	Support/Extension	Resources
What's in a rock? (10 min) Show students samples of a few minerals, and explain that a mineral is a single substance, which can be an element or a compound, that is found naturally. Tell students that most types of rock are mixtures of minerals. Display a sample of granite to illustrate this point.		
Modelling Earth's structure (30 min) Students label a diagram showing the structure of the Earth and include a brief description of each layer. They will then consider a student's model of the Earth in terms of how well it represents the internal structure. Students answer questions based on this model, before suggesting improvements and designing their own model of the Earth's structure.	**Support:** Prompt students to think about how different properties of the layers can be shown using materials in their proposed models.	**Activity:** Modelling Earth's structure

Plenary	Support/Extension	Resources
The Earth (5 min) Students place the layers of the Earth given on the interactive screen into the correct order, starting from the core. This step can be carried out using mini-whiteboards to increase class participation. Students should then offer descriptions of each layer.	**Extension:** Students may be able to re-order the layers of the Earth according to their depths, starting with the largest.	**Interactive:** The Earth
Describing the Earth (10 min) Provide students with mini-whiteboards and call out a layer of the Earth. Students write down as many facts as they can about that layer. Discuss answers given. This can be done as a competition to see who can give unique facts about each layer.		

Homework		
Students make models showing the structure of the Earth, as described in their activity sheet.		

Securing Mastery Goals

- 3.7.1 Explain why a rock has a particular property based on how it was formed. (Pt 1/3)
- 3.7.1 Identify the causes of weathering and erosion and describe how they occur.

Exceeding Mastery Goals

- 3.7.1 Predict planetary conditions from descriptions of rocks on other planets.

Enquiry processes

- 2.3 Make a conclusion and explain it.

Band	Outcome	Checkpoint	
		Question	**Activity**
Know	State a property of sedimentary rocks.	B	Starter 2, Plenary 1
	Describe how sedimentary rocks are made.	C, 1	Starter 1, Main 1, Main 2, Plenary 1, Plenary 2, Homework
	State the processes shown by different models of the stages in sedimentary rock formation.		Main 2
Apply	Explain why a sedimentary rock has a particular property based on how it was formed.		Homework
	Identify the causes of weathering and erosion and describe how they occur.	2	Lit, Main 2, Plenary 1, Homework
	Explain how a given model represents a particular process in the formation of sedimentary rock.		Main 2
Extend	Predict planetary conditions from descriptions of rocks on other planets.	3	
	Explain in detail each stage in the formation of a sedimentary rock.		Lit, Main 1, Main 2, Plenary 1, Homework
	Evaluate strengths and weaknesses for models of sedimentary rock formation, giving reasons.		Main 2

Literacy
Students organise and sequence information to explain the formation of sedimentary rocks in the student-book activity and for homework.

Key Words
sedimentary, igneous, metamorphic, porous, weathering, sediment, erosion, transport, deposition, strata

Answers from the student book

In-text questions	A igneous, sedimentary, metamorphic
	B Sedimentary rocks are porous. They are usually soft and can be scratched easily.
	C weathering, transportation (erosion), deposition, compaction/cementation
Activity	**Sedimentary sequence**
	Give credit for accuracy, clarity, and engagement of audience during the talk.
	Talk should include the individual stages of the sedimentary rock formation process: weathering (physical, chemical, or biological), transportation (by water, ice, wind, or gravity), deposition, compaction/cementation.

Summary questions	1 Weathering breaks rock into pieces. Erosion breaks rock into smaller pieces and moves them away from their original rock. Transportation moves sediments far away from their original rock. Deposition is the settling of sediments. Compaction involves the weight of sediment above making sediments stick together. (5 marks) 2 Physical weathering can occur as a result of changes in temperature. For example, in freeze-thaw weathering, water gets into a crack in a rock. When it is very cold, the water freezes. The ice pushes against the sides of the crack. This happens many times, and breaks the rock. Chemical weathering happens when acids in rain react with substances in the rock. Biological weathering happens when plants and animals break up rocks. (6 marks) 3 The rocks are made up of layers/strata. They might have been formed as sediments were laid down in layers, perhaps under water in a lake or sea. (3 marks)

Starter	Support/Extension	Resources
Sediments and rocks (5 min) Show students some sediment, for example sand, and a sedimentary rock, for example, sandstone. State that the sediment can be turned into the stone. Ask students to give ideas on how they think this happens.	**Support**: Show students wet sand as a visual aid. **Extension**: Students compare the properties of sand and sandstone.	
Observing rock types (10 min) Provide students with hand lenses and examples of sedimentary rocks (sandstone), metamorphic rocks (slate), and igneous rocks (granite). Ask them to list features they can see for each rock type and ask whether they think the rocks come from the same 'family' given their observations.	**Support**: Give students rock samples grouped by rock type, and ask them to justify the groupings using observations. **Extension**: Students sort rocks into different types, comparing similarities and differences in properties.	

Main	Support/Extension	Resources
Sedimentary rocks (10 min) Explain that rocks form over thousands of years. There are three types of rock: igneous, metamorphic, and sedimentary. Explain that the different rock types form under different conditions and have unique features. Introduce sedimentary rocks as rocks that form from small fragments of other rocks and matter, called sediments. Explain the properties of sedimentary rock, with examples, and introduce the stages of formation: weathering, transportation, deposition, and compaction/cementation. Animations to show the stages of formation are readily available on the Internet.		
Modelling sedimentary rock formation (30 min) Students carry out simple experiments that model sedimentary rock formation processes, and then answer the questions that follow.	**Extension**: Students offer reasoned evaluations of the models in this activity.	**Practical**: Modelling sedimentary rock formation

Plenary	Support/Extension	Resources
Sedimentary rocks (10 min) Interactive resource where students complete a crossword on key words from the topic. They then place the key words in order to describe sedimentary rock formation.	**Extension**: Students improve the clues by adding more detail.	**Interactive**: Sedimentary rocks
Guess the process (5 min) Give simple descriptions of a stage of sedimentary rock formation. Students write the stage name on a mini-whiteboard. This can be turned into a competition where the first person to hold up the correct answer will get to make up the next question.		

Homework	Support/Extension	
Students draw a cartoon strip to show how a small pebble that was loosened by weathering goes on to form part of a new sedimentary rock.	**Extension**: Students explain in their cartoons why sedimentary rocks are often soft and porous.	

7.1.3 Igneous and metamorphic rocks

Securing Mastery Goals
- 3.7.1 Explain why a rock has a particular property based on how it was formed. (Pt 2/3)

Exceeding Mastery Goals
- 3.7.1 Identify circumstances that indicate fast processes of change on Earth and those that indicate slower processes.

Enquiry processes
- 2.12 Make an experimental prediction.

Band	Outcome	Checkpoint	
		Question	Activity
Know	State one difference between igneous and metamorphic rocks.		Main 1, Plenary 1, Homework
	Describe how igneous and metamorphic rocks are formed.	B, 1	Starter 1, Starter 2, Main 1, Main 2, Plenary 2
	Describe what you see when a substance representing lava is cooled.		Main 2
Apply	Explain in detail how igneous and metamorphic rocks form.		Main 1, Main 2, Plenary 2, Homework
	Explain why igneous and metamorphic rocks have particular properties based on how they were formed.	3	Main 1, Main 2, Plenary 1, Plenary 2, Homework
	Predict observations when a substance representing lava is cooled at different temperatures.		Main 2
Extend	Discuss examples of rocks that illustrate the different methods of formation of igneous and metamorphic rocks.	B, 3, 4	Main 1, Plenary 2, Homework
	Identify circumstances that indicate fast processes of change on Earth and those that indicate slower processes.	4	Main 2
	Predict observations when a substance representing lava is cooled, using knowledge about igneous rock formation to explain the answer.		Main 2

Maths
Students calculate the mean amount of granite quarried per week at Rubislaw quarry when completing the student-book activity.

Students record numerical comparisons of crystal sizes in salol for their experimental observations.

MyMaths More support for the maths skills in this section can be found on MyMaths.

Literacy
Students organise ideas and information using scientific terminology when giving reasons for their hypotheses in their experiment.

Key Words
durable, magma, lava

Answers from the student book

In-text questions	**A** hard, durable, and not porous
	B Marble is formed when limestone below the Earth's surface is heated. Slate is formed when high underground pressure squashes mudstone.
	C Not porous and made up of layers so easily split into thin sheets.
Activity	**Granite quarry** Years = 1971 − 1740 = 231; weeks = 231 × 52 = 12 012; mass/week = 6 000 000 ÷ 12 012 = 500 tonnes/week

Summary questions	1 metamorphic, igneous, igneous, metamorphic, non-porous, crystals, hard (7 marks)
	2 Igneous rocks form when liquid rock cools and freezes. When liquid rock freezes slowly the particles have time to arrange themselves into big crystals. This is how granite is formed. When liquid rock freezes quickly the crystals are small because there is less time for particles to arrange themselves into crystals. This is how basalt is formed. (3 marks)
	3 Granite forms when liquid rock freezes. Its particles arrange themselves to form crystals. There are no gaps between the crystals, so granite is non-porous. (4 marks)
	4 Rock X has bigger crystals. This means that when it was formed from magma its particles had more time to arrange themselves into crystals. For this reason rock X formed more slowly. (3 marks)

Starter	Support/Extension	Resources
Giant's Causeway (5 min) Display a photograph of the Giant's Causeway. Students consider how the natural landmark was formed. Discuss that the causeway is actually a collection of basalt columns, which formed when lava cooled rapidly. This rapid cooling and contraction formed the shapes seen.	**Extension:** Ask students about the 'formation' of Stonehenge. They offer similarities and differences between the sites.	
What happens when a volcano erupts? (5 min) Show a video clip from the Internet of lava erupting from a volcano. Students recap where the lava comes from and what happens to it once it leaves the volcano. This recaps the structure of the Earth, before introducing the other two types of rock. Introduce the difference between magma (liquid rock underground) and lava (on the surface).	**Extension:** Students say where magma is found relative to the other layers that form the structure of the Earth.	

Main	Support/Extension	Resources
Igneous and metamorphic rocks (20 min) Introduce igneous and metamorphic rocks. Discuss that igneous rocks are formed when liquid rock cools down. This can happen slowly within the Earth's crust or rapidly outside the crust (including under water). Metamorphic rocks are formed when other types of rocks are under high pressures and/or temperatures but do not melt. Samples of basalt, granite, obsidian, slate, marble, and schist could be passed around so that students can observe the different properties of each rock type (e.g., both have crystals but some types of metamorphic rock have layers, neither are porous, and metamorphic rocks may contain distorted fossils whilst igneous rocks do not).	**Support:** Students recap properties of sedimentary rocks before moving on. They should focus on identifying properties of each rock under a hand lens. **Extension:** Students use observations to group the rock samples, and to compare differences in properties between the rock types.	
What determines crystal size in igneous rock? (20 min) Students read a short text that gives information about the formation and crystal sizes of granite and basalt, before writing a hypothesis on the relationship between crystal sizes in igneous rock and the temperature of the environment during formation. Students carry out a practical to mimic igneous rock formation using salol, and use their observations to answer questions that follow.	**Support:** The support sheet offers students a simpler text and a writing frame to help with their hypothesis.	**Practical:** What determines crystal size in igneous rock? **Skill sheet:** Hypothesis

Plenary	Support/Extension	Resources
Properties of rock types (10 min) Interactive resource where students complete a paragraph on the properties of the three types of rocks.	**Support:** Students explain how each property is observed.	**Interactive:** Properties of rock types
Modelling rock formation (10 min) Students walk randomly around the room whilst staying in contact with each other. Give 30 seconds for students to order themselves into lines. Repeat the process but only give 10 seconds. Students are likely to be in smaller lines. Moving one end of a line forces students to move to new places. Students describe how these models represent igneous and metamorphic rock formation.	**Extension:** Students should offer strengths and weaknesses of these models.	

Homework	Support/Extension	
Students complete the practical sheet. They then find names and pictures of a sedimentary, igneous, and metamorphic rock. They should describe the properties and uses of each.	**Extension:** Students link the properties of the rocks to their formation.	

7.1.4 The rock cycle

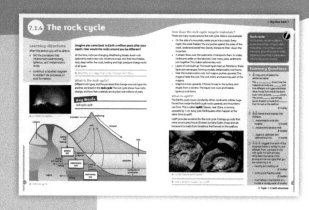

Securing Mastery Goals
- 3.7.1 Construct a labelled diagram to identify the processes of the rock cycle.

Exceeding Mastery Goals
- 3.7.1 Describe similarities and differences between the rock cycle and everyday physical and chemical processes.

Enquiry processes
- 2.3 Make a conclusion and explain it.

Enquiry processes activity
- 3.7.1 Model the processes that are responsible for rock formation and link these to the rock features.

Band	Outcome	Checkpoint	
		Question	Activity
Know ↓	Give simple facts about how a rock can be changed from one type to another.	A, 1, 2	Lit, Main 1, Main 2, Plenary 1, Plenary 2, Homework
	State what happens to wax in a model rock cycle.		Main 2
Apply ↓	Use the rock cycle to explain how the material in rocks is recycled.	A, 1, 2	Lit, Main 1, Plenary 1, Plenary 2, Homework
	Describe how changes in the wax used to represent a rock represent the real rock cycle.		Main 2
Extend ↓	Give a detailed description and explanation of the journey of material through the rock cycle.		Lit, Main 1, Plenary 1, Plenary 2
	Suggest similarities and differences between the rock cycle and everyday physical and chemical processes.	3	Main 2

Maths
Students consider the timescales taken for a rock to travel through the rock cycle, during this lesson.

Literacy
Students organise information effectively and in a logical order for the student-book activity.

Key Words
rock cycle, uplift

Answers from the student book

In-text questions	**A** One from: weathering breaks down existing rock, sediments join together to make new rock, lava freezes to make rock, high pressure and/or high temperature deep within the crust alters rocks of all types. **B** Uplift is the process by which huge forces inside the Earth push rocks upwards.
Activity	**Rock route** Paragraphs should describe processes of the rock cycle, be clearly organised, and have events in the rock cycle occurring in a logical order. An example is provided in the corresponding page in the student book.

Summary questions	**1** rock cycle, recycled, uplift, mountains, limestone (5 marks)
	2a melting (1 mark)
	  b cooling and freezing (2 marks)
	  c cementation or compaction (1 mark)
	3a Like rock being heated and melted underground to become magma. (2 marks)
	  b Like igneous rock being formed from magma. (2 marks)
	  c Like sediments falling to the bottom of a lake or sea. (2 marks)

Starter	Support/Extension	Resources
The rock cycle (10 min) Students find key words for the lesson in the wordsearch on the interactive resource. Students should suggest what they think new words mean and, as a recap, state the definition of words they have already met. This activity allows you to gauge the confidence levels of students in terms of their understanding of the topic so far.	**Support**: If this activity reveals gaps in students' knowledge of this topic, time should be spent recapping words that are not fully understood.	**Interactive**: The rock cycle
Chocolate rocks (5 min) Provide students with cut-up chunks of three different chocolate bars or cakes. Ask them to decide which rock type they most closely resemble and why. Students should be considering the arrangement of grains, presence of fossils, and so on. (A layered chocolate bar = sedimentary, marble effect chocolate = metamorphic, and chocolate honeycomb = igneous.) Ensure that students do not eat in the laboratory.		

Main	Support/Extension	Resources
Introducing the rock cycle (20 min) Display a diagram of the rock cycle on the board. Discuss that the materials that make up rocks are constantly recycled over millions of years and that, over this time scale, the particles that make up these materials will be part of several different rock types. Effectively, over millions of years, rocks change from one type to another over and over again.	**Support**: Students may be prompted to use a specific starting point for their routes.	
Ask students to work in pairs or small groups to identify a possible route around the rock cycle, using as many scientific key words (from Starter 1) as possible, before presenting possible routes in a class discussion.		
Modelling the rock cycle (20 min) This activity is one of the AQA Enquiry process activities. Students carry out a short practical where they use wax to model the processes in the formation of sedimentary, metamorphic, and igneous rocks as part of the rock cycle. They will then answer questions that follow, linking parts of the model to different rock formations, and evaluating the strengths and weaknesses of the models used.	**Support**: The accompanying support sheet provides students with a suggested table to record their observations during the experiment. **Extension**: Students answer question 3 in the Student book, which asks them to suggest similarities and differences between the rock cycle and everyday physical and chemical processes.	**Practical**: Modelling the rock cycle **Skill sheet**: Recording results

Plenary	Support/Extension	Resources
Rock cycle sentences (5 min) Students use as many key words as possible to write sentences about the processes within the rock cycle in a logical order. Students present their answers to each other in pairs.	**Support**: Allow students to work in small groups.	
Rock cycle describing game (10 min) In a clear open space, have the three rock type names written on large pieces of paper laid on the floor, placed as vertices of a triangle. Divide students in the class to make three groups and place each group on one vertex. Students must describe to another student how they move from one rock type to another. A correct answer allows the student to move; an incorrect answer means the student must sit back down. The winner is the person who can move around the rock cycle in the shortest amount of time.	**Extension**: Students describe the difference between intrusive and extrusive igneous rocks during their path.	

Homework	Support/Extension	
Students produce a coloured poster of the rock cycle, with full labels and descriptions of each possible stage.	**Extension**: Students must include the difference between intrusive and extrusive igneous rocks in their diagrams.	

Securing Mastery Goals
- 3.7.1 Explain why a rock has a particular property based on how it was formed. (Pt 3/3)

Exceeding Mastery Goals
- 3.7.1 Suggest how ceramics might be similar to some types of rock.

Enquiry processes
- 2.10 Write a fair test enquiry question.
- 2.11 Identify control variables.
- 2.13 Identify risks and hazards.
- 2.13 Identify control measures.

Band	Outcome	Checkpoint	
		Question	Activity
Know	List the properties of ceramics.	B, 1	Lit, Starter 2, Plenary 1, Plenary 2
	List some uses of ceramics.	C	Lit, Plenary 1, Plenary 2
	Suggest a simple method for comparing the strength of ceramic materials given a choice of apparatus.		Main 2
Apply	Use data on properties to decide which materials might be ceramics.	2	
	Explain why properties of ceramics make them suitable for their uses.		Lit, Main 1, Plenary 1, Plenary 2
	Plan a method for comparing the strength of ceramic materials, including devising a fair test question, identifying control variables, and identifying risks, hazards and control measures.		Main 2
Extend	Justify decisions made from property data about which materials might be ceramics.	2	
	Suggest how ceramic materials might be similar to some types of rock.	3	Main 1
	Plan a method for comparing the strength of ceramic materials, justifying choices of experimental techniques, apparatus and the measures to control risk.		Main 2

Maths
Students extract and interpret numerical data on hardness and melting points of ceramics from a table.

MyMaths More support for the maths skills in this section can be found on MyMaths.

Literacy
Students organise ideas and information, adapting their writing style towards their target audience, to write an interesting article on the properties and uses of ceramics in the student-book activity.

GCSE link
4.10.2.2 (GCSE Chemistry)/5.10.2.2 Ways of reducing the use of resources

Metals, glass, building materials, clay ceramics and most plastics are produced from limited raw materials. Much of the energy for the processes comes from limited resources. Obtaining raw materials from the Earth by quarrying and mining causes environmental impacts.

Key Word
ceramic

Answers from the student book

In-text questions	
	A Ceramic materials are compounds. They include metal silicates, metals oxides, metal carbides, and metal nitrides.
	B Four physical properties from: hard, brittle, stiff, solid at room temperature, strong when forces press on them but break easily when stretched, are electrical insulators.
	One chemical property from: unreactive with water, unreactive with acids, unreactive with alkalis.
	C Three from: buildings, electrical power-line insulators, jet-engine turbine blades, plates, bowls, mugs, or jugs.

Activity	**Splendid ceramics**
	The article should include information on the usefulness of ceramics presented in an interesting way for a general audience.
	Possible areas of focus:
	What are ceramics?
	Properties of ceramics and where these properties come from.
	Uses of ceramics in technical equipment and in everyday lives.
Summary questions	**1** silicates, oxides, brittle, hard, high, insulators (6 marks)
	2 Materials B, D, and possibly E could be ceramics. This is because they have high relative hardness and high melting points. (4 marks)
	3 Both granite and brick are non-porous.
	Granite is harder than brick, although both are difficult to scratch.
	Both are stiff and melt at high temperatures. (3 marks)

Starter	Support/Extension	Resources
Deduce the properties (5 min) Have an array of ceramic items around the room for students to look at, feel, and compare (bricks, roof tiles, pottery, porcelain, and bone china). They should be told that all the items are made from materials called ceramics. Students discuss properties of ceramics in pairs before discussing as a class.	**Support**: Students may be able to describe properties of everyday ceramics, such as plates. **Extension**: Students should justify their predictions of ceramic properties from their observations.	
Finding the properties of ceramics (10 min) Using a range of ceramic materials as stimuli (bricks, roof tiles, pottery, porcelain, and bone china) students must find the properties of ceramics hidden in the wordsearch on the interactive resource.	**Extension**: Students should suggest how they know ceramics exhibit these properties based on daily observations and general knowledge.	**Interactive**: Finding the properties of ceramics

Main	Support/Extension	Resources
What are ceramics? (15 min) Formally introduce ceramics, what they are, what they are made from, as well as their chemical and physical properties. Discuss reasons for these properties (their particles are joined together strongly) and discuss common uses of ceramics. Students should then match uses of ceramics to their physical or chemical properties to explain why ceramics are suitable for these uses.	**Extension**: Students discuss in pairs how ceramics are similar to specific rocks, for example limestone and basalt.	
Comparing ceramic strength (25 min) Students plan an investigation to compare the strength of different ceramic materials using the guidelines on the practical sheet. Students are required to select the correct apparatus, decide on a suitable method, and carry out a risk assessment before having one procedure for testing ceramic strength demonstrated to them (unless another lesson is devoted to the testing of this experiment). Students then record their observations in the results table provided.	**Support**: The accompanying support sheet includes a list of suitable apparatus for students to use in their method for this experiment.	**Practical**: Comparing ceramic strength **Skill sheet**: Planning investigations **Skill sheet**: Scientific apparatus

Plenary	Support/Extension	Resources
Reviewing ceramics (10 min) Revisit the ceramic items available at the start of the lesson and ask students to describe why each item can be classified as a ceramic, in terms of the physical and chemical properties they have learnt about in the lesson. Students should also link common uses of ceramics with their properties.		
Ceramic properties and uses (5 min) Students prepare a list of the properties of ceramics and suggest one use of ceramics that utilises each property, while distinguishing between chemical and physical properties.	**Extension**: Students should explain the origin of some of these properties based on the internal structure of ceramics.	

Homework		
Students complete the questions on the practical sheet for homework.		

7.2.1 The night sky

Securing Mastery Goals

- 3.7.2 Describe how space exploration and observations of stars are affected by the scale of the universe. (Pt 1/2)
- 3.7.2 Explain the choice of particular units for measuring distance.

Enquiry processes

- 2.15 Understand the role of a theory in science.

Band	Outcome	Checkpoint	
		Question	**Activity**
Know	Name some objects seen in the night sky.	A, 2	Starter 1, Starter 2
	State a unit that astronomers use to measure distance.	D	Starter 1
	Identify scientific evidence from secondary evidence.		Starter 1
Apply	Describe how space observation of stars is affected by the scale of the Universe.	B, C, 1	Starter 1, Starter 2, Main 1
	Explain the choice of light years as a unit of measuring distances in astronomy.	D	Starter 1
	Draw valid conclusions that utilise more than one piece of supporting evidence.		Main 2
Extend	Describe the structure of the Universe in detail, in order of size and of distance away from the Earth.		Main 1, Plenary 2
	Use the speed of light to describe distances between astronomical objects.	3	Plenary 1
	Assess the strength of evidence, deciding whether it is sufficient to support a conclusion.		Main 2

Maths
Understand number size and scale with reference to a billion.

Use light year as a unit of distance.

MyMaths More support for the maths skills in this section can be found on MyMaths.

Literacy
Read information from a range of sources about the objects in the night sky and prepare a podcast for the public.

Key Words
star, artificial satellite, orbit, Earth, Moon, natural satellite, planet, Sun, Solar System, **star, galaxy,** Milky Way, Universe, astronomer, **light year, exoplanet**

Answers from the student book

In-text questions	
	A the Moon
	B A body that gives out light, and which may have a solar system of planets.
	C A galaxy contains millions of stars.
	D The distance light travels in a year.

Summary questions	1 star, exoplanets, (8) minutes, (4) years (4 marks)
	2 The distances are very large (1 mark)
	The distances in km would take a long time to write down/have lots of zeros (1 mark)
	Writing light years is much simpler/uses smaller numbers. (1 mark)
	3 Extended response question (6 marks). Example answers:
	It takes fractions of a second for light to reach us from objects in orbit around the Earth, such as satellites or the International Space Station. Light takes minutes to reach us from planets close to us in the Solar System, such as Mercury, Venus, Mars, Jupiter. Light takes hours to reach us from distant planets in the Solar System. Light takes years to reach us from stars in the Milky Way galaxy. Our nearest star is about 4 light-years away. Light takes millions of years to reach us from other galaxies.

Starter	Support/Extension	Resources
What is in the night sky? (10 min) Students list what they can see in the night sky. Then use the interactive resource where students match items in the night sky with their definition. Discuss why the objects are visible. Emphasise that we are looking back in time because the light takes time to travel from the object to our eyes. Light travels fast, so the distances are huge. Define a light year.	**Support:** Suggest ideas and ask students what they have seen. **Extension:** Students identify reasons why they cannot see things well at night, for example, light pollution, clouds, or buildings.	**Interactive:** What is in the night sky?
What is in the sky tonight? (5–10 min) Use a star map to show what is visible in tonight's sky (e.g., from the National Schools Observatory website) or show a current video of Tonight's Sky from Hubble's website. Free downloadable programs such as Celestia and Stellarium make good alternatives.	**Extension:** Discuss if it is possible to tell between planets and stars using a telescope.	

Main	Support/Extension	Resources
What is in the Universe? (20 min) Use the Hubble website image gallery to show objects in the night sky (planets, nebulae – gas clouds where stars form, stars, black holes – remnant of collapsed giant stars, galaxies). Explain how objects fit together to form the Universe. This can be prepared in advance as a slide show with images and titles. Use the activity sheet to reinforce student perception of our place in the Universe.	**Support:** Show animations of satellites. An access sheet is available with easier text and comprehension questions. Graph paper is useful to give students an idea of one billion.	**Activity:** What is in the Universe? **Skill sheet:** Converting units
Satellites (20 min) Define a satellite as a smaller object orbiting a larger one. Give examples of natural satellites such as the Moon orbiting the Earth or planets orbiting stars. Remind students satellites always move and that they orbit the widest point of Earth but not necessarily over the equator. Discuss uses of man-made satellites and describe how scientists share data from these.	**Extension:** Discuss different orbits for satellites (vary in height, orientation, uses), for example, geostationary orbits, low polar orbits. Ask students to suggest benefits for scientists of sharing their ideas.	

Plenary	Support/Extension	Resources
How far are they? (10 min) Students rank objects in order of distance from Earth and matching distances in light-time, for example, Sun (8 light-minutes), Moon (1 light-second), Proxima Centuri (our nearest star, 4 light-years). Planet light-times vary as position in orbit varies, for example, Neptune (4 light-hours ±8 light-minutes) or Mars about 4–20 light-minutes. Students guess where the furthest man-made object has gone, and think of three reasons why we may, or may not, visit other astronomical objects.	**Support:** Provide a diagram for reference. **Extension:** Students estimate distances in light-time before you provide a list.	
What is in the Universe? (5 min) Students list objects found in the Universe. Rank them in size order, (e.g., Moon, planet, star, black hole, galaxy, Universe).	**Support:** Provide the list for students to rank.	

Homework	Support/Extension	
Make a model of a satellite identifying solar panels for power, rockets to control direction, communication antenna, and battery for power supply.	**Support:** Use Met Office template for satellite model, available from their website. **Extension:** Model a named satellite.	

7.2.2 The Solar System

Securing Mastery Goals

- 3.7.2 Describe the appearance of planets or moons from diagrams showing their position in relation to the Earth and Sun. (Pt 1/2)
- 3.7.2 Describe how space exploration and observations of stars are affected by the scale of the universe. (Pt 2/2)

Exceeding Mastery Goals

- 3.7.2 Make deductions from observation data of planets, stars and galaxies.

Enquiry processes

- 2.1 Identify patterns in data.
- 2.6 Develop an explanation.
- 2.3 Make a conclusion and explain it.
- 2.6 Communicate your idea, evidence and reasoning.

Band	Outcome	Checkpoint	
		Question	Activity
Know	Name some objects in the Solar System.	A, B	Starter 1, Plenary 1
	Explain how we see planets.	1	
	Identify some patterns in the Solar System.	3	Main 2
Apply	Describe how objects in the Solar System are arranged.	1	Starter 2, Main 1, Main 2
	Explain why we see objects in the Solar System, and describe how they appear to move.	1, 2	Main 1
	Describe how space exploration is affected by the scale of the Universe.	3	Main 2
Extend	Explain how the properties and features of planets are linked to their place in the Solar System.	3	Main 2, Plenary 2
	Explain why we see objects in the Solar System, and why they appear to move as they do.	2	Main 1
	Make deductions from observation data of planets, stars, and galaxies.		Main 2

Maths
Students extract and interpret data about the planets in the Solar System from a table.

MyMaths More support for the maths skills in this section can be found on MyMaths.

Literacy
For homework, students retrieve and collate information from a range of sources on space exploration, exploring the advantages and disadvantages of space travel, to summarise the information in a table.

Key Words
asteroid, dwarf planet

Answers from the student book

In-text questions	**A** There are eight planets in the Solar System. **B** Mercury, Mars, Venus, Earth, Neptune, Uranus, Saturn, Jupiter **C** It is reflected.
Activity	**Remember that order!** Students should choose a suitable mnemonic with the correct initial letters.
Summary questions	**1** four, four, asteroid belt, dwarf, great (5 marks) **2** Diagram to include: Sun with Earth and Mars in orbit. Lines drawn from Earth to Mars at different positions of Earth and Mars around the Sun. Lines projected to show that Mars appears to go backwards. All the planets orbit the Sun due to the force of gravity. The orbits are ellipses the planets travel at different speeds. This means sometimes they are moving one way in the sky, and at another time they move in the opposite direction. (4 marks)

3 Extended response question (6 marks). Example answers: As you move away from the Sun the temperature decreases. Less light reaches objects that are further away. Less energy is transferred from the Sun to objects that are further away. More distant planets should be colder than nearer planets. Venus should be colder than Mercury because it is further from the Sun. It is hotter than Mercury because it has an atmosphere that traps energy transferred the Sun.	

Starter	Support/Extension	Resources
What do you know? (5 min) Students sketch a diagram showing the objects they think are in the Solar System and their orbits. Use this to assess prior knowledge and draw out misconceptions. **Models of the Solar System** (10 min) Show the video clip 'Models of the Solar System – Earth, Sun and Moon' from the Institute of Physics website. Students list three to five points from the video.	**Support**: Provide a diagram for students to add labels to. **Support**: Point out models of Sun, Moon, and Earth in video. **Extension**: Students explain why we see 'wandering stars' (planets).	

Main	Support/Extension	Resources
The moving Solar System (15 min) Students make a moving model of Sun, Earth, and Moon in their books. This can also be done as a large demonstration model. Students add another planet, and use the model to explain why it seems to move forwards and backwards relative to Earth.	**Extension**: Students suggest improvements to their models, for example, scale.	**Activity:** The moving Solar System
The Solar System to scale (25 min) At this point, it is important to introduce the difference between inner planets and outer planets, in particular about the materials they are made from. This can be done from the student book. Using a long, narrow strip of paper, students can display relative distances of planets from the Sun by folding the paper, or by using a scale diagram. Discuss patterns in the separations and the scale of the Solar System. Students then work through the activity sheet individually. Discuss the problems with space travel arising from the scale of the Solar System.	**Support**: Introduce the idea of scale and give students 30-cm rulers. The support sheet includes a table of data to help students answer the questions. **Extension**: Provide data of light time to other stars in the Milky Way, and to other galaxies, and write a paragraph describing the problems associated with travelling outside the Solar System.	**Activity:** The Solar System to scale **Skill sheet:** Choosing scales

Plenary	Support/Extension	Resources
Objects in the Solar System (5 min) Interactive resource where students order objects in the Solar System according to size. **Which planet am I?** (5 min) Each student writes down clues so their partner can guess which planet they are thinking of.	**Support**: Ask students to focus on the relative sizes of the Sun, Earth, and Moon. **Extension**: Explain why we have only worked out the structure of the Universe in the last 100 years.	**Interactive:** Objects in the Solar System

Homework	Support/Extension	
Students research benefits and costs of space travel (e.g., spin-off technology, cost of manned versus unmanned expeditions). Two spin-off technologies from the Moon landing are baby formula and water filters. An alternative WebQuest homework activity is also available on Kerboodle where students research the planets of the Solar System.	**Support**: Students fill out a table with two columns: advantages and disadvantages. **Extension**: Students can add extra columns based on evidence and evaluation.	**WebQuest:** Solar System tourist

Securing Mastery Goals

- 3.7.2 Explain why places on the Earth experience different daylight hours and amounts of sunlight during the year.

Exceeding Mastery Goals

- 3.7.1 Predict patterns in day length, the Sun's intensity or an object's shadow at different latitudes.

Enquiry processes

- 2.1 Identify patterns in data.
- 2.3 Make a conclusion and explain it.

Enquiry processes activity

- 3.7.2 Relate observations of changing day length to an appropriate model of the solar system.

Band	Outcome	Checkpoint	
		Question	Activity
Know	Describe differences between seasons.	2	Starter 1
	Describe the motion of the Sun, stars, and Moon across the sky.	B, 1	Starter 2
	Describe patterns in data linking day length during the year.	2	Main 2
Apply	Explain the motion of the Sun, stars, and Moon across the sky.	A, B, 1	
	Explain why seasonal changes happen.	2	Main 1, Main 3
	Use data to show the effect of the Earth's tilt on temperature and day-length.	2	Main 2
Extend	Predict the effect of the Earth's tilt on temperature and day length.		Main 2
	Predict how seasons would be different if there were no tilt.	3	Plenary 2
	Interpret data to predict how the Earth's tilt affects temperature and day length.		Main 2

Maths

The student-book activity allows students to carry out simple calculations to work out the occurrence of a leap year.

During the activity students extract and interpret information from charts, graphs, and tables. They also represent changes in temperature and day length with changes in season graphically.

In order to answer questions, students must interpret graphs comparing day length, temperature, and season.

Literacy

The student-book activity asks students to summarise information using key words.

Students explain to each other phenomena caused by the moving Earth.

For homework, students write an account of changes experienced travelling from the Equator to the North Pole.

Key Words
axis, day, night, year, season, constellation

Answers from the student book

In-text questions	**A** Take a picture of the night sky over many hours. The stars make circular tracks. **B** east
Activity	**Spin and orbit** For example, one day is the time it takes for the Earth to spin once. The half of the Earth where sunlight does not reach is night. One year is the time it takes the Earth to orbit the Sun once. **February 29th?** 21 600 × 4 = 86 400 so 86 400 ÷ (24 × 60 × 60) days = 1 day

Summary questions	1 east, west, spins, year, orbit the Sun, longer, higher (7 marks)
	2a It is hotter because the days are longer so the Sun warms the Earth for longer. The rays from the Sun are more concentrated than they are in winter. (2 marks)
	b The Sun is higher in the sky at the Equator than it is in the UK because of the tilt of the Earth's axis. (2 marks)
	3 Extended response question (6 marks). Example answers: You would not have seasons. Days and nights would be equal length throughout the year. Shadow length at noon would be the same throughout the year. The height of the Sun in the sky at noon would be the same throughout the year. There would be no difference between the angle at which the Sun's rays hit the Earth at different times of the year. Temperature changes depend on the Sun's rays spreading out over a bigger area in the winter than the summer.

Starter	Support/Extension	Resources
An alternative question-led lesson is also available. **Different seasons** (5 min) Students list differences in seasons, for example, day-length, position of Sun, and weather. Students suggest why changes happen. **The Pole Star** (5 min) Discuss navigation without a compass. The North Pole always points towards the Pole Star because Earth tilts that way. Use a video clip from the Internet to show how to find the Pole Star and navigate using it.	**Support**: Students identify differences in day length and temperature. **Extension**: Students suggest differences on the same date in different parts of the Earth.	**Question-led lesson**: The Earth

Main	Support/Extension	Resources
Why we have seasons (15 min) Ensure students know the Earth always tilts towards the Pole Star, not towards the Sun. Use a paper star on a wall as the Pole Star. Move a globe (Earth) to tilt towards this star as it orbits around a central lamp (Sun). The North Pole tilts towards the Sun for part of the year only. Add a sticker on the globe to show the UK. Students should identify when the UK has winter and summer, and predict changes in day length. **Seasons and temperature** (10 min) Students may think winter is cooler because the Earth is further away from the Sun but it is because the Sun's rays spread over a larger area when Earth tilts away from the Sun. Stick a 1-cm wide strip of thermofilm from pole to pole, including the UK. Tilt the globe towards the lamp. The thermofilm by the UK warms up changing colour (summer). Tilt the globe away from the lamp, light spreads over a larger area and the thermofilm is cooler (winter). It is important to keep the separation of the lamp and section of the globe the same. **The seasons** (20 min) This activity is one of the AQA Enquiry process activities. Students complete questions on the activity sheet.	**Extension**: Students design their own model on paper to show this idea. **Support**: A support sheet is provided with labelled graph grids and fewer sets of data.	**Activity**: The seasons

Plenary	Support/Extension	Resources
The Sun and the seasons (5 min) Students complete the gap fill on the interactive resource to explain how seasons occur.	**Support**: Set as cloze exercise. **Extension**: Students draw diagrams explaining why some countries are cooler.	**Interactive**: The Sun and the seasons
A changing tilt (5 min) Students predict what would be different if Earth was not tilted (we would still be cooler than the Equator but day-length/temperature would be the same all year).	**Support**: Structure using questions with yes/no answers. **Extension**: Predict changes if Earth's tilt were greater.	

Homework		
Give students the temperature and day-length in a particular month for four countries between the equator and the North Pole. They write an account or postcards describing changes from the point of view of a tourist.		

7.2.4 The Moon and changing ideas

Securing Mastery Goals
● 3.7.2 Describe the appearance of moons from diagrams showing their position in relation to the Earth and Sun. (Pt 2/2)

Exceeding Mastery Goals
● 3.7.2 Compare explanations from different periods in history about the motion of objects and structure of the Universe.

Enquiry processes
● 2.1 Identify patterns in data.
● 2.3 Make a conclusion and explain it.
● 2.15 Understand the role of a theory in science.
● 2.15 Understand how scientific ideas have changed.

Band	Outcome	Checkpoint	
		Question	Activity
Know	Name some phases of the Moon.	A, 1	
	Explain simply why we see the Moon from Earth.	1	Main
	Show the different phases of the Moon using models provided.		Main
	Name the current model of the Solar System.	D, 1	
Apply	Describe the phases of the Moon.	1	Main, Starter 1, Plenary 1
	Describe the appearance of the Moon from diagrams of the Earth, Sun and Moon.	1	Main
	Explain phases of the Moon using the models provided.		Main
	Describe evidence that led to a change in the model of the Solar System.	1, 2	Main, Starter 2, Plenary 2
Extend	Predict phases of the Moon at a given time.		Plenary 1
	Explain how total eclipses are linked to phases of the Moon.	B	Main
	Predict the phases of the Moon using models provided.		Main
	Compare explanations about the motion and structure of the Universe from different periods in history.	2, 3	Main, Starter 2, Plenary 2

Maths

The student-book activity asks students to carry out a simple calculation to work out the distance between the Moon and the Earth at a given time.

MyMaths More support for the maths skills in this section can be found on MyMaths.

Literacy

Students use scientific vocabulary when writing about the phases of the Moon in the starter and plenary tasks.

Key Words
solar eclipse, phases of the Moon, total eclipse, partial eclipse, lunar eclipse

Answers from the student book

In-text questions	
A	full moon, waning gibbous, last quarter, waning crescent, new moon, waxing crescent, first quarter, waxing gibbous
B	Half the Moon is lit up at all times.
C	geocentric
D	heliocentric

Activity	**Farewell, Moon** Distance = your age × 3.8 cm/year = 11 years × 3.8 cm/year = 41.8 cm
Summary questions	**1** full, new, geocentric, heliocentric (4 marks) **2** In the geocentric model objects in the Solar System/Universe orbit the Sun Galileo observed objects that orbited something else - the moons of Jupiter. (2 marks) **3a** You see all the phases when a planet passes between the Earth and the Sun, such as Mercury and Venus. You see the outer planets as gibbous or full because they do not pass between the Earth and the Sun. (2 marks) **b** The light from the Sun hits the Earth at an angle close to 90° when you are at the Equator. It hits the Earth at an angle when you are in the UK. The Sun is higher in the sky when you are at the Equator than when you are in the UK. (2 marks)

Starter	Support/Extension	Resources
Check the facts (5 min) Check misconceptions/prior knowledge with five short questions. Students may think that the Moon changes shape or clouds change its appearance, that it always appears in the same part of the sky, and that it gives out its own light. Possible questions: Does the Moon change shape? Is the Moon bigger/closer than the Sun? What is a full/new moon? Is the Moon seen in the same place each night/during the night? **How have ideas changed?** (10 min) Students in groups write down as many ideas that people may have had about our Solar System/Universe. Next to each idea they write down one observation that supports that idea. Keep their ideas for later.	**Support:** Provide multiple choice answers. **Extension:** Students explain answers and offer more detail.	

Main	Support/Extension	Resources
Changing Moon (15 mins) Students use the model of the Earth, Moon and Sun that they used for eclipses to model the phases of the Moon using the instructions on the practical sheet. Students answer questions on the practical sheet. Students suggest whether planets, or the moons around other planets have phases. **Changing ideas** (20 mins) Students use their model from the previous activity to make the geocentric model of the Solar System. Give out a list of observations (or ask them to come up with a list of observations) involving the Sun, Earth, Moon, and other planets. Then they make the heliocentric model of the Solar System. Students write down observations that fit with each model, or both on pieces of different coloured card. Collect in the cards and read out the observations for each colour. Discuss the main pieces of evidence for the heliocentric model (retrograde motion, moons around Jupiter, phases of planets).		**Practical:** Changing Moon

Plenary	Support/Extension	Resources
What does it look like? (10 min) Draw a phase of the Moon (e.g., full moon). Students describe its appearance in future or the past, for example, in a week's time/two weeks' time/a week ago. This can be done in conjunction with the interactive gap fill as a summary. **From geocentric to heliocentric** (5 min) Students reorder statements provided on the interactive resource to describe how observations led to the geocentric model being discarded in favour of the heliocentric model.	**Support:** Provide cards with images to sort. **Extension:** Predict appearance (phases) of Earth for an astronaut on the Moon.	**Interactive:** What does it look like? **Interactive:** From geocentric to heliocentric

Homework	Support/Extension
Provide students with some websites about the history of ideas about the Solar System. They should make a poster about the people who have had ideas about our place in the Universe. They should describe the way that ideas about it have developed over time, and the evidence that the people used to produce their ideas.	

7 Earth: Checkpoint

Checkpoint lesson routes

The route through this lesson can be determined using the Checkpoint assessment.

Percentage pass marks are supplied in the Checkpoint teacher notes.

Route A (support)
In the first part, students carry out activities that collate the information they ultimately need to produce a diagram to show the rock cycle.

In the second part, students carry out a series of activities related to the universe topic.

Route B (extension)
Students review the information about the changing ideas about the solar system and produce a poster about the ideas and evidence that lead the model to be revised over the years from Ptolemy to the reclassification of Pluto to a dwarf planet.

Progression to *Apply*

Know outcome	Apply outcome	Making progress
Know that sedimentary rocks are made from layers of sediment; metamorphic rocks are formed from existing rocks exposed to pressure and temperature over a long time; igneous rocks are formed from magma, with minerals arranged in crystals.	Explain properties of rocks based on how they formed.	Show students examples of each type of rock and ask them to compare the appearance and hardness. In Task 1, students complete a gap-fill activity describing the properties of each type of rock. In Task 2, they use the information to classify unknown rocks from their image and description and explain their choices.
Know that is the wearing down of rock by chemical, physical or biological processes; erosion is the movement of rock by water, ice or wind.	Identify the cause of weathering and erosion and describe how they occur	Describe the difference between weathering and erosion. You could also show an appropriate video from the Internet. Students answer questions about the types of weathering in Task 3.
Know that sedimentary, igneous and metamorphic rocks can be interconverted over millions of years through weathering and erosion, heat and pressure, and melting and cooling.	Construct a labelled diagram to identify the processes in the rock cycle.	In Task 4, students complete a diagram of the rock cycle. It is possible to use the diagram provided as a starting point or students can create their own.
Know that our solar system is a tiny part of a galaxy, one of billions in the Universe.	Explain the choice of particular units for measuring distance.	Before Task 5, remind students about the definition of a light year. Ask students to look at distances to nearby galaxies in metres and in light years, and guide them towards realising why the unit of light year might be used instead of metres.
Recall that light takes minutes to reach the Earth from the sun, four years from the nearest star and billions of years from other galaxies.	Describe how space exploration and observations of stars are affected by the size of the Universe.	For Task 6, show students a list of data to show how long it took spacecraft to travel to the different planets in the solar system and how long it takes for a signal to be sent back to Earth. Ask them to use this data to identify potential issues with space exploration. Students use data about distances to stars and galaxies in light years to describe that stars we see may no longer exist.
Know that the planets rotate on tilted axes while orbiting the Sun, which explains day length, year length, and seasons.	Explain why different places on the Earth experience different amounts of day light hours and sunlight during the year.	Use a globe with a tilted axis and torch to demonstrate how the angle of the Earth affects the area that the light from a torch is spread over. In Task 7, students complete diagrams to show how the path the Sun takes across the sky at different times in the year varies. They complete questions about why the sun's intensity changes at different times in the year.
Know that the solar system can be modelled as planets rotating on tilted axes while orbiting the Sun, while moons orbit planets, this can explain the visibility of objects from Earth.	Describe the appearance of planets or moons from diagrams showing their position in relation to the Earth and Sun.	Model the phases of the Sun by using a light source and a ball. A projector is a good source of light. If students walk around the ball it is possible to see the shadows from different angles, illustrating the phases. In Task 8, students complete the diagram to show the phases of the Moon as it orbits around the Earth and explain why the Moon has phases.

156

Answers to End-of-Big Idea questions

1a One mark for each correct label. (3 marks)

b heliocentric (1 mark)

c one from: Jupiter had moons that orbit Jupiter/there are phases of Venus (1 mark)

2a C (1 mark)

b Igneous rock is formed from cooled magma that solidified/froze. (3 marks)

c The sedimentary rocks around the granite were softer, and eroded. (2 marks)

d Metamorphic rock is made under heating and pressure. The marble shown in the diagram was probably made from sedimentary rock that was heated by the cooling magma (that formed granite). 2 marks

3a Temperature of microscope slide (1 mark)

b Size of crystals (1 mark)

c To make the investigation fair (1 mark)

d Small crystals are made quickly. Larger crystals are formed more slowly. (2 marks)

4a Left: sunrise, east; Right: sunset, west; Centre: noon, south.
All correct (2 marks), one or two wrong (1 mark).

b A path that is lower in the sky at noon (1 mark) and that produces a smaller semicircle (1 mark)

c The Earth's axis is tilted (1 mark), in summer it is tilted towards the Sun, and in winter it is tilted away from the Sun (1 mark).

5 It would take minutes or hours for the signal to reach the spacecraft. There would be a long delay between asking a question and receiving an answer. (2 marks)

6 Extended response question (6 marks). Examples of correct scientific points:
- Sediments are removed from the surface of a rock by weathering.
- Sediments are transported by wind or water.
- Sediments are deposited.
- Sediment is compacted or cemented to make sedimentary rock.
- Rock is heated, without melting. Its particles rearrange to form crystals in a metamorphic rock.
- Rock is subjected to high pressures. Its particles rearrange to form crystals in a metamorphic rock.
- Liquid rock / magma / lava cools and freezes to make an igneous rock.
- Rock melts to form liquid rock / magma / lava.

7 This is an extended response question. Students should be marked on the use of good English, organisation of information, spelling and grammar, and correct use of specialist scientific terms. The best answers will be well presented and clearly organised, making references to the information provided in the table as well as to their scientific knowledge (maximum of 6 marks).
Examples of correct scientific points:
The seasons would be would be longer or shorter depending on the angle.
The angle of tilt of Mars, Saturn, and Neptune is about the same as Earth. The seasons on Mars, Saturn, and Neptune would be similar to Earth. The axis of Mercury is not tilted. Mercury would not have seasons.
You would hardly notice the seasons on Jupiter – the angle of tilt of Jupiter is so small.
Seasons are longer for planets further from the Sun because it takes longer for the planet to orbit the Sun.
Uranus has an angle of tilt of nearly 90 degrees, so rolls like a barrel on its axis as it moves around the Sun – seasons would last about 6 months.
Venus has very little difference between the seasons because the angle is very small – it is just spinning the other way.

Answer guide for Big Write

Know	Apply	Extend
1–2 marks	3–4 marks	5–6 marks
• Student picks out obvious points from the table given (e.g., year length is shorter, day length is longer) but little or no comparisons to other planets in the Solar System.	• Student shows comprehension that conditions probably too hot for life and that the same side would always face the star. • Some basic comparison with other planets in the Solar system.	• Student connects the idea that temperatures not suitable for liquid water so unlikely to have life. • Compares with other planets in the Solar System, e.g., rolls like Uranus.

kerboodle

7 Part 1 Checkpoint assessment (automarked)
7 Part 1 Checkpoint: Revision, 7 Part 1 Checkpoint: Extension
7.1 Progress task, 7.2 Progress task

8 Organisms

National curriculum links for this unit	
Topic	**National Curriculum topic**
8.1 Movement	Cells and organisation The skeletal and muscular systems
8.2 Cells	Cells and organisation

In this Big Idea students will learn:

- the parts of the human skeleton work as a system for support, protection, movement, and the production of new blood cells
- antagonistic pairs of muscles create movement when one contract and the other relaxes

- multi-cellular organisms are composed of cells, which are organised into tissues, organs, and systems to carry out life processes
- there are many types of cell. Each has a different structure or feature so it can do a specific job.

AQA Enquiry process activities

Activity	Section
3.8.1 Explore how the skeletal system and muscular system in a chicken wing work together to cause movement.	8.1.4 Movement: muscles
3.8.2 Identify the principal features of a cheek cell and describe their functions.	8.2.2 Plant and animal cells

Preparing for Key Stage 4 success

Knowledge	4.1.1.2 Animal and plant cells
Underpinning knowledge is covered in this Big Idea for KS4 study of:	4.1.1.3 Cell specialisation
	4.1.1.5 Microscopy
	4.1.3.1 Diffusion
	4.2.1 Principles of organisation
Maths	**2** Handling data
Skills developed in Big Idea 8:	**a** Find arithmetic means (8.1.3)
	c Construct and interpret frequency tables and diagrams, bar charts and histograms (8.1.3)
	f Understand the terms mean, mode and median (8.1.3)
	h Make order of magnitude calculations (8.2.1)
	3 Algebra
	a Understand and use the symbols (please insert) (8.2.1)
	d Solve simple algebraic equations (8.2.1)
	4 Graphs
	a Translate information between graphical and numerical form (8.1.3)
Literacy	Collaboration and exploratory talk (8.1.1, 8.2.3)
Skills developed in Big Idea 8:	Communicating ideas to a wide range of audiences (8.1.1)
	Use of scientific terms (8.1.1, 8.1.2, 8.1.3, 8.2.1, 8.2.2, 8.2.3, 8.2.4, 8.2.5)
	Making connections across a range of texts and from personal experience (8.2.3)
	Organisation of ideas and information (8.1.3, 8.2.1, 8.2.5)
	Legibility, spelling, punctuation, grammar and sentence structure (8.2.1, 8.2.4)
	Planning and adapting writing style to suit audience and purpose (8.2.1, 8.2.4)

Assessment Skills
- Extended response questions (8.1.2, 8.1.4, 8.2.1, 8.2.2, 8.2.3)
- Quantitative problem solving (8.1.3, 8.2.1)
- Application of Enquiry Processes (8.1.3), End-of-Big Idea questions, Q3

KS2 Link	Check before	Checkpoint	Catch-up
Know about the main body parts and internal organs.	8.1.1 Levels of organisation	Provide students with a blank diagram of the human body. Ask them to label the main organs and what they do.	Provide students with a list of the main organs in the human body and a description of what they do. Ask the students to match the organ to the description.
Humans and some other animals have skeletons.	8.1.2 The Skeleton	Ask students to make a list of animals that have and don't have a skeleton.	Provide images of animals with and without a backbone for students to sort.
Animals have a skeleton for support and production.	8.1.2 The Skeleton	Ask students to explain why they have a skull.	Ask students to feel their skull and their ribs, discuss that they are protecting their brain and heart.
Some animals have skeletons and muscles for support, protection, and movement.	8.1.4 Movement: Muscles	Discussion on 'Why do humans have skeletons and muscles?'	Ask students to put their hand around their upper arm, and bend the arm at the elbow and describe what they feel happening.
The functions of different parts of flowering plants: roots, stem, leaves, and flowers.	8.2.3 Specialised cells	Students label a diagram of a flowering plant, including the functions of each part.	Card sort of the main parts of a flowering plant and their functions.

Key Stage 2 Quiz: Biology
8 Organisms End-of-Big-Idea test (foundation)
8 Organisms End-of-Big-Idea test (foundation) mark scheme
8 Organisms End-of-Big-Idea test (higher)
8 Organisms End-of-Big-Idea test (higher) mark scheme

Answers to Picture Puzzler
Key Words
chin, egg, leaf, leg
The key word is **cell**.
Close Up
an amoeba cell

You can find additional support for the maths skills covered in this Big Idea on **MyMaths**, including carrying out calculations, and using standard and compound units.

8.1.1 Levels of organisation

Securing Mastery Goals
- M3.8.2 Explain why multi-cellular organisms need organ systems to keep their cells alive. (Pt 1/2)

Exceeding Mastery Goals
- 3.8.2 Suggest how damage to, or failure of, an organ would affect other body systems.

Enquiry processes
- 2.5 Use scientific vocabulary accurately, showing that you know its meaning and use appropriate units and correct chemical nomenclature.

Band	Outcome	Checkpoint	
		Question	**Activity**
Know	State what is meant by a tissue, an organ, and an organ system.	1	Main 1
	State the sequence of the hierarchy of organisation in a multi-cellular organism.	1	Lit, Starter 2, Main 1
	Use information provided to list the organs found in a given organ system, and state the function of that system.	2, 3	Main 1, Main 2
Apply	Define and state examples of tissues, organs, and organ systems.	B–D, 1–3	Main 1, Plenary 1
	Explain the hierarchy of organisation in a multi-cellular organism.	3	Lit, Main 1
	Interpret information provided to decide on the function of the individual organs and of the organ system.		Main 1, Main 2
Extend	Explain in detail the hierarchy of organisation in a multi-cellular organism, using a range of examples.	2	Main 1, Plenary 2
	Explain how the different tissues in an organ, and the different organs in an organ system function together.	3	Main 1, Main 2
	Interpret information to explain the functions of several organ systems.		Main 1, Main 2

Literacy
Students write and deliver a presentation on an organ system they have researched.

GCSE link
4.2.1/4.2.1 Principles of organisation

Cells are the basic building blocks of all living organisms.

A tissue is a group of cells with a similar structure and function.

Organs are aggregations of tissues performing specific functions.

Organs are organised into organ systems, which work together to form organisms.

Key Words
multi-cellular, cell tissue, organ, organ system, circulatory system, respiratory system, reproductive system, digestive system, muscular skeletal system, immune system

Answers from the student book

In-text questions	**A** cell
	B for example, nervous tissue
	C for example, skin
	D for example, circulatory system

Summary questions	1 cell – building blocks of life; tissue – group of similar cells working together; organ – group of tissues working together; organ system – group of organs working together; organism – group of organ systems working together (5 marks)
	2 For example, the digestive system is made up of the following organs: (pancreas,) stomach, liver, small intestine, large intestine. (2 marks)
	3 One mark for correctly ordering the levels of organisation; one mark for each correctly linked example. For example, nerve cell (cell) → nerve tissue (tissue) → brain (organ) → nervous system (organ system) → human (multi-cellular organism) (6 marks)

Starter	Support/Extension	Resources
Working together (5–10 min) Present students (either in a group or as a class demo) with the disassembled parts of plastic building blocks, which will build into a specific object, for example, a car. Ask them to build the object. Have a discussion in which the idea is that the individual bricks work together to make the whole object work. Each block might have its own function. **Building an organism** (5 min) Present students with a picture of a cell, tissue, organ, organ system, and an organism. Ask them to put the pictures into an order and to explain their decision. Ideally use images from a related organ system sequence. In a short discussion, focus in on groups that have selected a hierarchical structure.	**Extension:** Ask more probing questions in the discussion. Ask the students to make connections between this idea and a large plant or animal body. **Support:** Students work in groups. The images used could be more basic. **Extension:** Students explain their reasoning in detail.	

Main	Support/Extension	Resources
Organising a body (25 min) Begin by introducing the parts of the digestive system so that students can label the system on their activity sheet. Students then read through the information sheet, describing specialised cells, levels of organisation, and organ systems. Students extract information in order to answer the questions on the accompanying activity sheet. Alternatively, show students the animation on organisation in multi-cellular organisms. **Research and presentation** (20 min) Provide students with a variety of text books from a range of levels, or use the Internet if available. Divide the class into groups and give them time to research the organs and functions of a different organ system. Students should write brief notes in their books. Each group then gives a presentation about their organ system.	**Extension:** Students complete the extension activity to explain how the organs of the digestive system function together to digest food. **Support:** Organise students into groups so that some students can lead the task. Differentiate according to the quality of the texts available. **Extension:** Students should explain the role of each organ in the system in detail, and suggest how organ damage or failure would affect other body systems.	**Activity:** Organising a body **Animation:** Organisation in multi-cellular organisms

Plenary	Support/Extension	Resources
Cells, tissues, or organs? (5 min) Using the interactive resource, students organise a list of words according to the categories cells, tissues, and organs. **Which system am I?** (5 min) Produce a series of paper slips, each containing the name of one organ (plant or animal). Students must then find other students in the class with organs from the same organ system. They group together and name their system.	**Support:** Students can discuss answers in pairs before going through answers on the board.	**Interactive:** Cells, tissues, or organs?

Homework		
Ask students to create a table. The first column should have the seven life functions that students have encountered at KS2 (MRS GREN). In the second column, ask students to explain how this function is carried out in the human body, linking this to as many organs and organ systems as possible.		

8.1.2 The skeleton

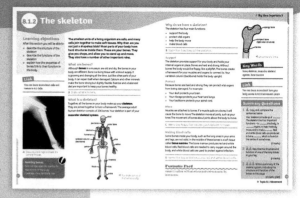

Securing Mastery Goals
- 3.8.1 Explain how a physical property of part of the skeleton relates to its function.

Exceeding Mastery Goals
- 3.8.1 Predict the consequences of damage to a joint, bone, or muscle. (Pt 1/3)

Enquiry processes
- 2.5 Add a diagram if it helps to make the meaning clearer.

Band	Outcome	Checkpoint	
		Question	Activity
Know ↓	Name the main parts in the skeleton.	D, 1	Main, Starter 1
	List the functions of the muscular skeletal system.	B, D, 1	Main, Plenary 1
Apply ↓	Describe the structure of the skeleton.	A, D, 1–3	Main
	Describe the functions of the muscular skeletal system.	B, D, 1–3	Main
Extend ↓	Explain the relationship between the bones and joints in the skeleton.		Main
	Explain the link between structure and functions in the muscular skeletal system.	D, 2, 3	Main
	Predict the consequences of damage to a bone.	EoBl 5	Plenary 1

Literacy
Students use scientific terminology correctly when linking skeletal structures to their functions.

They will also be required to communicate ideas, retrieving and collating information from a range of different sources when building a model of the skeleton.

GCSE link
4.1.2.3/4.1.2.3 Stem cells

Stem cells from adult bone marrow can form many types of cell including blood cells.

Key Words
bone, skeleton, **bone marrow**

Answers from the student book

In-text questions	**A** A living tissue with a blood supply, which is strong but slightly flexible.
	B To support the body, protect vital organs, help the body to move, and make blood cells.
	C muscle tissue
	D bone marrow
Activity	**Naming bones**
	patella, scapula, mandible
Summary questions	**1** bones, support, protect, blood, marrow (5 marks)
	2 Any four from:
	contains bone marrow, produces blood cells to fight disease/carry oxygen; rigid outer structure provides support, enables movement, and gives shape to body (4 marks)
	3 Extended response question (6 marks). Example answers:
	Bones/bone marrow produce blood cells. Red blood cells carry oxygen around the animal. White blood cells protect against infection. Bones are strong. They protect organs from being crushed. They also give structure to the organism. In conjunction with muscles, bones allow the animal to move.

Starter	Support/Extension	Resources
An alternative question-led lesson is also available. **What's in a skeleton?** (10 min) Present student groups with large flip chart paper and board markers and ask the question 'What is your skeleton, and why do you need it?' Allow them a few minutes to write down key words to answer the question, grouping key words into structural ideas or function. Discuss their answers, and correct any misconceptions. **Name those bones!** (5 min) An interactive resource that asks students to label a diagram of the skeleton, using the names of some of the major bones in the body provided.	**Support:** Students may be provided with an image of the skeleton as a visual prompt.	**Question-led lesson:** The skeleton **Interactive:** Name those bones!

Main	Support/Extension	Resources
Build your own skeleton (40 min) Students use the activity sheet and photocopied images of bones to build a skeleton. Students then use the model skeleton and the information in the student book as a resource to label the bones on their own activity sheet. Students then answer the questions that follow.	**Support:** Students should work in mixed-ability groups.	**Activity:** Build your own skeleton

Plenary	Support/Extension	Resources
What's the skeleton for? (5 min) Present images of the skeleton on the board and point to different regions of the skeleton. Ask students to suggest what the bones in these areas do. The regions should include the skull, the ribcage, and the long bones of the arm and leg.	**Support:** Students may be provided with a list of possible skeletal regions and functions to choose from. **Extension:** Ask students to predict what would happen if these bones were damaged.	
Table of functions (10 min) Students draw a table that lists several regions of the skeleton (skull, ribcage, long bones in the arm and leg) in the first column. Students then fill in the second column with the functions of the bones in these regions.	**Support:** Provide students with a pre-drawn table to fill in. **Extension:** Students should include in their functions an explanation of how the function is achieved.	

Homework	Support/Extension	
Provide each student with an image of a different animal and ask them to add annotations around the picture to describe how the animal achieves support, movement, and protection. Independent research will be required to complete this task.	**Extension:** Students can be given more unusual animals, (e.g., fish or arthropods) to test their understanding and application of knowledge. Students should also provide an explanation for how these animals achieve their skeletal functions in their annotations, linking functions to structures.	

8.1.3 Movement: joints

Securing Mastery Goals
- 3.8.1 Explain how antagonistic muscles produce movement around a joint. (Pt 1/2)

Exceeding Mastery Goals
- 3.8.1 Predict the consequences of damage to a joint, bone, or muscle. (Pt 2/3)
- 3.8.1 Consider the benefits and risks of a technology for improving human movement.

Enquiry processes
- 2.4 Design a table for the data being gathered.
- 2.12 Identify and record key features of an observation.
- 2.1 Calculate a mean from a data set.
- 2.2 Analyse strengths and weaknesses in your inquiry.

Band	Outcome	Checkpoint	
		Question	Activity
Know	State where joints are found in the body.	A, 1	Homework
	State how a muscle exerts force during movement.	C	Main
	Carry out an experiment to make simple observations.		Main
Apply	Describe the structure and function of joints.	1	Main, Homework
	Explain how to measure the force exerted by different muscles.	3	Main
	Carry out an experiment to make and record measurements of forces using the correct units.		Main
Extend	Explain how the parts of a joint allow it to function.	1, 2	Homework
	Explain the relationship between the forces required to move different masses.		Main
	Carry out an experiment to record measurements of forces in newtons, evaluating the accuracy and precision of the method chosen.		Main, Plenary 2

Maths
Students calculate means of their experimental results and plot a suitable graph to display their observations.

MyMaths More support for the maths skills in this section can be found on MyMaths.

Literacy
Students extract information from text in order to carry out the practical, and must organise their ideas concisely when using scientific terms to explain their findings in the experiment.

Key Words
biomechanics, **joint, cartilage, ligament,** newtons

Answers from the student book

In-text questions	A Where bones two or more join together.
	B knee and elbow
	C newton
Activity	**Health and safety**
	There is a high risk of causing injury to yourself, straining/spraining a muscle, and tearing a ligament if you drop the dumbbell on yourself.

Summary questions	1 bones, movement, hip/shoulder, cartilage, rubbing (5 marks)
	2 Diagram showing any three from
	two bones, ligament(s) joining the bones together, cartilage on ends of bones, fluid surrounding joint. (3 marks)
	3 Example answers (6 marks):
	measuring equipment – newton (bathroom) scale; muscle force measured from reading on newton scale; select named muscle (e.g. biceps); push onto newton scale using that particular muscle; record reading on scale; repeat reading to check for errors; calculate average force exerted on scale; repeat for second or subsequent muscle group(s)

kerboodle

Starter	Support/Extension	Resources
Walking skeletons (10 min) Show animations from the Internet, or from a film clip, which show a skeleton walking. Ask students why is it impossible for the skeleton to walk and the bones to move even though we know bones to be strong structures that are only slightly flexible. Discuss student ideas leading onto the need for joints, muscles, ligaments, cartilage, and tendons for movement.	**Support**: Focus on muscles and joints in the discussion. **Extension**: Students should explain the roles of different tissues used in movement.	
Arm movements (5 min) Using their own arms, ask students to identify where joints are and what range of movements they can achieve with these joints.	**Support**: Students should ignore the joints in the wrist and hand to avoid confusion. **Extension**: Students should consider if other types of joints are present around the body.	

Main	Support/Extension	Resources
Forces for lifting (40 min) Introduce the different parts of the arm needed for movement. Use scientific terminology such as biceps, triceps, and the different parts of a joint. Students then carry out an experiment investigating the forces required by the arm to lift different masses. Students will use a model of an arm with a hinge joint for the elbow to collect data in accordance with the method on the practical sheet. They will then display results on a graph to find a relationship between the two factors under investigation and answer the questions that follow.	**Support**: A support sheet is available with a suggested table of results and a graph grid with pre-labelled axes.	**Practical**: Forces for lifting **Skill sheet**: Calculating means **Skill sheet**: Choosing scales **Skill sheet**: Recording results

Plenary	Support/Extension	Resources
The role of joints in movement (5 min) The interactive resource requires students to use the definitions provided to fill in a crossword using key words in this topic.		**Interactive**: The role of joints in movement
Where, how, and why? (10 min) Evaluate the experiment as a discussion with students. Questions to consider include: Where in the experiment did you do something to make it fair? State the type of variable this is. How did you increase the accuracy in the experiment?	**Extension**: Students should offer detailed answers with explanations.	

Homework	Support/Extension	
Students apply their knowledge by writing a short paragraph about how a different joint elsewhere in the body works.	**Support**: Students should apply their ideas to another hinge joint, for example, the knee. **Extension**: Students should apply their knowledge to another type of joint, for example, a pivot or a ball and socket joint.	
An alternative WebQuest homework activity is also available on Kerboodle where students research hip replacements.	**Extension:** The WebQuest allows students to consider the benefits and risks of a technology for improving human movement.	**WebQuest:** Hip replacement

8.1.4 Movement: muscles

Securing Mastery Goals

- 3.8.1 Explain why some organs contain muscle tissue.
- 3.8.1 Explain how antagonistic muscles produce movement around a joint. (Pt 2/2)
- 3.8.1 Use a diagram to predict the result of a muscle contraction or relaxation.

Exceeding Mastery Goals

- Predict the consequences of damage to a joint, bone, or muscle. (Pt 3/3)
- Suggest factors that affect the force exerted by different muscles.

Enquiry processes

- 2.3 Interpret observations carried out during a dissection.

Enquiry processes activity:

- 3.8.1 Explore how the skeletal system and muscular system in a chicken wing work together to cause movement.

Band	Outcome	Checkpoint	
		Question	Activity
Know	State the function of major muscle groups.	1	Starter 1, Plenary 2, Homework
	State the definition of antagonistic muscles.	1	Lit, Starter 1, Plenary 1, Homework
	Carry out an experiment to study the muscle system in a chicken wing.		Main
Apply	Explain the function of different muscles within the body.	B, 1	Starter 1, Plenary 2, Homework
	Explain how antagonistic muscles produce movement around a joint.	3	Lit, Plenary 1, Homework
	Interpret observations in a chicken wing to describe how the muscles work together to cause movement.		Main
	Use a diagram to predict the result of a muscle contraction or relaxation.	2	Plenary 2, Homework
Extend	Explain how the muscle groups interact with other tissues to cause movement.	2	Plenary 2, Homework
	Explain why it is necessary to have both muscles in an antagonistic pair to cause movement.	4	Lit, Main, Plenary 1, Plenary 2, Homework
	Interpret observations in a chicken wing to explain how the muscles work together to cause movement.		Main

Literacy
Students apply their scientific knowledge and understanding, using the key words learnt during the lesson, when explaining how antagonistic muscle pairs are used in kicking a football (for their homework).

GCSE link
4.5.2/4.5.2 The human nervous system

The CNS coordinates the response of effectors which may be muscles contracting or glands secreting hormones.

Key Words
tendon, antagonistic muscle pair

166

Answers from the student book

In-text questions	**A** It consists of many cells contracting together to cause movement. **B** Any three from: neck muscles, shoulder muscles, biceps and triceps, abdominal muscles, thigh muscles, calf muscles, shin muscles. **C** The muscle gets shorter.
Activity	**Model limb** The model should include a pair of antagonistic muscles on either side of a joint. Muscles should not be able to push, they can only contract. When one muscle contracts, the other relaxes.

Summary questions	**1** tendons, contracts, pulls, joint, antagonistic (5 marks)
	 2a To pump blood around the body to deliver oxygen/nutrients to cells. (2 marks)
	   b To squeeze food through the digestive system so nutrients can be absorbed and waste products removed. (2 marks)
	 3a The lower leg will bend upwards from the knee, behind the upper leg. (1 mark)
	   b The foot will bend upwards from the ankle, in front of the shin. (1 mark)
	 4 Example answers (6 marks):
	   Muscles can only pull.
	   One muscle is required to bend the joint.
	   A second muscle is required to straighten the joint.
	   The muscles act on opposite sides of the joint.
	   As one muscle contracts, the other relaxes.
	   The muscle pair is antagonistic.
	   Diagrams depicting the bending and straightening of a joint.

Starter	Support/Extension	Resources
Muscle groups (10 min) Split students into small groups and provide each with a large image of a body showing the major muscle groups. Students should try to label the muscle groups and describe their function. **Flexing your muscles** (5 min) Ask students to lift a sizeable textbook. They need to observe any changes in the muscles of the upper arm and describe their observations to the class.	**Support:** Provide students with labels and descriptions for them to match to the correct muscle groups on their diagram. **Extension:** Students should be encouraged to offer their thoughts on why these changes occur.	
Main	**Support/Extension**	**Resources**
Investigating how a chicken wing works (45 min) This practical is one of the AQA Enquiry process activities. Students carry out a simple practical to explore how the skeleton and muscles work together within a chicken wing. They observe the bones, muscles, ligaments and tendons, and the structure of joints. Students record their observations as annotated diagrams and answer questions on how the individual and antagonistic pairs of muscles create movement in the wing.		**Practical:** Investigating how a chicken wing works
Plenary	**Support/Extension**	**Resources**
Revisiting antagonistic muscles (5 min) Students are presented with a summary of antagonistic muscles, where they must choose the correct words to fill individual gaps, using key words provided on the interactive resource. **Other muscle pairs** (10 min) Students apply their knowledge of antagonistic pairs to other parts of the body. They must find another antagonistic pair in the body (no names required) and explain how the muscle pair works in order to move the bones about the joint. Students pair-share their ideas, before offering these in a class discussion.	**Support:** Students concentrate on finding other antagonistic pairs of muscles around the body.	**Interactive:** Revisiting antagonistic muscles
Homework		
Provide students with a diagram of the leg with the hamstrings and quadriceps labelled. Students must write an account to explain how these muscles are used as an antagonistic pair during the kicking of a football.		

8.2.1 Observing cells

Securing Mastery Goals
- 3.8.2 Use a light microscope to observe and draw cells. (Pt 1/2)
- 3.8.2 Explain how to use a microscope to identify and compare different types of cell. (Pt 1/2)

Enquiry processes
- 2.5 Add a diagram if it helps to make the meaning clearer.
- 2.9 Use the measuring instrument correctly.

Band	Outcome	Checkpoint	
		Question	Activity
Know	State what a cell is.	A	Starter 1, Starter 2
	Describe how to use a microscope to observe a cell.	3	Main 1
	Use a microscope to observe a prepared slide, with assistance.		Main 1
Apply	Describe what a cell is.		Starter 2
	Explain how to use a microscope to observe a cell.	3	Main 1
	Use a microscope to observe a prepared slide and state the magnification.		Maths, Main 1
Extend	Explain what all living organisms are made of.		Starter 1, Starter 2
	Explain what each part of the microscope does and how it is used.	2	Main 1
	Use a microscope to observe a prepared slide calculating a range of magnifications.		Maths, Main 1

Maths

In the student-book activity, students use multiplication to calculate magnification.

MyMaths More support for the maths skills in this section can be found on MyMaths.

Literacy

In the student-book activity, students organise ideas and information to explain how to use a microscope.

GCSE link
4.1.1.5/4.1.1.5 Microscopy

An electron microscope has much higher magnification and resolving power than a light microscope. This means that it can be used to study cells in much finer detail. This has enabled biologists to see and understand many more sub-cellular structures.

Students should be able to carry out calculations involving magnification, real size and image size using the formula:

$$\text{magnification} = \frac{\text{size of image}}{\text{size of real object}}$$

Key Words
organisms, microscope, observe

Answers from the student book

In-text questions	A cells
	B cork cells that looked like tiny rooms
	C looking carefully/in detail at an object
	D eye-piece
Activity	**Magnification** $(10 \times 50) = 500$

Summary questions	
	1 cells, building, observe, microscope, magnifies (5 marks)
	2a magnifies object (1 mark) **b** holds microscope slide (or object) you are observing (1 mark) **c** produces a clear image of the object (1 mark)
	3 Extended response question (6 marks). It must be a logical answer, covering:
	Take a single petal and place on a slide/stage
	Add dye/stain to make it easier to see
	Using lowest magnification of objective lens
	Turn coarse focusing knob to see your object
	Focus image clearly using fine focus
	Repeat with higher magnification to observe petal in more detail

Starter	Support/Extension	Resources
A scaly problem (5 min) Ask students to draw an insect (or any small organism) on the board. Lead discussion to consider size. If the student makes a small drawing, extract the idea that it is difficult to see so should be drawn bigger. If the student makes a large drawing to start, ask why. Try to extract the idea that increasing the size of the object makes it easier to see. **Magnifying lenses** (5 min) Issue hand lenses and some objects, for example, insect wings. Ask students to look at the object. Ask students what has happened and why it has happened. Has the object changed size? What is the advantage of increasing the image size? In both cases, introduce the idea that all living things are made up of cells.	**Support**: Clearly focus on the idea that increasing size helps to see objects. Write key words for of magnification on the board. **Extension**: Consider how much bigger the image is, introduce the idea of quantifying magnification.	

Main	Support/Extension	Resources
Discovering the microscope (45 min) Divide the class into small groups and issue each group with a microscope. Provide only basic safety information; do not tell them how it works. Ask the students to use the microscope and find out how it works. Set a time limit of approximately 5 minutes. Initiate a class discussion to establish what they have found out. Try to extract the basic ideas about the parts, their names, and how to use these parts. Now issue each group with some slides, either pre-made or locust wings and a pair of glass slides. Ask students to use the microscope to observe the details of the object issued. Ask how they were able to see the object. Then issue practical sheets and ask the students to complete the tasks included.	**Support**: The support sheet lists parts of a microscope. Instead of producing a full leaflet, students can instead write a simple statement for each part of the microscope. **Extension**: Students label the sheet alone and produce a detailed leaflet. Lead students to calculate the magnification used during the practical. Encourage students to consider the different levels of magnification.	**Practical**: Discovering the microscope

Plenary	Support/Extension	Resources
What's in a name? (5 min) Use the interactive resource to check the students' knowledge of the names of the parts of the microscope. **Ordering game** (5 min) Produce a set of cards, each with a statement about how to use a microscope. Deal them out to the class. Each student needs to stand up and read their card when they think it is their turn.	**Extension**: Ask students to explain what each part does. **Support**: Identify the first card player.	**Interactive**: What's in a name?

Homework		
Students complete the production of the leaflet from the practical activity. An alternative WebQuest homework activity is also available on Kerboodle where students research the development of the microscope.		**WebQuest**: Development of the microscope

8.2.2 Plant and animal cells

Securing Mastery Goals

- 3.8.2 Use a light microscope to observe and draw cells. (Pt 2/2)
- 3.8.2 Both plants and animal cells have a cell membrane, nucleus, cytoplasm and mitochondria. Plant cells also have a cell wall, chloroplasts and usually a permanent vacuole.
- 3.8.2 Explain how to use a microscope to identify and compare different types of cells. (Pt 2/2)
- 3.8.2 Suggest what kind of tissue or organism a cell is part of, based on its features. (Pt 1/2)

Enquiry processes

- 2.9 Use the measuring instrument correctly.
- 2.13 Identify features of an investigation which are hazardous.
- 2.13 Identify ways of reducing the risk.

Enquiry processes activity:

- 3.8.2 Identify the principal features of a cheek cell and describe their functions.

Band	Outcome	Checkpoint	
		Question	Activity
Know	Identify one similarity and one difference between a plant and an animal cell.	C, 1, 3	
	Match some components of a cell to their functions.	B, 1	Starter 1
	With support, prepare and observe a microscope slide safely.		Starter 2, Main
Apply	Identify and compare the similarities and differences between plant and animal cells.	3	
	Describe the functions of the components of a cell.	1–3	
	Prepare and observe cells on a microscope slide safely.		Starter 2, Main
Extend	Explain the similarities and differences between plant and animal cells.	3	
	Explain the functions of the components of a cell by linking them to life processes.		Starter 1, Plenary 2
	Prepare and observe cells on a microscope slide safely, using scale and magnifications.		Starter 2, Main, Plenary 1

Literacy

Students access information to ascertain meaning, using word skills and comprehension strategies when reading instructions for preparing a slide for a microscope.

GCSE link

4.1.1.1/4.1.1.1 Eukaryotes and prokaryotes

Plant and animal cells (eukaryotic cells) have a cell membrane, cytoplasm and genetic material enclosed in a nucleus.

4.1.1.2 Animal and plant cells (*GCSE Biology and GCSE Combined Science: Trilogy*)

Most animal cells have the following parts:

- a nucleus
- cytoplasm
- a cell membrane
- mitochondria
- ribosomes.

In addition to the parts found in animal cells, plant cells often have:

- chloroplasts
- a permanent vacuole filled with cell sap.

Key Words

nucleus, cell membrane, cytoplasm, mitochondria, respiration, **cell wall, vacuole, chloroplast**

Answers from the student book

In-text questions	**A** nucleus, cell membrane, cytoplasm, mitochondria **B** controls the cell/contains genetic material **C** cell wall, chloroplast, vacuole **D** cell sap
Activity	**Prefixes** bio- = life; biology, biography photo- = light; photograph, photographer micro- = small; microscope, microwave
Summary questions	**1** vacuole – contains cell sap to keep the cell firm nucleus – controls the cell's activities cell wall – rigid structure that supports the cell cytoplasm – where chemical reactions take place chloroplast – where photosynthesis occurs cell membrane – controls what comes in and out of a cell mitochondria – where respiration occurs (7 marks) **2a** leaf cells (1 mark) **b** Leaf cells require chlorophyll to be able to photosynthesise. (1 mark) **3** Extended response question (6 marks). Example answers: Animal cells and plant cells have a nucleus, cytoplasm, cell membrane, and mitochondria. Plant cells also have a cell wall, chloroplasts, and a vacuole. Both cell types can respire (due to the presence of mitochondria). Only plant cells can photosynthesise (due to the presence of chloroplasts).

Starter	Support/Extension	Resources
Parts of a cell (5 min) Ask students to read the corresponding student-book spread and then use the interactive screen to name the parts of an animal cell. **Seeing cells** (10 min) Ask students why we can't see cells. Then lead them into explaining how scientists do see cells.	**Extension**: Ask students to explain the roles of the parts of the cell.	**Interactive**: Parts of a cell

Main	Support/Extension	Resources
Making a cheek cell slide (40 min) This practical is one of the AQA Enquiry process activities. It is important at this point to formally introduce students to the different parts of plant and animal cells. Issue the practical sheet with instructions explaining how to make a cheek cell slide. Ask students to read the sheet, and then list at least two health and safety risks. Students then make a cheek cell slide and set up the microscope. Students observe their slide through the microscope and produce a labelled diagram of a cheek cell.	**Support**: First, demonstrate the making of the slide, then help students to make the slide and set up the microscope if necessary. **Extension**: Ask students to calculate the magnification they are using.	**Practical**: Making a cheek cell slide

Plenary	Support/Extension	Resources
Another cell (10 min) Ask students to follow the instructions to make a slide of an onion cell. If time permits they can answer the corresponding questions. **Missing parts!** (5 min) Discuss with the students what they could observe in the cheek cell and what they could not see, for example, mitochondria. Why couldn't they see some parts? What other parts of a cell would you expect to see if you were looking at a plant cell?	**Support**: Return to the list of words on the board. Start as a checklist for drawing diagrams. **Extension**: Target able students with more probing questions.	

Homework		
Ask students to draw a summary table for the different components of both animal and plant cells, including their functions.		

8.2.3 Specialised cells

Securing Mastery Goals
- 3.8.2 Suggest what kind of tissue or organism a cell is part of, based on its features. (Pt 2/2)

Exceeding Mastery Goals
- 3.8.2 Deduce general patterns about how the structure of different cells is related to their function.

Enquiry processes
- 2.5 Use scientific vocabulary accurately, showing that you know its meaning and use appropriate units and correct chemical nomenclature.

Band	Outcome	Checkpoint	
		Question	Activity
Know	Name some examples of specialised animal cells.	1	Starter 1, Starter 2, Main 1, Main 2, Plenary 1
	Name some examples of specialised plant cells.	1	Starter 1, Starter 2, Main 1, Main 2, Plenary 1
	State structural adaptations of plant and animal cells, summarising this in a table or as a model.	C–E	Main 1, Main 2
Apply	Describe examples of specialised animal and plant cells.	2	Starter 1, Starter 2, Main 1, Main 2, Plenary 1
	Suggest what kind of tissue or organism a cell is part of, based on its features.		Main 1, Main 2
	Describe structural adaptations of plant and animal cells, summarising this in a table or as a model.		Main 1, Main 2
Extend	Describe examples of specialised animal cells, linking structure and function.	2, 3	Starter 1, Starter 2, Main 1, Main 2, Plenary 2
	Describe examples of specialised plant cells, linking structure and function.	2, 3	Starter 1, Starter 2, Main 1, Main 2, Plenary 2
	Compare and contrast structural adaptations of plant and animal cells, summarising this in a table or as a model.		Main 1, Main 2

Literacy
Students read a paragraph describing ciliated cells, interpreting the information given to draw a diagram of ciliated cells.

In the main activities students need to read information to ascertain meaning and to talk about their own cells in a presentation.

GCSE links
4.1.1.3/4.1.1.3 Cell specialisation

Cells may be specialised to carry out a particular function:
- sperm cells, nerve cells and muscle cells in animals
- root hair cells, xylem and phloem cells in plants.

Key Words
specialised cell, nerve cell, red blood cell, sperm cell, leaf cell, root hair cell, **structural adaptations**

Answers from the student book

In-text questions	A cells that can perform particular functions/jobs
	B transmit messages/electrical impulses around the body
	C nucleus
	D streamlined head and long tail
	E any two from: chloroplasts, vacuole, cell wall

Activity	Detailed descriptions Ciliated cells should appear as rectangular cells with nuclei inside and hairs on top of the rectangles labelled cilia.
Summary questions	**1** specialised, function, oxygen, chloroplasts, photosynthesis (5 marks) **2** Correct description of specialised features, for example, a red blood cell: no nucleus, disc-like shape. (2 marks) **3** A labelled diagram for a sperm cell is drawn, with the following features: streamlined head – enable it to move through water easily; tail – to 'swim'; many mitochondria – for respiration. (6 marks)

Starter	Support/Extension	Resources
An alternative question-led lesson is also available. **Mix and match** (5 min) Present students with a list of the main parts of plant and animal cells, and a list of the functions. Ask students to match each part to the function. This could be done with playing cards or on the board. **Becoming different** (5–10 min) The teacher shows a number of images of specialised cells from the Internet. Ask the students to identify special features in these cells not familiar to them from their previous knowledge of cells. They make suggestions about what the parts might be used for.	**Support:** Allow students to use the corresponding student-book spread. **Extension:** Ask students to give their own definition of the functions. **Extension:** Spend more time on what the parts are for.	**Question-led lesson:** Specialised cells

Main	Support/Extension	Resources
Building a cell (40 min) Students use textbooks (provided by the teacher) to research a specialised cell. Give students a box of scrap material, such as paper, string, packaging, dried pasta, and so on, and ask them to build a model of a specialised cell. Ask students to give a short presentation to the class about their cell, focusing on the special parts and their functions. **Speed dating** (40 min) Select up to eight cells. Divide the class into groups of the same number as the number of selected cells. Each student in the group is given time to research about one of the selected cells, either using text books, the internet, or an information card from the activity sheet. Then divide the group in half. Make two concentric circles, each facing the other. Students should be in pairs. Give each pair about three minutes to tell the other about their cell. Then move the outer circle around by one student. Continue until all pairs have been matched.	All students should be issued with the support sheet (blank table) to fill in regardless of the activity chosen. This table will be self-differentiating. **Support:** The teacher controls which cells are researched and built by which student/group. Give more difficult cells to the more able students/groups. **Extension:** Ask probing questions during the presentation and ask students to fill in the final column of the table.	**Activity:** Building a cell **Activity:** Speed dating

Plenary	Support/Extension	Resources
Matchmaking (5 min) Interactive resource where students link cells to their specialised feature and function. **Game of threes** (5 min) Students asked to pick three specialised cells. For each, name a special part and give a special function. This could be done on a mini-whiteboard.		**Interactive:** Matchmaking

Homework		
Students draw and label a specialised cell. They should label as many specialised parts as possible and describe the functions.		

8.2.4 Movement of substances

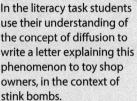

Securing Mastery Goals
- 3.8.2 Explain why multi-cellular organisms need organ systems to keep their cells alive. (Pt 2/2)

Enquiry processes
- 2.6 ecord observations using scientific words.

  2.9 Choose a suitable range for the independent and dependent variable.

  2.9 Gather sufficient data for the investigation and repeat if appropriate.

Band	Outcome	Checkpoint	
		Question	Activity
Know	Identify substances that move into or out of cells.	A, B	
	State simply what diffusion is.	1	Plenary 2
↓	Make sets of observations or measurements of diffusion of coloured gel, identifying the ranges and intervals used.		Main 1, Plenary 1
Apply	Describe the process of diffusion.	1	Plenary 2
	Collect data of diffusion of coloured gel, choosing appropriate ranges, numbers, and values for measurements and observations.		Main 1, Plenary 1
↓	Explain why multi-cellular organisms need organ systems to keep their cells alive.		Plenary 2
Extend	Explain which substances move into and out of cells.	A, B, 3	
	Explain the process of diffusion.	3	Plenary 2
↓	Choose and justify data collection methods of diffusion of coloured gel that minimise error, and produce precise and reliable data.		Main 1, Plenary 1

Maths
During the practical students will be required to measure times and volumes.

MyMaths More support for the maths skills in this section can be found on MyMaths.

Literacy
In the literacy task students use their understanding of the concept of diffusion to write a letter explaining this phenomenon to toy shop owners, in the context of stink bombs.

During the practical students need to read the method for information on how to complete the experiment. They will discuss their results with others in the group, and listen to the ideas of others, for explanations of their findings.

GCSE link
4.1.3.1/4.1.3.1 Diffusion

Factors which affect the rate of diffusion are:
- the difference in concentrations (concentration gradient)
- the temperature
- the surface area of the membrane.

Key Words
diffusion, concentration

Answers from the student book

In-text questions	**A** food particles/glucose, and oxygen **B** carbon dioxide
Activity	**Stink-bomb alert!** In diffusion, particles travel from an area of high concentration to an area of low concentration. Initially, the smell from the stink bomb is only found in the immediate vicinity but, through diffusion, the smell will spread until the concentration of stink bomb particles becomes constant.
Summary questions	**1** high, low, diffusion (3 marks) **2** The smell diffuses from an area of high concentration to one of low concentration. (3 marks) **3** Diagram should show understanding of the following concepts (6 marks): Substances moving in an out of red blood cells through diffusion, smells diffusing across a room, water diffusing into plant cells, including the difference between a healthy plant and a wilting plant. Credit correct use of diagrams.

Starter	Support/Extension	Resources
Wanted or not (5 min) Interactive resource with a list of molecules students need to decide whether or not the cell needs.		**Interactive:** Wanted or not
Observation skills (5 min) Pose two questions: 'What is the difference between an observation and a measurement?' and 'When making observations, how would you plan to make observations during an experiment?'. Give students some time to consider these questions then explore their answers. Try to lead the second answer to a series of observations during the course of the experiment.	**Support**: Change second question to two options, 'observe at the end only' or 'observe at intervals'. **Extension**: Ask students why a series of observations would be more useful.	

Main	Support/Extension	Resources
Observing diffusion (40 min) Give the students the practical sheet with a method. They will need to put a cube of coloured gel into water and make observations at times intervals. Do not lead students to expect any particular outcome. There should be a group discussion of their observations. Students need to consider the questions in the practical sheet to produce some explanation of the movement of molecules. They should link this to diffusion into and out of cells. For the conclusion, it is important to go through with students the definition of diffusion and which substances diffuse into and out of our cells.	**Support**: The support sheet contains a results table for students to use. Help students write in their observations by modelling good practice. **Extension**: Encourage students to explain the idea of diffusion and lead their group during the experiment. They might be able to discuss limitations with the technique or model.	**Practical:** Observing diffusion **Skill sheet:** Recording results

Plenary	Support/Extension	Resources
Class feedback (10 min) Groups feedback their ideas about what they have seen in the experiment. Students can write notes on 'What is diffusion?' in their books.	**Support**: Ask weaker students to describe the observations.	
Role play (10 min) Arrange the chairs in a large circle around the room with gaps to represent the cell membrane. Ask all of the students to stand outside the membrane and tell them they represent oxygen. Then ask them to diffuse into the cell. They need to become evenly spread. If they don't, ask them why they have gone wrong. Discuss with students why multi-celluar organisms need organ systems, such as the circulatory system, and cannot just rely on diffusion to transport materials around the body.	**Extension**: Encourage students to explain why this might have happened.	

Homework		
Ask students to produce a drawing of a red blood cell. Ask them to explain how oxygen would get into the cell. They can use a mix of labels or written prose, depending on ability.		

8.2.5 Uni-cellular organisms

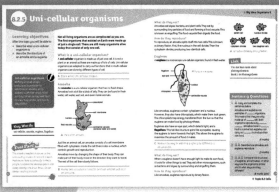

Securing Mastery Goals
● 8.3.2 Explain how uni-cellular organisms are adapted to carry out functions that in multi-cellular organisms are done by different types of cell.

Enquiry processes

● 2.9 Use the measuring instrument correctly.

Band	Outcome	Checkpoint	
		Question	Activity
Know	Name an example of a uni-cellular organism.	1	Starter 1, Starter 2
	Identify some structures in an amoeba.	B, C	Starter 1, Starter 2, Plenary 2
	Identify some structures in a euglena.	C	Starter 1, Starter 2, Plenary 2
↓	Select the appropriate apparatus to observe an amoeba and a euglena cell.		Main 1
Apply	Describe what a uni-cellular organism is.		Starter 1, Starter 2
	Describe the structure of an amoeba and a euglena.		Starter 1, Starter 2
	Explain how uni-cellular organisms are adapted to carry out functions that, in multi-cellular organisms, are done by different types of cell.	4	Main
↓	Select the appropriate magnification to observe an amoeba and a euglena cell through a microscope.		Main 1
Extend	Explain what a uni-cellular organism is and give detailed examples.	3	Starter 1, Starter 2, Plenary 2
	Describe the structure and function of an amoeba.	3	Starter 1, Starter 2, Plenary 2
	Describe the structure and function of a euglena.	3	Starter 1, Starter 2, Plenary 2
↓	Give justifications for the choice of magnification when observing an amoeba and a euglena cell through a microscope.		Main 1

Maths
During the practical activity, students use multiplication to calculate magnification.

MyMaths More support for the maths skills in this section can be found on MyMaths.

Literacy
Students produce a presentation to introduce amoeba and euglena, in order to discuss and show their understanding to others.

For homework, students are asked to write a summary of the differences between multi-cellular and uni-cellular organisms.

GCSE link
4.1.3.1/4.1.3.1 Diffusion

A single-celled organism has a relatively large surface area to volume ratio. This allows sufficient transport of molecules into and out of the cell to meet the needs of the organism.

Key Words
uni-cellular, amoeba, euglena, flagellum

Answers from the student book

In-text questions	A Organism made up of only one cell. B Any two from: cytoplasm, nucleus, cell membrane. C Any from: euglena carries out photosynthesis/has chloroplasts/has an eye spot/has a flagellum.
Activity	**Unicellular organisms** Some of the following points should be included: both uni-cellular organisms; amoeba looks jelly-like with no fixed structure; euglena are green with a tail-like structure.

Summary questions	1 uni-cellular, one, binary fission, engulf, photosynthesis (5 marks) 2 Nucleus in the parent cell divides, cytoplasm divides, two (daughter cells) produced. (3 marks) 3 Unicellular organisms have specialised cell components that perform specific functions. (1 mark) Any three named examples and functions, for example: euglena has a flagellum for movement (1 mark) euglena has chloroplasts for photosynthesis (1 mark) ameoba change the shape of the cell to move (1 mark) 4 Extended response question (6 marks). Example answers: Both uni-cellular, have a nucleus/cytoplasm, get rid of waste by excretory vesicles. Only euglena can photosynthesise. Both can move-euglena by flagellum, amoeba by pseudopods. Both cells can engulf food.

kerboodle

Starter	Support/Extension	Resources
Going it alone (5 min) Pose the questions 'Name some really small organisms that live in our environment'. Try to avoid bacteria but guide students to small animals and plants. Then challenge their ideas by showing a film from the internet of single-celled organisms such as amoeba. **How to go it alone** (5 min) Having shown a film of an amoeba, start a discussion about all the things that a cell has to do to survive. Ask students to consider any special parts a cell might need to carry out these tasks.	**Support**: Remind students about characteristics of life (MRS GREN) **Extension**: Ask students how these organisms carry out their life functions. In addition, find a second film of a more specialised organism, for example, paramaecium, and discuss the more special features.	

Main	Support/Extension	Resources
Observing amoeba and euglena (40 min) Formally introduce the idea of uni-cellular organisms and issue the practical sheet. Students should use the method on the practical sheet to make temporary slides with amoeba and with euglena. Students then observe the organisms using the microscope. If available, use a projection microscope as well so that students know what to look for. Students should draw labelled diagrams of the two cell types. Note: euglena in particular will be small and may be difficult to observe, so have images of these cell types to project for the students to observe and draw.	**Support**: Have projection images prepared. Students will need more help with the microscopes. Students may only observe the amoeba as it is larger and slower moving, therefore easier to see. The use of film clips or images may be used for the drawings rather than actual specimens but use real specimens so that students do see the real organism. **Extension**: Encourage more independent work. Students could also produce a series of diagrams to show amoeba moving.	**Practical**: Observing amoeba and euglena

Plenary	Support/Extension	Resources
Spot the difference (10 min) Use the interactive screen to look at a selection of different features found in cells. Students identify the common features of all cells, and the unique features of uni-cellular organisms. **Create a cell** (5 min) Ask students to design an imaginary cell that would live in water. Ask them to draw features onto the cell to help it carry out as many of the special functions as possible.	**Support**: Focus on the common features of cells. **Extension**: Try to discuss what the special features are used for. **Support**: List the life processes on the board, and discuss how cells might carry these processes out. **Extension**: Students look up single-celled organisms in a higher-level text book to incorporate real structures in their drawings.	**Interactive**: Spot the difference

Homework		
Ask students to produce a written description of the cells that they have observed. They should pay particular attention to how the cells are different to those studied in earlier lessons.		

Checkpoint lesson routes

The route through this lesson can be determined using the Checkpoint assessment.

Percentage pass marks are supplied in the Checkpoint teacher notes.

Route A (support)

Resource: 8 Part 1 Checkpoint revision

This revision activity is largely focused on improving knowledge and understanding of cells and the muscular skeletal system, and developing the ability to explain how the parts work. The activities are varied and include sentence completion, labelling diagrams, linking lines, and interpretation of a diagram of the joint.

Route B (extension)

Resource: 8 Part 1 Checkpoint extension

Students work through a series of tasks to answer the question 'What happens when runners get injured?'

They are supplied with information about sprains and strains and a bar chart to show the incidence of these and other injuries in one group of runners. They also have a worked example to show how to calculate the raw number from a percentage.

Progression to *Apply*

Know outcome	Apply outcome	Making progress
Know that the parts of the human skeleton work as a system for support, protection, movement.	Explain how a physical property of part of the skeleton relates to its function.	Use different strength elastic bands to try and pull a small object. If too elastic they cannot pull. Students can feel their own bones and muscles to compare texture. If available, students can look at models of joints to compare their structure and range of movement. Task 3 and 4 cover joints and movement.
Know that antagonistic pairs of muscles create movement when one contracts and the other relaxes.	Explain how antagonistic muscles produce movement around a joint. Use a diagram to predict the result of a muscle contraction or relaxation.	Students can use their own muscles to demonstrate. If they hold left arm out and pull biceps back with right hand just above elbow, the arm will bend. Then pull back the triceps at the back and watch arm lower. Then use normal movement to show biceps getting thicker. Try the exercise with various muscle sets around the body. Task 4 can be used to explain antagonistic muscle action.
Know that the muscular skeletal system is muscles and bones working together to cause movement and support the body.		Toy puppets that require strings to cause movement make the point that bones cannot move alone – if not available a video clip could show this. Task 4 shows the relationship between muscle, bones and ligaments.
Know that there are many types of cell. Each has a different structure or feature so it can do a specific job.	Suggest what kind of tissue or organism a cell is part of, based on its features.	Matching exercises work well. Provide students with a set of cards with cells on them and another set with cell functions on them. As students to match the cell to its function. You could then provide another set of cards with tissues or organs on and students can choose which cells are found in them. Each student in a group could find out how one cell shape is matched to its function and describe it orally to the group.
Use a light microscope to observe and draw cells.	Explain how to use a microscope to identify and compare different types of cells.	Remind students that explanations always require a statement followed by 'because' or 'so', for example, "I used the high power objective because the cell was too small to see with the low power". Task 1 covers how to use a microscope.
Know that both plant and animal cells have a cell membrane, nucleus, cytoplasm and mitochondria. Plant cells also have a cell wall, chloroplasts and usually a permanent vacuole.	This basic knowledge is used throughout all biology/science courses.	Students often muddle walls and membranes at GCSE. You could show them a range of animal and plant cells and ask them to identify the presence of a wall and membrane/no wall, membrane only. They should also be able to recognise other key features, such as cytoplasm. It is important they realise that animal cells do not have walls. Ideally use a range of images – for example, photos of microscope slides, digital images, and sketches. Task 1 and 2 cover cell structures and functions.

Answers to End-of-Big Idea questions

1a nucleus (1 mark)

 b trap light/carry out photosynthesis (1 mark)

 c W (vacuole) (1 mark)

 d Two from: nucleus, cytoplasm, cell membrane. (2 marks)

2 reproductive system–produces new organisms, digestive system–breaks down food so it can be absorbed, respiratory system–takes in oxygen, removes carbon dioxide, circulatory system–transports materials around the body. (4 marks)

3a microscope (1 mark)

 b add stain/dye/coloured liquid (1 mark)

 c It could transmit a disease or cause an infection as blood is removed. (1 mark)

 d Diagram should show a cell containing a nucleus, cytoplasm, and cell membrane. (3 marks)

4a A cell whose structure is adapted to suit its function. (1 mark)

 b red blood cell (1 mark), transport oxygen (1 mark)

  transmits messages (1 mark)

  carry out photosynthesis (1 mark), packed with chloroplasts (1 mark)

 c Water moves into the root hair cell by diffusion/osmosis.

  It moves from an area of high water concentration to an area of low water concentration, through a cell membrane. (3 marks)

5 a Uni-cellular organisms consist of one cell, multi-celluar organisms are made of many cells. (1 mark)

 b appropriate example, e.g., ameoba, euglena (1 mark)

 c For example:

  Transport systems are needed to deliver substances such as oxygen (1 mark) / remove waste (1 mark); transport distance is too far for diffusion (1 mark). Nervous systems are also needed to enable communication (1 mark).

6a ligament – X (1 mark), tendon – Y (1 mark)

 b cartilage covers the end of the bones (1 mark)

  cartilage is strong smooth tissue that prevents bones rubbing / wearing away (1 mark)

  fluid present makes cartilage slippery (1 mark)

 c Bones would rub together / not move freely/ movement would be restricted (1 mark)

  leading to pain / arthritis. (1 mark)

 d reference to antagonistic muscles (1 mark)

  one muscle contracts to move bone (1 mark)

  as extensor muscle contracts, arm bends (1 mark)

  as flexor muscle contracts, arm straightens (1 mark)

Answer guide for Big Write

Know	Apply	Extend
1–2 marks	3–4 marks	5–6 marks
• The article is not presented in a logical way, and little attention has been paid to the rules of this text type. • The student has stated at least one difference and one similarity between an amoeba and a human.	• The article is clearly presented. • The student has described at least two similarities and two differences in the structure and function of an amoeba and a human.	• The article is clearly presented and engaging, paying attention to the rules of this text type. • The student has clearly explained a number of similarities and differences in the structure and functions of an amoeba and a human.

kerboodle

8 Part 1 Checkpoint assessment (automarked)

8 Part 1 Checkpoint: Revision

8 Part 1 Checkpoint: Extension

8.1 Progress task, 8.2 Progress task

National curriculum links for this Big Idea	
Topic	**National Curriculum topic**
9.1 Interdependence	Relationships in an ecosystem
9.2 Plant reproduction	Reproduction in plants

In this Big Idea students will learn:

- organisms in a food web (decomposers, producers, and consumers) depend on each other for nutrients. So, a change in one population leads to changes in others
- the population of a species is affected by the number of its predators and prey, disease, pollution, and competition between individuals for limited resources such as water and nutrients

- plants have adaptations to disperse seeds using wind, water, or animals
- plants reproduce sexually to produce seeds, which are formed following fertilisation in the ovary.

AQA Enquiry process activities

Activity	Section
3.9.1 Use a model to investigate the impact of changes in a population of one organism on others in the ecosystem.	9.1.4 Competition
3.9.2 Use models to evaluate the features of various types of seed dispersal.	9.2.3 Seed dispersal

Preparing for Key Stage 4 Success

Knowledge	• 4.7.1.1 Communities
	• 4.7.1.3 Biotic factors
	• 4.7.2.1 Levels of organisation
	• 4.7.4.1 Trophic levels (biology only)
Maths	**1** Arithmetic and numerical computation
	c Use ratios, fractions and percentages (9.1.1, 9.2.2)
	d Make estimates of the results of simple calculations (9.1.4)
	2 Handling data
	a Find arithmetic means (9.2.3)
	c Construct and interpret frequency tables and diagrams, bar charts and histograms (9.1.2, 9.2.2, 9.2.3)
	d Understand the principles of sampling as applied to scientific data (9.1.4)
	f Understand the terms mean, mode and median (9.2.3)
	3 Algebra
	a Understand and use the symbols (please insert) (9.1.1, 9.2.3)
	4 Graphs
	a Translate information between graphical and numerical form (9.1.2, 9.2.2, 9.2.3)
Literacy	• Use of scientific terms (9.1.1, 9.1.2, 9.1.3, 9.1.4, 9.2.1, 9.2.2, 9.2.3)
	• Organisation of ideas and information (9.1.4, 9.2.3)
	• Legibility, spelling, punctuation, grammar and sentence structure (9.2.3)
	• Planning and adapting writing style to suit audience and purpose (9.2.3)
Assessment	• Extended response questions (9.1.1, 9.1.2, 9.1.3, 9.1.4, 9.2.1, 9.2.2, 9.2.3)
	• Quantitative problem solving (9.1.1)
	• Application of enquiry processes (9.2.3)

KS2 Link	Check before:	Checkpoint	Catch-up
Food chains include producers, predators, and prey.	9.1.1 Food chains and webs	Students write a food chain, labelling this using the key terms: predator, prey, producer, and consumer.	Show pictures of three organisms and ask students to build them into a food chain by talking about what each animal eats.
Living things are classified into groups according to common characteristics and based on similarities and differences.	9.1.1 Food chains and webs	Students offer different categories of organisms, for example, mammals, predators, and plants, describing the characteristics of each group.	Students sort images of different organisms into groups, justifying their choices.
Environments can change, posing dangers to living things.	9.1.2 Disruption to food chains and webs	Students make a list of different factors that can affect an ecosystem.	Show students a food web. Describe a number of situations and ask them what would happen. For example if the producers or top predators died?
The functions of different parts of flowering plants: roots, stem, leaves, and flowers.	9.2.1 Structure of a flower and pollination	Students label a diagram of a flowering plant, including the functions of each part.	Card sort of the main parts of a flowering plant and their functions.
The part that flowers play in the life cycle of flowering plants, including pollination, seed formation, and seed dispersal.	9.2.1 Structure of a flower and pollination	Name the main parts of a flower. What is the flower of a plant for?	Show a picture of a half flower. Identify the parts and what they are needed for.
The requirements of plants for life and growth (air, light, water, nutrients from soil, and room to grow) and how they vary from plant to plant.	9.2.2 Fertilisation and germination	Discussion on 'What conditions do plants need to grow? Is this different for seeds growing to seedlings?'	Link back to MRS GREN for all living things.

Key Stage 2 Quiz: Biology
9 Part 1 End-of-Big Idea test (foundation)
9 Part 1 End-of-Big Idea test (foundation) mark scheme
9 Part 1 End-of-Big Idea test (higher)
9 Part 1 End-of-Big Idea test (higher) mark scheme

Answers to Picture Puzzler
Key Words
plant, orange, leg, light bulb, egg, nest
The key word is **pollen**.
Close Up
A pollen grain

MyMaths

You can find additional support for the maths skills covered in this Big Idea on **MyMaths**, including making estimates, using mean, median and mode, and drawing and interpreting graphs.

9.1.1 Food chains and webs

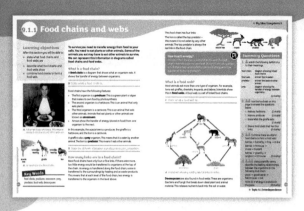

Securing Mastery Goals
- 3.9.1 Combine food chains to form a food web.

Band	Outcome	Checkpoint	
		Question	**Activity**
Know ↓	State the definition of a food chain.	A, 1	Starter 1, Starter 2, Main, Plenary 2
	State the definition of a food web.	C, 1	Main, Plenary 2
Apply ↓	Describe what food chains show.	B, 1	Starter 1, Starter 2, Main, Plenary 1, Plenary 2, Homework
	Describe what food webs show.	2	Main, Plenary 1, Homework
	Combine food chains to form a food web.	3	Main, Homework
Extend ↓	Explain the link between food chains and energy.	1, 4	Maths, Main
	Explain why a food web gives a more accurate representation of feeding relationships than a food chain.		Main, Plenary 1

Maths
Students carry out simple calculations using percentages to calculate the amount of energy that is transferred between different levels of food chains.

MyMaths More support for the maths skills in this section can be found on MyMaths.

Literacy
Students describe and explain food chains and food webs using scientific terminology.

GCSE link
4.7.2.1/4.7.2.1 Levels of organisation

Students should understand that photosynthetic organisms are the producers of biomass for life on Earth.

Feeding relationships within a community can be represented by food chains. All food chains begin with a producer which synthesises molecules. This is usually a green plant or alga which makes glucose by photosynthesis.

Key Words
food chain, predator, prey, **food web**, consumer, producer, decomposer

Answers from the student book

In-text questions	**A** It is a diagram that shows what an organism eats. It shows the flow of energy between organisms. **B** A predator eats other animals, whereas prey are eaten by other animals. **C** A set of linked food chains.
Activity	**How much energy?** First level = 1000 kJ, Second level = 0.1 × 1000 kJ = 100 kJ, Third level = 0.1 × 100 kJ = 10 kJ 10 kJ would be passed to the top predator.
Summary questions	**1** food chain – diagram showing the flow of energy through organisms food web – diagram showing linked food chains predator – animal that eats another animal prey – animal that is eaten (4 marks)

182

2a giraffe/impala/zebra (1 mark) **b** acacia tree/grass (1 mark) **c** acacia tree (1 mark)

   d Credit any suitable answer. For example, grass → impala → leopard → lion

     (1 mark for correct order of organisms, 1 mark for arrows in correct direction)

3 1 mark for all arrows pointing in correct direction.

  1 mark for two food chains correctly interlinked.

  1 mark for third food chain correctly interlinked.

4 Example answers (6 marks):

  Grasshopper eats grass, field mouse eats grasshopper, owl eats field mouse.

  The producer is the grass. The herbivore is the grasshopper. The carnivores are the field mice and the owls.

  The predators are the field mice an the owls. The prey are the grasshoppers and the field mice. The top predator is the owl.

  500 kJ of energy are transferred to the grasshopper.

  50 kJ are transferred to the field mouse.

  5 kJ are transferred to the owl.

Starter	Support/Extension	Resources
Who eats who? (10 min) Students share ideas in pairs about some of the key words in this lesson (food chain, carnivore, herbivore, omnivore, predator, and prey), as students will have met simple food chains in KS2. Discuss as a class before using the interactive resource to complete some simple food chains.	**Extension**: Encourage students to use scientific terms throughout the activity.	**Interactive**: Who eats who?
Feeding definitions (5 min) Prepare a set of cards, each with a key word or a definition. Students match the words with their definitions. Cards should include: food chain, carnivore, herbivore, omnivore, producer, consumer, decomposer, predator, and prey. Students use what they have learnt from the key words to make simple food chains.	**Extension**: Challenge students to make food chains that are three, four, and five levels long.	

Main	Support/Extension	Resources
Food chains and webs (40 min) Introduce the definition of a food web and show an example. Students discuss in pairs what they see before discussing as a class. You can assess students' understanding of the key terms in this lesson by using mini-whiteboards during questioning, increasing class participation. Students then make their own food webs using the organisms provided on the activity sheet, and answer the questions that follow.	**Support**: The support sheet provides students with a reduced number of organisms to make food webs. Images of organisms are accompanied by short notes explaining what they eat and what they are eaten by.	**Activity**: Food chains and webs

Plenary	Support/Extension	Resources
Chains from webs (5 min) Present students with a food web and ask them to write as many food chains as possible from that web using mini-whiteboards. Alternatively, present students with several food chains, and ask them to construct a food web from the food chains provided.	**Extension**: Students suggest the merits of using food chains and food webs as a scientist.	
Role-playing food chains (10 min) Project a jumbled-up list of organisms on the board. Students work in small groups of three to five to act out a food chain from the organisms provided in three minutes. Watch the role plays, and students evaluate each other's role plays using the definitions of food chains and food webs.	**Extension**: Encourage students to work towards longer food chains and where possible, team up with another group to act out a food web.	

Homework		
Students construct a food web from a different environment of their choice. Students include as many organisms as they can in their food web, before choosing one food chain from their food web to annotate using key words.		

Disruptions to food chains and webs

Securing Mastery Goals
- 3.9.1 Explain issues with human food supplies in terms of insect pollinators.
- 3.9.1 Describe how a species' population changes as its predator or prey population changes. (Pt 1/3)
- 3.9.1 Explain effects of environmental changes and toxic materials on a species' population. (Pt 1/2)

Exceeding Mastery Goals
- 3.9.1 Develop an argument about how toxic substances can accumulate in human food.

Enquiry processes
- 2.4 Decide the type of chart or graph to draw based on its purpose or type of data.
- 2.4 Label the x axis with the name of the independent variable and the y axis with the dependent variable.
- 2.4 Mark out an equal scale showing what each square of graph paper represents.

Band	Outcome	Checkpoint	
		Question	**Activity**
Know	State that one population of organisms can affect another.	1, 2	Lit, Starter 2, Main 1, Plenary 2
	State that toxic material can get into food chains.	C, 1	Main 2, Plenary 2, Homework
	Present population data as a graph, and describe simple patterns shown.		Main 1
Apply	Describe the interdependence of organisms.	B, 1, 2	Lit, Starter 2, Main 1, Plenary 2, Homework
	Explain effects of toxic materials on a species' population.	C, 1, 4	Main 2, Plenary 2, Homework
	Present population data as a graph to describe trends and draw conclusions.		Main 1
	Explain issues with human food supplies in terms of insect pollinators.	3	Plenary 2
Extend	Explain the interdependence of organisms.	1, 2	Lit, Starter 2, Main 1, Plenary 2, Homework
	Explain how toxic materials can accumulate in human food sources.	3	Main 2
	Present population data as a graph, explaining trends and drawing detailed conclusions from data provided.		Main 1

Maths
Students interpret numerical data given in tables, and plot graphs.

They also interpret and sketch graphs to demonstrate changes in populations for different organisms.

MyMaths More support for the maths skills in this section can be found on MyMaths.

Literacy
Students use scientific terminology when carrying out discussions on factors affecting populations and causes of bioaccumulation.

Key Words
interdependence, **population**, bioaccumulation

GCSE link
4.7.1.1/4.7.1.1 Communities

Within a community each species depends on other species. If one species is removed it can affect the whole community. This is called interdependence.

4.7.1.3/4.7.1.3 Biotic factors

Biotic (living) factors which can affect a community are: availability of food, new predators, new pathogens.

Answers from the student book

In-text questions	A bees (or any other appropriate answer) B The population of consumers will decrease. C The build-up of (toxic) chemicals through a food chain.

Activity	**Interpreting food webs** Credit sensible suggestions for what would happen to other organisms in the food web if disease reduced the population of frogs.

Summary questions	**1** interdependence, decrease, bioaccumulation (3 marks)
	2a Rabbit population would increase as it has no predators/it will not get eaten. (2 marks)
	  b The hawk and fox population may decrease as they have reduced food supplies.
	    The insect population may increase as they have fewer predators. (4 marks)
	3 Any three from:
	  Insects act as pollinators. This ensures seeds are produced to produce future crops. This also ensures fruits are produced. If insect numbers decrease, the amount of foods produced would drop. (3 marks)
	4 Extended response question (6 marks). Example answers:
	  Insecticide runs into river. Taken up by plankton. DDT accumulates in fish when they eat the plankton. One fish eats lots of plankton, but not enough to cause death. DDT accumulates in birds when they eat the fish. One bird eats many fish. DDT level is now so high/concentrated that it causes death in the bird.

Starter	Support/Extension	Resources
Key words and definitions (10 min) Write the key words interdependence, population, and bioaccumulation on the board. Students should discuss possible definitions in pairs, before offering these in a class discussion. **Up or down?** (5 min) Interactive resource where students predict how populations will change for different organisms in different circumstances.	**Extension**: Students should offer explanations to justify their answers.	**Interactive**: Up or down?

Main	Support/Extension	Resources
Changes in population (25 min) Students are given data about the population of gannets on the island of Grassholm over a period of 18 years. Students present the information using a suitable graph, and answer questions that follow. **What killed the herons?** (15 min) Students play a card game in groups of three using the sort cards provided to work out the mystery of 'What killed the herons?' The cards give small pieces of information that add together to explain the process of bioaccumulation. Use the animation to reinforce the concept of bioaccumulation.	**Support**: Pre-labelled graph axes are provided on the accompanying support sheet. **Support**: Prompt students towards the first card in the sequence. **Extension**: Students research mercury poisoning in humans.	**Activity**: Changes in population **Skill sheet:** Drawing graphs **Information:** What killed the herons? **Animation:** Bioaccumulation

Plenary	Support/Extension	Resources
Best and worst (5 min) Students work in pairs to discuss features needed for the best and worst pesticides farmers can use. Follow up with a class discussion of ideas. Students can use mini-whiteboards to hold up the features that they think are most important. **Human impact** (10 min) Students work in pairs to think up as many ways as possible that humans can affect a population of organisms. Students write this down and swap ideas with another group. Groups must then work out what effect the human activities listed will have on a population (increase or decrease) and explain their answers to each other.	**Support**: Give prompts, such as, good pesticides would be species-specific, biodegradable, and insoluble. **Extension**: Remind students of the importance of insect pollination in the production of food crops. Students consider the advantages and disadvantages of pesticides.	

Homework	Support/Extension	
As an extension to the activity Changes in population, ask students to write a prediction on the population of gannets for each of the following scenarios: • A new competitor for the gannet arrives. • An oil spill has resulted in a temporary fall in fish stocks in the area. • The local farmer starts to use vast quantities of insecticides toxic to animals. Students must give explanations for their answers.	**Extension**: Students should sketch the corresponding population curve for each scenario given.	

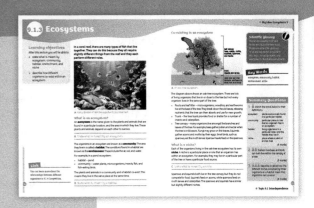

This spread covers prerequisite knowledge and key words for AQA KS3 Science topic 3.9.1 Interdependence.

Securing Mastery Goals

- 3.9.1 Explain effects of environmental changes and toxic materials on a species' population. (Pt 2/2)
- 3.9.1 Describe how a species' population changes as its predator or prey population changes. (Pt 2/3)

Enquiry processes

- 2.9 Apply sampling techniques if appropriate.

Band	Outcome	Checkpoint	
		Question	**Activity**
Know	State that different organisms can co-exist.	A, 1	Lit, Starter 1, Main, Plenary 1
	State the definition of the term niche.	C, 1	Lit, Starter 1, Main, Plenary 1
	Record data from sampling an ecosystem.		Main
Apply	Describe how different organisms co-exist within an ecosystem.	2, 3	Main, Plenary 1, Plenary 2, Homework
	Identify niches within an ecosystem.	3	Main, Plenary 1, Plenary 2, Homework
	Use quadrats to take measurements in an ecosystem, describing trends observed.		Main
Extend	Explain why different organisms are needed in an ecosystem.	2, 3	Main, Plenary 2, Homework
	Explain why different organisms within the same ecosystem have different niches.	2, 3	Main, Plenary 2, Homework
	Use quadrats and transects to take unbiased measurements in an ecosystem, describing trends observed in data.		Main

Maths

Students must show an understanding of number size and scale when carrying out sampling techniques using quadrats and transects.

Some students will also estimate the number of a named plant in a given area using sampling data provided.

MyMaths More support for the maths skills in this section can be found on MyMaths.

Literacy

Students use scientific terminology, including their definitions, when describing trends shown by their sampling technique, and when discussing the co-existence of organisms in an ecosystem.

GCSE link

4.7.1.1/4.7.1.1 Communities

An ecosystem is the interaction of a community of living organisms (biotic) with the non-living (abiotic) parts of their environment.

Key Words

ecosystem, community, habitat, environment, niche

Answers from the student book

In-text questions	**A** Name given to plants and animals found in a particular location, and the area/habitat in which they live.
	B The area in which an organism lives.
	C A particular place or role occupied by an organism within an ecosystem.
Activity	**Scientific glossary**
	Credit key words from this chapter given with definitions. Each key word should be accompanied by an example or a diagram where possible.

Summary questions	**1** ecosystem – living organisms in a particular area, and the habitat they live in community – plants and animals found in a particular habitat habitat – place where a plant or animal lives niche – particular place or role that an organism has in an ecosystem (4 marks) **2** Bees and birds have different niches. They eat different things. Bees require nectar from flowers, whereas birds live off insects living on the leaves. (2 marks) **3** Extended response question (6 marks). Example answers: A niche is the place or role that an organism has in a habitat. For example, many organisms live in an oak tree (or suitable example). Not every organism lives in the same part of the tree. Microorganisms at the base of the tree break down old leaves. This gives the tree further nutrients to absorb for growth. Insects live in the tree trunk. The insect larvae are food for birds that may live in the canopy. Squirrels and bees also live in the canopy. Bees gather pollen and nectar when the tree is in blossom. Squirrels gather acorns as food. The activities of each organism do not conflict each other, and so different organisms can co-exist.

kerboodle

Starter	Support/Extension	Resources
Ecosystem key words (5 min) Interactive memory matching game where students match key words to their definitions (ecosystem, niche, environment, community, co-existence, habitat, population).	**Extension:** Ask students to suggest definitions before starting the game.	**Interactive:** Ecosystem key words
Sampling techniques (5 min) Show students a quadrat or an image of a quadrat on a grass field. Talk about the sampling techniques used to count the number of plants in a field.	**Extension:** Introduce the idea of using transects when sampling to control bias.	

Main	Support/Extension	Resources
Investigating the distribution of a plant (45 min) Introduce students to the idea of ecosystems, habitats, communities, and niches. Explain to students how different organisms can co-exist in the same environment. Take the class onto the school field and split into small groups. Issue each group with a transect line (30 m long, marked at metre intervals) and a quadrat (1 m² or 0.25 m²). Students use sampling techniques to measure the abundance of a named plant on the school field (e.g., dandelion), and record observations. Students then return to the classroom to answer the questions on their practical sheets.	**Extension:** Encourage students to estimate the plant population of the whole field, from their results. Students also discuss whether their estimate is accurate, explaining in terms of dependence on light, competition, and other factors on the distribution of plants.	**Practical:** Investigating the distribution of a plant **Skill sheet:** Recording results

Plenary	Support/Extension	Resources
Key word definitions (5 min) Revisit the seven key words from the start of the lesson (ecosystem, habitat, community, niche, population, co-existence, and environment) and ask students to provide the definition for each key word using a mini-whiteboard.	**Extension:** Encourage students to use each key word in a sentence.	
Living together (5 min) Divide the class into groups of three. Each student in the group is assigned one of three organisms found in the school field: grass, earthworm, and starling. Students describe how the organisms are able to all live in the habitat and how they interact, identifying the roles of each organism in this habitat.	**Extension:** Add additional organisms to introduce the idea of different niches. For example, dandelions as competitors, or grasshoppers with a different niche to the earthworm.	

Homework	Support/Extension
Students research an ecosystem. They produce an image of their chosen ecosystem and select a number of different organisms within ecosystem to write a short explanation on how these organisms can live together.	**Support:** Provide students with a list of terms to use in their explanation, for example, niche.

9.1.4 Competition

Securing Mastery Goals
- 3.9.1 Describe how a species' population changes as its predator or prey population changes. (Pt 3/3)

Exceeding Mastery Goals
- 3.9.1 Suggest what might happen when an unfamiliar species is introduced into a food web.
- 3.9.1 Make a deduction based on data about what caused a change in the population of a species.

Enquiry processes
- 2.1 Identify patterns in data.
- 2.3 Make a conclusion and explain it.

Enquiry process activity
- 3.9.1 Use a model to investigate the impact of changes in a population of one organism on others in the ecosystem.

Band	Outcome	Checkpoint	
		Question	**Activity**
Know	State some resources that plants and animals compete for.	A, B, 1	Starter 1, Main 1, Plenary 1, Homework
	Interpret secondary data to describe simple predator–prey relationships.		Maths, Main 2
Apply	Describe some resources that plants and animals compete for.	1	Starter 1, Main 1, Plenary 1, Homework
	Interpret secondary data to describe trends and draw conclusions about predator–prey relationships.		Maths, Main 2
Extend	Explain the effect of competition on the individual or the population.	1	Main 1, Plenary 1, Homework
	Make a deduction based on data about what caused a change in the population of a species.	2	Main 2
	Suggest what might happen when an unfamiliar species is introduced into a food web.	3	

Maths
Students draw, extract, and interpret information from graphs about predator–prey populations.

MyMaths More support for the maths skills in this section can be found on MyMaths.

GCSE link
4.7.1.1/4.7.1.1 Communities

Plants in a community or habitat often compete with each other for light and space, and for water and mineral ions from the soil.

Animals often compete with each other for food, mates and territory.

4.7.1.3/4.7.1.3 Biotic factors

Biotic (living) factors which can affect a community:
- one species outcompeting another so the numbers are no longer sufficient to breed.

Key Words
competition, adaptation

Answers from the student book

In-text questions	A food, water, space, and mates
	B light, water, space, and minerals
	C Interdependence means that changes in the population of one animal directly affects the population of the other.

Activity	**Predator–prey graphs**
	Graph of fox population against rabbit population should resemble that of the snowshoe hare and the Canadian lynx in the student book. When the population of the rabbit is high, the fox population increases. This reduces the number of rabbits, which in turn reduces the number of foxes, and the whole cycle starts again.
Summary questions	**1** compete, resources, mates, light (4 marks)
	2 When there are lots of prey, the population of predators increases.
	The large predator population will cause the prey population to decrease.
	There is now not enough food for all the predators so the predator population decreases.
	The prey population will now increase as less are being eaten.
	The cycle starts again.
	(3 marks)
	3 Example answers (6 marks):
	Initially, the population of European ladybirds will increase significantly because they can feed on aphids and other ladybird species.
	Eventually their food supply will decrease, which will lead to starvation for many seven-spotted ladybirds.
	The population of seven-spotted ladybirds will decrease, which allows the population of aphids to increase.
	The cycle then starts again.
	(Students must include a correct predator–prey graph.)

kerboodle

Starter	Support/Extension	Resources
Competitions galore (10 min) Ask students to think about as many competitions as they can. Most will talk about competitions in sport, music, or the arts. Steer students towards competition for living organisms to survive. Students then complete the interactive activity to decide whether the environment or competition is causing an effect on the organisms.	**Support:** Allow students to work in small groups	**Interactive:** Competition or environment?
Predator and prey (5 min) Provide students with a list of animals for them to sort into predators and prey organisms. Ask them to discuss what the organisms have in common.		

Main	Support/Extension	Resources
What does an organism need to survive? (10 min) Ask students in pairs to produce two spider diagrams to show what plants and animals need to survive. Discuss the similarities and differences between both lists. Discuss how competition for these resources limits population size.		
Predator–prey relationships (20 min) This activity is one of the AQA Enquiry process activities. Students plot a graph to show the number of Canadian wolves in Quebec 2001–13. This graph is drawn on top of an existing graph showing the number of caribou in the same period. Students must interpret the graphs to answer the questions that follow.	**Support:** An access sheet is provided where the predator–prey graphs are already drawn and the questions are simpler.	**Activity:** Predator–prey relationships

Plenary	Support/Extension	Resources
The result of competition (10 min) Give students the hypothetical situation where two wolf packs have moved into the same area of forest. Students pair-share ideas on what the two packs will compete for, and what is likely to happen in terms of outcome for this competition. Finish this activity as a class discussion.		
Competitive graphs (5 min) Students sketch a graph for a predator–prey relationship, with a third line to show the effect of competition on populations. For example, students consider the populations of zebras, cheetahs, and hyenas when cheetahs and hyenas are hunting the same prey.	**Support:** Students should concentrate only on the basic predator–prey sketch graph.	

Homework	Support/Extension	
Students research the adaptations of a squirrel and the population difference between red and grey squirrels. Students should then use what they have learnt this lesson to suggest reasons for their relative population sizes in terms of competition and its effects.		

Securing Mastery Goals
- 3.9.1 Insects are needed to pollinate food crops.
- 3.9.2 Flowers contain the plant's reproductive organs.
- 3.9.2 Pollen can be carried by the wind, pollinating insects or other animals.
- 3.9.2 Identify parts of the flower and link their structure to their function.

Exceeding Mastery Goals
- 3.9.2 Suggest how plant breeders use knowledge of pollination to carry out selective breeding.
- 3.9.2 Describe similarities and differences between the structures of wind pollinated and insect pollinated plants.

Enquiry processes
- 2.9 Use the measuring instrument correctly.
- 2.9 Carry out the method carefully and consistently.

Band	Outcome	Checkpoint	
		Question	Activity
Know	Name the parts of a flower.	1	Starter 1, Main, Plenary 1
	State what is meant by pollination.	2	Homework
	Name two methods of pollination.	C, 2, 3	
↓	Follow instructions to dissect a flower.		Main
Apply	Identify the main structures in a flower and link their structure to their function.	1	Starter 1, Main, Plenary 1
	Describe the process of pollination.	A–D, 2	Lit, Plenary 1, Homework
	Describe the differences between wind- and insect– pollinated plants.	3	Main, Homework
↓	Use appropriate techniques to dissect a flower into its main parts.		Main
Extend	Explain how the structures of the flower are adapted to their function.	1	Starter 1, Main
	Suggest how plant breeders use knowledge of pollination to carry out selective breeding.		Homework
	Explain the processes of wind and insect pollination, comparing the similarities and differences between the two.	3	Lit, Main, Plenary 1, Homework
↓	Record detailed observations from a flower dissection.		Main

Literacy
Students must use scientific terminology correctly when naming key parts of the flower and describing their function.

Key Words
petal, sepal, stamen, anther, **pollen**, filament, **carpel**, stigma, style, ovary, **ovule**, **pollination**

Answers from the student book

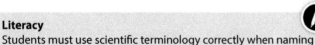

In-text questions	**A** attract insects **B** anther **C** wind, insects, or other animals **D** sweet, sugary fluid (that bees use to make honey)

Activity	**Cartoon strip**
	The cartoon strip should include the following steps: brightly coloured petals to attract insects; an insect visiting the flower; pollen transferred from the anther to the insect; insect moves to another plant; pollen is transferred from insect to stigma

Summary questions	**1** anther – produces pollen
	  filament – holds up the anther
	  stigma – this is sticky to 'catch' pollen grains
	  style – holds up the stigma
	  ovary – contains ovules
	  petal – brightly coloured to attract insects (6 marks)
	2a Transfer of pollen from anther to stigma. (2 marks)
	  b Cross-pollination is when pollen from one flower is transferred to stigma of another flower. Self-pollination is when pollen is transferred to the stigma in the same flower. (2 marks)
	3 Extended response question (6 marks). Example answers:
	Insect pollinated (maximum of 3 marks)
	large, brightly coloured petals and sweetly scented; usually contain nectar, a sweet sugary fluid; smaller quantities of pollen produced; pollen is often sticky or spiky, to stick to insects; anthers and stigma held firm inside the flower, so insects can brush against them; stigma has a sticky coating, so pollen sticks to it
	Wind pollinated (maximum of 3 marks)
	small petals, often brown or dull green; no nectar; pollen produced in large quantities as lots never reach another flower; pollen is very light, so it can be blown easily; anthers are loosely attached and dangle out of the flower, to release pollen into the wind; stigma hangs outside the flower to catch drifting pollen

Starter	Support/Extension	Resources
Parts of a flower (5 min) Students must link the key parts of a flower to their function using the interactive resource. **Beginning of life** (10 min) Hold a discussion based on the question. 'How do plants reproduce?'. This will then lead on to the main parts of a flower, what they do, where the sex cells come from, and how are they are fertilised.		**Interactive:** Parts of a flower

Main	Support/Extension	Resources
Flower dissection (40 min) Each student should be presented with a simple flower. They use forceps to dissect out the four key parts of the flower carefully. These parts should then be drawn onto the practical sheet and labelled. Students then answer the questions that follow.	**Support:** Demonstrate flower dissection in small groups and use larger flowers that are easier to dissect, for example, fuchsias.	**Practical:** Flower dissection

Plenary	Support/Extension	Resources
Pollination role play (10 min) Divide the class into groups of 6–8 and ask them to design a role play where they take on the roles of insects and the parts of the flower required for pollination. Give groups two minutes to prepare and ask for volunteers to perform their role play. Students should consider the importance of insect pollination in terms of producing crops for humans.	**Support:** Students should be told which roles to play in their groups, to limit the role play to its essentials.	
Pollen grains (5 min) Show students images of pollen grains or samples in a sealed container. Ask students to decide on the type of pollination they represent based on their adaptations, such as the presence of air sacs or hooks.	**Support:** Students should focus on physical features of the pollen observed.	

Homework	Support/Extension	
Write an account that describes the process of insect or wind pollination. If Plenary 1 was chosen, the account should be of wind pollination to test for understanding across both types. Accounts of insect pollination should include the importance of insect pollination in human food security.	**Extension:** Briefly introduce the concept of selective breeding. Students then write an account of how plant breeders use knowledge of pollination to enable them to produce plants with desired characteristics.	

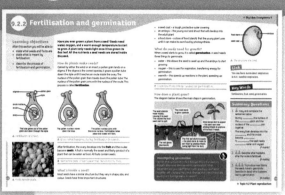

Securing Mastery Goals
- 3.9.2 Describe the main steps that take place when a plant reproduces successfully. (Pt 1/2)

Enquiry processes
- 2.9 Prepare a table with space to record all measurements.
- 2.9 Carry out the method carefully and consistently.
- 2.1 Select relevant data and do calculations.

Band	Outcome	Checkpoint	
		Question	Activity
Know	State what is meant by fertilisation in plants.	A, 1	Main
	State what seeds and fruit are.	B, 1	Main
↓	Make and record observations of germination.		Main
Apply	Describe the process of fertilisation in plants.	A, 1	Main, Homework
	Describe how seeds and fruits are formed.	B, 1, 2	Main
↓	Make and record observations in a table with clear headings and units, using data to calculate percentage germination.		Main
Extend	Explain the process of fertilisation in plants, explaining the role of each of the parts involved in the process.	1, 2	Homework
	Explain how the germination of seeds occurs.	3	Starter 1, Main, Homework
↓	Make and record observations in a table, using data to calculate percentage germination, evaluating experimental procedure.		Main

Maths
Students carry out simple calculations when working out the percentage of successful germination from experimental data, and draw graphs using this data by selecting appropriate scales for the axes on the graphs.

MyMaths More support for the maths skills in this section can be found on MyMaths.

Literacy
Students discuss the conclusions of their experiment using scientific terminology, and evaluate the validity of the experiment using key terms such as accuracy and precision.

GCSE link
4.6.1.1/4.6.1.1 Sexual and asexual reproduction

Sexual reproduction involves the joining (fusion) of male and female gametes:
- sperm and egg cells in animals
- pollen and egg cells in flowering plants.
In sexual reproduction there is mixing of genetic information which leads to variety in the offspring. The formation of gametes involves meiosis.

Key Words
fertilisation, fruit, seed, germination

Answers from the student book

In-text questions	A The pollen grain and ovule nuclei fuse.
	B ovary
	C water, oxygen, warmth
Activity	**Investigating germination**
	Experimental procedure should include placing the same number of seeds in the same apparatus set-up, placed in different conditions, changing one factor at a time. The experiment can be based on the practical provided with this lesson.

Summary questions	1 fertilisation, pollen, ovule, fruit, seeds, germinate, warmth (7 marks)
	2 Ovule develops into a seed.
	Ovary develops into the fruit. (2 marks)
	3 QWC question (6 marks). Example answers:
	Seed absorbs water and swells.
	Hard seed coat starts to split.
	Root grows downwards transferring energy from food store in seed.
	shoot starts to grow upwards
	first leaf starts to emerge
	plant starts to photosynthesise to produce its own food using light from the Sun.

Starter	Support/Extension	Resources
Germination (10 min) Introduce the idea of the germination of seeds. Students then complete gap-fill activity using the interactive resource to consolidate their knowledge and understanding.		**Interactive**: Germination
Seed-packet detective (5 min) Students look at the instructions on a packet of seeds. They discuss the weather conditions indicated on the packet that are required for seed germination and growth.	**Support**: Use seed packets designed for children and recap on MRS GREN.	

Main	Support/Extension	Resources
Successful seeds (40 min) Students carry out a practical to investigate germination with different amounts of water. Students analyse the results by calculating the percentage of successful germinations and plotting a graph of their results. They then answer the questions that follow, relating to the experiment itself and the content learnt this lesson. Students will require the use of the student book in order to answer questions. For this practical to be successful, a demo of this experiment could be set up three to four days in advance so that students may use the sample set of results for their analysis.	**Support**: A support sheet is available with a suggested table of results and a pre-labelled graph grid.	**Practical**: Successful seeds **Skill sheet**: Recording results **Skill sheet**: Calculating percentages **Skill sheet**: Choosing scales **Skill sheet**: Drawing graphs

Plenary	Support/Extension	Resources
Accuracy and precision (5 min) Write 'accuracy' and 'precision' on the board and give students a few minutes in groups to discuss the two words. What do they mean? How did they make their results both accurate and precise?	**Extension**: Students should offer their ideas for an evaluation of this experiment.	**Skill sheet**: Accuracy and precision
Why graph? (10 min) Ask why the ability to plot and interpret graphs is important in science. Lead a short discussion, culminating in the conclusion that visual presentation is easier to interpret than tables of numerical data.	**Extension**: Show a range of graphs depicting experimental data and ask students to explain what the graphs show, justifying the choice of graphs drawn.	

Homework	Support/Extension	
Students produce labelled diagrams of fertilisation of a plant and germination of a seed.	**Extension**: Students should explain the role of each part of a plant in fertilisation.	

9.2.3 Seed dispersal

Securing Mastery Goals

- 3.9.2 Describe the main steps that take place when a plant reproduces successfully. (Pt 2/2)
- 3.9.1 Suggest how a plant carried out seed dispersal based on the features of its fruit or seed.
- 3.9.2 Explain why seed dispersal is important to survival of the parent plant and its offspring.

Exceeding Mastery Goals

- 3.9.2 Develop an argument why a particular plant structure increases the likelihood of successful production of offspring.

Enquiry processes

- 2.10 Identify a dependent variable.
- 2.10 Identify an independent variable.
- 2.11 Decide how to vary the independent variable between planned values.
- 2.9 Prepare a table with space to record all measurements.
- 2.9 Carry out the method carefully and consistently.

Enquiry process activity

- 3.9.2 Use models to evaluate the features of various types of seed dispersal.

Band	Outcome	Checkpoint	
		Question	Activity
Know	State what is meant by seed dispersal.	1	Starter 1, Starter 2
	Name the methods of seed dispersal.	A, 1	Starter 1
	Plan a simple experiment, stating the variables, when given a hypothesis.		Main
Apply	Describe methods seed dispersal, and use the features of seeds and fruit to explain how they are adapted to their method.	A, 1, 2	Starter 1, Main, Homework
	Explain why seed dispersal is important to survival of the parent plant and its offspring.	C, 3	Plenary 1
	Plan a simple experiment to test one hypothesis about seed dispersal, identifying a range of variables.		Main
Extend	Explain how the adaptations of seeds aid dispersal.	C, 3	Starter 2, Plenary 1
	Develop an argument why a particular plant structure increases the likelihood of successful production of offspring.		Lit
	Plan and design an experiment to test a hypothesis about seed dispersal, clearly explaining all the variables involved.		Main

Maths

Students collect data from which they can calculate arithmetic means using simple calculations.

As part of the homework activity, they will plot a graph of their results, deciding on the most appropriate graph to draw given the nature of their variables, as well as choosing the appropriate scales for the axes.

MyMaths More support for the maths skills in this section can be found on MyMaths.

Literacy

In the student-book activity, students synthesise information and make predictions about how seed features increase the likelihood of plants producing successful offspring. Students will use scientific terminology correctly when writing a concise experimental procedure from their plan.

Key Words
seed dispersal

Answers from the student book

In-text questions	**A** wind, animal, water, explosive **B** Any two from: blackberries, strawberries, tomatoes, goose grass, burdock. **C** light/able to float/waterproof **D** pea/gorse
Summary questions	**1** dispersed, competition, nutrients, wind, animals (5 marks) **2** Internally – seeds contained within fruit that animals eat. The seed passes through the animal without getting damaged, reaching the ground in animal droppings. Externally – seeds may have hooks on them, which stick to animals as they walk past. The seeds eventually drop off onto the ground. (4 marks) **3** Extended response question (6 marks). Example answers: Wind dispersion: seeds are light, seeds have parachutes/wings. Dispersion by being eaten by animals: sweet/brightly coloured fruit. Dispersion by being stuck on animal's fur: have hooks. Dispersion by water: light, float, waterproof. Dispersion by explosion: fruits burst open.

Starter	Support/Extension	Resources
Seed dispersal (10 min) Show photographs or a short film clip about seed dispersal. Discuss why plants go to such lengths to move away from the parent plant. Students suggest a definition of seed dispersal. **Sycamore seeds** (5 min) Drop a few sycamore seeds from head-height as a demonstration. Ask students to describe what they have observed. Discuss why the seeds spin, and where the seeds land in relation to the parent plant (you). This demonstration can be adapted for other seeds.	**Extension**: Students should suggest how this particular seed is adapted to aid its dispersal.	

Main	Support/Extension	Resources
Investigating seed dispersal (40 min) This activity is one of the AQA Enquiry process activities. This practical requires students to consolidate all their ideas about what makes a good practical. Students should be shown a range of apparatus available to them, before deciding on their own hypothesis to investigate, and the apparatus that will be needed in their experimental procedure. Students must describe their method on the worksheet in terms of the independent, dependent, and control variables. For safety reasons, it is important that students are aware that they must not begin their experiment until you have signed off their procedure. This is a long planning and practical session, so students will be required to analyse their results, and answer the questions that follow for homework.	**Support**: An access sheet is available that guides students through the planning process using a given hypothesis. The access sheet also includes a suggested table of results.	**Practical:** Investigating seed dispersal **Skill sheets:** Planning investigations Recording results Calculating means Drawing graphs Choosing scales

Plenary	Support/Extension	Resources
Wind and animal dispersal (5 min) A range of characteristics of seeds belonging to either wind or animal dispersal methods are shown on the interactive resource. Students must group these characteristics accordingly. **Experimental conclusions** (5 min) Discuss students' findings from their experiments. Did their experiments work according to plan? What were their conclusions with respect to their hypotheses?		**Interactive:** Wind and animal dispersal

Homework	Support/Extension	Resources
Students should complete the questions on the practical sheet, analysing their data, and drawing a graph of their results. They should also write a conclusion for their experiment.	**Extension**: Students should offer a basic evaluation, offering one way to improve their experimental procedure.	

Checkpoint lesson routes

The route through this lesson can be determined using the Checkpoint assessment.

Percentage pass marks are supplied in the Checkpoint teacher notes.

Route A (support)
Students complete a range of tasks on the revision sheet. The questions are broken down into steps and the grid below provides guidance for how to support students. Hints are given to guide the writing in the questions that require a longer written answer.

Route B (extension)
Students are given information about Redonda Island, which they must use to complete the tasks on the sheet.

Progression to *Apply*

Know outcome	Apply outcome	Making progress
Know that organisms in a food web depend on each other for nutrients.	Combine food chains to form a food web.	Look at the food web in Task 1 and discuss the importance of producers and why some consumers are linked together. Provide students with cards, each containing the name of an organism from the food web. Ask them to make some food chains and then combine them to make a food web. Students can then complete the task.
Know that the population of a species is affected by the number of its predators and prey, disease, pollution and competition between individuals for limited resources	Describe how a species' population changes as its predator or prey population changes. Explain effects of environmental changes and toxic materials on a species' population.	Use the Task 1 food web, or another familiar one, to introduce the impact of a change in one population on the other organisms. Ask them to suggest what would happen if there were no buzzards or the number of rabbits rapidly increased. Guide them towards answering question 2 by discussing what animals and plants need to survive and what might interfere with survival.
Know that plants reproduce sexually to produce seeds, which are formed following fertilisation in the ovary.	Identify the parts of a flower and link their structure to their function.	Use the diagram in Task 2 to revise the parts of a flower and the functions of the parts. Explain how to use the table to summarise the information. An alternative is to give students cut outs of the parts of the flower and get them to put them together to produce a cross section through a flower head. Or they could make their own flower head from modelling clay and add labels.
Know that pollen can be carried by the wind and insects.	Describe the main steps that take place when a plant reproduces successfully.	Revise the difference in flower structure between insect and wind pollinated flowers. Use a variety of illustrations as examples. Instead of completing Task 3, students could design their own wind or insect pollinated flower and produce a poster, annotating why they have added each feature.
Recall that flowers contain the plant's reproductive organs.	Describe the main steps that take place when a plant reproduces successfully.	Outline the sequence of processes in plant reproduction and produce a flow diagram. Task 4 asks students to reorder a sequence of statements. Apply students could be expected to do this without the flow diagram to prompt them.
Know that plants have adaptations to disperse seeds using wind, water or animals.	Explain why seed dispersal is important to survival of the parent plant and its offspring.	For Task 5, discuss the methods of dispersal in general terms. Show real examples (or illustrations) of various fruits and seeds and ask how they are dispersed. Use beads on a tray with a barrier to keep them close together, remove the barrier and allow beads to spread. Discuss the advantage of spreading the 'seeds' over a wider area.

Answers to End-of-Big Idea questions

1a A filament, **B** anther, **C** petal, **D** stigma, **E** style, **F** ovary (6 marks)

  b brightly coloured/smell/nectar (1 mark)

2a corn → mouse → owl (1 mark) **b** corn (1 mark)

  c Producers have energy transferred from glucose.
     Consumers have energy transferred from the organisms they eat. (2 marks)

  d The spider population would increase as less organisms eat them. (2 marks) (Alternatively, spider population
     stays the same/decreases as shrew and mice population increase due to no predators, so eat the excess spiders.)

3a Any two from:
   Pollen produced in large quantities.
   Pollen is very light.
   Anthers are loosely attached and dangle out of the flower.
   Stigma hangs outside the flower. (2 marks)

  b Any two from: large, brightly coloured petals, sweetly scented, contain nectar, smaller quantities of pollen
     produced, anthers and stigma held firmly inside the flower. (2 marks)

  c Pollen is transferred from the anther to the stigma. (2 marks)

  d Any four from:
   Pollen tube grows.
   Pollen tube grows down the style into the ovary.
   Nucleus of the pollen grain travels down the pollen tube.
   Joins with the nucleus of the ovule/fertilisation.
   Ovary becomes a fruit. Ovules turn into seeds. (4 marks)

4a The mice population would increase as there are no predators/nothing would eat them. (2 marks)

  b The grasshopper population would decrease as shrews and spiders would need to eat more of them to survive. (2 marks)

  c Mice and shrews occupy different niches because they eat different foods. (2 marks)

  d Any three from: toxic chemical builds up in the food chain. Owls eat many other organisms so owls receive a higher
     dose of the toxic chemical. High levels can cause death to an organism. Correct use of term bioaccumulation. (3 marks)

5 This is an extended response question. Students should be marked on the use of good English, organisation of
   information, spelling and grammar, and correct use of specialist terms. The best answers will be organised clearly in
   paragraphs, describing the main structures, and linking these ideas to their functions (maximum of 6 marks). Examples
   of correct scientific points:
   petals – brightly coloured to attract insects
   sepals – special leaves which protect
   unopened buds
   stamen – male reproductive part
   anther – produces pollen
   filament – holds up the anther
   carpel – female reproductive part
   stigma – sticky to 'catch' grains of pollen
   style – holds up the stigma
   ovary – contains ovules

Case Study

Know	Apply	Extend
1–2 marks	3–4 marks	5–6 marks
The control of key variables is not considered. A plan is evident, but may lack detail or be poorly sequenced. Few scientific words are used correctly.	Most key variables are identified. A plan has been produced which uses some appropriate equipment. Some key scientific terms have been used correctly.	Key variables are identified. A logical plan has been produced which would lead to a valid investigation. A range of key scientific terms are used correctly.

9 Part 1 Checkpoint assessment (automarked)	9 Part 1 Checkpoint: Extension
9 Part 1 Checkpoint: Revision	9.1 Progress task, 9.2 Progress task

10 Genes

National curriculum links for this unit	
Topic	**National curriculum topic**
10.1 Variation	Inheritance, chromosomes and genes
10.2 Human reproduction	Reproduction in animals

In this Big Idea students will learn:

- there is variation between individuals of the same species
- some variation is inherited, some is caused by the environment, and some is a combination
- variation between individuals is important for the survival of a species, helping it to avoid extinction in an always changing environment

- the menstrual cycle prepares the female for pregnancy and stops if the egg is fertilised by a sperm
- the developing fetus relies on the mother to provide it with oxygen and nutrients, to remove waste and protect it against harmful substances.

AQA Enquiry process activities

Activity	Section
3.10.1 Graph data relating to variation and explain how it may lead to the survival of a species.	10.1.2 Continuous and discontinuous
3.10.2 Relate advice to pregnant women to ideas about transfer of substances to the embryo.	10.2.4 Development of a fetus

Preparing for KS4 success

Knowledge	4.6.1.1 Sexual and asexual reproduction 4.6.1.4 DNA and the genome 4.6.2.1 Variation

Maths and literacy	**2** Handling data
	  a Find arithmetic means (10.1.3)
	  c Construct and interpret frequency tables and diagrams, bar charts and histograms (10.1.2, 10.1.3)
	  f Understand the terms mean, mode and median (10.1.2)
	  h Make order of magnitude calculations (10.2.3)
	3 Algebra
	  a Understand and use the symbols (please insert) (10.1.3)
	4 Graphs
	  a Translate information between graphical and numerical form (10.1.2, 10.1.3)

Literacy	Collaboration and exploratory talk (10.2.1) Use of scientific terms (10.1, 10.1.2, 10.1.3, 10.2.1, 10.2.2, 10.2.3, 10.2.4, 10.2.5) Making connections across a range of texts and from personal experience (10.1.3) Organisation of ideas and information (10.2.1, 10.2.4) Legibility, spelling, punctuation, grammar and sentence structure (10.1.1, 10.2.1, 10.2.4) Planning and adapting writing style to suit audience and purpose (10.2.1, 10.2.4)
Assessment	Extended response questions (10.1.1, 10.1.2, 10.1.3, 10.2.3, 10.2.5) Quantitative problem solving (10.2.4)

KS2 Link	Check before	Checkpoint	Catch-up
Living things produce offspring of the same kind but are not identical to their parents.	10.1.1 Variation	Students discuss the question 'Are we all the same?'	Students write down differences between themselves. State that this is called variation.
Animals and plants are adapted to suit their environment in different ways. Adaptation may lead to evolution.	10.1.3 Adaptation	Students discuss hypothetical situations, for example, whether a shark can survive on land, explaining their answers.	Give one further hypothetical situation before allowing students to give their own. State that an adaptation is a feature which helps an organism to survive.
Environments can change, posing dangers to living things.	10.1.3 Adaptation	Pick a topical environmental change, for example, deforestation. Students discuss how this change has affected wildlife.	Show a picture of a polar bear, discussing the loss of the ice sheets and how this has impacted the total population of polar bears.
The changes as humans develop from birth to old age.	10.2.1 Adolescence	Ask students 'What is the difference between a child and an adult?'	List obvious differences between boys and men, girls and women.
The life cycles of a mammal, an amphibian, an insect, and a bird.	10.2.1 Adolescence	Name parts of the life cycle of different animals. What do they have in common?	Group stages in the lifecycle into a table. Column headings: mammals only, amphibians only, insects only, birds only, common to all.
The life process of reproduction in some plants and animals.	10.2.2 Reproductive systems	Pose the question 'Where do babies come from?'	Spot the difference in biological artwork of men and women.

Key Stage 2 Quiz: Biology
10 Part 1 End-of-Big Idea test (foundation)
10 Part 1 End-of-Big Idea test (foundation) mark scheme
10 Part 1 End-of-Big Idea test (higher)
10 Part 1 End-of-Big Idea test (higher) mark scheme

Answers to Picture Puzzler
Key Words
grape, ant, magnet, elephant, toe, earth
The key word is **gamete**.
Close Up
sperm and egg

You can find additional support for the maths skills covered in this Big Idea on **MyMaths**, including making estimates, using mean, median and mode, making order of magnitude calculations, and drawing and interpreting graphs.

10.1.1 Variation

Securing Mastery Goals

- 3.10.1 Explain whether characteristics are inherited, environmental or both. (Pt 1/2)

Exceeding Mastery Goals

- 3.10.1 Critique a claim that a particular characteristic is inherited or environmental.

Enquiry processes

- 2.12 Identify and record key features of an observation.
- 2.12 Write a scientific description of the observation, using key words.
- 2.6 Suggest a scientific idea that might explain the observation.
- 2.6 Describe the evidence for your idea.

Band	Outcome	Checkpoint	
		Question	**Activity**
Know	State what is meant by the term variation.	A, 1	Main, Plenary 2
	State that variation is caused by the environment or inheritance.	C, D, 1	Starter 1, Starter 2, Main, Plenary 1
	Record observations of variations between different species of gull.		Main
Apply	Describe how variation in species occurs.	1, 3	Starter 1, Starter 2, Main, Plenary 2, Homework
	Explain whether characteristics are inherited, environmental, or both.	1–4	Starter 1, Starter 2, Main, Plenary 1, Homework
	Record and categorise observations of variations between different species of gull.		Main
Extend	Explain how variation gives rise to different species.		Main, Plenary 2, Homework
	Critique a claim that a particular characteristic is inherited or environmental.		Starter 1, Starter 2, Main, Plenary 1
	Record and categorise observations of variations between different species of gull to suggest species boundaries.	1	Main

Literacy

Students test their spelling of key words used in the student-book activity.

They will then use scientific terminology to describe and suggest reasons for the variation in different species of seagulls.

GCSE link

4.6.2.1/4.6.2.1 Variation

Differences in the characteristics of individuals in a population is called variation and may be due to differences in:

- the genes they have inherited (genetic causes)
- the conditions in which they have developed (environmental causes)
- a combination of genes and the environment

Key Words

variation, species, inherited variation, environmental variation

Answers from the student book

In-text questions	**A** Differences in characteristics within a species. **B** A group of organisms which share very similar characteristics (and are able to produce fertile offspring). **C** Variation between organisms in a species due to the characteristics inherited from their parents. **D** Variation caused by a person's surroundings and lifestyle.
Activity	**Spelling key terms** Working with a partner, students test their spelling of species, variation, adaptation, inherited, environmental.

Summary questions	**1** species, characteristics, offspring, variation, environmental, inherited (6 marks)
	2 Environmental: tattoo, scar. Inherited: blood group, eye colour. Both: body mass, intelligence (6 marks)
	3 Identical twins have the same inherited characteristics.
	  Any differences must therefore be caused by environmental factors. (2 marks)
	4 Extended response question (6 marks). Example answers:
	  Variation is the difference in characteristics within a species. Inherited variation depends on characteristics inherited from parents. For example, lobed or lobe-less ears, eye colour, and blood type. Environmental variation depends on changes in a person's surroundings and/or lifestyle. For example, dyed hair, tattoos, and scars. Many characteristics are affected by both inherited and environmental variation. For example, height. Some characteristics are not affected by environmental factors at all. For example, eye colour, blood group.

Starter	Support/Extension	Resources
What is variation? (10 min) Students work in pairs to discuss what the word variation means, and give a possible definition with examples. Give an example of inherited variation (e.g., dog breeds), environmental variation (e.g., colours of flamingos), and variation affected by both (e.g., height). Students suggest a reason for the variation of each type.	**Extension:** Students suggest other factors for each category of variation.	
Causes of variation (5 min) Students read a short passage of text provided on the interactive resource about a day at the zoo, and select types of variation dependent on inherited factors, environmental factors, or both.	**Extension:** Students suggest a definition for inherited and environmental variation.	**Interactive:** Causes of variation

Main	Support/Extension	Resources
Variation (40 min) Formally introduce the key words for this lesson: variation, inherited variation, environmental variation, and species. Discuss possible variation in humans due to the three types of factors (inheritance, environmental, or both) before moving on to the activity. In the activity students study images of different species of seagulls and record variations within the different species, then answer the questions. It is important to go through differences within a species (e.g., dog breeds) and differences between species (e.g., kangaroos and wallabies) before issuing this activity.	**Support:** A support sheet is available where students are given a list of possible variations within the gulls to choose from.	**Activity:** Variation

Plenary	Support/Extension	Resources
Variation in humans (10 min) Working in small groups, students list human variations, and categorise them as inherited, environmental, or variations affected by both. Discuss their lists as a class. **Variation definitions** (5 min) Students give the definitions of variation, inherited variation, and environmental variation.	**Extension:** Ask students to justify their chosen categories for each characteristic. Students should be encouraged to question each other's choices if they disagree with any of the stated categories.	

Homework	Support/Extension	
Provide students with a list of four pet animals. For example, two different dogs (e.g., a Labrador and a Yorkshire terrier), a rabbit, and a goldfish. Ask students to list as many variations between the animals as possible, classify the variations, and suggest possible causes.	**Extension:** Students use their list to explain why the dogs are the same species but dogs, rabbits, and goldfish are different species.	

Securing Mastery Goals

- 3.10.1 Explain whether characteristics are inherited, environmental or both. (Pt 2/2)
- 3.10.1 Plot bar charts or line graphs to show discontinuous or continuous variation data.

Enquiry processes

- 2.4 Select a good way to display data.
- 2.4 Explain the choice of type of graph.
- 2.4 Explain why different kinds of data are better displayed on different kinds of graphs.

Enquiry processes activity

- 3.10.1 Graph data relating to variation and explain how it may lead to the survival of a species.

Band	Outcome	Checkpoint	
		Question	Activity
Know	State that there are two types of variation.	1, 2	Starter 2, Main, Plenary 1
	State the two types of graphs that can be drawn when representing the two types of variation.	1	Maths, Main, Plenary 2
	Record results in a table and plot a graph on axes provided.		Main
Apply	Describe the difference between continuous and discontinuous variation.	A, B, 4	Starter 2, Main, Plenary 1
	Use knowledge of continuous and discontinuous variation to explain whether characteristics are inherited, environmental, or both.	1, 3	Main, Plenary 1, Homework
	Plot bar charts or line graphs to show discontinuous or continuous variation data.		Maths, Main, Plenary 2
	Record results in a table and plot a histogram.		Main
Extend	Explain the causes of continuous and discontinuous variation.	3, 4	Main, Plenary 1
	Record results in a table, and identify and plot an appropriate graph to show variation within a species.		Maths, Main, Plenary 2

Maths

Students suggest the appropriate type of graph to draw for different continuous and discontinuous variations in the student-book activity.

Students will then display the results of the class experiment on arm span in an appropriate graph, and interpret results to answer questions relating to mode, mean, and range.

MyMaths More support for the maths skills in this section can be found on MyMaths.

Literacy

Students use scientific terminology when describing the differences between continuous and discontinuous data, and when drawing conclusions from results of the class experiment to measure arm span.

GCSE link

4.6.2.1/4.6.2.1 Variation

Differences in the characteristics of individuals in a population is called variation and may be due to differences in:

- the genes they have inherited (genetic causes)
- the conditions in which they have developed (environmental causes)
- a combination of genes and the environment

Key Words

discontinuous variation, continuous variation

Answers from the student book

In-text questions	A Characteristics that can only result in certain values.
	B Characteristics that can take any value within a range.
	C bar chart
	D histogram, often with a line added

Activity	**Which graph?** **a** bar chart **b** histogram **c** histogram **d** histogram

Summary questions	**1** discontinuous, continuous, graph, bar chart, histogram (5 marks)
	2 Continuous: length of arm, maximum sprinting speed, average leaf size.
	    Discontinuous: hair colour, shoe size. (5 marks)
	3a Most people are of an average height, around 150 cm. Few people are very short, below 135 cm. Few
	    people are very tall, above 170 cm. (3 marks)
	  b Height is affected by both inherited and environmental factors. If your parents are tall, you are also
	    likely to be tall (inherited). However, growth can be affected by environmental factors, for example,
	    malnourishment. (3 marks)
	4 Extended response question (6 marks). Example answers:
	    Continuous variation is variation that can take any value within a range. For example, height, body mass, arm
	    span, hair length, or length of feet. Continuous data should be plotted on a histogram. A line is often added
	    to the histogram to see the shape of the graph. This type of variation usually produces a curve known as a
	    normal distribution. Discontinuous variation is variation that can only result in certain values. For example,
	    gender, blood type, eye colour, or shoe size. Discontinuous variation should be plotted on a bar chart.

Starter	Support/Extension	Resources
Types of variation (10 min) Ask students to look around them. List as many sources of variation as they can just by looking at their classmates. Students should suggest different ways they can categorise the variations listed, justifying their suggestions using examples. Feedback as a class discussion.	**Support:** Students concentrate on listing variations, not grouping them.	
Discontinuous or continuous (10 min) Introduce the difference between discontinuous and continuous variation using examples. Students will then apply their new-found knowledge to group variations given on the interactive resource into the correct category.	**Extension:** Students should offer other variations to add to the existing list.	**Interactive:** Discontinuous or continuous

Main	Support/Extension	Resources
Investigating arm span (40 min) Formally introduce the difference between continuous and discontinuous variation. For students struggling to grasp this idea, parallels can be drawn to continuous and discrete data. Demonstrate how to measure arm span before issuing the practical sheet. **Variation** (40 min) This is an AQA Enquiry Processes activity. Students complete a guided worksheet where they draw graphs for data that is provided on a species' characteristics. They then analyse the data and make conclusions to explain how the variation may help the species to survive under different conditions.	**Support:** A labelled graph grid is available for students in the accompanying support sheet.	**Practical:** Investigating arm span **Activity:** Variation

Plenary	Support/Extension	Resources
Causes of discontinuous or continuous variation (5 min) Ask the class to work in pairs to list eight ways humans vary. Students should categorise these variations into continuous and discontinuous variations, and suggest possible causes for these (inherited, environmental, or both).	**Extension:** Students should spot trends in their results, for example, that most inherited variations are discontinuous.	
Which type of graph? (5 min) Call out different types of continuous (e.g., hair length) and discontinuous variations (e.g., tongue-rolling), for students to decide on the correct type of variation using a mini-whiteboard. Students should also suggest the type of graph needed to display the results.	**Extension:** Students should justify their choice of graph and draw a sketch-graph for one of the variations mentioned.	

Homework	Support/Extension	
During the lesson, draw a tally chart on the board with a list for eye colour. Students should add their eye colour to the tally during the course of the lesson, copy the tally at the end of the lesson, and prepare a suitable graph to display results for homework.	**Extension:** Students should state the type of variation this is, and describe possible trends shown by the graph.	

10.1.3 Adapting to change

Securing Mastery Goals

- 3.10.1 Explain how variation helps a particular species in a changing environment.
- 3.10.1 Explain how characteristics of a species are adapted to particular environmental conditions.

Exceeding Mastery Goals

- 3.10.1 Predict implications of a change in the environment on a population.
- 3.10.1 Use the ideas of variation to explain why one species may adapt better than another to environmental change.

Band	Outcome	Checkpoint	
		Question	**Activity**
Know	Name an environmental change.		Starter 1, Main 1
	Give a possible reason for adaptation or extinction.		Starter 2, Main 1, Main 2, Homework
Apply	Explain how organisms are adapted to their environments.	B	Lit, Starter 2, Main 1, Main 2, Homework
	Explain how variation helps a particular species in a changing environment.	1, 4	Starter 1, Main 1, Main 2
	Describe how organisms are adapted to their environments.	3	Lit, Starter 2, Main 1, Main 2, Plenary 2, Homework
Extend	Explain how organisms are adapted to seasonal changes.		Starter 1, Plenary 1
	Explain how competition or long-term environmental change can lead to evolutionary adaptation or extinction and the role variation plays in a species success.	2, 3, 4	Starter 2, Main 1, Main 2, Homework
	Predict implications of a change in the environment on a population.	4	Main 1

Literacy

Students read and extract information from text to answer questions that follow.

Students use scientific terminology when describing adaptations, seasonal changes, and population changes.

GCSE link

4.7.1.4/4.7.1.4 Adaptations

Organisms have features (adaptations) that enable them to survive in the conditions in which they normally live. These adaptations may be structural, behavioural or functional.

Some organisms live in environments that are very extreme, such as at high temperature, pressure, or salt concentration. These organisms are called extremophiles. Bacteria living in deep sea vents are extremophiles.

Answers from the student book

In-text questions	A Characteristics that enable an organism to be successful, and so survive.
	B Any two from: saves energy, nutrients can be reused, provide a layer of warmth/protection at the base of the tree.
	C hibernation, migration, grow thicker fur

204

Activity	**Nocturnal animals**
	Credit suitable information poster on a nocturnal animal of the student's choice (e.g., owl), and how the animal is adapted for hunting at night.
	Poster should include features of the animal with special adaptations, explained using as many scientific terms as possible.
Summary questions	**1** characteristics, variation, survive, extinction (4 marks)
	2 Changes to a habitat cause an increased competition for survival. Those organisms best adapted to the change will survive and reproduce. This increases the population of that species. Unsuccessful organisms will have to move to another habitat, or die. (3 marks)
	3 Any three from: waxy layer, spines instead of leaves, large root system, stems which can store water. (3 marks)
	4a One mark for plausible suggestion (1 mark) with reasoning (1 mark) and effect on population (1 mark)
	For example, If the atmosphere is warmer, there may be less snow (1 mark)
	This means that the hare would be less well camouflaged if white (1 mark) and so be more likely to be eaten / so population would decrease (1 mark).
	b If any change in fur colour from reddish-brown to white is caused by a drop in temperature (1 mark), any increase in temperature would cause no response, so the hare would retain its reddish-brown colour (1 mark) meaning it remains well adapted to its habitat (1 mark). *OR* Other species may have white fur (1 mark) which means they would lose their camouflage (1 mark) if the temperature rose and snow melted (1 mark).

Starter	Support/Extension	Resources
In six months' time (10 min) Students describe possible changes to the organisms in the school grounds in six months' time. Students should suggest why these changes have occurred as an adaptation to seasonal changes.	**Support:** Prompt students to think about deciduous trees and hibernating animals.	
Winners and losers (10 min) Show an image or a short film of a cheetah hunting. Students identify the adaptations of the cheetah that make it a successful hunter. Introduce the hyena and that cheetahs have low stamina. They often lose their food to hyenas in the wild.	**Extension:** Encourage students to offer further examples of changes in environment. This can lead the discussion to evolution and extinction.	

Main	Support/Extension	Resources
Climate change and polar bears (20 min) Students read an article about the environmental changes in the Arctic and the effects of these changes on polar bears and their population, before answering questions that follow.	**Support:** Read text as a class or in small groups to ensure students can understand the material given.	**Activity:** Climate change and polar bears
Competition and adaptation (25 min) Formally introduce the idea of competition for resources, and the importance of adaptations in different organisms. A video such as 'The Adaptation Song' from the Internet could be shown.	**Support:** Students should concentrate on two or three adaptations for the image provided.	**Activity:** Competition and adaptation
Divide the class into small groups of four or five students, and give each group an image of a different organism. Students must use the images to highlight four adaptations of the organism in the table provided on their activity sheet, before answering the questions that follow.		

Plenary	Support/Extension	Resources
Deciduous trees (5 mins) Students produce a time line of the changes that take place throughout the year and how this is linked to seasonal changes.	**Extension:** Students give adaptations for another organism such as a camel	
Something fishy! (10 min) Interactive resource where students link adaptations of a fish with the function of the adaptation that helps it survive.		**Interactive:** Something fishy!

Homework		
Ask students to carry out research on a pair of organisms similar to the cheetah and the hyena (where one organism has adapted better than the other). Students write a short paragraph about each of their adaptations, and explain how the population of one has been affected by the other.	**Extension:** Students should include an explanation of how species' survival is linked to the level of variation within the species, when environmental change occurs.	

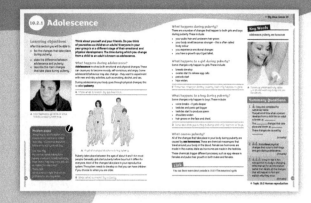

This spread covers prerequisite knowledge for AQA KS3 Science topic 3.10.2 Human reproduction.

Enquiry processes
- 2.5 Write in a style to fit purpose and audience.
- 2.5 Use clear language and well formed sentences.

Band	Outcome	Checkpoint	
		Question	Activity
Know ↓	State the definitions for adolescence and puberty.	A, B, 1	
	State changes to the bodies of boys and girls during puberty.	C, D, 2	Lit, Main, Plenary 1
	Interpret observations given, as changes that occur in boys or in girls.		Main, Plenary 1
Apply ↓	State the difference between adolescence and puberty.	A, B, 1	Main
	Describe the main changes that take place during puberty.	3	Lit, Main, Plenary 1
	Interpret observations given, to categorise the changes during adolescence.		Main, Plenary 1
Extend ↓	Explain the different between adolescence and puberty.	1	Main
	Explain the main changes that take place during puberty.	3	Lit, Plenary 2, Homework
	Interpret observations given, to categorise and explain physical and emotional changes during adolescence.		Main, Plenary 1

Literacy
Students pay attention to what others say in discussions, ask questions to develop ideas, and make contributions to discussions.

When writing answers to questions they need to use scientific terms confidently and correctly.

4.5.3.4/4.5.3.3 Hormones in human reproduction
During puberty reproductive hormones cause secondary sex characteristics to develop.

Key Words
adolescence, puberty, sex hormones

Answers from the student book

In-text questions	
	A The period of time in which a person changes from a child into an adult.
	B The physical changes a person's body experiences when changing from a child to an adult.
	C Any two from: breasts develop, ovaries release eggs, periods start, hips widen.
	D Any two from: voice breaks, testes/penis get bigger, testes start to produce sperm, shoulders widen, growth of facial/chest hair.

Activity	**Problem pages**
	The reply should include the following points:
	Kyle is undergoing puberty, caused by male sex hormones. He is changing from a child into an adult.
	A number of changes will occur, including his voice deepening, getting taller, and his genitals growing.
	The whole process takes several years but the precise start and finish time is different for everyone. This is something that happens to everyone and we cannot stop puberty. It is nothing to worry about.
Summary questions	**1** adolescence, physical, puberty, hormones (4 marks)
	2 pubic hair/underarm hair growth, body odour, growth spurt (3 marks)
	3 Give two marks for general changes (pubic hair/underarm hair growth, body odour, emotional changes, and growth spurt).
	Give two marks for male-only changes (voice breaks, testes/penis get bigger, shoulders widen, facial/chest hair).
	Give two marks for reasons (hormones/ released from testes/ chemical messengers/ reproductive system needs to become fully functional).

Starter	Support/Extension	Resources
What's the difference? (10 min) Working in groups, students discuss what changes occur as we change from a child into an adult. They put their ideas or observations on a sheet of paper and present them to the class in a short opening discussion. For classes with very shy students, it may be easier for students to come up with their own ideas, write them onto sticky notes, and place these anonymously into a container for you to choose from.	**Support:** Students may find it easier to focus on physical changes, either observed in themselves or observed in their older siblings.	
Growing up (10 min) Pose the question: 'Why do we need to grow up?' Write suggested answers on the board, for example: • We grow up to be physically able to have children. • Growing up is just getting physically bigger. • Growing up is just getting more sensible. Discuss the statements and decide which statement is most accurate.	**Extension:** Students should offer their own suggestions for the definition of growing up.	

Main	Support/Extension	Resources
Changes during adolescence (40 min) Students are given a set of cards with statements about changes experienced during adolescence. Students must sort these cards according to changes that occur in girls and in boys, then answer the questions that follow.	**Support:** Take out cards relating to emotional changes, which are marked with a letter E, to allow students to solely focus on the physical changes that occur during adolescence.	**Activity:** Changes during adolescence

Plenary	Support/Extension	Resources
Changes in puberty (5 min) Students sort a list of changes that occur during puberty into changes that happen to boys, girls, or both boys and girls.		**Interactive:** Changes in puberty
No worries! (5 min) Ask one student to suggest one typical problem a teenager might have about the changes that they experience during adolescence. Another student then gives advice to that student by explaining what is happening, and so on. (This is an opportunity to allay students' own concerns.)	**Support:** Students should concentrate on physical changes only.	

Homework	Support/Extension	
Produce an information leaflet with an outline of a human (gender neutral) in the middle. Put the heading 'Changes in a boy at adolescence' on one side, and 'Changes in a girl at adolescence' on the other side. Students then fill in this leaflet.	**Extension:** Students may wish to annotate the diagram in the centre of the page.	

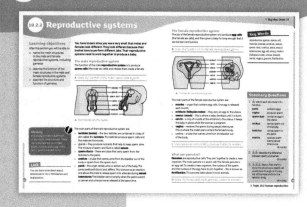

10.2.2 Reproductive systems

This section covers prerequisite knowledge and key words for AQA KS3 Science topic 3.10.2 Human reproduction.

Securing Mastery Goals
- 3.10.2 Use a diagram to show stages in development of a fetus from the production of sex cells to birth. (Pt 1/3)

Enquiry processes
- 2.5 Use scientific vocabulary accurately, showing that you know its meaning and use appropriate units and correct chemical nomenclature.

Band	Outcome	Checkpoint	
		Question	**Activity**
Know	Name the main structures of the male and female reproductive system, including gametes.	C, D, 1	Lit, Starter 1, Starter 2, Main, Plenary 1, Plenary 2
	State a function of the main structures of the male and female reproductive system.	A–C, 1	Lit, Starter 1, Main, Plenary 1, Plenary 2
	Extract information from text to state structures and functions of the key parts of the reproductive systems in a table.		Main
Apply	Describe the main structures in the male and female reproductive systems.	3	Starter 1, Starter 2, Main, Plenary 1, Plenary 2
	Describe the function of the main structures in the male and female reproductive systems.	1	Starter 1, Main, Plenary 1, Plenary 2
	Extract information from text to describe structures and functions of the key parts of the reproductive systems in a table.		Main
Extend	Explain how different parts of the male and female reproductive systems work together to achieve certain functions.	3	Starter 1, Main, Homework
	Explain the adaptations of some of the main structures that help them function.		Starter 1, Main, Homework
	Extract information from text to explain structures and functions of the key parts of the reproductive systems in a table.		Main

Literacy
Students extract information from text in the student book, before summarising this material in tables using scientific terms.

GCSE link
4.6.1.1/4.6.1.1 Sexual and asexual reproduction

Sexual reproduction involves the joining (fusion) of male and female gametes:
- sperm and egg cells in animals
- pollen and egg cells in flowering plants.

In sexual reproduction there is mixing of genetic information which leads to variety in the offspring. The formation of gametes involves meiosis.

Key Words
reproductive system, sperm cell, **testicles** (testes), scrotum, semen, sperm duct, urethra, **penis,** sexual intercourse, egg cell, **ovary, oviduct (fallopian tube), uterus (womb),** cervix, **vagina fertilisation, gamete**

Answers from the student book

In-text questions	A Produce sperm and release them inside the female.
	B Produce egg and allow a baby to grow until it is ready to be born.
	C uterus (womb) D female: egg cell, male: sperm

Activity	**Glossary**
	The students' glossaries should contain key words from Big Idea 10.
Summary questions	**1** 1 mark for each correct match. (6 marks)
	penis – carries sperm out of the body
	vagina – receives sperm during sexual intercourse
	sperm duct – carries sperm to the penis
	oviduct – carries an egg to the uterus
	testicles – produce sperm
	ovaries – contain eggs
	2 Sperm are the male sex cells; semen is a fluid containing both sperm and the nutrients to keep sperm alive. (2 marks)
	3 4 marks for identifying the correct structures, 1 mark for the correct order, and 1 mark for a well organised flow chart. testicles → sperm duct → urethra/penis → vagina

Starter	Support/Extension	Resources
Reproductive structures (10 min) Introduce the structures of the male reproductive system. Outline the functions of each of the key structures. This would be best achieved using a model of the structures or an image on the board. Repeat for the structures of the female reproductive system.		
Label these parts! (10 min) Introduce the structures within the male and female reproductive systems. Students should then consolidate their knowledge using the interactive resource, which asks students to label the different parts of these systems.	**Support**: Limit the structures introduced only to those listed on the interactive.	**Interactive**: Label these parts!

Main	Support/Extension	Resources
Male and female reproductive systems (40 min) This activity requires students to extract information from the student book in order to label diagrams of both reproductive systems, fill in tables summarising structures and functions, and answer questions that follow.	**Support**: A support sheet is provided for students with partially filled-in tables, linking structures and functions of the two reproductive systems.	**Activity**: Male and female reproductive systems

Plenary	Support/Extension	Resources
Making connections (5 min) Produce a set of playing cards with the names of the main reproductive structures on half of them, and their functions on the other half. Give each student one card; select one student to read their card. The student whose card matches must read theirs out. If correct, they get to pick the next student. Continue until all cards have been played out.	**Support**: Give students name cards rather than function cards, to test understanding rather than literacy skills.	
Word volleyball (5 min) Ask all the students to stand. Pass a soft sponge ball to a student who has to name a structure. That student then passes the ball to another standing player who has to state the function. They then name another structure, and the game continues. Once they get a correct answer they can sit down. The game ends when they have all sat down. (For every student to participate in this game, the set of key structures and functions may be repeated several times.)		

Homework	Support/Extension	
Produce a crossword with as many names of the parts of the reproductive systems as possible. Students must also produce all of the clues.	**Support**: Students may write simple definitions of each structure as the clue. **Extension**: Students should be encouraged to give clues relating to how that part is adapted to its function.	

Fertilisation and implantation

Securing Mastery Goals
- 3.10.2 If an egg is fertilised it settles into the uterus lining.
- 3.10.2 Use a diagram to show stages in development of a foetus from the production of sex cells to birth. (Pt 2/3)
- 3.10.2 Describe causes of low fertility in male and female reproductive systems.

Exceeding Mastery Goals
- 3.10.2 Make deductions about how contraception and fertility treatments work. (Pt 1/2)

Enquiry processes
- 2.5 Use scientific vocabulary accurately, showing that you know its meaning and use appropriate units and correct chemical nomenclature.

Band	Outcome	Checkpoint	
		Question	Activity
Know ↓	State what is meant by a person being infertile.		Main, Plenary 2, Homework
	State what is meant by fertilisation.	1	Starter 2, Main
	State that if an egg is fertilised it settles into the uterus lining.	C, 1	Main
Apply ↓	Describe some causes of infertility.	2	Main, Plenary 2, Homework
	Describe the process of fertilisation and where it occurs in the body.	A, B, 1	Main, Plenary 1
	Use a diagram to show the main steps that take place from the production of sex cells to the formation of an embryo.		Plenary 1
Extend ↓	Discuss some causes of infertility and how these may be treated.	2	Main, Plenary 2, Homework
	Explain the sequence of fertilisation and implantation.		Main, Plenary 1, Homework

Maths
Students carry out simple calculations using magnification and scale to calculate the actual sizes of egg and sperm cells.

MyMaths More support for the maths skills in this section can be found on MyMaths.

Literacy
The homework task requires students to use scientific terms correctly using a storyboard format to convey complex ideas to a KS3 audience.

GCSE link
4.6.1.1/4.6.1.1 Sexual and asexual reproduction

Sexual reproduction involves the joining (fusion) of male and female gametes:
- sperm and egg cells in animals
- pollen and egg cells in flowering plants.

In sexual reproduction there is mixing of genetic information which leads to variety in the offspring. The formation of gametes involves meiosis.

Key Words
cilia,
ejaculation,
embryo,
implantation

Answers from the student book

In-text questions	A moved along by cilia
	B Penis releases sperm/semen into the vagina.
	C Fertilised egg (or embryo) attaches to the lining of the uterus.
Summary questions	1 fertilisation – the nuclei of the sperm and egg cell join together
	ejaculation – semen is released into the vagina
	implantation – the fertilised egg attaches to the lining of the uterus
	cilia – the little hairs that move the egg cell along the oviduct (4 marks)

2a Penis becomes erect and vagina becomes moist. Penis inserted into vagina. Sperm/semen released/
  ejaculated into vagina. (3 marks)

  b male: low sperm count/sperm that do not swim properly (1 mark); female: egg cells not being released/
  blocked fallopian tubes (1 mark)

3 Example answers (6 marks):

  Eggs are larger; sperm are smaller.

  Sperm can swim; eggs must be moved by cilia.

  Eggs are made before birth/only mature; sperm are made constantly.

  Only one egg released per month; millions of sperm released each ejaculation.

Starter	Support/Extension	Resources
Egg and sperm cells (5 min) Students use the interactive resource to complete a paragraph on egg and sperm cells. **What we will learn today!** (10 min) List the three main key words from this lesson on the board: ejaculation, fertilisation, and implantation. Ask students to guess what these words mean, and then write their guesses in their books in pencil. Students should revisit their definitions at the end of the lesson, and make amendments.		**Interactive**: Egg and sperm cells

Main	Support/Extension	Resources
Fertilisation and implantation (40 min) This activity sheet is split into two main sections plus one optional task. **Task 1 – The size of egg and sperm cells** Students use diagrams provided to carry out simple calculations using magnification size and scale to deduce the actual size of egg and sperm cells. **Task 2 – Sexual intercourse** Students connect phrases together to sequence events that occur during sexual intercourse. You may wish to discuss this topic first. **Task 3 – Fertilisation and implantation (optional)** Show the short film on fertilisation and cell cleavage, which shows the process of fertilisation and the splitting of the fertilised egg. The process of implantation is not covered in detail in this video. Discuss with the class the events shown on the film, and introduce the homework task (described below). Where appropriate, discuss the different fertility problems that can occur for couples who are trying for a baby.	**Support:** An access sheet is available where questions of lower demand are given and students are not required to carry out calculations for Task 1. **Extension:** If the video is used, students should carry out an evaluation of the video shown for Task 3.	**Activity:** Fertilisation and implantation **Video:** Fertilisation and implantation

Plenary	Support/Extension	Resources
Sequencing (10 min) Write the words/phrases below on the board in any order. Students should then place the words in the correct order according to the sequence of events, defining each term. implantation, fertilisation, intercourse, gamete production, cell division **Fertility problems** (5 min) Students summarise the key causes of low fertility, classifying each issue as a problem affecting males or females.	**Support:** Students can be given the sequence on a sheet of paper, so they only need to focus on the definitions, or vice versa. **Extension:** Suggest how each of the conditions may be able to be treated.	

Homework	Support/Extension	
Students complete the storyboard of their own educational film to cover the entire topic. Students should indicate the images they would like to use, as well as the commentary, for each artwork. An alternative WebQuest homework activity is also available on Kerboodle where students research fertility treatment.	**Support:** The access sheet includes prompts for each frame of the video. **Extension:** Students should include explanations using scientific terminology.	 **WebQuest:** Fertility treatment

Securing Mastery Goals
- 3.10.2 Explain whether substances are passed from the mother to the fetus or not.
- 3.10.2 Use a diagram to show stages in development of a fetus from the production of sex cells to birth. (Pt 3/3)

Exceeding Mastery Goals
- 3.10.2 Predict the effect of cigarettes, alcohol or drugs on the developing fetus.

Enquiry processes
- 2.5 Use clear language and well formed sentences.
- 2.5 Use scientific vocabulary accurately, showing that you know its meaning and use appropriate units and correct chemical nomenclature.

Enquiry processes activity
- 3.10.2 Relate advice to pregnant women to ideas about transfer of substances to the embryo.

Band	Outcome	Checkpoint	
		Question	**Activity**
Know	State the definition of gestation.	1	Plenary 2
↓	State how long a pregnancy lasts.	A, 1	Main, Plenary 2
Apply	Describe what happens during gestation.	1, 2	Main, Plenary 2
	Describe what happens during birth.	D	Main, Plenary 2
↓	Explain whether substances are passed from the mother to the foetus or not.	1, 2	Main
Extend	Describe accurately the sequence of events during gestation.	C, 2, 3	Main, Plenary 2
↓	Explain in detail how contractions bring about birth (Level 8).	D	Main, Plenary 2
↓	Predict the effect of cigarettes, alcohol, or drugs on the developing fetus.		Plenary 2

Maths
Students carry out simple calculations to compare gestation periods.

Literacy
Students collate information from different sources, using scientific terms confidently to summarise their ideas.

GCSE link
4.6.1.2/4.6.1.2 Meiosis

Gametes join at fertilisation to restore the normal number of chromosomes. The new cell divides by mitosis. The number of cells increases. As the embryo develops, cells differentiate.

Key Words
gestation, fetus, placenta, umbilical cord, amniotic fluid

Answers from the student book

In-text questions	A about 9 months (40 weeks)
	B nutrients and oxygen
	C about 4 weeks
	D Cervix relaxes and uterus muscle contracts, pushing the baby out of the vagina.
Activity	**Elephant gestation**
	$22 \times 4 = 88$ weeks. This is more than twice the length of the gestation period in humans (40 weeks).

Summary questions	1 fetus, uterus, gestation, amniotic fluid, umbilical cord, blood, 40 (7 marks)
	2 Any three from:
	Substances transferred between maternal and foetal blood.
	Occurs in the placenta.
	Oxygen and nutrients diffuse from mother to baby.
	Waste substances, like carbon dioxide, diffuse from baby to mother. (3 marks)
	3 Extended response question (6 marks). Example answers:
	Placenta is area where substances pass between the mother's and foetus blood. It acts as a barrier, stopping infections and harmful substances reaching the foetus.
	Umbilical cord connects the foetus to the placenta. It carries the foetus blood/oxygen/nutrients from the placenta to the baby and carries carbon dioxide from the foetus to the placenta.
	Amniotic fluid acts as a shock absorber/protects the foetus from bumps.

Starter	Support/Extension	Resources
Key word cascade (5 min) Write a key word on the board. Ask students to suggest another word that is connected to the key word. Add this to the board. Repeat the process until all the links are exhausted. Suggested key words include pregnancy, fetus, and placenta.	**Extension:** Students should justify why words are linked.	
Egg to baby (5 min) Ask students how an egg from the ovaries turns into a baby. Invite ideas and lead a short discussion about the ideas of development. This is a good opportunity to dispel possible misconceptions.		

Main	Support/Extension	Resources
Development and birth (45 min) This activity is one of the AQA Enquiry process activities. This activity is split into three sections, and is run in the format of home and expert groups. Students should be split up into groups of three (mixed ability), called the home group, before the activity begins. Each section should take 15 minutes.	**Support:** The information cards are ramped.	**Activity:** Development and birth
Task 1 – Becoming experts Each member of the home group moves to a designated table to collect information from the resource card available. They must not remove the cards, although they can summarise the information as a diagram on a piece of paper. You may wish to introduce a word limit to prevent students from copying the resources.		
Task 2 – Returning home Students return to their home group and have five minutes to teach each topic to one another.		
Task 3 – Answering questions Students then attempt the questions on the activity sheet.		

Plenary	Support/Extension	Resources
Development links (5 min) Students link key words in this topic to their definitions using the interactive resource.		**Interactive:** Development links
Egg to baby – revisited (5 min) Students revisit their ideas from the beginning of the lesson, comparing what they thought originally to what they know now. Students should focus on the terms 'gestation' and 'birth' in particular.	**Extension:** Students should predict the effect on the development of a healthy baby of smoking, drinking alcohol or taking drugs.	

Homework	Support/Extension	
Write an account of the development of the baby using the notes obtained from the activity. The account should include scientific words used in a logical and coherent manner.	**Support:** Students should be provided with a different information card (one other than about birth) to summarise.	

10.2.5 The menstrual cycle

Securing Mastery Goals
- 3.10.2 The menstrual cycle lasts approximately 28 days.
- 3.10.2 Identify key events on a diagram of the menstrual cycle.

Exceeding Mastery Goals
- 3.10.2 Make deductions about how contraception and fertility treatments work. (Pt 2/2)
- 3.10.2 Explain why pregnancy is more or less likely at certain stages of the menstrual cycle.

Enquiry processes
- 2.4 Decide the type of chart or graph to draw based on its purpose or type of data.

Band	Outcome	Checkpoint	
		Question	Activity
Know	State the length of the menstrual cycle.	A	Starter 2, Main
	State the main stages in the menstrual cycle.	1, 2	Starter 1, Main, Plenary 1, Plenary 2
↓	Present key pieces of information in a sequence.		Main
Apply	State what the menstrual cycle is.		Starter 1, Main, Plenary 1
	Identify key events on a diagram of the menstrual cycle.	1, 2	Starter 1, Main, Plenary 1, Plenary 2
↓	Present information in the form of a graphical timeline.		Main
Extend	Explain why pregnancy is more or less likely at certain stages of the menstrual cycle.	3	Main, Plenary 2
	Make deductions about how contraception methods work.		Homework
↓	Present information in the form of a scaled timeline or pie chart.		Main

Literacy
Students are required to understand scientific terminology when interpreting information, and to present this information using a different method.

GCSE link
4.5.3.4/4.5.3.3 Hormones in human reproduction

Oestrogen is the main female reproductive hormone produced in the ovary. At puberty eggs begin to mature and one is released approximately every 28 days. This is called ovulation.

Several hormones are involved in the menstrual cycle of a woman.

4.5.3.5/4.5.3.4 Contraception

Fertility can be controlled by a variety of hormonal and nonhormonal methods of contraception.

Key Words
period,
menstruation,
menstrual cycle,
ovulation,
contraception,
condom,
contraceptive pill

Answers from the student book

In-text questions	**A** 28 days **B** The release of an egg cell from one of the ovaries. **C** condoms and the contraceptive pill **D** barrier method
Summary questions	**1** menstrual cycle, lining, vagina, period, condoms, pregnancy (6 marks) **2** period – lining is lost as blood through the vagina ovulation – egg is released

Uterus lining thickens ready for a fertilised egg to implant.

If egg is not fertilised, the lining breaks down and the cycle starts again. (4 marks)

3 Around day 14 (1 mark) as this is when an egg is present/ovulation has just occurred to meet the sperm (1 mark) and the lining of the uterus if thick to receive a fertilised egg. (1 mark)

4 Extended response question. (6 marks) Example answers:

Condoms are used by males during intercourse. They are an example of the barrier method of contraception. The barrier method protects against STIs and is highly effective at preventing pregnancy.

The contraceptive pill is taken by females. It must be taken daily and gives no protection against STIs. It is highly effective at preventing pregnancy.

Starter	Support/Extension	Resources
An alternative question-led lesson is also available. **Cycles in nature** (5 min) Ask students to suggest as many events in nature as they can that occur in cycles. Ask them to feed their ideas back to the class. The aim is to introduce the idea of cycles and to produce a simple definition of a cycle in nature. **Menstrual cycle facts** (10 min) Interactive resource in which students complete a paragraph on the menstrual cycle. Students may copy the corrected summary into their books for future reference.		**Question-led lesson:** The menstrual cycle **Interactive:** Menstrual cycle facts
Main	**Support/Extension**	**Resources**
Timeline of the menstrual cycle (40 min) Students are presented with key events in the menstrual cycle as a series of text boxes that have been jumbled up. Students are required to read and interpret the information, sequence the boxes in the correct order, and answer the questions that follow.	**Support:** Students are simply required to sequence the text boxes in order. **Extension:** Students should arrange the timeline against a scaled axis of time, using graph paper or, as an extra challenge, students could present the sequence in a circle as a pie chart.	**Activity:** Timeline of the menstrual cycle
Plenary	**Support/Extension**	**Resources**
Loop game (10 min) Write down a list of events during the menstrual cycle as a pack of cards, with one event on each card. Students can then place the cards in the correct sequence to form a loop. Students discuss why each event is important while working on the loop game. **Menstrual cycle in a minute** (5 min) Write down a list of events during the menstrual cycle as a pack of cards, with one event on each card. Split students into groups with one statement per group. Present the class with a clock and students must scale the events of the menstrual cycle to one minute. They will need to call out their key events in the cycle at the correct point in that minute. Give students a few minutes of thinking time before commencing the activity.	**Extension:** Students should highlight within their loop the times when a person is more likely to become pregnant. **Support:** Students should work on the scale of two seconds = one day.	
Homework	**Support/Extension**	
Students should prepare five questions on the reproduction topic so far, one for each lesson, together with a mark scheme. Show students a condom, and the contraceptive pill (or use the information in the student book). Ask students to find out how each of these forms of contraception work.	**Support:** Students concentrate on short questions between 1–3 marks each. **Extension:** Students should write questions requiring higher-order-thinking skills, where each question is worth 3–5 marks.	

Checkpoint lesson routes

The route through this lesson can be determined using the Checkpoint assessment.

Percentage pass marks are supplied in the Checkpoint teacher notes.

Route A (support)
This revision activity focuses on improving students' knowledge and understanding of inherited and environmental variation, male and female reproductive systems, and the development of a fetus. The tasks include drawing graphs, labelling diagrams, and writing short answers.

Route B (extension)
Two options are provided for students to choose from.

Option 1: Students are supplied with information about moth populations and asked to use their knowledge and the information provided to complete two tasks, including writing a persuasive letter to their local council.

Option 2: Students are given information about the menstrual cycle and factors affecting ability to get pregnant. They act as a doctor in a fertility clinic to answer questions and produce a poster about contraception.

Progression to *Apply*

Know outcome	Apply outcome	Making progress
Know that there is variation between individuals of the same species. Some variation is inherited, some is caused by the environment and some is a combination.	Explain whether characteristics are inherited, environmental, or both.	For Task 1, show photos of the different varieties of snapdragon. There are two distinct ranges of sizes that are genetically controlled. The variation within each range is due to the environment. Use flower colour and height to discuss types of variation – perhaps use other more familiar examples to lead students in.
Recall that continuous variation is where differences between living things can have any numerical value and discontinuous variation is where difference can only be grouped into categories.	Plot bar charts or line graphs to show discontinuous or continuous variation data.	In Task 2, students decide when to use bar charts or histograms/line graphs. Discuss the axes and how to choose a scale. Draw an outline on the board to guide students if necessary. For the histogram/line graph, get students to group the various heights before plotting the graph.
Know that variation between individuals is important for the survival of a species, helping it to avoid extinction in an always changing environment.	Explain how variation helps a particular species in a changing environment.	At the end of Task 2, students discuss the effect of putting tall shrubs between other plants. Ask them how the environment changes. Explain that plants cannot grow without sufficient light/soil nutrients/space.
Recall that variation is the differences within and between species.	Explain how characteristics of a species are adapted to particular environmental conditions.	In Task 3, students use diagrams of birds' feet and descriptions of how they live to explain how their feet are adapted to their needs. Start by showing photos of animals or plants with exaggerated characteristics that help them to survive. For example, show a camel and tell students that the hump stores water. Students should be able to come up with possible ways it could help the organism survive.
State that if an egg is fertilised it settles into the uterus lining.	Use a diagram to show stages in development of a fetus from the production of sex cells to birth.	In Task 4, students label male and female reproductive systems before adding the function of certain parts (provided on the sheet). Ask students to compile a list of the parts of the reproductive system before attempting the labelling. Suggest they trace the pathway of sperm with a finger or pencil from testis to fallopian tube and egg from ovary to uterus.
Know that the developing fetus relies on the mother to provide it with oxygen and nutrients, to remove waste and protect it against harmful substances.	Explain whether substances are passed from the mother to the foetus or not.	For Task 5, discuss what a developing fetus will need to grow – remind students that these will be the same things that all animals need to survive. Ask students how these things get to and from the fetus. It may help to show a diagram of a fetus that clearly shows the placenta.
Know that menstrual cycle prepares the female for pregnancy and stops if an egg is fertilised. Recall that the menstrual cycle lasts about 28 days.	Identify key events on a diagram of the menstrual cycle.	Before Task 6, revise the key words associated with the menstrual cycle. Key words on the board will prompt *Know* students.

Answers to End-of-Big Idea questions

1a Arctic (1 mark)　　**b** white fur– camouflage　　large feet– to stop the bear sinking into snow

thick fur– insulation　　sharp claws – to catch prey (4 marks)

2　Girls – breasts develop, periods start. Boys – testes produce sperm, voice deepens.

Both – pubic hair

grows, growth spurt. (6 marks)

3a A – oviduct, D – cervix (2 marks)

　b vagina (1 mark)

　c uterus (1 mark)

　d An egg is released from an ovary. (2 marks)

4a umbilical cord (1 mark)

　b surrounded by (shock absorbing) amniotic fluid (1 mark)

　c Cervix relaxes, muscles in uterus wall contract, baby pushed through vagina. (3 marks)

　d Any three from the following:

Allows maternal and fetal blood to flow close together.

Supplies oxygen/nutrients.

Removes waste/carbon dioxide.

Prevents infections/harmful substances passing to the foetus. (3 marks)

5a Differences in a characteristic within a species. (1 mark)　　**b** balance/(bathroom) scales (1 mark)

　c histogram (1 mark)　　**d** *x*-axis for mass of student, *y*-axis for number of students (2 marks)

　e Each student's body mass could take any value (between the smallest and largest mass). (1 mark)

　f Some variation is passed on in genes (from parents). This is inherited variation. Diet/exercise/lifestyle also affect body mass. This is environmental variation. Overall body mass is a result of both environmental and inherited variation. (4 marks)

Answer guide for Case Study

Know	Apply	Extend
1–2 marks	3–4 marks	5–6 marks
• The cartoon shows some of the main steps in fertilisation. • An attempt has been made to label the main structures in the male and female reproductive system.	• The cartoon illustrates the main steps in fertilisation. • The main structures in the male and female reproductive system are labelled and the process of fertilisation has been explained, but may lack detail.	• The cartoon is well structured and illustrates the main steps in fertilisation. • The structures in the male and female reproductive system are fully labelled and the process of fertilisation has been clearly explained.

kerboodle

10 Part 1 Checkpoint assessment (automarked)	10 Part 1 Checkpoint: Extension
10 Part 1 Checkpoint: Revision	10.1 Progress task, 10.2 Progress task

Index

Great Clarendon Street, Oxford, OX2 6DP, United Kingdom

Oxford University Press is a department of the University of Oxford.
It furthers the University's objective of excellence in research,
scholarship, and education by publishing worldwide. Oxford is a
registered trade mark of Oxford University Press in the UK and in
certain other countries

British Library Cataloguing in Publication Data
Data available

978 0 19 840826 0

10 9 8 7 6 5 4 3

Paper used in the production of this book is a natural, recyclable
product made from wood grown in sustainable forests.
The manufacturing process conforms to the environmental regulations
of the country of origin.

Printed and bound by CPI Group (UK) Ltd, Croydon, CR0 4YY

Content for this title has been authored by Simon Broadley, Philippa
Gardom Hulme, Jo Locke, Mark Matthews, Helen Reynolds, Victoria
Stutt, and Nicky Thomas.

Activate author acknowledgements
The authors would like to thank Yon-Hee Kim for keeping everything on
track, as well as for her great patience and attention to detail. You have
done an excellent job.

Philippa Gardom Hulme would like to thank Barney Gardom, Catherine
Gardom, and Sarah Gardom for their help, support, and patience. She is
also grateful to the man in the computer shop who sold her the biggest
computer monitor ever.

Jo Locke would like to thank her husband Dave for all his support,
encouragement, and endless cups of tea, as well as her girls Emily and
Hermione who had to wait patiently for Mummy 'to just finish this
paragraph'.

Helen Reynolds would like to thank Michele, Janet, Liz and Carol, and
all at OUP.

Andy Chandler-Grevatt would like to thank the editorial team at OUP,
the awesome author team, and Geoff.